THE GENERAL & Mrs. Washington

THE UNTOLD STORY OF A MARRIAGE & A REVOLUTION

Bruce Chadwick

SOURCEBOOKS, INC.®
NAPERVILLE, ILLINOIS

Cover and internal design © 2007 by Sourcebooks, Inc.
Portrait of George Washington (1732-99) after a painting by Gilbert
Stuart (1755-1828) (oil on canvas) by Durand, Asher Brown (1796-1886)
© Collection of the New-York Historical Society/Bridgeman Art Library
The Marriage of Washington (1732-99) 1849 (oil on canvas) by Stearns,
Junius Brutus (1810-85)
© Butler Institute of American Art, Youngstown/Bridgeman Art Library
Museum Purchase 1966
Internal photos used by permission as noted in captions
Sourcebooks and the colophon are registered trademarks of Sourcebooks, Inc.

Published by Sourcebooks, Inc.
P.O. Box 4410, Naperville, Illinois 60567-4410
(630) 961-3900
Fax: (630) 961-2168
www.sourcebooks.com

Originally published in hardcover by Sourcebooks, Inc.

Library of Congress Cataloging-in-Publication Data
Chadwick, Bruce.
   The general and Mrs. Washington : the untold story of a marriage and a revolution /
Bruce Chadwick.
      p. cm.
   Includes bibliographical references and index.
   1. Washington, George, 1732-1799--Marriage. 2. Washington, Martha,
1731-1802--Marriage. 3. Married people--United States--Biography. 4.
Generals--United States--Biography. 5. Generals' spouses--United
States--Biography. 6. United States--History--Revolution, 1775-1783.
I. Title.

E312.19.C47 2006
973.4'10922--dc22
[B]

2006006324
Printed and bound in the United States of America
VP 10 9 8 7 6 5 4 3 2

AUTHOR TO READER

Just before she died in 1802, Martha Washington burned the hundreds of letters that she had exchanged with her husband George during the Revolutionary War. No one knew why. Were the letters too private? Was George, so careful in his public statements, overly critical of others in that correspondence? We'll never know. The destruction of those private letters, which must have revealed much about the Washingtons' personal relationship, was a great loss to historians and to the country. The letters surely would have provided a more complete look at the way the mind of George Washington worked during the Revolution and, just as important, his concerns for his wife and family.

Washington, as the commander in chief of the Continental Army and later as the first president of the United States, wrote thousands of letters during his life and kept most of them. Just about all have been published somewhere. The letters, in war and peace, helped historians to construct a comprehensive portrait of him.

Martha did not write many letters. However, a lengthy study of the letters written by her and to her, and about her by others, enabled me to write a rather full description of the first First Lady. (The term did not come about until 1849. Martha was called the President's Lady, or Lady Washington, but I use First Lady because Americans are so familiar with it.) These descriptions of her, and assessments of her inner strength and mercurial personality, came from farflung sources—important figures such as Thomas Jefferson, Abigail Adams, and an assortment of public officials, newspaper editors, and foreign diplomats. But they were also jotted down by unknown people—men who rode past her on roads, little girls who rode in carriages with her, merchants, farmers, and the many soldiers who met her during the Revolution.

Using all of these sources, I tried to write a biography of the Washingtons that not only established their place in history but also captured their personalities and the deep love they had for each other. I tried to explain, too, what at first seemed unfathomable—the extraordinary love of the American people for the country's First Couple. That is rather easy in George's case because he was the conquering war hero. Understanding the respect for his wife, who led no charges and fired no guns, was much harder. In the end, though, I think I did so by explaining the brand-new Americans of the Revolutionary era. Americans were then, and remain today, a people who admire men and women of great character and integrity, men and women who risk all for freedom.

Such a couple was George and Martha Washington.

ACKNOWLEDGMENTS

One would think that writing a biography about the most famous man in United States history and his wife would not be a difficult task. After all, every schoolchild knows their story. The problem I had was not telling the story that everybody knew, but the story that people did not know.

To do so, I had to write about the Washingtons within the context of the extremely complicated and, at times, stormy era in which they lived. How did George Washington go from being a bungling field commander to the most famous man in the world in just two weeks, following the crossing of the Delaware River on Christmas 1776, on his way to stunning victories at Trenton and then Princeton? If women were invisible and powerless in the eighteenth century and lived only for the men in their lives, how did a rather ordinary-looking woman such as Martha Washington become so cherished by men as well as women throughout the land?

The answers lay in the political, economic, social, and cultural changes taking place in the United States at the same time that the struggling colonies were attempting to defeat the British Empire in what eventually became the most successful revolution in the history of the world. It is that cultural landscape that I address throughout the book, hopefully painting a picture of the entire country and its people that will enable the reader to see how the Washingtons fit into that portrait and, in fact, became the centerpiece of it.

I had the help of many kind people along the way. First and foremost was Mary Thompson, the historian of Mount Vernon, Washington's magnificent estate in Virginia on the banks of the Potomac. The cherubic Ms. Thompson, one of the nation's finest scholars in her own right and the author of a work on Martha Washington, was kind enough to read through the manuscript and offer many constructive suggestions.

Librarians everywhere helped me in my research, cheerfully handing me yet ten more books to read, twenty more journals to dissect, and one more stack of original letters to go through. Most helpful were the librarians at New Jersey City University, Rutgers University, Washington and Lee University, the Morris County (N.J.) Library, Randolph (N.J.) Library, New York Public Library, the Valley Forge and Morristown National Historical Parks, and those at the historical societies of Massachusetts, New York, Connecticut, New Jersey, Pennsylvania, Delaware, Virginia, and Maryland.

I had assistance from photo experts at the New York Historical Society and Dawn Bonner at Mount Vernon, plus Scott Houting at Valley Forge National Historical Park, Johnni Rowe at the Morristown National Historical Park Andrea, Ashby-Leraris at Independence National Historical Park in Philadelphia, and Christine Jochem and Suzanne Gulick at the Morristown-Morris Township Library.

Special thanks go to Jo Bruno and Liza Fiol-Matta at New Jersey City University for giving me travel grants to complete work on this project.

I would like to thank Hillel Black, the executive editor of Sourcebooks, who urged me to write about George and Martha and did a wonderful job editing the manuscript. This is my third book about the Revolutionary era for Sourcebooks in what has been a happy relationship. Thanks, too, to Michelle Schoob, Heather Moore, Tara VanTimmeren, Alison Syring, Megan Dempster, Scott R. Miller, and Libby Topel at Sourcebooks.

Many thanks to my literary agents, Elizabeth Winick and Jonathan Lyons, of McIntosh & Otis, both history lovers, who were so encouraging about my work on this book.

Finally, as always, thanks to my wife, Marjorie, who assisted with the research and shared the joy of this journey with me.

CONTENTS

The Presidency

CHAPTER ONE

GEORGE AND MARTHA

S he did not expect to see him at the home of her friend
William Chamberlayne that March afternoon in 1758.

Martha Custis and her two small children had been invited to
spend the day at Chamberlayne's modest two-story brick home
on his plantation, Poplar Grove, on the banks of the Pamunkey
River in New Kent County, Virginia. Chamberlayne was a
vestryman at nearby St. Peter's church, where she worshipped.
He knew Martha because her late husband, Daniel Custis, and
her father, John Dandridge, were also vestrymen. His daughters
had been classmates of hers at the local school. She knew everyone at the Chamberlayne home from other receptions and parties
she had attended at the sprawling plantations throughout the
Tidewater area of the colony and in the large mansions of
Williamsburg, the capital of Virginia. Martha, twenty-seven, had

been a widow for eight long months. She had become a member of the colony's gentry in 1750 when she married Daniel Custis. He was a planter twenty years older than she; she was just nineteen when they wed.

Daniel Custis was the third-richest man in Virginia and one of the wealthiest men in America. He owned more than fifty thousand acres of valuable land near Williamsburg and several town lots in that community. He also owned 287 slaves, and had made a fortune raising and selling tobacco on his plantation, White House, on the banks of the Pamunkey. The Custises lived in a well-appointed home at White House and owned one of the largest mansions in Williamsburg, a well-designed, spacious brick house with lawns and gardens, whose six tall chimneys could be seen from anywhere in the community. Custis had died suddenly of bilious fever and heart complications in 1757 at the age of forty-six, leaving Martha the richest widow in Virginia.

Martha Custis was a very small woman, barely five feet tall in her stockings, overweight and "plump," as many who knew her said. She had tiny hands and her face was oval, with a small mouth, high forehead, and rounded chin. She had beautiful white teeth—a rarity in the era. Her face was highlighted by her short brown hair and soft hazel eyes. Martha had a thin, slightly hooked nose and was, by all accounts, rather plain-looking. Martha was not an educated woman and rarely read books at that time; her penmanship was nearly illegible and her spelling atrocious, much like the spelling of most Virginians of the day.

The charm of Martha Custis, though, was her personality. Family members and friends acknowledged that she was no beauty, but all who knew her enjoyed her company. She was friendly, compassionate, and always seemed vitally interested in what a companion had to say. She shared in the joys of others when they married or gave birth, but she also grieved with them upon the deaths of loved ones.

Daniel Custis's widow luxuriated in any discussion of children and family. She could carry on conversations about any mundane topic, from the weather to Sunday's church sermon. Those who met her said Martha could carry on an interesting conversation about what roadway a guest followed that morning, and she always seemed to know somebody acquainted with a guest. People who knew her when she first began to attend social events in Williamsburg as a girl readily acknowledged that she was not physically attractive but quickly added that people were drawn to her because of her cheerful disposition. Perhaps John Enys, an Englishman who met her later in her life, described her best when he compared her to a fictional British heroine, writing of Martha, "She appears to me to be a plain good woman very much resembling the character of Lady Bountiful, is very cheerful and seems most happy when contributing towards the happiness of others." A relative wrote that it was her personality that "caused her to be distinguished amid the fair ones who usually assembled at the court of Williamsburg."

She was the daughter of a successful planter and had grown up in comfortable surroundings. She was groomed all of her life to be a fine lady of the Virginia upper class. She loved beautifully made clothes, ornate carriages, expensive furniture, good food, and elegant homes. Her refinement, as well as her amiable ways, had made her popular as a girl and as the young wife of Daniel Custis.

Martha was as surprised as everyone else when the well-known colonel in charge of the state militia regiment, the 6'3, two-hundred-pound George Washington, uninvited and unannounced, arrived at Chamberlayne's that afternoon. Washington and a white manservant, Thomas Bishop, a tall man himself, had been riding back to Washington's farm at Mount Vernon on the southern bank of the Potomac River, the northern border of Virginia. They had casually ridden north on a narrow dirt road from Williamsburg, where Washington had been to see a doctor about his health. Bishop had been asked to work for Washington by General William Braddock, as Braddock lay dying on a battlefield during the French and Indian War three years earlier. Bishop would work for Washington on and off for forty years. As they approached the ferry slip, Washington realized he was right across the river from the plantation of Chamberlayne, a friend. On the spur of the moment, he reined in his horse and headed for the small wooden public ferry that carried visitors and their horses across the Pamunkey River towards the Chamberlayne estate.

George Washington had a physical presence that impressed all who met him, whether the dirt-poor, shabbily dressed farmers on the frontier who relied on him and his soldiers to protect them from the Indians, or the wealthy, finely dressed patricians who lived in the large brick mansions on the neat, well-planned, tree-lined streets of Williamsburg. Washington was a very tall man, six feet, three inches in height and two hundred pounds, and he walked ramrod straight, head high, making him appear even larger to those who were introduced to him. He looked even more intimidating on top of one of his horses; later, a French soldier in the Revolution who saw him for the first time wrote that Americans must be "a band of giants." He had a thick torso, long arms and legs, wide hips, and very thick thighs. The colonel had huge hands, so wide that the hands of other large men disappeared inside his when they greeted each other, prompting the Marquis de Lafayette to remark, "I never saw so large a hand on any human being." Washington wore size thirteen shoes. His face was oval, highlighted by blue-gray eyes and a large nose.

The colonel's hair was reddish-brown and tied in a cue. His skin was pale and burned easily in the hot Virginia summer sun. It was covered with light pock marks from his near-fatal bout with smallpox at age nineteen. His smile, when it could be seen, was enigmatic. The colonel always seemed overly grave to most people when they first met him because he rarely smiled or laughed, probably afraid to show the defective teeth that he worried about all of his life. Yet some found his countenance easy and amiable, especially when he was with friends. One man wrote of the colonel's looks that "in conversations they become animated."

The shape of his eyes always seemed different to people. One person who met him would remark about how grim his eyes appeared and another would describe them as alert, especially when he was intrigued by something. "His eyes were...indicative of deep thoughtfulness, and when in action, on great occasions remarkably lively," wrote a later friend, Jedidiah Morse.

There was an air of authority about him, even at age twenty-seven. His friend George Mercer wrote about him that "in conversation, he looks you full in the face, is deliberate, deferential and engaging. His demeanor is at all times composed and dignified. His movement and gestures are graceful, his walk majestic." Another man wrote, "His general appearance never failed to gain the respect and esteem of all who approached him."

Later, when he was selected as commander in chief of the Continental Army, John Adams would tell people that one of the reasons Congress gave him the job was that nobody had ever met a man who looked more like a general than Washington. Adams's wife Abigail, stumbling for words, wrote of him that "not a king in Europe but would look like a valet by his side." Throughout his life, all who met him were taken by his appearance. A chaplain wrote that anyone who saw him had to believe that he "was reserved for some great destiny," and a teenager who met him said that "so superior did he seem to me to all that I had seen or imagined of the human form." During the war, a doctor wrote, "His personal appearance is truly noble and majestic."

On the afternoon that he stopped off at Chamberlayne's house, though, there was little majesty or nobility about him. Washington had been suffering from dysentery for more than six months. He appeared pale and gaunt, seemed tired, and found it hard to carry himself as well as he usually did.

He knew that guests were in the house as he walked toward the front door because he saw activity throughout the building and horses and coaches in front of it. Washington did not know who they were, however. He was surprised to see Martha Custis as he entered, and all were surprised and pleased that the dashing Colonel Washington, the hero of the French and Indian War, had decided to drop by. They had read about him in the *Virginia Gazette* and had heard about him in the taverns of Williamsburg.

George and Martha had probably met before. They traveled in the same social circles and had been at several of the same functions.

The pair had some of the same friends. Colonel William Fitzhugh, as an example, was a friend of Daniel Custis and also a friend to Washington because he and George shared a passion for race-horses. Fitzhugh not only bred horses, but he also owned a race-track where contests were staged for horses owned by planters in the colony. Washington attended many of them. George and Martha, however, apparently never had the opportunity to engage in lengthy conversation with each other at any of those encounters. There, at Chamberlayne's on that chilly March 5 afternoon, they finally had that chance.

The guests noticed that George and Martha had drifted into a deep conversation as the afternoon wore on. There was small talk with the other guests and Chamberlayne, but everyone there realized that the pair only had eyes for each other. Dinner was served in late afternoon and both George and Martha talked with the others around Chamberlayne's table, enjoying a variety of meats and wines brought into the dining room by servants. Following dinner, George and Martha went into the parlor alone and continued talking in front of a roaring fireplace. Martha, nine months older than George, told him of the death of her husband, her troubles running the plantation, and the woes of trying to be a businesswoman.

And then there were the deaths of her children. Virginians had large families because diseases sometimes took children. The Custises, though, had been struck by genuine tragedy. Two of Martha's four children had died before the age of five. Washington offered his condolences to her on their deaths and on the passing of her husband, and she commiserated with him on the death of his brother Lawrence six years before. She must have felt compassion for him as he explained his years in the military with great frustration, outlining a controversy over a slain French diplomat, the debacle at a stockade called Fort Necessity, and the death of General Braddock. And, too, he lamented, his first effort into politics had met with disaster when he was defeated in his campaign for the House of Burgesses, the Virginia state legislature, in the 1758 elections. Reportedly, it was because he did not buy enough drinks for the men who turned out to vote, an illegal but common practice in Virginia politics.

Neither realized that darkness had started to fall and that all of the other guests had gone home. Martha had planned to stay over, but George had to go on to Mount Vernon. The Chamberlaynes, who, like everyone else in the house, realized a romance was blooming in their parlor, insisted that the colonel remain overnight. They also encouraged the pair to continue talking as the fire burned and, within moments, the Chamberlaynes said good night, rather early, and conveniently disappeared. George and Martha talked long into the night, retiring only when the embers of the fire had died out, leaving the room in near darkness.

In the morning, with the sun enveloping the parlor on the eastern side of the home, the Chamberlaynes mysteriously disappeared once more. Alone again for the next several hours, George and Martha continued their conversation of the previous evening. George's manservant, Bishop, tipped off by Chamberlayne the night before, spent the evening sleeping at their host's house, too, and in the morning chatted with workers as his boss continued to talk, and talk, and talk to Martha Custis. Finally, in early afternoon, George Washington said good-bye to Martha after accepting an invitation to visit her a few weeks later at White House; she wished him good luck with his health. They had talked for over fourteen hours and had genuinely enjoyed each other. It was more than that, however. As she said good-bye to him and he stepped onto the wooden planks of the ferry, both realized that there was a quiet chemistry between them. Something serious had started.

George Washington was ready for marriage. He had courted numerous women in Virginia and in New York, but the relationships never amounted to much. Many of his friends had been married for several years and already had families. He was twenty-seven and it was time for him to settle down. Martha had been a widow for almost a year. A widow in the eighteenth century, especially one with small children, found herself in an extremely awkward position. She had to grieve for her husband

and yet, after an appropriate interval, was expected to remarry. She was invited to social functions and always attended alone. The widow, who knew very little about running her husband's farm, shop, or plantation, had to grapple with his debts and pay-rolls and attempt to run his business. As the widow of a slave-holder, she also had to oversee the lives of the slaves on the family plantation; the management of Custis's over two hundred slaves was an enormous chore. Martha already employed overseers for the slaves, and she hired lawyers and business managers to help her care for the Custis plantations and tobacco exporting business, but she was tired of it.

She was suddenly faced with the management of the Custis plantations at White House, her home there, and her magnificent brick mansion in Williamsburg. She had been brought up to be a plantation wife, not a plantation administrator. She did not know how to manage the business operations of the farms, keep books, buy and sell necessary goods, and oversee the work and lives of her slaves. She needed a man to do that. She knew, too, that it could not be just any man. It had to be a good businessman, some-one with an eye for detail and, most important, someone who spoke and acted with authority.

She was the mother of two children, the adorable two-year-old girl, Patsy, and Jacky, her rambunctious, almost-four-year-old son. Martha had domestics to help her with the children, but they needed a father. It could not be just any father, though. It had to be a man who would not simply care for Patsy and Jacky as stepchildren, but someone who would love them as his own. Their father had to be a man that they grew to genuinely admire.

Martha Custis was a young woman who needed a husband. She enjoyed a good relationship with Daniel Custis, but at nine-teen she was an inexperienced and apprehensive young bride. He was thirty-five. There was love and comfort, but little electricity. Now, at twenty-seven, she wanted a loving mate. Martha was rich and enjoyed a very good life in Virginia, but she was lonely. She wanted to share all the good things in her life with a man her own age, a man she could respect and love. She saw in George

Washington the possible answer to all of her needs. And, she thought, like any young woman, that there was something dashing about a military hero.

The colonel had needs, too, and they were immediate. Mount Vernon was an incomplete home and in disrepair because he was always away on military business and was rarely around to supervise workers refurbishing the house, a challenging project that involved raising the roof to create a full second floor. He had purchased thousands of dollars worth of furnishings and farm equipment and was in debt. He needed money. Washington was at the age when he knew he should have a family. The military had begun to frustrate him, and he yearned for a return to civilian life. He wanted to take his place in Virginia high society, as he had always dreamed, but he had never had the financial and land resources to do so. He also wished to establish Mount Vernon as the grandest estate in Virginia, with a wife who could, with him, welcome guests, and stage dinners, parties, and balls. And he, too, was lonely. He had never met the right woman, and the woman he had fallen deeply in love with, gorgeous Sally Fairfax, was married to his best friend.

In Martha Custis, Washington saw the answer to his own needs. Marriage to her would immediately make him one of the wealthiest men in Virginia and permit him to lead the life of comfort that he had always dreamt about as a member of the gentry. She would give him an immediate family. Her arrival at Mount Vernon as his wife and sexual partner would also, hopefully, put an end to his infatuation with Sally Fairfax and permit him to move on with his life—and his new wife.

And he liked Martha Custis. There was something charming about her that intrigued him.

Washington next saw Martha in late March, when he took her up on her offer to visit at her White House plantation. They met again during the first week of May when she asked him to spend several days at White House. He had been in Williamsburg on business and stopped off at her home for a two-day stay on the way back to Mount Vernon, about sixty miles from White House. There, after getting to know her better and meeting and playing with her two children, he asked Martha Custis to marry him, and she accepted. A pleased Washington immediately ordered a wedding ring from Philadelphia that cost him two pounds and sixteen shillings.

They did not see each other for months afterwards because Washington had to rejoin the Virginia regiment at Fort Cumberland. The regiment was part of a force that captured Fort Duquesne (now Pittsburgh) from the French that summer and renamed it Fort Pitt.

He wrote Martha a tender letter on July 20, 1758, just after the march to Fort Duquesne commenced: "I embrace the opportunity to send a few words to one whose life is now inseparable from mine. Since that happy hour when we made our pledge to each other, my thoughts have been continually going to you as another self. That an all-powerful Providence may keep us both in safety is the prayer of your ever faithful and affectionate friend."

Washington had decided that if the regiment had some success he would retire. He had put in five years of near-continuous service. He had joined the army to pursue his goal of becoming a British officer. It was clear that he would never get that appointment because he was an American. He had no future in the military, and his growing affection for Martha Custis, and his decision to marry her, was the perfect reason to leave it. He did so and returned to White House to visit Martha and her children again during the last week of December. They finalized their plans for a January 6, 1759, wedding, an event that brought him great joy.

There was more good news. Washington had been elected to the House of Burgesses, representing Frederick County, on his second attempt. The colonel had not only been elected, but was the leading vote-getter with 307 votes, well ahead of runner-up Colonel Thomas Martin, who received 240 votes. He did not campaign because he was with the army, but this time, following the advice of local politicians, he made certain that his campaign manager, Colonel James Wood, provided plenty of drinks for those who turned out on election day. To guarantee the landslide, Wood not only arrived at the polls with a barrel of spiked punch, but added thirty-five gallons of hard cider and also bought dinner for all those who voted for Washington.

The wedding of the Washingtons was one of the highlights of the social season in Virginia. Friends and relatives of the pair were quite pleased with the match. Virginians in the gentry were always encouraged to marry into similarly comfortable families, and this merger of the Custis and Washington families fit that tradition. It was Martha's second marriage and, understandably, could have been a small affair. She may have insisted on a lavish ceremony in order to please her husband and to let everyone in the colony know that their marriage was important. They chose January 6 because that was the traditional date of Twelfth Night, the English holiday that celebrated the close of the Christmas season. Christmas was a religious holiday; Twelfth Night was the holiday for dinners, parties, and dancing. It was a date that everyone remembered, and the Washingtons wanted all to remember the day they were joined in matrimony.

The site of the wedding remains uncertain. Some accounts place the ceremony in St. Peter's Episcopal Church, and there is a painting of the marriage in a church. Others contend the event occurred in the parlor of Martha's home at White House. It was an elaborate affair, and the bride and groom wore expensive clothes ordered from London for the occasion. George wore an elegant blue cloth suit with a white satin waistcoat, breeches, and new shoes with shiny gold buckles. White dress gloves covered his large hands. The groom's clothes were tight, as always, because even the best tailors in Great Britain could not properly fit a man of his gargantuan size.

According to family lore, Martha wore an elegant gold damask dress trimmed with lace over a petticoat of white fabric decorated with silver threads. She walked down the aisle in purple satin high-heeled slippers embellished with silver metallic thread, sequins, and pearl jewelry. Later, she made a silver handkerchief out of part of her petticoat that she kept as a memento. The two children wore new clothes specially ordered for the event, too. Washington's manservant, Bishop, was resplendent in one of his British Army uniforms.

The ceremony was conducted by the pastor of St. Peter's, the Rev. David Mossom. Martha arrived in an elegant horse-drawn carriage, and George rode the handsome horse given him by General Braddock. The wedding took place on a cold day, and the countryside around White House was stark; guests arrived dressed in winter coats and gloves, and most shivered a bit as they stepped down from their horses or carriages.

The reception at White House was elegant. Martha Custis's parlor was filled with tables overladen with meats and desserts. Servants brought in wines and ales. Later, in the parlor, guests danced until late in the evening. The reception reportedly continued for three days.

Guests filled every bedroom of White House; others slept in hastily arranged guest quarters in the outbuildings of the plantation. The invited comprised a "Who's Who" of Virginia politics and high society. They included the royal governor, William Fauquier, in scarlet robes, a shoulder-length wig, and a ceremonial sword at his side, and his wife; several members of the state legislature, all dressed in their finest coats; the brothers and sisters of George and Martha; and friends and neighbors from both the Potomac and Pamunkey River regions. It is not known whether George's feisty mother, Mary Ball Washington, was in attendance.

One week after he married Martha, Washington received a very moving congratulatory note on his retirement from the army and also on his wedding from the members of the Virginia Regiment. In it, the men called him "the soul of the corps." Washington wrote an emotional note back, thanking them for their service to the colony and to him, and added tenderly that no one could appreciate the pangs he felt upon parting with a regiment "that has shared my toils and experienced every hardship and danger which I have encountered. Gentlemen, with uncommon sincerity and true affection for the honor you have done me—for if I have acquired any reputation, it is from you I derive it. I thank you also for the love and regard you have all along shown me. It is in this I am rewarded. It is in this I glory."

It was a letter written to show his deep affection for the soldiers that fought with him on the Virginia frontier and to say farewell to the military life. It would also explain why, seventeen years later, Washington would be back in uniform and tens of thousands of other men would risk their lives for him.

The newlyweds opted not to honeymoon and remained at White House plantation for three months. They left only for a visit to Williamsburg for the legislative session, where they were greeted by friends as man and wife for the first time. During the final week of March, George and Martha Washington and their children climbed into their elegant, horse-drawn carriage as trees and flowers began to bloom throughout Virginia. They proceeded north for the banks of the Potomac River and their new home, Mount Vernon.

CHAPTER TWO

COLONEL WASHINGTON

When Martha Washington died in 1802, the Washington family's total assets in money, slaves, land, and their gorgeous mansion on the Potomac—Mount Vernon—made it one of the wealthiest in America. When the first Washington, John, came to America from England in 1656, he was surely one of the poorest.

John Washington, a tall, muscular, robust man, was a victim of the English Civil War that took place in the mid-seventeenth century. His father Lawrence, a rector, lost his post because he sided with the Royalists, not the opposition, and he died in reduced circumstances. His sons John and Lawrence fled to America, nearly penniless. They joined the thousands of people who braved the hard sea passage across the Atlantic.

John Washington labored harder than most when he arrived in America, and he began to buy up parcels of land in the central and northern regions of his new home, Virginia. He also purchased slaves to work on his farms, as so many men did. His sons and grandsons followed this practice of purchasing land and slaves over the next seventy years. They all prospered by growing tobacco, a product much in demand in the British Isles and in Europe.

His grandson Augustine was also a giant of a man. Height and strength were already hallmarks of the Washington men by the time Augustine married Jane Butler. She gave birth to three sons, Butler, Lawrence, and Augustine, and a daughter, Jane, before her death in 1728. Augustine then married Mary Ball, an attractive twenty-three-year-old orphan who already had a reputation as being an excessively strong-willed, highly opinionated woman. The spirited Mary bore him six children at their farm, Pope's Creek Plantation, in the central region of the state. The first child was George, who came into the world on February 22, 1732.

George would have three half brothers, Butler, Lawrence, and Augustine; one half sister, Jane, who died at age two; three brothers, Samuel, John Augustine (Jack), and Charles; and two sisters, Betty and Mildred. He would wind up with twenty-five nephews and nieces from their families, plus five more nephews and nieces from the family of Martha Custis. He maintained close relationships with his brothers and sisters, particularly Jack, throughout their lives.

Augustine Washington moved his family to Ferry Farm, a rather flat piece of land across the Rappahannock River from the tiny but bustling town of Fredericksburg, in order to run an iron foundry nearby. He died young, at forty-nine, as did many of the men in his family, and bequeathed most of his land to his sons by his first marriage. That angered Mary Ball. Lawrence was given a large farm on the southern shore of the Potomac River that he named Mount Vernon, after a military leader he had served under during a brief stint in the British Army. George, eleven at the time, had to be satisfied with the relatively tiny Ferry Farm, its small farm house, and its nineteen slaves. There, he and his mother oversaw the production of wheat, tobacco, and corn. They also earned some money from the operation of a small ferry that crisscrossed the Rappahannock River.

Lawrence Washington married into the wealthy and politically influential Fairfax family soon after taking up residence at Mount Vernon. He told his stepmother that the Fairfaxes had considerable influence and might be able to help young George, then fourteen, obtain an appointment in the British Navy. Perhaps he would be made a cabin boy for a famous sea captain and embark on a career, becoming a captain himself one day, a position of great prestige in society.

The overly protective and irascible Mary would hear none of it. She knew that life in the navy would take George away from her on long and dangerous sea voyages. Seamen visiting different ports, especially in the Caribbean, often contracted fatal diseases, too, such as smallpox and tuberculosis. Her half brother, Joseph Ball, who lived in London, supported her decision, writing to her that not only was navy life unhealthy, but that officers would "use him like a Negro, or rather like a dog." He advised her that her son would be better off as "an apprentice to a tinker" than a seaman.

George had no great desire to join the navy, either, even though he seemed fascinated by military life, and raised no objections to his mother's decision to keep him home at Ferry Farm.

George was intrigued by Virginia society and was determined, even as a young teenager, to find an avenue that would permit him to enter it. Toward that goal, he read whatever he could; simple books at first and, later, popular novels such as *Don Quixote* and *Tristram Shandy*. One of his favorite works was *The Rules of Civility and Decent Behavior in Company and Conversation,* a short guide on how to become a gentleman. Washington read it several times and even copied the entire work in his own handwriting. It would be, he hoped, his guide to upward mobility.

By seventeen, he became a land surveyor, a profession that he thought might help him move into the circles of the rich and influential. Washington had become an expert horseman and learned to read maps and use surveyors' tools left to him by his father. The work gave him a chance to earn money and, best of all, spend long days riding through the countryside. He loved horses almost as much as he loved the rolling farmlands of Virginia. Riding was

a recreation that he enjoyed as a teenager and liked even more as
he grew into a young man. He would ride horses just about every
day of his life. Even then, onlookers were impressed with Washington's grace and skills as he rode various mounts. "He is a very
excellent and bold horseman, leaping the highest fences and going
extremely quick without standing upon his stirrups, bearing on
the bridle, or letting his horse run wild," noted a man who frequently rode with him. Others said that only the veteran express
couriers on their fleet mounts could make the distance between
Winchester and Williamsburg faster than Washington.

There was a great need for Washington's services, but many
planters had all of their money invested in land, slaves, and farming
equipment and could not pay Washington in cash. So they gave him
land, a rather common practice, and in a few years the aggressive surveyor owned fourteen hundred acres in addition to Ferry Farm. He
also surveyed for counties and towns, earning fees for that work.

Washington had grown into a tall, strong young man. He was
often described as "a giant" or "gigantic." He was a muscular man.
He had powerful arms and was able to hurl stones and pieces of
wood great distances. Once, joking with his friend Fielding Lewis,
he bent down, picked up a flat stone, and tossed it quite some distance across the Rappahannock River.

His brother Lawrence convinced him to leave Ferry Farm and
move in with him. Moving north to Mount Vernon was full of
opportunity to help Lawrence, whom he admired; to meet new
people and make friends in Virginia society; and to put some distance between himself and his overbearing mother.

Lawrence's house at Mount Vernon was not a grand mansion
at the time. The residence was actually a one-and-a-half story
structure with dormer windows jutting out from the roof on the
second level—modest compared to most of the plantation homes in
the area and downright puny compared to the lavish, three-story-
high brick manor house with its huge porch and lengthy driveway
at Belvoir, the neighboring plantation, where the Fairfaxes resided.

There at Mount Vernon, having just turned eighteen, George
slowly began to indulge himself in the social life of the Virginia

wealthy, a dream since boyhood. He attended Lawrence's dinner parties and those of friends at nearby plantations. He frequented the taverns of Alexandria, Norfolk, Fredericksburg, and Williamsburg and thoroughly enjoyed the camaraderie and entertainment there. Washington became a dedicated card player, keeping close track of his winnings and losings in games at the raucous taverns that served as the center of social life in those communities. He enjoyed drinking tankards of good ale and listening to funny stories and ribald jokes. Although he spoke little and seemed stoic for someone so young, he was an easy man to get along with and soon assimilated into this new world.

Washington learned how to dance, and dance well, during this time, and enjoyed the fast-paced Irish jigs and Virginia reels as much as the traditional, slow minuets. People marveled at how gracefully he moved for such a big man. His superb dancing made him a sought-after guest. His physical strength and endurance made it possible for him to dance for hours, and it was common for him to dance well past midnight at the lavish parties and balls that were frequent throughout the colony. He developed a love of the stage as he approached the age of twenty and went to the theater in Williamsburg as often as he could to see plays presented by local companies or traveling theater troupes, some from London.

The tall surveyor also developed a fondness for ladies during his travels to Williamsburg and, rumor had it, spent time with some of the actresses in the plays he enjoyed so much. Some of these relationships seemed serious to him at the time, and there were a number of them. Many of his paramours were quite young, such as Mary Fairfax, just fourteen. She reminded him of another type of beauty. He wrote to a friend that the girl "revives my former passion for your lowland beauty, whereas was I to live more retired from young women, I might in some measure alleviate my sorrows by burying that chaste and troublesome passion in the grave of oblivion or eternal forgetfulness."

There were a number of lowland beauties in Washington's pre-martial life. He frequently saw Mary Bland, of Westmoreland County. There was Lucy Grymes, who married Henry Lee and whose grandson was Robert E. Lee. There was Betsy Fauntleroy, just fifteen, who lived on the large Naylor's Hole plantation on the banks of the Rappahannock.

None of these relationships worked out, though. Washington sulked in letters to friends about his romantic failures, and at times he was reluctant to strike up a new relationship with a woman because he feared that it too would result in rejection.

He was, after all, not a scion of a wealthy family or the descendant of British royalty. He was not a physician or lawyer, just a lowly surveyor. As a soldier later, he was merely an American—not a British—officer. Unlike many of the rich young men of Virginia, he had never sailed to England or toured Europe and had no money for such adventures. He was well-read but had not spent much time in a formal school.

Although he comported himself well in small groups of men, he had great difficulty socializing with women. The gift of easy conversation in mixed company eluded him. ("Speak seldom. A dictatorial style, though it may carry conviction, is always accompanied by disgust," he later wrote.) Washington was the son of a domineering mother who would drive any young woman to distraction and, on top of all that, he had bad teeth. To the young women of Virginia, George Washington was a man who did not have much of a future.

But there was something about Washington that all women and men noticed early. Even while still a teenager, friends recalled that he had always looked calm, poised, and possessed of unusual self-assurance. George Mason, a friend, said he had a "commanding countenance." Thomas Jefferson later wrote that he could not remember Washington speaking for more than ten minutes at any session of the Virginia legislature, but always "to the main point, which was to decide the questions." Another man who knew him well wrote that he was "a modest man, but sensible, and speaks little...like a bishop at his prayers." This stoic persona would serve him well all of his life.

The social life at Mount Vernon that he enjoyed disappeared rapidly in the early 1750s. George found that he had to spend much of his time caring for his brother Lawrence, who suffered with crippling tuberculosis. Doctors told Lawrence that a trip to a warm-weather climate might help him recover, so in 1751 he and George sailed to Barbados, in the Caribbean. Lawrence did not heal under the hot Caribbean sun, however, and his tuberculosis became worse, not better. George, his caretaker, derived no enjoyment from the tropical island, either. He contracted a bad case of smallpox and was confined to his bed on the hot, sultry island. He survived, but he had light pock marks on his face for the rest of his life.

They returned to Mount Vernon in far worse condition than when they had left. George came home right away and Lawrence sailed to Bermuda for more rest. When Lawrence finally returned to Mount Vernon, his wife, Anne, and George did what they could to care for him, but Lawrence took a turn for the worse and died in the summer of 1752. He left Mount Vernon and its twenty-five hundred acres to his wife. She remarried a year later and leased the plantation to George, who was next in line to inherit it.

Shortly after entering into the lease agreement, the grieving Washington joined the army. Lawrence had used his connections to the Fairfax family to secure George a commission as an adjutant in one of Virginia's two militia companies. The Fairfax family again interceded for George to enable him to fill Lawrence's old post as an officer in the state regiment. The Fairfaxes had considerable political clout in the colony and George Washington knew it. In a letter that showed his own understanding of the need for influential friends, he wrote to his brother Jack that he should get to know the Fairfaxes: "Live in harmony and good fellowship with the family at Belvoir, as it is in their power to be very serviceable upon many occasions to us as young beginners. I would advise your visiting often as one step towards the rest, if any more is necessary, your own good sense will sufficient dictate; for to that family I am under many obligations, particularly to the old gentleman."

Recognition was always important to George. He wrote to William Byrd in 1755 that he was joining the army out of patriotic fervor, but added, "If I can gain *any credit* or if I am entitled to the least countenance or esteem, it must be from serving my country."

He was direct about his desires to use his connections for success, too, writing to his brother Jack a short time later that he planned to make the utmost of his appointment as one of General Braddock's aides so that he could "push my fortune in the military way."

George Washington's militia service came during a time of considerable tension in the colonies. The French government had started to show some swagger in its possessions in the Ohio River valley, and also in the Great Lakes, building forts and securing trade agreements with the Indian tribes of the Iroqouis Confederation residing there. The British and their American colonists feared Indian raids on colonial towns and farms, and a French takeover of the vast North American territories.

Washington entered the service because he saw the military as another stepping stone to the successful life he sought. British officers were held in high esteem in the colonies.

The French incursion into the middle of America made Virginia governor Robert Dinwiddie apprehensive. England insisted that their holdings in the Americas extended all the way to the Mississippi River, halfway across the continent and, some optimistically argued, all the way to the Pacific Ocean. The French countered that they did not. Dinwiddie wanted a strong message sent to the French demanding their evacuation of the area; he chose his brand-new adjutant, young Washington, twenty-one, to carry it.

Washington, the guide Christopher Gist, and a small party traveled from Virginia to a French compound, Fort Le Boeuf, in what is now northern Pennsylvania, in the months of November and December to deliver the message. At the fort they met with the French commander, Jacques Le Gardeur, sieur de Sainte Pierre, and a prominent Indian chief, Half King, who represented the powerful Iroquois Confederation. Washington wrote that the French officer quickly dismissed the governor's letter, "Telling me that it was their absolute design to take possession of the Ohio and by G——they would do it." Washington remembered, too, Half King's contention that the land contested between the French and

English actually belonged to the Indians who lived there. The rejection, and apprehension about the well-armed French soldiers and Indian warriors all around them, made Washington nervous. He wrote in his journal, "I can't say that ever in my life I suffered so much anxiety as I did in this affair."

In Dinwiddie's name, he graciously accepted the French rejection and the Indian warning. He also took a close look at the French soldiers, their weapons, ammunition, and the architecture of their fort, committing all to memory in case he wound up fighting them later.

His return trip to Virginia was far more arduous than his trek north. He and Gist left in mid-December, after winter had set in. Their trip home was plagued by cold fronts, rain, sleet, and storms that dumped several inches of snow on the land. Their first passage was down a shallow creek with fast-running water. Gist wrote, "We were forced to get out, to keep our canoes from oversetting, several times; the water freezing to our clothes."

They later reached the Allegheny River and traveled down it by raft, but the fast-running waters and sizable chunks of ice caused the raft to become unstable. Washington wrote, "We expected every moment our raft to sink, and ourselves to perish." Shortly thereafter, the current became too strong for anyone to successfully pole the raft, even the muscular Virginian officer. A beleaguered Washington wrote, "The rapidity of the stream threw [ice sheets] with so much violence against the pole that it jerked me out into ten feet of water." He nearly drowned, but was lucky enough to grab the side of the raft as it sailed past him.

A party of Indians had followed them for several days and confronted the men. One fired his musket point-blank at Washington but missed. The Virginians fashioned snowshoes and walked the rest of the way back to Williamsburg, exhausted, hungry, half frozen, and having failed in their mission.

The trip had its benefits, however. First, this initial foray into military life intrigued Washington. Second, it showed him that he— anyone—could live through bitter winters if they were ingenious and resilient. Third, it gave him a little taste of fame. Governor

Dinwiddie asked him to keep a diary of his trip and urged him to publish it upon his return. The pamphlet, *The Journal of Major George Washington,* was reprinted in several colonial newspapers and in magazines in Great Britain. Washington found the notoriety much to his liking.

In 1754, Washington was back in the service and ordered to take charge of a half-built fort at the intersection of the Monongahela and Allegheny rivers in western Pennsylvania. On the way, he learned that the French had seized the garrison, completed construction, and named it Fort Duquesne. Then, his men, along with Indian allies, encountered a small French force of thirty-two soldiers and attacked them. Unfortunately for Washington, Monsieur Joseph Coulon de Villiers, sieur de Jumonville, a diplomat, was one of the French soldiers killed in the attack, which had turned into a massacre when the Indians set upon the enemy.

Washington wrote a letter to his brother that was forwarded to Virginia newspapers. In it, he gloated, "I heard the bullets whistle and believe me there was something charming in the sound." The remark, on the heels of the controversial slaying of the diplomat, in what was said to be the first battle of the French and Indian War, brought mixed reaction. The residents of Virginia seemed to appreciate Washington's self-confident and daring language, but his superiors in London were angered. Even King George II was annoyed by the braggadocio, and said of Washington and his bullets that "he would not say so, if he had been used to hear many."

Washington, fearful of other enemy war parties, ordered the construction of the aptly named Fort Necessity nearby. On July 3, a force of eleven hundred French soldiers and Indian allies, led by the slain de Villier's brother, arrived and laid siege to the wooden stockade and captured it. Washington and his men were permitted to march home, humiliated.

Washington came under withering criticism from many sides. Virginia's governor and the House of Burgesses tried to make the best of the rout, even passing a proclamation praising Washington and his men for "gallant and brave behavior."

Badly shaken by his failed first military engagement and the criticism he received, an angry young Washington resigned. Still, even in departure, he acknowledged his love of the military life. He wrote to a friend, William Fitzhugh, "My inclinations are strongly bent to arms."

He did not remain retired for long. A year later, in 1755, determined to let the world know who controlled North America, England sent one of its best generals, Edward Braddock, with a large and well-supplied army, to march through the Virginia, Pennsylvania, and Ohio regions and crush any French or Indian forces he encountered.

To young Washington, still sulking at Mount Vernon, this was the chance of a lifetime. If he could join this army he would not only have the opportunity to redeem himself, but would share the glory of an historic victory. Best of all, he would serve with the much-heralded Braddock, a man of enormous stature who could surely secure a British Army commission for him. Braddock was glad to have him because Washington knew the landscape, but he took Washington on as an American volunteer and captain, not a British officer.

George Washington possessed two great skills throughout his military life. One, he never made the same mistake twice. Two, he learned everything he could about the enemy. He had done so in his winter trek northward to see the French and in his disastrous encounters with the French and Indians at Fort Necessity. He had learned that Indians traveled light, unencumbered with wagon trains full of supplies. They struck quickly and, if they lost, escaped just as quickly. Indians never attacked an enemy head-to-head in an open field. They lurked in the woods and fought in the brush, or they ambushed a foe.

He gave that information to General Braddock as the highly visible British Army, with its armada of wagons and military bands, inched slowly and noisily westward. Indians had trailed the army, picking off stragglers and scalping them. Washington could feel their ominous presence in the woods. He begged Braddock to move faster.

Washington fell ill with a high fever and stayed behind; he did not catch up with the army until July 7. The sick Virginian arrived on his horse, fragile and still extremely weak, the pains in his stomach bothering him, a pillow tied to his saddle to ease a case of painful hemorrhoids. The very next day the army was ambushed by the French and Indians as it marched down a narrow dirt road in a forest in the Pennsylvania wilderness, just as Washington had feared.

The French soldiers and their Indian allies were in the woods when the ambush started. Braddock began to line his soldiers up in standard defensive military formations in the center of the clearing near the edge of the road where they were trapped. The soldiers were easy targets in their bright red coats and rigid formations. To Washington, they seemed immobilized. Washington sought out Braddock and told him that those types of formations would not work in the battle that was commencing. They had to attack the Indians in the woods and not leave large groups of men exposed and practically defenseless in the open. He asked for permission to take several hundred men into the forest and assault the French and their Indians, fighting the Indians just as the Indians fought everyone else. Braddock turned him down.

There was no time for a second plea because the attack against the British began with a thunderous volley of guns, accompanied by shrill war whoops as the Indians emerged from the woods. A rain of arrows flew through the air along with the musket balls, and within minutes dozens of British soldiers began to fall, dead or wounded, their blood splattering on the crisp, clean uniforms of those standing next to them. The redcoats had little chance in the ambush, as Washington could see from his position on the field. The problem for the English was that most of the men being killed were officers. Braddock lost sixty-three of his eighty-six officers in the skirmish; there were few officers left to direct the men as the fusillade of musket balls continued.

Washington reined in his horse and began to ride across the battlefield to direct men himself. It was a bold move, and he nearly paid for it with his life. He had two horses shot dead underneath him. He himself was shot four times; miraculously, the musket balls merely tore into his clothing and did not hit his body. Apprehensive, but fearless, the Virginian continued to rally the troops.

Then, across the field, he watched as General Braddock was shot in the chest and fell. The general was severely wounded; now there was no leadership. Washington turned and rode toward the wounded general, surrounded by some officers. It was an eerie scene. Braddock was bleeding badly, his shirt and jacket soaked in crimson, and his men were trying to save him amid the roar of gunfire and the hailstorm of musket balls. All around them men fell to the ground screaming.

Displaying a coolness under fire that would later become his trademark, Washington dismounted and began to give orders. He had several men get a stretcher. At Washington's direction, the general was lifted up, placed on it, and hastily carried off the field. The Virginian then began to shout precise orders for an organized retreat. He took command of the army and moved them out of the clearing and through a wooded area back toward the road on which they had arrived.

The British had suffered a devastating defeat that day, with nine hundred of their fourteen hundred troops killed or wounded. Braddock died a few days after the battle; he thanked Washington for saving the regiment and for trying to save his life. To protect Braddock's body from mutilation by the Indians, Washington ordered him buried beneath the roadway and the ground covered over to make it appear undisturbed. Washington then had the army move out in an attempt to put as much distance as possible between the British and the enemy. It worked. The army escaped without a further attack, was able to regroup, and then make its way to safety. Washington's actions had prevented a disaster.

Upon his return to Williamsburg, the twenty-three-year-old officer was applauded for his bravery and leadership. His uncle, Joseph Ball, wrote to him that it was the rash conduct of Braddock that had brought about the defeat, and praised his nephew. "You have behaved yourself in such a martial spirit in all your engagements with the French [since the] Ohio. Go on as you have begun; and God prosper you."

He was the hero of the hour, a man who showed courage under fire. The grateful governor promoted him to colonel, gave him a bonus, and put him in charge of the entire one thousand-man Virginia regiment. Dinwiddie wrote to the state legislature about the soldiers and Washington that "the natural bravery of our countrymen, if ever questioned, is now established beyond a doubt, by those Virginia forces who purchased, with their lives, immortal glory to their country and themselves on the banks of the Monongahela."

Washington's newfound prominence was pleasing for a while, but the French and Indian War was not fought in Virginia. Most of the activity took place in Canada, New York, and the New England states, with some action in the Ohio territory. There was little for Washington to do with his new post except serve as an administrator of several frontier forts. In that capacity he led several campaigns against rumored Indian raiding parties, but found few. He recruited troops for the frontier militia, represented the state with local public officials, and supervised the construction of some garrisons. He gained a reputation as an able administrator, an efficient military leader, and a harsh disciplinarian who meted out frequent lashings for soldier transgressions. He boasted that he had a gallows in his fort and was not afraid to use it to punish his men if necessary.

Over his years in the service, Washington had become a highly praised officer, even though his efforts to gain a commission had failed. He kept his superiors and political figures well-informed about the activities at his posts, was honest with them and his men, and seemed hardworking and productive. He was a military administrator who demanded order and discipline in his camps and forts, and he was an officer who paid attention to every tiny detail. He was directly involved in every aspect of the management of his military posts. These were all skills that would serve him well when he became the administrator of a large plantation when he returned to civilian life, and even more so when events later brought him back to the military.

There was little action for the Virginia regiment on the frontier, though, and Washington became bored. He was appalled when the 1757 militia draft in Virginia produced several hundred fewer soldiers than the required twelve hundred. He complained that the soldiers had no training, telling the governor that they were "[incapable of] defending themselves...or afford any protection to the inhabitants."

Washington was frustrated and began to engage in small political feuds with Dinwiddie, who found fault with his work as head of the regiment. Washington insisted that Dinwiddie pay him the respect he had earned in his years on the frontier. Washington wrote, "No man that was ever employed in a public capacity has endeavored to discharge the trust reposed in him with greater honesty and more zeal for the country's interest than I have done."

He knew, too, that even though he had impressed all of the officers in Braddock's army, he could not obtain a commission as an officer in the regular army because he was a Virginian. He had been an American officer with the army or the state militia since the age of twenty and now, at twenty-four, he was no closer to a much-desired commission. He vented his frustrations to John Campbell, the Earl of Loudon, the new British general in Virginia, in the winter of 1756–1757, telling him that the orders he received were "full of ambiguity" and left him "like a wanderer in the wilderness."

Friends and family tried to convince him to remain in the service and assured him that all Virginians thought highly of him, as did his officers, who lionized him. His half brother Augustine wrote to him, "I am certain that your character does not in the least suffer here. You are in as great esteem as ever with the governor here and especially the House of Burgesses. Don't give up your commission."

At the same time, he realized that Mount Vernon had fallen into disrepair because of his absence. Buildings had collapsed, some cattle and hogs had vanished, and crops were badly harvested. The plantation was in such dismal shape that the front lawn of the main house had turned brown and had to be reseeded. Washington had ordered a large amount of supplies from London to refurbish the home, including parts of a chimney, wallpaper for five rooms, mahogany tables and chairs, and two hundred and fifty window panes, but he was not around to receive them. Washington's neighbor and close friend, George Fairfax, along with a plantation manager, John Patterson, had to oversee repairs to the main house, outbuildings, and slave quarters in Washington's continued absence. They needed decisions from him concerning the renovations, but he was far away.

But the talk around Virginia in the winter of 1757–1758 was not about repairs to Mount Vernon or whether or not Washington would remain in the service. People began to wonder when, or if ever, George Washington would settle down, marry, and raise a family. He was nearly twenty-six, past the age when most men in the gentry married.

All of the colonel's problems were put aside when, at the end of the winter of 1757, George Washington became gravely ill. He fell victim to dysentery, which afflicted many in that era, but his doctors on the frontier had no cure for it. His army doctor, James Craik, a Scotsman, bled Washington several times, the standard practice of the day, to rid his body of tainted blood. It did no good and Washington became bedridden and "unable to walk," according to Craik. The doctor told army officers that their colonel's problems in his bowels and lungs seemed to be incurable by bleeding and medicines. A medicine to cure him of one thing made him ill with something else or, as the confused Craik wrote, "as what is good for him in one respect hurts him in another." He told the colonel to go home, rest, and hope for the best.

Washington's condition deteriorated, and he was bedridden at Mount Vernon for nearly six months. Washington wrote to Dr. Craik that his health was getting worse, not better. He, too, assured him that all he needed to be cured was plenty of rest. Washington was so ill that he actually thought he was going to die, writing an army friend that "wherever I go, or whatever becomes of me, I shall always possess the sincerest and most affectionate regards for you."

It was at that time that the tangled romance he shared with the lovely Sally Fairfax reached its apex. He had met the slim, beautiful, dark-haired Sally, the eldest of the four Cary sisters, daughters of a wealthy Virginia businessman, nearly ten years before when he moved to Mount Vernon to live with his brother Lawrence. Sally had married his friend and next-door neighbor George Fairfax. Washington and Sally had become close friends— very close. Young Washington had become infatuated with the adorable Sally, who was two years older than he. His feelings for her grew deeper as the years went by, despite his friendship with her husband.

George and Sally exchanged letters frequently, beginning in 1755, when Washington was on the frontier with the army. The contents were unknown, but the few that survived indicated that Sally was a hopeless flirt, and George was smitten with her. Ordinary letters from friends in the Potomac region or from those who visited Mount Vernon in his absence often carried postscripts that Sally had sent her regards, or wished him well, or was looking forward to his return.

In 1755 he came back to Mount Vernon after General Braddock had been killed to find a letter from William Fairfax welcoming him. In her lovely handwriting, Sally took it upon herself to write the tantalizing postscript: "Dear sir, after thanking heaven for your safe return, I must accuse you of great unkindness in refusing us the pleasure of seeing you this night. I do assure you that nothing but our being satisfied that our company would be disagreeable should prevent us from trying if our legs would not carry us to Mount Vernon, but if you will not come to us tomorrow morning very early, we shall be at Mount Vernon."

George's brother John "Jack" Augustine, who had been spending time at Mount Vernon, had married and moved far away, leaving the ailing George alone with his servants in the mansion on the Potomac when he returned so sick from the army. At that same time, William Fairfax died. His son George had to travel to England for several months to settle his father's estate. He left his wife Sally alone at Belvoir, next door to Washington.

It was apparent that winter and summer, even as he was planning to marry Martha Custis, that Sally and George tumbled deeper into a romance, the depth of which is not clear. He sent her a note upon his arrival at Mount Vernon to let her know how sick he was and asked if she could help him obtain medicines in Alexandria. These included jellies, hyson tea, and a wine mixed with gum arabic. She did so immediately, riding to Alexandria herself or sending slaves. She could see how sick he was when she saw him the day after his return. Sally visited him frequently at Mount Vernon in her newfound role as nurse. No one knows how often Mrs. Fairfax traveled to see her bachelor neighbor in his bed, how long she stayed, or what was said between them. There is no record of what servants, if any, lingered in the house while she was there in George's bedroom, helping him recover.

Sally was a classic coquette. She was gorgeous and she knew it. Men were attracted to her and she enjoyed their arousal. She flirted with older men as well as young ones, and even flirted with General Braddock when he passed through Alexandria. Sally was a tease and continually kept Washington dangling throughout the years prior to George's marriage. In his letters, Washington constantly asked her, in a roundabout way, if she loved him. There was never a concrete answer. He asked her to write to him frequently but she did not. Early on, in 1756, she even told him to stop writing to her because she did not think the relationship a healthy one. At another point, she said he should only communicate with her through a girlfriend. Sometimes he was welcomed at Belvoir and sometimes he was not. She even had her sister write Washington a curt note telling him to leave Sally alone. He did not. The two played out a classic dance of courtship for years, although no one knows how far it actually went.

The pair developed very deep affection for each other during those years and might have been in love with each other by 1757. Washington's only two existing letters to her clearly indicate this. He wrote her this halting, disorganized, but heartfelt letter on September 12, 1758:

"I profess myself a votary to love. I confess that this lady is known to you. Yes, madam, as well as she is to one, who is too sensible of her charms to deny the power, whose influence he feels and must ever submit to. I feel the force of her amiable beauties in the recollections of a thousand tender passages that I could wish to obliterate, till I am bid to revive them. But experience alas! sadly reminds me how impossible this is—and evinces an opinion which I have long entertained, that there is a destiny which has the sovereign control of our actions, not to be resisted by the strongest efforts of human nature.

"The world has no business to know the object of my love, declared in this manner to you—when I want to conceal it. One thing, above all things in this world I wish to know, and only one person of your acquaintance can solve me that, or guess my meaning, but adieu to this, till happier times, if I shall ever see them."

In the letter, in direct and unmistakable language, Washington told Sally that they were destined for each other, even if in secret. He told her that "the world has no business to know the object of my love, declared in this manner to you."

Two weeks later, on September 25, he sent her another tender letter, referencing secret lovers in the 1713 novel *Cato*. He wrote, "Do we still misunderstand the true meaning of each other's letters? I think it must appear so, though I would feign hope the contrary as I cannot speak plainer without—but I'll say no more, and leave you to guess the rest…I should think my time more agreeable spent, believe me, in playing a part in *Cato* with the company you mention and myself double happy in being the Juba to such a Marcia as you must make."

But perhaps the strongest sentiments he expressed to Sally did not come then, when he was a young man, but long afterward, in 1798, just before he died. Sally's husband George Fairfax had died in England, and Washington wrote Sally one last letter, approved by his wife. In it, he told her that "the happiest moments in my life" were the ones "I have enjoyed in your company." Belvoir had burned down in 1783 in a fire that might have been caused by lightning. George Washington often rode over to Belvoir, each time looking at the ruins and remembering events there. He wrote to the Fairfaxes a line surely intended for Sally, "I could not trace a room in the house [in the ruins] that did not bring to my mind recollections of pleasing scenes."

Sally's loving care and frequent visits in 1757 and the crude medicines of local doctors did very little to help him, though, and his health did not improve as winter deepened and several snow-falls covered the grounds of Mount Vernon. Finally, in March 1758, fed up with his doctors and angry that he was not getting any better, Washington traveled to Williamsburg to visit to Dr. John Anson, one of the colony's most experienced surgeons, in his office on one of the town's narrow lanes. Washington had convinced himself that he never had dysentery. He was certain that he actually had tuberculosis, the same disease that killed his brother Lawrence. Anson, he believed, would tell him that. But the physician did not. The doctor gave Washington a thorough examination and confirmed earlier diagnoses of dysentery. He did not have tuberculosis, Anson said; he would get better, and would hopefully live a long life.

Although his health was still fragile, Washington's spirits now soared. He could return to the regiment. Anson probably told him to remain at Mount Vernon for a few more weeks or months until he was better. The doctor gave him some medicines to help ease his pain. Washington left Williamsburg on horseback a week later, accompanied by Thomas Bishop. On his way home, he realized that he was close to the home of friend William Chamberlayne and decided to take a ferry across the Pamunkey River, a branch of the wider York River, and pay him a visit.

There he saw Martha Custis.

CHAPTER THREE

THE WIDOW
CUSTIS

Martha Custis's childhood was not much different from that of most girls who grew up in the world of very wealthy Virginians. She was born shortly after midnight on June 2, 1731, in one of the upstairs bedrooms of the home of her father, the well-to-do tobacco planter John Dandridge. The house sat on Dandridge's five-hundred-acre plantation on the banks of the Pamunkey River in New Kent County, some twenty-five miles west of Williamsburg, the pristine capital of the Virginia colony. The home on the plantation, named Chestnut Grove, was a two-story wood-frame residence with three rooms on each floor. A wide hallway separated the rooms on both levels. The family's kitchen was housed in one of several small outbuildings nearby, as were most in that era, so that uncontrolled kitchen fires would not burn down the house, and also to avoid heat from cooking in the hot summers.

Martha was the first child of John and Frances Dandridge. She would be joined by three brothers: John, William, and Bartholomew, and four sisters: Anna Maria, Frances, Elizabeth, and Mary. A victim of tragedy all of her life, Martha experienced the pain it brought early as three of her siblings died young. John died at seventeen, Frances at thirteen, and Mary at the age of seven.

Martha's mother, Frances, was the descendant of a clergyman, Reverend Rowland Jones, who arrived from England in 1674 after a monthlong ocean voyage. He became the first vicar of Bruton Parish Church in Williamsburg. His son Orlando Jones became a prominent lawyer and was elected to the House of Burgesses. He married Martha Macon; their daughter was Frances.

John Dandridge was one of many British citizens who left their homeland and sailed to America to take advantage of newfound economic opportunities, especially in the fertile farmlands of the Tidewater region of Virginia, on the shores of the Chesapeake Bay. He certainly was aware that fortunes could be made there, raising tobacco with the labor of thousands of slaves. He arrived with his older brother William. For years William had been an officer in the British Navy, a position of great prominence in the colonies. William became a successful merchant and a member of the influential Royal Governor's Council. John obtained a job as the deputy court clerk of New Kent County and later married the clerk's daughter. His father-in-law died shortly afterward and Dandridge replaced him. It was lucrative position because the clerk was paid an annual salary—one thousand pounds of tobacco, sometimes more—and earned extra fees for each legal transaction in which he participated. These transactions included recording all deeds and leases, registering land patents, probating wills, filling out papers for indentured workers, issuing warrants, collecting bail, and making copies of all paperwork. In rapidly growing Virginia, this was profitable work. Dandridge used his income to acquire tracts of land and slaves, sold them at a profit, and moved to his five-hundred-acre plantation on the banks of the narrow Pamunkey River around 1731.

There, in a relatively uninhabited region of Virginia, Dandridge and his large family prospered. He purchased more slaves to work in his growing tobacco fields and earned substantial profits shipping bales of tobacco to England, where Virginia tobacco was in great demand. The thriving planter was asked to become a vestryman at nearby St. Peter's Anglican church, a small, handsome brick church where the county residents worshipped. The vestrymen ran the church, hired the minister, oversaw the maintenance of the church and parsonage, and organized relief drives to aid the poor of the parish. They assessed and collected monies from parishioners for these purposes. The invitation that he accepted was a sign of his success in Virginia society.

Dandridge's five-hundred-acre estate was small by Virginia standards. Many planters owned thousands of acres; the Fairfax family was said to own over one million acres in the central and northern regions of the state and along the southern banks of the Potomac River. It is unknown how many slaves Dandridge owned, but it could not have been more than a dozen or so. The wealthier families in the region, such as the Fairfaxes and Carters, owned several hundred.

Dandridge was not rich, but he was successful enough to raise his children within the social circles of the upper class of Virginia, and Martha, his eldest, in many respects grew up just like the other daughters of plantation owners. She was trained by her mother on how to be a proper young lady and learned how to run a kitchen, cook meals for her family, make drinks, produce clothes on a spinet, sew by hand, study the Bible, and learn what she could of the crude medicines of the era. She was expected to marry a planter like her father. Then, Martha would have the responsibility of not only caring for her own family, but as the mistress of the plantation would assume responsibility for the care of slaves, indentured servants, and tenants who leased land from the planter and paid for it with percentages of their crops.

From her mother, Martha Dandridge learned to love fine clothing, especially dresses from London, as did many women in New Kent County. The Dandridges, like most, imported their suits and dresses from expensive shops in London. Martha appreciated luxurious dresses and bonnets at an early age and enjoyed the company of other girls who enjoyed being well-dressed.

Martha was probably educated at a nearby school, although records do not give its exact location. It was common in Virginia at that time for a planter to build a one-room school near his house. A tutor, usually from England, would be hired to educate his children in the tiny school, well-equipped with books, chairs, and desks. Some planters invited the children of neighboring families to enroll, too. The tutor was paid a salary and usually lived in the planter's home and dined with his family (this sometimes became uncomfortable when the parents would grill the children on lessons during meals and, if unsatisfied, would complain to the tutor, who was sitting there, that he was not doing his job). Martha reportedly attended a school with children from nearby homes for four or five years and received a good education.

There were also free schools throughout Virginia for the children of lower-income families. These schools, and their teachers, were supported by county taxes. From time to time the wealthy tried to sneak their children into the free schools to save money, but they were almost always found out.

Martha was tutored in mathematics, reading, and writing, with an emphasis on grammar, but she was probably also given some musical instruction and dancing lessons at the school or at home in order to be able to participate in dances held at planters' homes or at lavish balls in Williamsburg. Dancing was the major form of entertainment in Virginia. Many planters hired dancing masters to visit their homes at regular intervals to instruct their children. There, with accompanying music in a refined atmosphere of grace, they learned how to dance the minuet, the Virginia reel, and rousing Irish jigs. The dancing classes were quite popular.

The Dandridge family history is sketchy, and accounts of it by nineteenth-century writers are vague, but reportedly young Martha also learned how to ride horses and enjoyed the experience. She also became quite proficient at lawn bowling, a popular pastime in the region.

But the teenager's life was in some ways different than those of other girls in Virginia's vast plantation world. As the firstborn daughter of the Dandridges, she was doted upon by her parents. Her mother gave birth to seven more children; Martha, as the eldest daughter, often found herself helping to run the household in her pregnant and/or bedridden mother's place—caring for her brothers and sisters, especially when they were sick, overseeing the preparation of meals with domestic slaves, sewing and repairing clothes, and helping in the management of the slaves who worked inside the Dandridge home. She helped her mother with her social calendar and assisted in the care of the many guests who visited and slept over at Chestnut Grove, in an era when frequent visits from friends and neighbors was an important part of Virginia social life. These skills, learned at a young age, enabled her to be a good wife and mother later.

⁓⦚⦚⁓

When Martha turned fifteen, her parents decided that it was time to find her a husband. Most women in Virginia married as teenagers, and there were brides as young as twelve. One wealthy planter called his daughter "an antique virgin" because she was twenty. Single women in their twenties were rare because men outnumbered women two to one in Virginia in the eighteenth century. There were so few women and so many marriage-hungry men that the English government encouraged their women to travel to America and even made a practice of sending women in British prisons to the colonies, especially Virginia, to balance the gender gap (over seven thousand female felons from 1700 to 1799).

Well-to-do families did everything they could to marry off their daughters to sons of other comfortable families. The most appropriate way to enable a daughter to meet eligible young men in the gentry was a social debut in Williamsburg. The town was not only the capital of the colony, home to the royal governor and the Houses of Burgesses, it was the colony's center of cultural life. People rode there in carriages from all over Virginia to partake in its balls, plays, and musical concerts. Women loved to visit the city to buy new clothing and household goods and to make appointments with the hairdressers located there. Men enjoyed the gambling, drinking, and card playing that went on in the town's raucous taverns and, in good weather, they would attend horse races held at the large oval track.

Martha's parents were eager for her to make her formal debut in order to meet hopeful suitors. Many eligible bachelors attended the balls to meet prospective wives. The gala Williamsburg balls were held at different times of the year. Young women were not formally presented to those invited to the ball, as they are at debutante balls today, but they simply attended and were introduced to different people they saw there amid the whirling couples on the dance floor.

The debut was nerve-racking for any young woman. Expensive clothes had to be ordered from London far in advance of the event because it took ships three weeks to cross the Atlantic. Since dressmakers never saw their clients, dresses and men's suits often did not fit properly and had to be home-tailored. The girl had to remember all the dance steps she had learned in her numerous lessons, observe all the social manners of the day, remember to curtsy for the royal governor and his wife, and properly greet those she met. She worried that no one would ask her to dance in the spacious, ornate ballroom in the large governor's mansion. It was located at the end of tree-lined Palace Street, a few blocks from the Duke of Gloucester Street, Williamsburg's main thoroughfare that was crowded with its inns and shops. In addition, the young lady had to deal with the pressure generated by the purpose of her visit—to attract a young man for a husband.

Martha did not attract any of the young men there, but she caught the eye of Daniel Parke Custis, thirty-five, heir to one of the largest fortunes in Virginia and a neighbor she had known casually most of her life. Custis was a kind and gentle man from a family of rogues and eccentrics, led by the impulsive and irascible Daniel Parke, who had scandalized various regions of the British Empire for years.

The egotistical, outlandish, and short-tempered Daniel Parke was a character. As a young man, in a fit of anger, he had challenged the governor of Maryland to a duel. The governor would not have anything to do with the wild-eyed Parke. He then became involved in a lengthy dispute with Doctor Blair of Williamsburg and challenged him to a duel, but Blair declined. Incensed, Parke then announced that the Blair family pew at Bruton Church in the capital belonged to him, and one quiet Sunday morning he physically yanked a very surprised Mrs. Blair out of it, an ill-advised decision that made Parke the target of gossipy Virginians for months.

Daniel Parke married a Virginia girl, Jane Ludwell, when he was seventeen, and they became the parents of two daughters. Unhappy with his wife, Parke departed the colonies, sailed to England, and joined the British Army. Through connections, he managed to become an aide to the Duke of Marlborough and served with him at the battle of Blenheim. It was Parke who was sent to bring news of the great victory to Queen Anne.

Parke arrived back in Virginia shortly afterwards, accompanied by his mistress, whom he referred to as his cousin, and their child, who, in a burst of historic enthusiasm, he had named Julius Caesar. Soon after returning to Virginia and his first family, Parke remembered why he had left in the first place and sailed right back to England. Later, Parke was appointed the governor of the Leeward Islands in the Caribbean, with headquarters at Antigua. A man with a tempestuous personality who was a terrible administrator, Parke was murdered on December 9, 1710, by a mob of local citizens who accused him of rampant corruption and the sexual conquests of local women, many of them married. He was accused of fathering at least one illegitimate child in Antigua.

The two daughters by Jane Ludwell that Parke had abandoned in Virginia married well. Lucy married William Byrd II, one of the wealthiest planters and largest slave owners in America. Frances, a strong-willed and obstinate woman, just like her father, married John Custis IV. The Custis marriage was a tumultuous union from the beginning and the couple fought constantly. Legend had it that he became so upset in an argument with her while riding that he drove their carriage into the Chesapeake Bay.

She haughtily asked him where he was going and he told her that he was going to hell. Not missing a beat, she sneered that was fine with her, that life in hell would be better than life with him.

The pair lived together the best they could, but, based on the inscription of Custis's tombstone, presumably failed. Under his name it read: "Aged 71 years, and yet lived but seven years, which was the space of time he kept a bachelor's home at Arlington, on the eastern shore of Virginia."

The Custises had four children, two of whom died young. A son, Daniel, and a girl, Fanny, survived. In 1715, Frances died of smallpox. John Custis inherited his wife's estate and her portion of the Parke family fortune. What should have been a welcome financial largesse became a monetary albatross. Parke had given Frances, and on her death John Custis, his estate but wrote in his will that she, and then Custis, had to pay all of his debtors. They were legion and included several people who claimed to be his illegitimate children and an entire family in the Leeward Islands that identified him as their husband and father. Parke also owed money to an assortment of businessmen in the Leewards, England, and America. To obtain their money, they all sued John Custis in what the courts wrapped into one massive case called the "Dunbar suit," taking the name from one of the litigants, Thomas Dunbar. The tangled legal claims caused endless aggravation—and the financial drain of legal fees to the Custis family—for more than fifty years.

John Custis never remarried, retiring to Williamsburg where he built a huge brick mansion called Six Chimneys. He also became an accomplished horticulturist and devoted most of his time to his beautiful Williamsburg gardens. He emerged from his rows of roses and azaleas, though, when he learned that his son Daniel was about to marry Martha Dandridge. He had become a cranky old man and maybe he just wanted to make life miserable for his son. Or perhaps, as gossips said, he wanted his son to marry a wealthy woman whose money he could use to fight the Dunbar suit. He certainly did not admire Martha and vehemently opposed the marriage.

His dislike for Martha Dandridge was known by many. He had offered Matthew and Ann Moody some plates and silverware as gifts. Mrs. Moody declined and suggested he give them to his son and his fiancée. Later, she told a court that Custis exploded and ranted "that he would rather [I] have them than any Dandridge daughter or any Dandridge that ever wore a head...Mr. Dandridge's daughter was much inferior to his son."

Daniel Custis was distraught. His father followed through on his threats. He had wrecked several opportunities for Fanny to marry, and when she defied him he disinherited her. For years his father had ruined his own chances to marry, and he was about to do so again. Custis IV had wrecked courtships Daniel had conducted with several women and caused Daniel to remain a bachelor, one of the few in the colony who was in his late thirties. His father had disapproved of every woman that Daniel ever met. John Custis even disapproved of a marriage between Daniel and the daughter of the wealthy William Byrd II.

John Custis IV saw Martha Dandridge as a fortune hunter. She was the daughter of a family that, although comfortable, was rather low in the social strata of Virginia. He became so angry at the prospect of his son's marriage to her that he denounced her in several public places in Williamsburg and then, as a final gesture of his fury, announced that his son would be disinherited if he married Martha. Not only that, he told one and all, but he would leave everything he had to an illegitimate black son he had fathered named Mulatto Jack, whom he had previously freed.

Daniel remembered how he had disinherited Fanny and knew that he would do the same to him. Some of his friends suggested that he simply ignore his father and marry Martha without his approval, but Daniel rejected that idea. The prospective groom could not discuss the matter with his angry father, so he wisely asked friends of his father to intercede for him. These were friends who understood how badly Daniel had been hurt by his father over the years. One of them, attorney James Power, was successful. He spent the night at Custis's home and talked him into approving of the marriage. He wrote to Daniel that Custis told him "he rather you should have her than any lady in Virginia" and that "he was as much enamoured with her character as you are with her person." Ironically, Custis told Power that he changed his mind after he remembered a conversation he had with Martha that he had enjoyed. No one noted what conversation it was, but he relented and the couple won his blessing.

The crusty John Custis, newly enlightened, did not live long enough to see his son's wedding. He died a few months after his consent, on November 22, 1749. His death not only sent his son into a period of mourning, despite their differences, but severely shook young Martha Dandridge.

It was the second dramatic family death in a span of just four months. Martha's younger brother John, seventeen, with whom she was close, drowned while swimming in the Pamunkey River in July. Martha and everyone in the colonies knew that the children of many families died young. There was no preventive medicine to protect colonists from the waves of smallpox that swept the Atlantic seaboard and no medicines to help stricken patients fight off the diseases of the day, especially malaria and meningitis in the southern colonies. And, as in John's case, people died accidentally. There were so many childhood deaths, and people were so cognizant of them, that many parents purposefully had many children, fearful that they would lose some. That sad knowledge did not lessen the grief of Martha Dandridge at the death of her brother, though. Then, a short time later, her future father-in-law died. Within a few years, she would lose two more siblings. She did not get over any of the deaths, as others seemed to do, at least outwardly. They tore her apart and always would. These deaths were the start of a long train of tragedy that would haunt Martha all of her life. The grieving couple postponed the wedding so that everyone could mourn. They were finally married, probably at Chestnut Grove, on May 15, 1750.

Martha moved to Daniel's home at White House plantation following the wedding and quickly became the plantation mistress she had been trained to be since childhood. She oversaw the cooking at the manor house, increased her sewing, which she loved, and taught sewing to the domestic slaves working in her home. She supervised the laundry cleaning, the homemade production of soap and candles, and the mending and purchase of clothing for the slaves. As the wife of a planter, she was in charge of the medical care of her family and the slaves who lived on their farms.

Life at White House, and with Daniel Custis, was quite different from her life at Chestnut Grove. Upon the death of John Custis, Daniel was the sole owner of his vast plantations in several counties in Virginia. Altogether, they covered more than seventeen thousand acres. Daniel was master of more than two hundred slaves on the different plantations and worked with dozens of overseers and farm managers. He was the sole administrator of one of the largest collections of tobacco producing farms in America.

However, Custis soon found himself under considerable stress, stress so bad that it eventually made him physically ill. An immediate problem was his father's will. John Custis may have given his consent for Daniel's marriage to Martha, but he later gave him much aggravation when his will was read. There were two bizarre provisions in it. The first stipulated that none of his descendants could inherit any of his money unless they were named Parke. In another provision, he formally freed his illegitimate son Mulatto Jack and ordered Daniel to turn over to Jack a sizable piece of land, build him a large house, and give him money annually.

Mulatto Jack wound up living at White House with the newlyweds while Daniel Custis, unhappy with the will, consulted lawyers about John Custis's staunch desire to take care of his illegitimate son. Then, suddenly and mysteriously, Jack died. He was bedridden at White House with a severe pain in his neck. Doctors had no idea what ailed the now-freed boy. They treated him with the standard blood-letting procedures of the day, but he died. His odd death ended what appeared to be an insurmountable problem for Daniel Custis and his new wife concerning the deceased father's will.

⁓⊗⊃

Those problems faded when the Custises welcomed their first child, Daniel Parke, into the world in November 1751. A daughter,

Frances, was born in 1753 and another son, John, nicknamed Jacky, in 1754. The Custises had a fourth child, Martha Parke Custis, nicknamed Patsy, in 1756. Their four small children brought them much happiness—for a time.

Tragedy continued to stalk the Custis and Dandridge families. In February 1754, Martha's first child, Daniel, died. Six months later, her father John Dandridge died after collapsing on an excessively hot day at a racetrack in Fredericksburg. Then, in April 1757, another of Martha's children, Frances, died. Martha was crushed by the losses of her father and two children in such a short period.

Daniel Custis was worried about the health of his wife. She had plunged into a deep and dark depression following the deaths of both John and Frances. Her husband commissioned artist John Wollaston to paint life-sized portraits of her two other children, Jacky and Patsy, and had them hung in the large first-floor passageway at White House so that Martha could look at them every day. The permanence of the portraits, he may have told her, would assure the two remaining children of long lives.

It was right after the death of Frances that Martha made a critical decision. She would not succumb to the accepted philosophy that there was little parents could do to prevent the passing of children. Martha made up her mind that she would do everything in her power, for the rest of her life, to protect her remaining children, Patsy and Jacky. She would always be there at home to watch over them, keep servants close to them, take them everywhere she went, and spend any amount of money to bring in every possible medical specialist to treat them if they fell ill. She did not care if the two children believed her to be overprotective; she could not lose them.

And then, as if all the sorrow over losing her first two children was not enough, Martha lost her husband.

Daniel Parke Custis, forty-six, a man of generally good health, became overly worried, along with his wife, when Jacky fell ill in early June 1757. His wife was distraught because she thought she was going to lose another child and that Jacky's death would be just months after Frances's. An alarmed Daniel Custis sent an urgent message to Doctor Carter, one of Williamsburg's best physicians, and implored him to ride immediately to White House to treat his son. Carter arrived shortly after he received the urgent note and began administering largely ineffective medicines to Jacky, whose health did not improve.

Doctor Carter rode back to White House again, his horse galloping as fast as it could, when he received word in early July that not only was Jacky no better, but now Daniel Parke Custis was very sick, probably of heart problems, and bedridden. Martha was frantically trying to care for both husband and son. Carter gave Daniel Custis an array of medicines. They did not help and he expired on July 8, 1757. Martha had now lost her husband, her father, and two of her four children, in addition to three of her siblings. She plunged into mourning, once again donning specially made black mourning clothes for the funeral and burial of her devoted husband.

At first, the young widow found herself overwhelmed in the aftermath of her husband's demise. Jacky was still sick, although improving, and she spent much of her time caring for him and for his younger sister. Martha had planned Daniel's funeral herself and ordered a headstone to be placed at her husband's grave later. She had to alert friends and acquaintances in New Kent County and in Williamsburg that her husband was gone; she also had to inform all of her husband's business partners that he had died, and that she would do her best to take care of the financial affairs of his vast plantations.

Daniel had handled all of the plantation's business, leaving the running of their house and the caring of the children to Martha. Consequently, his wife had little experience as an administrator or businesswoman, and her first meager efforts to master such jobs were frustrating. It was a common experience for widows in the colony. One, Eliza Carrington, wrote that she had no skills to run her husband's estate. "What will become of me?" she said in what was a common refrain for widows.

The laws of Virginia made life for widows a judicial nightmare. A widow was not allowed to act on her own behalf in court and had to have a man act as her surrogate in all legal matters. Fathers and brothers could be surrogates, but the courts always preferred a husband. To avoid that custom, most men named male estate managers or overseers to act for their wives to protect them; Custis, not foreseeing his early demise, did not.

Taking care of Daniel Custis's complicated business proved a daunting task. It meant overseeing the harvesting of a large tobacco crop on several plantations and transporting it to seaports for delivery to England; maintaining dozens of teams of horses; managing more than two hundred slaves and providing food, clothing, and medicine for all of them; plus taking care of her tenant farmers, overseers, and her own family. Most southern businessmen had little cash in their bank accounts because they invested their money in land and slaves, counting on the profits from their tobacco crop to pay their bills. This meant that most planters owed money to businessmen in America or in England; many died in debt.

The widows of wealthy colonial planters who died owing money usually faced immediate lawsuits from their creditors; the payments of debts, or settlements, was not only time-consuming, but it produced acrimony on both sides and genuine distress for a widow who had never been involved in legal suits before. Businessmen took advantage of their inexperience and bereavement and pounced upon widows, filing lawsuits demanding their money within weeks, even days, after their husbands' funerals. Creditors not only filed suits but also pressured relatives and friends of the widow to induce her to pay them immediately, painting her as a scoundrel if she did not.

Lawsuits and smear campaigns against widows were common throughout the colonial and antebellum era in the South, so common that women whose husbands passed away prepared for them. Mrs. Martha Richardson wrote of the suits she was certain that she would face, "I know that every plan will be pursued to cross and vex me," and added, "They have endeavored to make me an outcast in my family."

To prevent such distress, friends stepped forward to help Daniel Custis's amiable young widow. Robert Carter Nicholas, a state legislator and friend of the family, wrote to her less than a month after Daniel's death and told her she had to hire a manager for all of the plantations. She needed to employ a man who could run them and, more important, take care of the buying and selling and oversee the books.

It was a kind and supportive letter, the type she needed in her state of affairs. "I dare say your friends will ease you of as much trouble as they can," it stated. Nicholas went on to suggest quick steps. "It will be absolutely necessary that some person should administer upon the estate," he told her. "As the estate is very large and very extensive…you had better not engage with any but a very able man, though he should require large wages."

Nicholas told her that he and other friends of the Custises would oversee the sale of her tobacco to make certain that she was not shortchanged by factors, or middlemen, in Virginia and in London. They even went to the ports and checked off each shipment from White House as it was put on each vessel in order to keep an accurate record for her.

Nicholas assured her, "If you desire it, we will cheerfully go up to assist in sorting your papers, forwarding invoices, etc., and any other instance that you think I can serve you."

Nicholas and other friends helped her but, most of all, Martha Custis helped herself. By September, Jacky's health was back to normal. Showing surprising self-confidence, she then plunged into the work of running her plantations and tobacco business, oversaw the care of her slaves, wrote letters to banks and creditors, collected money owed to her family, made loans to members of her family, and obtained power of attorney authorization from the best lawyers in Williamsburg to collect debts owed her from companies in England. Her letters, such as one mailed to John Hanbury & Company, her tobacco factor in London, were as professional as that of any planter in Virginia: "I now enclose the bill of lading for the tobacco which I hope will get safe to your hands, and have reason to believe it is extremely good. I hope you will sell it at a good price. Mr. Custis's estate will be kept together for some time and I think it will be proper to continue his account in the same manner as if he was living."

She had other problems besides the detailed business operations of her newfound tobacco empire. The Dunbar suit hung over her, as it had hung over Daniel, and would for years. Neither she nor Daniel had paid George Mercer, the attorney handling the Dunbar suit for them, and he began to send her angry letters demanding his fees, writing to her that without him she would lose the complex and annoying suit. He was demanding £4,000, a large sum of money.

The suit was so aggravating and complex, and would prove so costly if Martha lost it, that she even contemplated, at a lawyer's suggestion, obtaining a legal guardian for three-year-old Jacky to protect him, as an heir, from becoming the target of any lawsuits. In what must have been a prescient look into the future for Mercer, he outlined just the kind of man who should bring up her son. He wrote, "He must not only be a man of fortune and character, but a man of interest and reputation in England."

Martha also had to decide the fate of the elegant Six Chimneys mansion in Williamsburg, the home of her late father-in-law, John Custis IV. She elected to let her brother Bartholomew use it while he attended William and Mary law school in the capital.

And then there was her husband's estate. Daniel Custis died intestate, with no will. The benefit for Martha, with her children, was that she was awarded all of his property, money, and possessions. Normally, a man bequeathed homes, land, and money to his wife and children, but also to parents, siblings, relatives, friends, neighbors, and business associates. A man was usually named as the executor of the estate and told the widow what to do. Martha had everything, making her one of the richest woman in America the day after his passing. The downside of the will was that tallying up all of his property and possessions for the legal papers, work done by male lawyers because Martha was a woman, took a considerable amount of time and effort.

In the middle of all that stress, Martha's thirteen-year-old sister Frances died at Chestnut Grove and the bereaved widow once again had to put on her mourning clothes, once again attend a funeral service, and once again listen to a minister's kind words over a grave of a loved one.

Throughout all of her problems, she drew strength from her rosy outlook on life, telling a friend, "I have learned from experience that the greater part of our happiness or misery depends upon our disposition, and not upon our circumstances."

As the months went by, Martha Custis realized that she did not want to continue to be burdened with all of the work of business and family. She knew that she needed to remarry, but that endeavor was full of problems. There were many men who would happily marry a widow who was now the third-wealthiest individual in Virginia, and Martha knew that.

Marrying for money was common in the Virginia upper class. Children were taught by their parent to hunt wealthy spouses. One frustrated mother wrote of future marriages for her children, "I wish a suitable offer would come Elizabeth's way...and that Berkeley would find some nice girl with a little money to get married to." A Georgia lawyer of the era was just as blunt. "If there was a prospect of plantation or slaves as a dowry there was a rush into matrimony."

Men who needed the practice explained had to look no further than the pages of their local newspaper, where writers constantly reminded readers that a woman's dowry was more important than love or, as a writer in the *Raleigh Register* pointed out, "When a young man is about to get him a wife, the first inquiry he makes is, has such a young lady much property?"

Newspaper accounts of weddings underscored the popularity of rich brides. One story that ran in the *South Carolina Gazette* the same year that Martha was introduced to society at the governor's ball in Williamsburg told its readers that the bride was "possessed of an amiable disposition and handsome fortune," and another wedding announcement informed readers that another bride was "a very amiable lady with a fortune of 1000 lbs sterling."

Some men would marry anybody if the woman had a sizable bank account. John Posey owed George Washington money and could not pay him. In a plea for more time, he wrote that after his wife died he considered marrying an unappealing wealthy local woman just to get money to pay his debts. There were drawbacks. "She is as thick as she is high and gets drunk three times a week...and has violent spirits when drunk," Posey told Washington. He did not marry her because, he admitted, his first wife was just as bad. "I believe I should run the risk [of marrying again] if my last wife had been an even-tempered woman, but her spirit has given me such a shock that I am afraid to run the risk again."

Society also disdained old maids and widows. Newspapers published columns called "The Old Maid" to chastise women who had never married or, if widowed, remained single. A writer for the *Star Gazette* of North Carolina sneered that all widows and old maids were "cranky, good-for-nothing creatures," and that all they did in the community was "take up room."

One genuine suitor for Martha was Charles Carter, the son of Robert "King" Carter, the richest planter in Virginia. Carter was twenty years older than Martha, though, and already had twelve children. She wanted a young man as her second husband and certainly did not want to care for fourteen children. Her first husband had died in his forties and everyone knew that three-quarters of men died before the age of fifty. Her bitter experience with her first father-in-law, John Custis, might have made her fearful of marrying into the Carter family, run by the dogmatic Robert Carter.

There was another reason that she spurned marriage into the Carter family, which might have made her the richest woman in all of America. Older widowers in the colonial South constantly chose very young women as their second, or third, wives. It was common for a wealthy planter in his late forties whose wife had died to marry a teenaged girl; some older men took second brides as young as fifteen. Martha did not want to be just one more young second or third wife. She had been married to one older man; she did not want another.

Friends constantly invited her to their homes for balls, receptions, barbecues, and birthday and anniversary parties. There, all of them tried to play matchmaker, introducing her to dozens of men. They were from diverse backgrounds, earned considerable income, and could provide a comfortable life for her and her two children. She had no interest in any of them.

She was being pressured by family and friends to remarry, but she did not let that force her into a union that she did not want. If all of the tragedies in her young life had any unintended benefit, they had served to harden Martha Custis. The deaths in her family had given her an inner strength that she would retain all of her life, a strength that she would need in the historic adversities that lay ahead for her and her family.

She always accepted the invitations to parties, often taking her small children with her, just to be sociable. Alone at White House, she also appreciated the company of friends. Although she had not met any men that interested her, she enjoyed the parties. And perhaps, as friends insisted, there was a good man out there somewhere who would make a suitable husband and reliable stepfather for her children.

So when the invitation came to visit the home of William Chamberlayne for an afternoon social to be held on March 5, 1758, she accepted. He was the father of her childhood friends and schoolmates, and she had spent so many happy hours in his home as she grew up. That day, Martha talked casually with Chamberlayne and the others and sipped her cup of tea. She was just as surprised as everyone else in the parlor when an uninvited visitor, the much-heralded Colonel George Washington, head of the Virginia Regiment, the man whom the newspapers had written about so often, walked through the front door.

CHAPTER FOUR

THE WASHINGTONS AT MOUNT VERNON

G eorge Washington loved Mount Vernon. He proudly told a friend later in life, "I can truly say that I would rather be at Mount Vernon with a friend or two about me than to be attended at the seat of government by the officers of state and the representatives of every power in Europe." He thought it majestic, writing that "no estate in America is more beautifully situated than this. It lies in a high, dry, and healthful country three hundred miles by water from the sea…and on one of the finest rivers in the world."

The grounds impressed everyone. Reverend Andrew Burnaby, a British minister who toured America in 1759 and 1760, wrote that "the house is most beautifully situated on a very high hill on the banks of the Potomac, and commands a noble prospect of water, of cliffs, of woods, and plantations."

Washington was worried, though, that his new bride Martha, whom he affectionately called Patsy from time to time, would not be happy with Mount Vernon. After all, the home, even though it had been renovated into two full stories over the previous autumn and winter, was much smaller than her mansion at White House Plantation, and it paled in comparison to Six Chimneys in Williamsburg. All of Mount Vernon's farms together were less than three thousand acres, or almost one-sixth the size of her lands. There were only a few dozens workers, most of them slaves, at Mount Vernon, compared to over two hundred slaves at Custis's plantations.

Washington's home was not even finished. The renovations on the house that had been started the previous summer had not been completed by the time the happy newlyweds arrived in early April. The dark wooden bannister on the new, two-story staircase had not been completely installed and the painting of the interior walls of the home remained unfinished because the painter left and stole all of Washington's paint mixture. Washington's lengthy absences had contributed to the disrepair at Mount Vernon, but he also blamed his workers and plantation managers for ignoring the upkeep of the home.

The new groom, eager to make an impression, had sent a frantic note to his manager, John Alton, urging him to spruce up Mount Vernon for the arrival of his bride and her children just twenty-four hours before they were due. He wrote, "You must have the house very well cleaned, and were you to make fire in the rooms below it would air them. You must get two of the bedsteads put up, one in the hall room, and the other in the little dining room that used to be, and have beds made on them against we come. You must also get out the chairs and tables and have them very well rubbed and cleaned; the staircase ought also to be polished in order to make it look well."

He did not want the Custis clan to think he would starve them, and added, "Inquire about in the neighborhood and get some eggs and chickens and prepare in the best manner you can for our coming."

There is no record of Martha Washington's reaction to her arrival at Mount Vernon. It was a different plantation from White

House. Her farms were located in a rather flat region, but Mount Vernon sat in the middle of rolling countryside that was pleasing to the eye. White House rested near the narrow, slowly meandering Pamunkey River, but Mount Vernon sat on a small slope overlooking the wide Potomac, one of America's larger and more impressive rivers. Mount Vernon faced the water, and regardless of what she thought of the smaller house, the view of the majestic Potomac must have been breathtaking. She must have thought the moderate home lovely, too, sitting next to an enormous pecan tree and near sprawling orchards of cherry, poplar, and apple trees, with a few dozen evergreens, cedars, and magnolia trees growing throughout the farm.

The new Mrs. Washington and her children settled in at Mount Vernon rather easily. George and Martha had initially argued about where to reside. White House was a much larger home, but George insisted on living at Mount Vernon. He appreciated everything about Mount Vernon. He enjoyed rising in the morning and looking out at the river, dotted with small sailboats and ships, as it meandered past to the Chesapeake Bay. He loved the way his farms looked in the fall, when the leaves turned into a painter's palette of colors, and in winter, when a thin blanket of freshly fallen snow sometimes covered them. George reveled in riding his favorite horses across his and neighboring lands, splashing through creeks and leaping over fallen trees and narrow ravines and "leaping the highest fences exceedingly quick," according to the Marquis de Chastellux, who rode with him, trying his best to keep up. His best friend George Fairfax lived next door. His brother Lawrence, whom he admired greatly, had died there.

The move to Mount Vernon was a huge step for Martha and her children. She had a number of friends in New Kent County, worshipped with them at St. Peter's Church, and attended balls, parties, and barbecues with them. The heavily wooded northern region of Virginia, where Mount Vernon was located, was fifty miles from Williamsburg—a five-day carriage ride—and still considered the frontier. The main town in the region, Alexandria, was a tiny ferry stop; Martha had never been there. She had no friends or relatives in the area and had no idea if there were children on nearby plantations who could serve as playmates for Jacky and Patsy. Her late husband, two children, father, brothers, and sisters were buried on or near White House.

But Martha agreed to do what her husband wanted her to do; there would be no going back once she agreed to move to Mount Vernon. Martha was so determined to put the past behind her and start the next chapter of her life, and her second marriage, that, except for some furniture, she left all of her belongings at White House. The only remnant from her past life that she brought to Mount Vernon was the elegant carriage that she arrived in with her children. She and her husband would buy all new clothes, books, housewares, horses, and toys for the children at their new home, including cloaks for Jacky and a "fashionably dressed" baby doll for Patsy. Her large new wedding ring tight on her finger, Martha left White House and all of its memories behind, with Mount Vernon and George Washington as her future.

Upon his marriage, George became one of the wealthiest men in Virginia and immediately took steps to increase the size of his lands, purchasing nearby tracts, tripling the size of his work force, and trying to harvest more and better tobacco for sale in London.

Mount Vernon was actually five plantations in one, run by Washington and several overseers, and it included several very small farms leased by tenants who paid rent in cash or in percentages of their crops. Over the years, he purchased tracts of land adjacent to his farms, nearly doubling their size. He hired more overseers for Mount Vernon and the Custis plantations and eventually brought in his cousin Lund Washington as his general manager.

Washington, like all of the rich planters in Virginia and other southern colonies, saw his plantation as a personal kingdom, a duchy within the colony of Virginia. Because of its vast size and considerable population of family, paid workers, and slaves, he saw it as its own country. Some planters might have the blood of English nobility, like the Fairfaxes, but most, like Washington, did not. They could live like English lords, though, by acquiring land

and slaves and building mansions. The estates fulfilled, Robert Beverley wrote, "the ambition each had of being Lord of a vast...territory."

The Virginia estates, like those of their forebearers in Britain, were anchored by a large manor house with as many chimneys as possible for both warmth and appearance. That home was surrounded by outbuildings of varying sizes for stables, tanners, carpenters, shoemakers, weavers, knitters, liquor distillers, blacksmiths, kitchens, food and supply storage, carriage houses, bake houses, and a school. Sizable plantations such as Mount Vernon usually contained large dairy and poultry houses plus pens for the cattle and hogs that were slaughtered for food. The paid white craftsmen, indentured workers, and slaves who labored there made up a large village of people who cared for a substantial community.

The manor houses sat in the middle of plantations like the elegant castles of Europe. Colorful, carefully laid-out gardens graced the grounds to the rear of the home. Smooth brick pathways, some encrusted with oyster shells, crisscrossed the lawns around the house. A long dirt driveway, often as wide as fifty feet, that often cut through rows of cherry or poplar trees, brought travelers to the manor house from the county road.

The main houses themselves were large and impressive. The Carter home, Nomini Hall, was two stories high, seventy-six feet wide by forty-four feet deep. Most homes were smaller, but planters often added wings, as did the Washingtons, to make them larger. A typical planter's home contained a parlor or ballroom, library, and dining room. Some had a second dining room just for the children and a billiard room that contained card tables. Bedrooms filled the upstairs.

These huge plantations were owned by a small percentage of the residents of Virginia. Most Virginians were subsistence farmers who lived in tiny homes on small farms and toiled from dawn to dusk to produce enough food to feed their families. Only about one-quarter of all southerners owned any slaves at all, and most of those only owned one or two to assist with farming. Many families on the frontier, in the western section of the state, lived in one- or two-room cabins and barely survived. Their primitive mode of living startled any wealthy planter who traveled through the region.

William Byrd rode through while doing some surveying work and stayed with several families. The patrician planter was aghast at their living conditions, writing disdainfully that in one home all nine members of the family lived in one room, where they "all pigged lovingly together." Washington, too, was appalled by the frontier life. On one of his surveying trips he stayed with a family that had no shelter. The family, and Washington, slept around a campfire. The horrified squire of Mount Vernon wrote that they were "a parcel of barbarians" and that they slept on makeshift hay beds around the fire "like a parcel of dogs and cats."

The wealthy planters were an anomaly, but it was their huge homes that most travelers visited or saw from the main highways that ran through the state. It was these sprawling fiefdoms that they wrote about in their diaries, journals, and letters. Frenchman Abbe Robin, who traveled through Virginia in 1781, was one of many impressed with homes like Mount Vernon and noted that they were very different from the homes he had seen in the New England and Middle Atlantic states, and that the South appeared an entirely different country.

"As we advance towards the south," he wrote, "we observe a sensible difference in the manners and customs of the people. We no longer find, as in Connecticut, houses situated along the road at small distances, just large enough to contain a single family, and the household furniture nothing more than is barely necessary; here are spacious habitations, consisting of different buildings, at some distance from each other, surrounded with plantations that extend beyond the reach of the eye."

Those who approached homes by river, such as Englishman William Grove, were even more impressed. He wrote, "The north side [of the river]...is thick seated with gentry on its banks within a mile or at most two miles from each other...Most of these have pleasant gardens and the prospect of the river render them very pleasant [and] equal to the Thames from London."

This was the face of Virginia that appeared in travelers' accounts published in newspapers and magazines; it was this Virginia that soon became the setting for so many romantic novels of the era.

These little kingdoms in Virginia, called "country seats" by some, were not just landscapes. They represented victory by the owners over nature and civilization. Planters lived far from each other and from cities. Their large farms created a splendid isolation for them from the colony and the world. The many visitors who drove up to the fronts of their opulent homes were made to feel, psychologically as well as metaphysically, that they truly had arrived in a kingdom. And few kingdoms were as appealing as Mount Vernon.

⧼⧽

One of the reasons Martha Washington had chosen George as a husband was because she needed a good administrator to take care of her estate, including the running of her plantations in York, New Kent, King William, Accomac, and Hanover counties, the overseeing of her slaves, growing and shipping of her tobacco, and the handling of the Dunbar suit. George moved quickly to take over all of those responsibilities, as he had promised. He hired some of the best lawyers in Virginia to turn over her one-third of the Custis estate to him as her husband and they arranged for him to assume the management of the estates of Jacky and Patsy, all routine at the time.

Washington immediately sent terse letters to all the businessmen with whom Martha dealt and her middlemen in the tobacco business in Virginia and England, plus the Robert Cary Company that acted on her behalf in her purchases in London, telling them that they had to deal with him now.

He acknowledged to Cary, and all the others, that the combined plantations of White House and Mount Vernon would mean enormous profits for them. He asked for statements from each outlining what they could do for him, reminding them in abrupt language that if his own profits were not high enough, he would take his business elsewhere. He also warned them against cheating him. He wrote to Cary, "Take some pains to inform your-selves exactly [on prices], because should the prices differ from those of the estate I might possibly think myself deceived and be disgusted."

His wife had no objections to his complete takeover of her estate. It was common in the southern colonies; women simply shrugged and accepted it. Women in the northern colonies were forced to accept policies such as this, too, but they did not like it. Abigail Adams, the wife of John Adams, fumed, "Even in the freest countries our property is subject to the control and disposal of our partners, to whom the laws have given a sovereign author-ity. Deprived of a voice in legislation, obliged to submit to those laws which are imposed upon us, is it not sufficient to make us indifferent to the public welfare?"

In the South, however, women did not share Abigail's beliefs. Martha certainly did not. She assumed the same wifely duties at Mount Vernon that she had handled at White House. The running of the manor house and its acres of gardens, long green lawns, and grounds was Martha's primary responsibility. She oversaw activ-ities in the kitchen, smokehouse, dairy, and the home itself, super-vising a staff of twelve men and women house slaves. These people worked as cleaners, butlers, cooks, and nannies for her children. She also oversaw a group of slaves who became expert spinners and produced most of the clothing for the slaves at Mount Vernon in a special spinning house. Along with George, she purchased wines, food, and other items for her home.

People who worked for the new Mrs. Washington, or met her, liked her instantly. They told friends that "her eyes were dark and expressive of the most kindly good nature; her complexion fair; her features beautiful and her whole face beamed with intelli-gence. Her temper, though quick, was sweet and placable, and her manners were extremely winning. She was fond of life, loved the society of her friends, always dressed with scrupulous regard to the requirements of the best fashions of the day, and was in every respect a brilliant member of the social circles."

She had moved into a small, refurbished home that still needed work, but knew of her husband's elaborate plans to turn Mount Vernon into a much larger and more beautiful home with well-manicured grounds and gardens full of sweet-smelling flowers not only as lovely as any in Virginia, but as impressive as any that could be found in London itself.

She had only been with George Washington a few times during their courtship and knew him, as all did, as a hardworking and rather tough colonel in the Virginia Regiment and, prior to that, a competent surveyor. She knew that he was a strong, athletic man and a fine horseman. He played cards, bought lottery tickets, went to the racetrack, and loved to spend long evenings drinking with his male friends at taverns. He exhibited all the characteristics of a tough, manly army officer.

What she discovered upon her arrival at Mount Vernon in those first few months of her marriage, though, was a man with an extra dimension that she must have adored. George Washington, unlike most men of the era, loved the finer things in life, whether elegant carriages, finely made clothes, ornately decorated dishware and wine decanters, handsome furniture, elegant candleholders, or pretty gardens. Martha recognized this characteristic during their first few months together at White House, but it was crystallized when she arrived at Mount Vernon and joined him in the renovation of the home that would take up all of their lives.

George Washington was a fashion plate. All of the men and women in the Virginia upper class were very conscious of the latest fashions from London that they read about in colonial and British newspapers and magazines. The colonists always strove to maintain their connections to England, and one of the most direct ties was fashion. They purchased men's suits and women's dresses that were popular in England because it was not only a way to look good, but it was also to continue to be members of Britain's much envied social world, even if they were three thousand miles and a wide ocean away. As early as 1619, reports were filed that the men of Virginia, even menial workers, dressed in rich silks on Sunday.

There was a difference in the taste in clothes exhibited by George and Martha. George was a flashy dresser who insisted on wearing the most fashionable men's shirts, jackets, and breeches from London, expensive stockings, and expensive shoes with shiny brass buckles. He was usually the best-dressed man wherever he went, whether it was to the meetings of the state legislature, the taverns of Williamsburg, the governor's balls, or the racetrack. He reveled in expensive hats and jackets and ordered them with the fastidious care of a fashion designer.

Martha's tastes were elegant, but simple. Mrs. Washington always opted for plain dresses over the lavish gowns that most of her high-society contemporaries favored. She preferred that her children wear simple clothing and insisted on it for Patsy when she became a teenager and began to yearn for the expensive dresses her friends wore. Whenever she sent an order for goods to the Carys in London, Martha stipulated that the buyers should not purchase the most expensive types, but look for cheaper ones. In one invoice, she wrote that she desired a fashionable lace dress with ruffles, cap, and handkerchief, but "not to exceed 40 lbs." She requested a firestone necklace and earrings, but "not to exceed 7 lbs.," and a hand fan "at a guinea."

Cost-wary Martha often complained that the prices in London were too high and that she was being overcharged. In an angry letter she signed with George, she wrote that a London store had sent her daughter a dress but did not include a cap and tippet that was supposed to go with it. She threatened to return the dress. She argued that five caps she purchased "might have been bought in the country at a much less price" and insisted that when she said she wanted a dress for 40 lbs, the buyers should not send her a higher priced one. She wrote that she showed several women an expensive dress she had purchased via her London buyers and that "all agree that they are most extravagantly high charged."

Martha's individually designed ballroom gowns and party dresses were costly, but also plain. She never appeared in public dressed like the "feathered birds" that many men complained about. When working around the home, she wore a plain day dress, perhaps with an apron tied around her waist. Visitors always commented on her ordinary clothing because it contrasted with the elegant dress of other wealthy women.

She maintained her simple appearance all of her life. Later, Claude Blanchard, a Frenchman, used to women in spectacular gowns, met her at Mount Vernon and was surprised at her appearance. He wrote that "she was dressed very plainly and her manners were simple in all respects." Another man, Olney Winsor, was also struck by her lack of glamour. He wrote that she "was dressed in plain black satin gown, with long sleeves, a figured lawn apron and handkerchief, gauze french night cap with black bows—all very neat, but not gaudy." Years later, when Martha was the First Lady, Abigail Adams wrote her sister that Mrs. Washington "received me with great ease and politeness. She is plain in her dress, but that plainness is the best of every article."

Martha and her husband were usually happy with orders from London, but they complained loudly when they received damaged goods or when purchases were missing. One shipment was deposited at a wharf on the wrong river and had to be transported to Mount Vernon at Washington's expense. Another shipment did not contain a full trunk of items for Patsy that the girl had longed for over several months; George painstakingly searched the entire hold of the ship, angry, and could not find it. Machinery arrived with parts missing. Wine bottles were stolen by the crew or smashed in a storm. He sometimes received what would today pass for the generic brand of dishes or kitchenware. When merchants in London learned that their goods were going to America they generally added 10 percent to the price. Washington fumed at this treatment. On one occasion he caustically told a friend that the goods from London were "mean in quality, but not in price, for in this they excel." On another, he snarled about "the latest in fashion" that the clothes he received "could only have been used by our forefathers in the days of yore."

Martha was angry about shipments, too, but the clothes she received were usually suitable. Martha could not have known it then, in her first years of marriage to George Washington, but her impressive, yet frill-less, simple, no-nonsense style of dressing would make her a woman that every woman in America, regardless of fortune or social standing, could connect to when she became the First Lady of the United States. Her simple look made her a distinctly American woman.

⁓

George Washington was not only a productive farmer, but a savvy one. He continued to raise tobacco, the most popular crop in the Chesapeake region, almost ninety thousand pounds of it each year, as his brother Lawrence had done. He also grew hundreds of acres of wheat and corn for sale and to feed his family and the slaves on his plantations, just as Lawrence had done. All of the planters in Virginia did the same, relying on tobacco leaves for profits and other crops for food. Tobacco had been so profitable for so long that it had come to represent Virginia life. Washington's problem, though, was that the soil on his farms was just not suited for the production of excellent tobacco plants. Tobacco middlemen in Virginia and London explained that was why they could never sell his tobacco for the same price they received for tobacco from most other Virginia farms, despite his efforts of using five different strains of tobacco. His tobacco failures frustrated Washington. He wrote to Robert Cary, "I confess it to be an art beyond my skill, to succeed in making good tobacco, as I have used my utmost endeavours for that purpose this two or three years past."

Instead of cursing his luck, George turned to other means of making money off his farms. Washington, unlike most farmers, kept a careful eye on the prices and popularity of tobacco in Europe. They were both declining by the mid-1760s. He then drastically cut back his production of tobacco, and he increased the production of wheat after reading reports that several bad wheat harvests in Europe had created a new demand for it from America. He not only provided tons of wheat, but he also experimented with a new style of cutting wheat. Washington's innovatively grown wheat was soon considered the best in America and sold well in England. He also planted more corn and sold it, plus oats, rye, barley, peas, potatoes, and turnips. He complained that the cost of clothing for his slaves was too high, so he set aside large acreage for the raising of sheep. The animals were shorn and the wool turned over to his wife who, with dozens of domestic slaves, used spinners to turn it into clothing. To provide meat for his plantations he raised herds of cattle, each animal branded "G.W." He bred horses and then added mules, animals he thought better suited for work on the plantation. The resourceful planter even tried to raise buffalo.

Over the years, Washington read every book he could find on soil management and engaged in a lengthy correspondence with British farming expert Arthur Young and implemented some of his suggestions. Washington started to alternate the crops he grew on Mount Vernon soil in order to better utilize the earth. Most farmers rotated three crops in three years to keep the soil fresh, but Washington rotated four crops and later seven. He grew all kinds of grass and was one of the first to experiment with manure as fertilizer to successfully improve his soil. Washington improved on the construction of plows and wagons and designed and produced his own tools. He grew flax and hemp and then hired weavers to assist Martha's tiny factory of spinners to turn them into clothing for his slave family.

A few years after he brought Martha to Mount Vernon, George built his own flour mill. He also bought a fully equipped fishing schooner expressly for the purpose of catching fish in the fertile Potomac and Chesapeake to use them for food for his farm families, black and white, and for commercial sale. His slaves caught over one million fish each year that they salted, sealed in barrels, and sold in America and in the West Indies at enormous profits. Always looking for a way to make money, Washington even turned to whiskey later in life, building at Mount Vernon what became the largest distillery in America.

Washington was a land speculator. He bought seventeen hundred acres of wooded land from a nearby planter and, emboldened, set about with others in attempting to buy or lease substantial tracts of disputed land in the far reaches of Virginia near the Ohio River and in a large marshy area south of the Chesapeake called the Great Dismal Swamp. Although neither of these ventures brought him any profit at first, they showed not only his ambition to acquire property but also his newfound ability to do so with his bride's fortune.

These ventures also showed that Washington could be nasty in some of his business transactions. One of his investors in a land project complained that he was being shortchanged. The colonel sent him a heated letter. He accused the man of "sottishness," "stupidity," and "rudeness" and told him of his accusation, "I am not accustomed to receive such from any man, nor would have taken the same language from you personally, without letting you feel some marks of my resentment."

Washington worked as hard as his slaves and the men he employed. He rose before dawn every morning and spent more than an hour going over his records. Just prior to the Revolution, the Washingtons added a wing to the southeast corner of their home. George went to the high-ceilinged first-floor study of that wing to go over plantation paperwork, account books, and letters before having breakfast with Martha, who rose just after sunup. The fifteen-foot-square room, where he washed, shaved, and dressed so as to not awaken his wife upstairs in their bedroom, was illuminated by candlelight that early, and later by sunlight streaming through two high, narrow windows on the southeastern wall. Following his morning paperwork, he walked some fifty yards south, down a slight incline, to his horse stable, opposite the barn for his carriages. Six stable boys worked there full time and one saddled a horse for the tall planter, who hoisted himself onto the mount and rode off to his farms for a long day of work.

His overseers were up early, too, because they knew that shortly after 8 a.m. they would be able to spot Washington crossing the fields at a leisurely gallop. The huge man and his handsome horses were familiar figures as the sun climbed over the Potomac early in the morning. In the field, Washington did not merely issue work orders for the day. He spent the days working next to his slaves to plant corn, harvest wheat, renovate buildings, and bale tobacco. As an example, one winter he decided to move the bricklayer's house at one of his Mount Vernon farms several hundred yards, so, as he wrote in his diary, he "went out early myself and continued with my people till one o'clock by which time we got the house about 250 yards."

He had his overseers write notes to him constantly so that he knew the problems they encountered at each of his plantations. They were instructed to tell him about medical problems, too, so that he could attend to them. Most were trivial, but some were alarming, such as a January 19, 1760, note from overseer Christopher Hardwick at the Bullskin plantation describing a smallpox epidemic that had just hit nearby farms.

Washington always checked up on the overseers, and they were severely reprimanded when they could not be found. On January 26, 1760, he scolded an overseer named Williamson for being absent from his post at his Muddy Hole farm. Two days later, he chastised another overseer for "indolence." He once complained bitterly in the fields to anyone within earshot that horses he had requested from another of his farms were so "abused" by "my rascally overseer Hardwick" that they were not fit to work.

Washington had to be careful about his overseers and his white craftsmen, such as carpenters, that he hired. Unlike his slaves, the craftsmen did not have to remain at Mount Vernon. Craftsmen were in great demand and many would quit following a dispute, or if they felt they had been insulted. One craftsman had been given cornbread for breakfast, instead of the usual wheat bread that the members of another planter's family ate, and quit. Another who felt the planter was too critical of him threw his set of keys at him and stormed off, never to return.

The squire of Mount Vernon was always trying to produce more and better crops and cut more and better contoured wood planks for house construction. He could be unnerving to workers in his efforts to do so. As an example, he once asked four carpenters how many feet of wood they had cut from downed trees the day before. They told him 120 feet. He suggested that they could produce more. They answered that they could not. He told them to go to work and sat there all day watching them with a watch, tracking the amount of time it took to cut the wood. He wrote in his diary that night that "it appears very clear…that they ought to yield 125 feet while the days are at their present length and more as they increase." Washington had spent an entire day to discover that working nonstop, with him watching, his workers could increase woodcutting productivity by 4 percent.

He was an obsessive micromanager who felt it necessary to be completely involved in every aspect of the work at Mount Vernon and its vast farms. It was an insatiable attention to detail that would benefit him greatly when he took command of the Continental Army a generation later.

Washington kept a close watch on the weather at all times in order to avoid losing crops to heavy rains, snows, or frosts. His care for detail in his weather notes was amazing, such as a remark he jotted down in the winter of 1760 as he observed the sky, "The wind got to the north and often clouded up and threatened rain but in the evening at sunset it cleared and seemed to promise fair weather." He kept meticulous weather diaries and tracked his harvests against the weather, becoming quite an expert meteorologist. His careful attention to weather would later become vital when he took over the army.

The love of the finer things in life that they shared, and could certainly afford, led the Washingtons to renovate Mount Vernon and its enormous grounds continually. George Washington would work on the expansion at Mount Vernon throughout all of his life. All of the many thousands of hours he devoted over the years to the care and improvement of his home and plantation were never a chore to him because he loved the endeavor. George and Martha discussed the furniture, bedspreads, paintings, and china they ordered from London for the house, with Martha's sense of style and interior design enabling them to obtain furniture as fine as any in the mansions of the South. They talked about doubling the size of the house by adding wings on each side of it, and also creating a spacious dining room, but that would not come about for another fourteen years.

One thing they did accomplish right away was the complete renovation of the grounds behind and in front of the main house. Washington did not have the money to build a colossal manor house, but he thought that he could give Mount Vernon just as much grandeur with beautifully planned and manicured grounds that would be pleasing to the eyes of any visitors as they rode up in a horsedrawn carriage or on horseback.

One of the first things Washington did was plant his gardens. In fact, among the first books he ordered after his marriage was *Langley's Book of Gardening,* one of several volumes on building produced by Batty Langley, an English architect. George was at first disappointed that he could not plant gardens at the rear of the house, where tradition dictated they be situated, because the ground there sloped down towards the river, making gardens impractical. He decided to put them in the front of the house, but feared that the two outbuildings west of the main house that housed slaves would throw off the symmetry of the property.

So he built two more outbuildings on the east side of his home to balance the others. One was the kitchen and the other the smokehouse. He then connected these buildings to the main house with walkways of low brick walls and wooden canopies. He eventually constructed eight outbuildings, all balanced around the main house. Washington decided to plant not one but two quite large gardens, closed off by brick walls to keep out animals. One was a four-acre fruit garden where he grew plums, apples, cherries, peaches, pears, and berries, plus some vegetables. The other was a flower garden that was tended by several full-time gardeners.

The best way to make the main house and outbuildings functional was to connect them to each other and the county road by a vast circular roadway, and not a straight drive, from the road to the home. When finished after several years, this meant that any visitors' first look at the Washington home was across about four hundred yards of open green lawn, a sweeping and impressive view. This architectural look, forced upon him by the lay of the land, not only enabled him to enjoy his gardens, but it also left the gorgeous slope of land down to the water at the rear of the house unfettered by anything. It provided the Washingtons a majestic view of the Potomac when they woke up in the morning and afforded their thousands of guests over the years one of the most striking views in all of America.

CHAPTER FIVE

MARTHA WASHINGTON: THE MISTRESS OF MOUNT VERNON

M artha Washington had been trained to be the typical plantation wife since childhood. In Virginia, she lived in a patriarchal society in which men dominated politics, business, and their marriages, and women had no power or influence outside of the home. Women who married knew that they had no rights within the union.

The husband owned everything, and a man who married a widow was given ownership of all of her property and monies. She might protest his decision on where they would live (as Martha apparently did), but in the end the wife had to reside in a place of his choosing. The husband not only could dictate how their children should be brought up during his lifetime, he could also dictate it after his death in his will, which the wife had to honor. The husband owned everything the wife either brought with her to the marriage or acquired. He owned all of her clothing, shoes, and horses, and he had the right to bequeath them to someone else in his will. The man of the house had an unrestrained right to hit his wife if he was unhappy with her (George never did). Her husband was responsible for her behavior and could chastise her, in private or public, and was expected to do so if he did not approve of her actions. She was not permitted to argue with her husband in public, to interrupt others when they spoke, or to offer her opinions about public matters. These women did not champion political causes, write letters to the editors of newspapers, or engage in public debates. Books, magazines, and newspapers constantly reminded them of the rules of marriage. A woman was expected to obey her husband at all times and, no matter how poorly he behaved, to put up with him.

Dr. Benjamin Rush, a prominent Philadelphia physician and later the chief surgeon in the Continental Army, told a woman about to be married, "From the day you marry you are to have no will of your own...the subordination of your sex to ours is enforced by nature, by reason, and by revelation" and reminded her that she had to do what her husband wanted no matter how much she disagreed. "The happiest marriages I have known have been those when the subordination I have recommended has been most complete." Another famed Philadelphian, Benjamin Franklin, was just as blunt, telling women, "Nature, and the circumstances of human life, seem indeed to design for man that superiority."

Obedience was urged in the numerous publications of the era. In a popular pamphlet on marriage, "The Well Ordered Family," Benjamin Wadsworth wrote that "the husband and wife should respect and honor each other, though the husband is ever to be esteemed the superior, the head, and to be reverenced and obeyed as such." In his bestselling book, *Sermon to Young Women,* Rev. James Fordyce told women that they did not have as much "vigor" as males and that "your business chiefly is to read men, in order to make yourself agreeable and useful."

The wife's role among the middle and working classes in the mid-seventeenth century was not much different than that of the wealthy spouse. Both were expected to leave politics, commerce, and all public matters to their husbands and spend their time tending to their families, homes, and gardens. They were assured that in the domestic sphere they would find the same satisfaction the men found in the world outside the home. Ironically, given the future lives of the Washingtons, one woman author saw the man of the house as "the warrior" full of "stern ambition" and the woman at his side to raise his family.

Thomas Nelson Page, an antebellum fiction writer who gained fame with his Old South and "Cavalier" novels, described the colonial wife well in his nonfiction book, *Social Life in Old Virginia:* "Her life was one long act of devotion, devotion to God, devotion to her husband, devotion to her children, devotion to her servants, the poor, to humanity...the training of her children was her work. She watched over them, inspired them, led them, governed them; her will impelled them; her word to them, as to her servants, was law."

Women were also expected to shun public debates and business in return for the comforts of family. "Woman naturally shrinks from public gaze and from the struggle and competitions of life," wrote George Fitzhugh, of the Virginia Fitzhughs, friends of the Washingtons.

The women, and their men, became part of what journalists and fiction writers soon came to call "the sunny South," a world of noble cavalier husbands and happy spouses where everybody, oppressed wives and slaves included, appeared content in a neat and well-run patriarchal world.

Wives were stuck; there was no legal divorce in Virginia. The only way for a wife to be rid of her husband was to run away with someone else or return to her mother's home. Many wives did so and managed to get back at their husbands by writing vicious letters to the editor of their local newspaper explaining why they had left them.

In one savage letter, Elizabeth Moore fumed about her husband, Filmer: "As [he] has publicly said that his mother would sooner live in a hollow tree than with me and has removed me to my father's house, with promise to come and live with me until I could be better provided for, but since has falsified his word, and has perfidiously absented, and kept himself from me these six months, without any provocation from me (*so that he has eloped from me, and not I from him*), I do here declare that I intend to remain in the situation he has placed me until he does come and account for the undeserved scandalous treatment which I have received at his hands. And as he has forbid all persons from crediting or entertaining me, I can prove this to be only spite and ill will; for I have not run him in debt one farthing, nor removed from my station wherein I was placed by him."

Martha Washington was no Elizabeth Moore; she was the model wife in this male-dominated society. Her life revolved around her husband and family. Martha worked hard to be the cheerful, obedient wife who complemented her husband and never overshadowed him. Her job was to make him happy and, with him, raise their children to be good Virginians. There were a few women who spoke out against the patriarchal world in which they were trapped. Abigail Adams was probably the most noted. In her famous "remember the ladies" letter to her husband John, she wrote that "all men would be tyrants if they could. If particular care and attention is not paid to the ladies we are determined to forment a rebellion." Martha Washington was not one of those women; there would be no wives' rebellion in Virginia.

Like all wives of wealthy planters in the southern states, Martha Washington played many roles within her immediate family and the "family" of tenant farmers, indentured servants whose contracts George purchased, paid white laborers, hired craftsmen, and the several hundred slaves who lived at Mount Vernon.

Just taking care of her immediate family and main house staff proved very time-consuming. She was responsible for overseeing slaves who helped her with the meal cooking for her home. The Washington household had a full breakfast of fish, fowl, Virginia ham, other meats, breads, tea, coffee, and chocolate just after 7 a.m. each day. Most Virginia tables also had Indian cakes, a pancake of cornmeal, with honey—that was all George ate because it was easier on his teeth and prevented him from gaining too much weight. The Washingtons ate in an elegant twenty-by-fifteen-foot dining room, with fireplace, at the front of the mansion facing the driveway; they could watch visitors arrive through two large windows. After the Revolution, when they entertained many guests, they would eat in the new, much larger dining room in the northern wing of the home. George always finished breakfast by downing a small cup of tea and then left the house to work in the fields. The two Custis children went off to their tutor or to play under the supervision of a nanny.

Virginians did not have lunch, but enjoyed an early dinner at 3 or 3:30 p.m. That was the main meal of the day, and Martha had to prepare it with her cooks and servers. These dinners were elaborate. Dining among the upper-class families, especially those like the Washingtons who had dinner guests several times each week, had become an important part of the day. It was a multi-course meal of soups, breads, and meats. A single dinner might include a ham, goose, pickled pork, boiled turnips, apple dumplings, cinnamon, sugars, beef, mutton, fowl, lamb, turkey, tongue, turtle, pigeon sausage, eggs, vegetables, and mince pie. The Washingtons often ate fish, usually herring and shad, caught by the fishermen that operated George's schooners on the Chesapeake. Desserts at a single dinner seating might include jellies, custards, cakes, and pies. The entire meal might be topped off with several bowls of fresh fruit and the nuts that George loved (many Virginians devoured ice cream for dessert; George would not cherish it until he became president).

Meals had become so important that, by the 1760s, British cookbooks were ordered by plantation wives with other goods from England so that they could prepare more extensive dinners. The cookbooks not only had hundreds of recipes, but some, such as Hannah Glasse's popular *The Art of Cookery: Made Plaine and Easy,* also offered readers carefully prepared antidotes for mad dog bites and plagues, and even gave printed instructions on how to avoid infestations of bugs.

Martha spent much of the day in the three-room outbuilding that served as the kitchen, which was highlighted by a single large brick fireplace. Sometimes there was a supper later, at 9 p.m., but that was a far lighter meal. George rarely participated in this evening meal, preferring to end his day with some tea and toast around 7 p.m. The Washingtons were deluged with dinner guests. Mount Vernon records show that they had as many as 677 people a year for dinner in hospitality-mad Virginia; many guests slept over in rooms upstairs. Martha had to oversee the preparation of all their afternoon dinners and breakfasts for them the next morning, too.

In addition to the preparation of food for so many people, Martha was responsible for the sewing and mending of all the clothing for the Washington family, the domestics who worked in the house, and the massive family of laborers and slaves. Once the clothing was made or mended for the year, she had to pack the varied shirts, pants, and stocking into boxes, mark them, and supervise the shipping of them to the numerous Washington farms.

Mrs. Washington also had to oversee the production of all the quilts for the beds at Mount Vernon, their repair, and their continual cleaning and airing, plus the linen for the beds that was changed constantly because of their hundreds of guests. This was an arduous task and took up considerable time. One plantation wife complained that she spent two months out of every year just working with domestics to sew, writing, "I never was so tired of sewing in my life; my fingers are worn out." Another wrote that she dreaded the time of year when she had to make clothes for the hundreds of slaves and her family. "My mind dwells upon the one subject that I find it necessary to be actively engaged—I have been making up clothes for the Negroes."

Many women understood the need to create clothes, but simply tired of it. One woman lamented of housework, "It has been a week of great toil and no comfort or peace to body or mind" and another wrote, "Rose in the morning...and went to weaving yet not very willingly for though I love that, it likes me not and I am in the mind that I shall never be well as long as I weave."

Martha Washington turned an outbuilding into a bustling clothing factory. As a child in New Kent County, she had been taught how to use spinning wheels and other machines to produce clothing, and had also become an expert sewer and a wizard at needlepoint; she had mastered the production of quilts. She, in turn, taught the domestics at Mount Vernon how to sew, and from time to time, hired local women to assist in the production of clothing. Martha spent much time teaching these women how to mend clothes, especially stockings and jackets, that were easily torn while laborers and slaves completed outdoor work on the plantation. Mrs. Washington had small but exceedingly quick fingers and a good eye for mending and, as the years went by, she showed many women on the plantation how to work just as speedily and with the same talent as she did. It was a skill that would serve her well later in the Revolution.

Mrs. Washington, who always carried dozens of keys to buildings on the plantation and to rooms in the main house on a ring with her, oversaw the work of the people who tended the gardens at Mount Vernon. She had to oversee the chopping of wood for fires in the kitchen and in the fireplaces of the home during the cold months. She had to make certain that workmen in the house finished their chores unimpeded by domestics running from floor to floor trying to do theirs. She was in charge of the plantation dairy and had to make certain that the milk that the cows produced was delivered to her kitchens and stored properly. She also had to oversee the cutting up of cattle carcasses for meats to be hung and cured in the smokehouse. Winter was the hog killing season, and she had to oversee the dismembering of the slain hogs that George's men sent her, working with her domestics to chop the animal into pieces, dipping the ham shoulders and flanks into brine, processing the fat into lard, and stuffing the intestines with sausage.

She was in charge of making hundreds of pounds of soap for the Washingtons and their hundreds of slaves, as well as dipping and manufacturing hundreds of candles each year. She oversaw the prodigious task of spring cleaning, making certain all of the beds for the family and guests were carefully washed and cleaned.

This task took weeks every April and May. A far more constant task was the scrubbing and cleaning of all the pots and pans in the kitchen, which were continually needed for their many daily meals. Mrs. Washington spent time in the washhouse, where all the clothes and linens for the family and guests were washed with soap and then hung to dry on thin rope lines, wooden frames, or spread out on the grass.

At the end of her first year at Mount Vernon, as the workload increased and the number of slaves to be clothed and fed began to rise towards three hundred, Martha was worn out. In 1765, she implored George to hire a housekeeper and other help to assist her in the supervision of the daily operations of the main house. Washington also asked overseers' wives to help Martha in dairy and poultry operations and hired new overseers with the understanding that their wives would do the same. Most women put their daughters to work as "deputy housekeepers," but Patsy was too ill to work. She had epilepsy from birth and it was a real problem for her as a teen.

The relationships between Martha and the domestic laborers and slaves were close. These men and women served as waiters for meals, nurses and nannies for her children, valets, and house cleaners. Martha was in contact with them all day and developed attachments to them, despite their master/slave relationship. The nannies, especially, were close to the Washingtons because they helped them raise their children. Girls often formed early and strong attachments to their nannies.

In addition, like any wife, Martha cared for her husband and children. Her husband arrived home at three for dinner, exhausted from a long day in the fields that had begun at dawn. She had dinner on the table for him and engaged him in lengthy conversations about his workday, as did many wives. In the evening they spent time with each other and their children or entertained their numerous guests, yet another task that fell to Martha as a wife in a socially active plantation home.

Most planters did little to help their wives. Their spouses had to oversee all of the gardens alone, keep track of food supplies, do all of the ordering of clothing and supplies for the family, write all of the family letters, and work with their children's tutors. Happily for Martha, her husband helped considerably. A tireless workaholic, George took it upon himself to do all the ordering of the supplies for Mount Vernon from local wholesalers and his buyers in London.

An important part of the work of a wife on a large slave plantation was supervising the medical care of the family and the workers. Medical care was primitive in that era, but every little bit helped. Doctors prescribed different medicines to act as sedatives to make patients sleep. They gave them "physics" to make them vomit and cleanse their digestive systems. Drugs such as calomel, opium, rattlesnake root, and tree bark were used. Herbs of all kinds were administered, along with foul-tasting elixirs. Doctors had to be summoned from nearby communities, such as Alexandria, often put up overnight, fed, and entertained. Beds had to be ready for any plantation slave that fell ill and needed a doctor's care. Medicines had to be purchased and stored. Mount Vernon was the size of a small town, and medical care involved a considerable amount of work.

Most plantation wives were prepared for this responsibility. Their mothers and grandmothers had passed down written instructions for the making of medicinal teas, herbs, and other concoctions, along with boxes full of written prescriptions, some brought over from England a generation before. At Mount Vernon, George Washington assumed some of those responsibilities, too. His diaries were filled with stories about summoning doctors for his wife, children, and farm workers. He often rode to Alexandria himself to buy needed medicines. Sick slaves were not left alone in their cabins, but moved to cabins set up as small hospitals. Washington frequently summoned doctors to treat workers and slaves.

Martha's contribution to the medical care of the people who lived at Mount Vernon included making homemade bromides for ailments that she had been mixing for sick people since she was a teenager, as the women of most Virginia households did. The inexactitude of medical science demanded that the woman of the house experiment with herbs, vegetables, and ointments to concoct handmade medicines. One of Martha's odder remedies, unproven, was a combination of chicken soup and ale, which she prescribed to cure tuberculosis, a disease that had killed several people in her family and George's brother Lawrence. A more effective creation of hers was a mixture of molasses and onions, administered for sore throats. She prepared this concoction because her husband, outdoors often, frequently came down with severe sore throats and sometimes even found breathing difficult when phlegm gathered in his throat. Her remedy worked quickly and always helped him recover. Later, in the Revolution, her personal sore throat cure would help to save his life.

Martha dabbled constantly at Mount Vernon. She used recipes from a cookbook handed down to her from the Custis family. She had special flower bouquets cut from her gardens to freshen up rooms; she even invented a perfume that could keep a room fresh all day long. Martha invented a special toothpaste for the Washingtons: a fine powder of crushed fishbone. She wrote, "It will preserve your teeth and keep them white and clean and preserve from a toothache." Martha, George, and her children used the powder to brush their teeth every day.

George, an amateur gardener, took it upon himself to supervise the work of the gardeners, stable boys, and others who worked near the mansion. It was George who worked with the tutors and was later the liaison to Jacky's tutors at his boarding school. It was George who wrote almost all of the family correspondence. George's intervention in household affairs was not resented, but welcomed. His help freed Martha to do what she wanted to do the most, care for her children.

Each of the newlyweds faced difficult tasks in their first year together. George had to not only embark on married life after years as a bachelor, but also had to detach himself from the military. The change from military to civilian life must have been hard for him, and to do so as a married man must have been even more challenging. He could not bark orders at his wife, and she certainly did not have to do everything he wanted her to do, as his troops did. George had decided to dramatically enlarge Mount Vernon, buy and employ more slaves, and fit into his new role as a wealthy planter who had both business and social roles to fill. The former colonel had to learn how to bring up, and love, two stepchildren. Most of all, he had to get to know and love his new wife and to rearrange his living patterns to accommodate hers. All men have to adjust to marriage, and Washington was no different. And, too, he had to end his love for neighbor Sally Fairfax in order to succeed in his marriage to Martha.

He worked hard at the marriage, apparently exerting great self-control in treating Sally as merely a good friend, changing some of his own habits to please his wife, and striking up good relationships with her children. He struggled to increase his affection for Martha, whom he barely knew when they married. This he found rather easy as time passed and he got to know the amiable woman better.

Martha Washington had even more formidable obstacles to happiness in their marriage. She had left her home county, where she had spent all of her life, to live in Washington's home in a county where she knew no one. Just as George had to learn to live with her eccentricities, she had to adapt to his lifestyle. Most men slept as late as they could in the morning; he was up before dawn. Most men let their wives run all the domestic operations of the plantation; he meddled in everything. Most newlywed husbands were full of joy; he was as reserved and stoic as ever.

Martha, like George, accommodated. She was happy to rise when the sun came up and oversee the preparation of breakfast long after he had risen and begun his daily work. She tried her best to make him more animated and often succeeded. She welcomed their parties and balls and loved to watch him dance. He enjoyed riding and she did, too; they both loved fast carriage rides.

And there was Sally. Martha surely heard the rumors about George and Sally in Virginia's gossipy society and must have been apprehensive about living next door to her. She may well have met Sally on several occasions in Williamsburg when she was married to Daniel Custis and knew that she was a beautiful flirt.

Martha Washington was not intimidated. She was determined to give her new husband the emotional and sexual love that any man needed so that he would not be tempted by other women.

Instead of fearing Sally, Martha embraced her. The two women became close personal friends, visited each other often, as George Washington's letters and diaries indicate, went shopping together, and helped each other through the hard times of their lives. Neither had a better friend than the other. No one truly knows if there was anything beyond friendship between George and Sally after George's marriage, but there was certainly no sign of it as the two couples settled into a deep friendship that would last until they were separated much later by one of history's great events.

Throughout those years, George's ardor for Sally Fairfax was contained. He had learned self-control in the military, and now he had to use it and stay away from Sally. His control in avoiding other women, holding in his anger, refusing to gossip about friends and neighbors, not yelling at his children, not beating his slaves, and his general emotional restraint and stoic demeanor were admired by all. Landon Carter, who had very little self-control, said admiringly of Washington in 1776 that "he was the master of himself!"

George and Martha helped the needy in their part of the colony. He and Martha donated generously to Bruton Parish Church in Williamsburg; their local parish church, Pohick; and to the alms funds for the county. One of George's jobs at the local church was to head up a committee that donated funds to the poor of the area.

The Washingtons were churchgoing Christians. They were both members of the Anglican Church, later the Protestant Episcopal Church, and attended services on Sunday as often as they could. They were members of the large, brick Pohick Church in the Truro Parish in Fairfax County, whose construction was supervised by George, and Christ Church in Alexandria. They also belonged to Bruton Parish Church in Williamsburg where, as substantial contributors, they had their own pew. George was a vestryman at Pohick Church. Throughout his life, George constantly referred to Providence in his letters and speeches, befriended ministers, urged his troops to go to church on Sunday, and espoused the values of Christianity.

Martha, like George, was a churchgoer and read the Bible each morning after breakfast. She raised her children as Christians, and had close ties to local churches throughout her life. George had also been a Freemason since 1752. He had joined the Masons, a very moralistic society, with three others in the first Fredericksburg chapter. He would remain a Mason all of his life, becoming the highest-ranking Mason in America, and he led meetings at winter camps during the Revolution.

Their first year together as man and wife certainly brought problems. Washington, who had spent well over his head upon marriage, did not have cash for an installment payment on land he had bought to expand Mount Vernon and nearly lost the parcel of land. He was unable to pay another debt and had to give up one of his prize horses in compensation. One ship carrying his tobacco to England was lost in a storm on the Atlantic and another was seized by a French warship. Four slaves died at Mount Vernon during the winter, and two slaves and an overseer died at one of the Custis plantations when a smallpox epidemic struck the area.

And then the plans the Washingtons had made to celebrate their first anniversary as man and wife on January 6, 1760, were wrecked by an epidemic of measles that spread throughout the region, felling several slaves at Mount Vernon and putting Martha in her bed for more than a week. Her husband's reaction to her illness was far more symbolic of their feelings for each other after a year together than any celebratory party.

Martha caught the measles on Tuesday afternoon, New Year's Day. Her body was covered with them and her appearance startled her husband upon his return from a day at work. Alarmed, he stayed home from work the next several days. She took a turn for the worse on Friday, and Washington sent a rider with a note to Rev. Charles Green, pastor of Truro Parish and a former doctor, that asked him to see Martha. George also sent for Sally Fairfax, who arrived by carriage to help nurse her. Rev. Green arrived the following morning and administered some medicine to Martha.

Still worried about his wife, Washington asked a second physician, Dr. James Laurie of Alexandria, to accompany his friend Walter Stewart to dinner at Mount Vernon that night so that he, too, could treat her. The household staff was also told to take extra special care of Mrs. Washington. Martha, with the help of two doctors, Sally, and the staff—all summoned by her very worried husband—was back on her feet by the following Monday.

The measles episode was a minor event, but it illustrated how affectionate George Washington had become to his wife by the end of their first year of marriage.

The first months of marriage for George and Martha were a bit rocky, as many marriages are, and did not resemble those in the romantic novels he enjoyed reading. Later in life, he wrote his stepgranddaughter, herself about to marry, a letter that probably conveyed some of his own feelings on the early days of his marriage. "Be assured, and experience will convince you," he told her, "that there is no truth more certain than that all of our enjoyments fall short of our expectations, and to none does it apply with more force than to the gratification of the passions."

He told her not to "look for perfect felicity before you consent to wed. Nor conceive, from the fine tales the poets and lovers of old have told us of the transports of mutual love, that heaven has taken its abode on earth. Love is a mighty pretty thing, but like all other delicious things, it is cloying; and when the first transports of the passion begin to subside, which it assuredly will do ... it serves to evince that love is too dainty a food to live on alone, and ought not to be considered further than as a necessary ingredient for that matrimonial happiness that results from a combination of causes: none of which are of greater importance than the object on whom it is placed should possess good sense, a good disposition, and the means of supporting you in the way you have been brought up."

Even so, by the autumn of 1759, after eight months of marriage and five months of living together at Mount Vernon, life had settled into a very satisfactory and loving routine for the Washingtons. When he was a boy, he had copied a simplistic poem into one of his books, a poem that may have expressed his inner yearnings at that time. Part of it read:

These are things that once possess'd,
Will make a life that's truly blessed.
A good estate on healthy soil,
Not got by vice nor yet by toil;
Round a warm fire, a pleasant joke,
With chimney ever free from smoke;
A strength entire, a sparkling bowl,
A quiet wife, a quiet soul

George was so pleased with his bride and married life toward the end of that first year that he wrote to his cousin Richard Washington with great confidence, perhaps remembering that poem, "I am now, I believe, fixed at this seat with an agreeable consort for life and hope to find more happiness in retirement than I ever experienced amidst a wide and bustling world."

Nobody disputed that. As a visitor to Mount Vernon wrote of the Washingtons, "They are to all appearances a happy pair."

CHAPTER SIX

THE
WASHINGTONS
IN HIGH
SOCIETY

D uring the first week of October 1772, George Washington and his family arrived at Annapolis, Maryland, a fast-growing harbor town on the shores of the Chesapeake Bay that was highlighted by large brick mansions, expensive inns, crowded docks, and a large harbor jammed with handsome sailing vessels. Annapolis was home to some of the wealthiest families in the state. The Washingtons were in the town for the highly publicized weeklong festivities that opened the annual horse racing season there. The beginning of the season, sponsored by the exclusive Jockey Club and its rich and influential members, attracted the gentry from all over the Chesapeake and rich merchants from as far away as New York City and Philadelphia. They came by carriage and boat, but few were as distinguished as the Washingtons.

The family arrived in their elegant white horse-drawn carriage, with its red Moroccan leather seats and the family crest emblazoned on the sides of the doors, driven by a meticulously dressed servant. George was resplendent in one of his new suits from London and his wife looked lovely in a simple new dress made for her just for the trip. Their children—sixteen-year-old Patsy, and Jack, almost eighteen—were well-dressed and eager to have a good time in the busy city, especially after their stepfather gave them some spending money.

The Washingtons had made reservations at one of the most reputable inns in Annapolis, bought tickets for several plays at the town's new theater, made plans for dinners at the best taverns, and registered for the lavish balls and musical concerts that would kick off the social season. Other rich planters invited them to parties and dinners. At these affairs, Washington became quite friendly with the governor and was sometimes an overnight guest at his home. Accompanying them, pristinely dressed, as always, was a small retinue of black servants who took care of their needs.

The Jockey Club's gala events would be the highlight of the year for almost everyone there, but for the wealthy Washingtons it would just be another event on their busy social calendar in a life of entertainment and fine living in which they were able to obtain the best of everything that money could buy.

George and Martha Washington began to spend money lavishly as soon as they were married in 1759. The first letter that George sent to Cary & Company, his buyers in London, contained a lengthy list of goods that he wanted them to purchase and send to Virginia by ship. The list took up several pages and contained so many orders that Washington wrote in shorthand to fit them all onto its pages. What he bought represented not just foods and apparel for consumption and wear, but extravagant purchases that represented all the grandeur of high society in Virginia.

Included were orders for casks of wine and delicacies such as cheeses, nuts, candies, teas, sweetmeats, citrus products, refined sugar, spices, and soaps. George ordered some of the most expensive pairs of shoes and boots, and over the years, would order dozens more. There were multiple pairs of well-tailored breeches, vests, and jackets, plus an elegant saddle, a fancy sword, furniture, beautiful china and pewter, the best silverware, a bedstead seven and a half feet high with "fashionable blue or blue and white curtains," four chairs for their bedroom "to make this room uniformly handsome and genteel," a large couch, fifty yards of "the best" floor matting, a half dozen pairs of men's "neatest" shoes, "fine soft calf skin" for a pair of boots, and an elegant white carriage.

It was the first of many large shipments of books, furniture, foods, and china that would be used to turn Mount Vernon into one of the finest mansions in the South and a home where the newlywed Washingtons would become two of the most important members of Virginia society. Shipments of goods from London increased in their lavishness over the years.

An order that arrived in 1772, thirteen years after their marriage, was a good example: four handkerchiefs of jackolet muslin with borders, women's caps of minionet lace, India Chintz, a blue satin bonnet, ivory combs, six pairs of white kid mittens, four pairs of women's white silk gloves, clogs made especially for Martha at a shop in Covent Garden, eight damask tablecloths, jars of the best raisins, thirty pounds of almonds, anchovies, French olives, walnuts, an expensive white saddle, Chinese ivory table knives, "fashionable" glass decanters, a black velvet gentleman's hunting cap, a silver pencil case, silver spurs "of the newer fashion," a china set of coffee cups and saucers, a woman's suit of tambour-worked muslin, a pair of red Morocco slippers and, last but not least, a silver-capped hunting whip engraved with George's name.

George and Martha quickly took their place among the leaders of Virginia's upper crust. Martha's fortune and the income from their combined plantations enabled them to host receptions, travel extensively, wear the most beautiful clothes, ride in elegant carriages, participate in every imaginable entertainment, and send their children to the best schools. They anticipated spending their entire lives in a fast-spinning world of dinner parties, balls, and barbecues, attended by dutiful servants and welcomed by all.

Virginia in the 1760s was a colony whose citizens bragged was a world unto itself. Many residents had become rich growing tobacco raised by slaves, and these men and women lived well.

The colony had a small but handsome capital, Williamsburg, finely trained militia companies, busy seaports at Norfolk and Yorktown, a rapidly growing population, schools for the rich, and a vibrant social life.

The heart of that social world was a unique system of hospitality. Because Virginians lived so far from cities, and so far apart, they spent much of their leisure time visiting each other. Everyone opened their doors to neighbors, relatives, friends, business associates, and even total strangers who were passing by on the narrow dirt highways that crisscrossed the colony. Guests were given drinks, dinners, and snacks and invited to stay for a night or two. Their hosts, such as the Washingtons, took them riding and entertained them in every way they could.

This hospitality enabled Virginians to maintain ties with relatives who lived miles away, and see friends and travel to their homes as guests, but the frequency of guests could be uncertain. George Washington kept meticulous records of people who arrived for visits, dinner, or overnight stays. The Washingtons were often surprised by travelers riding through the county who stopped off for a visit or dinner after a lengthy ride in their carriages or on horseback down Virginia's dusty roads, people who could not find inns and believed that "you ride in where two brick chimneys show there is a spare bed and lodging and welcome." These unannounced, weary guests had to be taken in with the same graciousness as relatives invited a month before. As an example, Washington wrote in his diary that on January 2, 1771, he finished work and, surprised, "upon my return home found Mr. Piper, Mr. Muir, and Doctor Rumney there, who dined and lodged."

The Washingtons entertained more than four hundred visitors a year throughout the 1760s and early 1770s, and more later, after Washington retired from the presidency. They usually hosted two or three people each night, but sometimes had eight, and once played host to eleven, including one man's entire family. The Washingtons had so many drop-in daily visitors, dinner companions, and overnight guests that a day without guests seemed like an event. In fact, on June 4, 1771, George scribbled in his diary, apparently with some astonishment, "at home all day without company." On another occasion, he rebuked his nephew, Fielding Lewis, for *not* dropping in while Lewis was visiting others in the area.

The Washingtons spent a fortune on food and drink for guests at Mount Vernon. They served nothing but the best. George ordered "carving knives and forks, handles of stained ivory and bound with silver," "fashionable china branches and stands for candles," and a "fashionable set of dessert glasses" in order to be seen as a successful host. Washington insisted on the finest wines from London, buying "from the best house in Madeira a pipe of the best old wine." A London buyer assured him that he had procured "a pipe of wine which although very dear we hope will prove satisfactory in quality in which as well as the color we have endeavored carefully to please you."

Overseeing preparations for guests was a large part of life for women like Martha Washington, who had done it since she was a little girl on the Dandridge plantation. Other wealthy Virginia women, such as Mrs. Robert Carter, who lived at Nomini Hall, the Carter's immense mansion, remembered that she not only oversaw the preparation of meals and ran the domestic side of the plantation all day prior to a dinner party or ball, but also helped the slaves round up the poultry to be slaughtered for dinner. She was so busy that she did not change out of her long silk party dress but, gathering in her hoop skirt and running as fast as she could in her expensive gown with its tight stays and her high-heeled shoes, chased the chickens as adroitly as the slaves.

Family reputations were established by the number of signatures in their visitors' books. People seemed relieved that they had pleased guests, especially important ones. When Governor Alexander Spotswood arrived at the home of William Byrd one day, the host flew into a hospitality frenzy, providing eight dinner dishes, dessert, and numerous bottles of wine. When the governor departed, Byrd wrote with relief that "the governor seemed satisfied with his entertainment." Some men and women were so eager for visitors, and to build their social standing, that they stationed slaves on highways to invite passersby to the house for dinner and drinks.

Virginia hospitality, such as that at Mount Vernon, astonished travelers. One Swiss man traveling through Virginia wrote, "It is possible to travel through the whole country without money…even if one is willing to pay, they do not accept anything, but they are rather angry, asking, whether one did not know the custom of the country. At first, we were too modest to go into the houses to ask for food and lodging, which the people often recognized, and they admonished us not to be bashful, as this was the custom of rich and poor."

The Washingtons welcomed these unknown drop-in visitors. On one occasion, George returned from the fields in the early evening just as a late supper was being served, and Martha was sitting down with a group of guests. They were all complete strangers who had dropped in several hours earlier. George had no idea who they were. He handed his coat to a servant, walked into the dining room, smiled thinly, and introduced himself to each guest. He explained that he had eaten dinner with his family in late afternoon, was not hungry, felt exhausted from work on his farms, and could not join them. Washington went upstairs to go to sleep, and Martha then continued playing the gracious hostess to people she had never met in her life.

Of course, there were guests who overextended their welcome. Every planter had a story of visitors who "dropped in" and stayed for a week or more. Some people stayed for two and three weeks. Some travelers went from plantation to plantation, remaining a week or more at each, finding it possible to spend most of the summer on an extended vacation as the guests of Virginia families. Most were well-behaved, but some were bores, becoming drunk and loud at dinners, using coarse language, and insulting hosts. One host cringed when a guest tried to seduce his maid; a planter's wife fended off a similar assault by striking her overly amorous guest over the head with a chamberpot.

No one set a finer table for guests than the Washingtons. The long table in their spacious dining room was filled with meats, cheeses, and a variety of drinks for guests. The Washingtons' servants were not only industrious, but well-dressed and courteous.

The same could not be said for others, whose domestics, visitors complained, worked very slowly and dressed shabbily. "I have frequently seen in Virginia, on visits to gentlemen's houses…young Negroes and Negresses from sixteen to twenty years old, with not an article of clothing, but a loose shirt, descending halfway down their thighs, waiting at table," wrote the Marquis de Chastellux, a Frenchman. Others complained that too many servants got in each other's way, creating havoc in the dining room.

One British visitor to Mount Vernon, Nicholas Cresswell, who described George Washington as a "just man, exceedingly honest," described the family's hospitality well: "He keeps an excellent table and a stranger, let him be of what country or nation, he will always meet with a most hospitable reception at it. His entertainments were always conducted with the most regularity and in the genteelest manner of any I ever was at on our continent (and I have been at several of them). Temperance he always observed, was always cool-headed and exceedingly cautious himself, but took great pleasure in seeing his friends entertained in the way most agreeable to themselves. His lady is of a hospitable disposition, always good-humored and cheerful, and seems to be actuated by the same motives with himself, but she is rather of a more lively disposition."

Elizabeth Powel, a friend of Martha's from Philadelphia, thanked her for inviting her to Mount Vernon and complimented her on "the elegant hospitality exercised at Mount Vernon, where the good order of the master's mind, seconded by your excellent abilities, pervades everything around you and renders it a most delightful residence to your friends."

Martha Washington appeared to all to be an amiable, cheerful woman who maintained an upbeat attitude about life no matter who the guests at her table were or, concerning her husband, what was happening politically during the highly charged times of the late 1760s and early 1770s. An American architect, Benjamin Latrobe, wrote of her as a hostess that she possessed a "good humored, free manner that was extremely pleasing and flattering." A Polish count visiting America wrote that "she has something very charming about her" and referred to her "gay manner" and "bright eyes." Joshua Brookes, an English visitor who had dinner with the entire family, remembered that "Mrs. Washington and Miss [Patsy] Custis pleased me most, especially the former."

The Washingtons enjoyed their often-lengthy dinner parties, filled with people engaged in animated conversation. George loved wine. He was able to drink large quantities of wine without getting drunk. After the Revolution, Alexander Hamilton told John London, of Wilmington, Delaware, of Washington's imbibing. "Hamilton told us that General Washington, notwithstanding his perfect regularity and love of decorum, could bear to drink more wine than most people. He loved to make a procrastinated dinner—made it a rule to drink a glass of wine with everyone at the table and yet always drink three to four or more glasses of wine after dinner, according to his company."

Colonel Washington loved to nibble on nuts of all types and always made certain there were sizable bowls full of them on his table, especially almonds and Brazil nuts. Chastellux, who dined at Mount Vernon after the war, wrote that "after dinner the cloth was taken off, and apples and a great quantity of nuts were served, which General Washington usually continues eating for two hours, toasting and conversing all the time."

Travelers to the homes of Virginia planters were impressed with the people they met. They had created a colony, many thought, that compared favorably to England itself. Lord Adam Gordon, who visited Virginia in 1764, wrote of gentry such as the Washingtons, "I had an opportunity to see a good deal of the country and many of the first people in the province and I must say they far excel in good sense, affability, and ease than any set of men I have yet fallen in with, either in the West Indies or the Caribbean…as sensible, conversible, and accomplished as one would wish to meet with."

Yet another guest, John Bernard, wrote of women like Martha Washington, "Of the planter's ladies I must speak with unqualified praise; they had an easy kindness of manner, as far removed from the rudeness as from the reserve, which being natural to them…was the more admirable…to the influence of their society I chiefly attribute their husbands' refinement."

Whenever the Washingtons traveled, whether to Williamsburg for a month of politics and parties or just to Alexandria for shopping, they conducted themselves with great decorum and grace. Elizabeth Jones, the daughter of Martha's cousin Frances, discovered this one morning when she accompanied Martha to Alexandria on a shopping expedition. The small child leaped up into the coach and onto the seat opposite Martha. The little girl settled in as the driver yanked on the reins to get the horses to move forward. They did so very quickly, jolting the carriage and knocking the child forward, out of her seat, and into Martha's lap. An angry Martha took the child by the shoulders and shook her hard. "Child, can't you keep your seat like a lady? Do you wish people to think you are not in the habit of riding coaches?" she said.

The chastised child was mad at Martha all morning, but forgave her later when Mrs. Washington bought an expensive doll in an Alexandria shop and gave it to her as a present and told her she was sorry she had been angry with her.

Families would also invite dozens of guests to a barbecue on the grounds of a plantation or ask them to join them for a picnic in a meadow or, at Mount Vernon, along the banks of the Potomac.

Parties were held on special days, such as Christmas, and these often combined musical concerts and theatrical plays with traditional dining, drinking, and dancing. "Mrs. Galloway flashed upon them in her muslin dress, attended by her admiring spouse in his rock of Gibralter coat," wrote a woman of her well-dressed, self-centered hosts at a Christmas ball in Chester Town, Maryland. "They had sixteen couples and spent an agreeable evening." The next night the host presented a play at his home. It was enjoyed by all, even though some of the inebriated young men broke a window.

Weddings were galas in Virginia. These events, which carried on for several days, combined dinners, breakfasts, drinking, and dancing and gave colonists a chance to mingle with distant friends.

Molly Tilghman wrote of the marriage of Betsy Worrell, "So superb a wedding was never seen here. A number of the most elegant clothed six bridesmen and maids...Between fifty and sixty people were present at the ceremony, who danced 'til 4 o'clock [in the morning]. Some of the company retired at 12, being afraid, I suppose, of injuring their health by keeping such riotous hours. They kept up the ball til Monday."

Dinners and parties at Mount Vernon and other plantations were opulent and guests talked about them for months, but they were nothing compared to the social life in Williamsburg.

Williamsburg was the social center of the colony because the royal governor resided there, and it was home to the courts and the House of Burgesses, the state legislature. The courts and legislature met for one month in October and another in March or April, and those months became the social seasons in the capital. The town was inland, situated two miles from both the York and James Rivers and their seaports, and therefore could not enjoy the benefits of the shipping business. The community had no large artisan community, farms, or other commerce except government business. There was no real work there besides jobs in taverns and inns, menial jobs at the College of William and Mary, and gardening work at some of the finer homes in the city. Consequently, Williamsburg never grew in size, like the northern port cities of Philadelphia, New York, and Boston. The town was home to fifteen hundred residents year-round in the 1760s, but the population tripled in size when the state legislature and courts were in session, and several thousand people from all walks of life descended upon it in elegant carriages, simple overloaded wooden wagons, on horseback, and on foot.

Since the gentry had money, Williamsburg became lively during these months. Anyone could earn cash off the rich who arrived in the pretty Virginia town. Moneylenders met in the grassy, sun-lit courtyard behind the brick capitol building to loan and collect money. Food sellers set up hastily constructed stalls along shady streets. Entertainers of all kinds, from fiddlers to acrobats, performed for tips on narrow city lanes, delighting wide-eyed children as well as adults. Strong men engaged in bloody, barefisted boxing matches, wrestled each other, and participated in the rather crude sport of "gouging," in which participants tried to gouge their opponents' eyes out, to the satisfaction of cheering, paying crowds. Fleet-footed teenagers raced each other up and down streets for prizes. Whores rented rooms on the second floors of the taverns and entertained customers by candlelight.

The town's main thoroughfare was the tree-lined Duke of Gloucester Street, a wide mile-long avenue that connected the handsomely designed, H-shaped, two-story brick legislative building surrounded by dozens of trees and cobblestone walkways on one end and the handsomely designed College of William and Mary on the other. The street was lined with shops of all kinds, residences, and taverns, such as the Raleigh, where businessmen and politicians spent time and where, a Scottish visitor observed, "more business has been transacted than on the exchange of London or Amsterdam."

A dozen or so lanes intersected the avenue; they contained more residences, from tiny, two-room white clapboard cottages to the lovely two-story brick mansion of prominent lawyer George Wythe. The capital also contained an attractive house of worship, Bruton Parish Church, where the Washingtons attended, a county jail, and a three-story-high brick insane asylum, one of the first in the country. The public buildings and larger homes were a mix of Renaissance Italian architecture with columns, gardens, and porticos in the popular British styles created by architect Sir Christopher Wren.

Visitors to the town were impressed by it. Johann Doehla, a Hessian soldier who was stationed in the community in 1781, wrote: "It [is] among the beautiful cities of America...It has some beautiful churches and steeples with clocks to see, and also some buildings otherwise worth seeing. The broad and straight main street of the city is nearly one mile long. There is also a beautiful large state house, where the general court assembles."

The Washingtons brought their two children and servants with them to Williamsburg on almost every visit to the capital for

George's political business as his county's representative in the legislature. Her parents had discovered that Patsy was an epileptic and
had nursed her through frightening seizures during her childhood;
they did not want to leave her at home. They wanted to take Jacky
to the capital because both parents were proud of him and wanted
to show him off to their friends. George especially loved taking his
stepson to the parties and local horse racing track to give him an
introduction to manhood. It was also a chance for the children to get
to know and play with the children of other friends visiting town
and the children of Willliamsburg residents.

The Washingtons usually stayed at local inns because they
rented out Six Chimneys, their elegant mansion. George sometimes came to town alone on business and usually stayed in one of
the rooms at Christiana Campbell's two-story, white clapboard
tavern, with its front porch where men could sit at twilight and
catch the evening breezes while they drank and talked. George
also resided at Jane Vobe's Raleigh, where guests could eat, drink,
gamble, hold meetings, and buy theater and concert tickets.
Sometimes when rooms were difficult to procure, he stayed in a
small room at one inn and his wife and children stayed in rooms
at another.

George Washington was a man who adored horses and racing.
He went to racetracks whenever he was in Williamsburg, Richmond, Norfolk, Annapolis, or when he visited his mother in Fredericksburg, sometimes remaining for a week of contests. When he
traveled to Annapolis, he usually brought his wife and children
and took his wife to the balls in the evening.

The middle and lower classes descended upon Williamsburg
for its twice-yearly entertainment, too, and they added another
dimension to the world of George Washington. The middle class
consisted of farmers who might have owned a few slaves or had
none and simply tilled their land with their families. It was also
made up of laborers, indentured servants, craftsmen, tutors, overseers, and sailors from bustling seaports such as Norfolk or Yorktown. A British officer characterized them as "a strange mixture
of characters, and of such various descriptions of occupations that

it is difficult to find their exact criterion or leading feature. They are, however, hospitable, generous, and friendly." The lower classes, this officer wrote, were friendly, too, but generally "rude, illiberal, and noisy, with turbulent disposition."

The middle and lower classes enjoyed rubbing shoulders with the rich, but in private their descriptions of them could be sarcastic. A tutor, James Reid, wrote that "if a man…has money, Negroes, and land enough he is a complete gentleman. These…hide all his defects, usher him into the best of company, and draws upon him the smiles of the fair sex. His madness then passes for wit, his extravagance for flow of spirit, his insolence for bravery, and his cowardice for wisdom. Learning and good sense; religion and refined morals…have nothing to do in the composition."

The Washingtons also enjoyed the fireworks there, accompanied by drinking at taverns and the firing of cannon to celebrate British military triumphs. Washington was one of the many Virginians who attended those fireworks, paying for his tickets. Horses often ran off at the sound of celebratory cannonfire, and some people complained that their drunken neighbors were too noisy. One claimed that a man on his street was "as drunk as a lord and has been endeavoring to imitate a cannon."

Some of the games that the Washingtons enjoyed playing, or watching, included horseshoe pitching, pell mell (the forerunner of croquet), badminton, handball, nine pins (bowling), and a game called trap ball, an early version of baseball, in which batters hit lightweight balls pitched by a spring-powered contraption on a mound. Men especially enjoyed going to cockfights. Washington probably did not enjoy them; he attended one, but never went again.

The main cultural attraction in Williamsburg was its theater, one of the few in America. Most of the plays were Shakespearean, but the season also included contemporary British dramas, such as *She Stoops to Conquer, Cato, The Recruiting Officer,* and *The Beggar's Opera.* Every once in a while a small ballet company toured the colonies. Vaudeville shows were presented with sets featuring eleborate machinery that dazzled the audiences. In 1772, the theater at

Williamsburg staged a production that featured a fiery land and sea battle between two armies, navies, rows of booming cannon, sea monsters, and, for a finale, an indoor fireworks.

George Washington loved the theater. He had attended plays since his first visits to Williamsburg as a teenager and was a regular as a young man. It is unknown how interested Martha was in the stage before she married George, but she accompanied him to the theater often whenever they were in Willliamsburg. Washington's diaries showed that he and Martha would attend several plays a week each season that they were in the capital, and it was not unusual for them to spend four out of six nights at plays. They went alone or with other couples; George sometimes brought along a half dozen politicians or business associates as his guests.

And it was in Williamsburg where the Washingtons attended the most elegant balls and parties in Virginia, where musicians played for men and women who ate, drank, and danced throughout the evening. George and Martha were not merely invited guests at these much anticipated events; they were often the center of attention.

Lavish balls were presented at the Governor's Palace at Williamsburg, especially when the state assembly was in session, and also on the King's birthday. Invited guests at these balls spared no expense in clothing to impress everyone. Martha Washington ordered fine materials for dresses and often invited a Mrs. Cox to Mount Vernon to make and alter ball gowns for herself and Patsy.

Prominent political figures hosted balls that attracted so many guests that the galas had to be held in public buildings. One year a man leased the red brick capitol building and held balls there every night that the court was in session. One professor hosted balls in the courtroom of the one-story courthouse for his college students, as did Anne Shields, proprietress of Shield's tavern. The Freemasons leased Christiana Campbell's tavern for balls, clearing out the tables on the first floor for dancing. The Raleigh Tavern had a separate room for its parties.

Professional hosts even hired musicians, staged weekly balls, and sold tickets to them. Some hosts advertised exotic entertainment to lure people to their balls, such as a widow who promised guests that they would see "several grotesque dances never yet performed in Virginia." Other hosts promised to auction off their slaves to the highest bidder at the ball. "A likely young Virginia Negro woman fit for house business and her child" were auctioned off at one.

All of the larger towns in Virginia offered similar, but smaller, social lives for planters. The Washingtons lived close to Alexandria and frequented balls there that often attracted close to one hundred celebrants. The Alexandria parties not only drew husbands and wives of the gentry, but also elderly widows, mothers who brought young children, and single teenaged girls. Women arrived in their finest dresses and spent hours on their makeup before climbing into their carriages to go to the parties. One visitor thought they overdid it, writing that they were "dressed and powdered to the life."

Balls in Annapolis were held in the statehouse, the council chambers of town hall, and other public buildings, in addition to private mansions. The gentry at these balls, including the Washingtons, were among the best dressed and coiffed in America. One Annapolis woman even employed a full-time French hairdresser to make certain that she maintained her position as the queen of the colony's social set.

The women at the parties and balls in Annapolis that the Washingtons frequented were stunning. Wrote one bedazzled man, "In a word, there are throughout these colonies very lovely women, who have never passed the bounds of their respective provinces and yet, I am persuaded, might appear to great advantage in the most brilliant circles of gaiety and fashion."

Balls were hosted at the larger plantation mansions and many even had a ballroom on the first floor. Smaller planters' homes did not have a ballroom, but owners easily transformed their parlor into one by removing the rugs and furniture.

The balls were elaborate affairs. Some were parties that lasted two or three days as guests slept over in any room with a bed.

Most were one-evening affairs that began in late afternoon with a dinner (most of the time guests all dined together, but sometimes women dined with each other, followed by the men). Different rooms in the manor house were set up for card playing, smoking, and drinking. The drinks included lemon punch, toddies, cider, and, especially at Mount Vernon, wines (Madeira was Washington's favorite). In the years just prior to the Revolution, when most people talked about politics, the drinking rooms were often filled with men and women, often inebriated, singing patriotic songs or sarcastic ditties denouncing the king. Those who heard their songs hoped that if there was a revolution, it would have more success than the singers.

The ball itself was arranged as a series of dances; first minuets, then jigs, then the Virginia Reel, then country dances. Marches would be held at different times throughout the evening; the atmosphere was festive. Philip Fithian, a tutor who attended many of them, wrote that "the ladies are dressed gay and splendid, and when dancing their silks and brocades rustled and trailed behind them."

The governor could afford to hire a sizable number of musicians with different instruments, and the wealthy usually had two or three violinists and a French horn. Some people needed little more than one man with a musical instrument. Wrote Boston's Nancy Winslow, "In the evening, young Mr. Waters, hearing of my assembly, put his flute in his pocket and played several minuets and other tunes, to which we danced mighty cleverly."

Dancing was popular in Virginia. Dancing masters enjoyed a steady business traveling throughout the colony to give lessons to the children of the rich. A full-time dancing school was established in Williamsburg in the 1720s, and by the 1770s there were two. Dancing was so important that parents stipulated in their wills that money be set aside for dance lessons for their surviving children. The Washingtons had a dance master hold classes at Mount Vernon for several years. All of the Washingtons tried to play instruments, but without much success. George bought a flute, but there is no report of him playing it. He ordered a small harpsichord for his daughter and wife; they both took lessons, but no records show that either entertained anyone with their playing, unless for the immediate family.

Dancing was a standard part of the day for a tutor who ran a small school or lived on a plantation and mentored the children who lived there and their friends. The dancing lessons, which could run from an hour to more than four, depending on the frequency of the dancing master's visit, were not mere socials; they were hard work. The teacher taught the children their steps slowly and made them repeat them hundreds of times. He was a stern taskmaster and often complained if they showed lack of enthusiasm or had forgotten the previous lesson. Teenaged boys, particularly, came under the teacher's scrutiny for laziness.

In time, the children improved. A tutor wrote about an afternoon dance, monitored by a dance master, "There were several minuets danced with great ease and propriety; after which the whole company joined in country dances, and it was indeed beautiful to admiration, to see such a number of young persons, set off by dress to the best advantage, moving easily to the sound of well-performed music and with perfect regularity."

Dancing consumed the lives of some teenaged girls. Anne Blair of Virginia wrote of her young niece that dancing filled "her thoughts by day and dreams by night." A tutor joked about Virginians that "they will dance or die."

Single men saw dances as a natural way to meet women. Some women did not agree, such as Molly Cooper, of New York, who wrote of one party, "Some men stay to dance, greatly against my will."

Some saw dancing as the devil's work. Quakers and many New England puritans, such as John and Abigail Adams, frowned upon it. Adams frumped that men who were good dancers were rarely good at anything else.

The women at the balls danced well despite being dressed in their cumbersome hoop skirts. Women of the lower classes ignored the fancy gowns and danced with loose-fitting homespun dresses and, some said, ended their evenings with rather *daring* Irish Jigs. One participant at such a party in Alexandria wrote, "The people very merry, dancing without either shoes or stockings."

Martha Washington had only a mild interest in dancing and enjoyed the marches and minuets, but usually sat down after those, and happily so. George, though, was one of the very best dancers in Virginia, perhaps in America, and would dance for hours. He was an athletic man, and the rigors of army life had helped him to stay in good shape, unlike many of the gentry husbands. His athletic prowess contributed to his skill at dancing and permitted him to dance much longer than most people. He was such an enthusiastic and expert dancer that at parties and balls many women insisted on at least one dance with him; these dances apparently did not create any jealousy in Martha, who was proud of all of her husband's many skills. There were legends about Washington dancing nonstop at one ball in Virginia, until the sun rose and most guests had gone to bed. In the middle of the Revolution, on a dare, he danced continuously for three hours with Kitty Greene, the wife of a general.

Balls were a vital part of the social life in upper-class Virginia and hosts, whether the governor or a country planter, were expected to offer sufficient food, drink, and entertainment to ensure that guests enjoyed themselves. The men and women of the gentry could be savage in their gossip about balls at which the food was sparse and the drinks infrequent or substandard. The Washingtons were as critical as others of ill-planned balls. George wrote caustically of one party in Alexandria, "[The food] abounded great plenty of bread and butter, some biscuits, with tea and coffee, which the drinks of could not distinguish from hot water sweetened." He scoffed at the lack of table linens, writing that "pocket handkerchiefs served the purpose of tableclothes and napkins and that no apologies were made for either" and finished with a flourish, sarcastically calling it "the bread and butter ball."

Washington's humor was rare, but he often found it when describing these balls. He attended another in which a needed extra man was procured at the last minute to serve as the partner of an extra woman. Washington wrote, "Happy, thrice happy for the fair who were assembled, that there was a man to spare; for had there been seventy-nine ladies and only seventy-eight gentlemen, there might, in the course of the evening, have been some disarray among the caps."

Gambling was another favorite pastime in Virginia and many of the wealthy eagerly participated. Men bet on horse races, played cards and billiards, rolled dice, and purchased thousands of lottery tickets. Gambling, like dancing, was a part of life. It reflected the competitiveness of the men of Virginia, their willingness to take risks, and any victory gave them a sense of joy and accomplishment.

Men bet on anything. One man bet another than he could not produce seven hundred gallons of wine on his plantation in a single year. Another laid odds of sixteen to one that Alexander Spotswood would become governor. (He did.) One man bet another one thousand pounds of tobacco that he could seduce a servant girl before his friend could accomplish the task. The dispute over who succeeded turned into a scandal, the subject of gossips for months, and wound up in Virginia's highest court.

Gambling at the racetrack, card tables, and elsewhere had become so prevalent, and so costly, that as early as 1752 the royal governor begged legislators to end it and to urge the constituents in their districts to end it when they returned home from Williamsburg. None paid any attention to him.

Gambling was George Washington's great passion. He was an avid lottery player; lotteries were not only a lucrative gambling scheme in colonial Virginia, but also a source of much-needed income for institutions, such as churches and schools. Houses of worship of just about any denomination turned to lotteries to raise funds to build new physical structures, repair roofs and windows, and fix up the pastor's home. They counted on churchgoers to buy tickets and get their friends to do the same. Local governments raised money for road and river navigation projects through lottery sales. Men in debt sold tickets to raise money to pay them.

Late one night, Washington was playing cards at a tavern in Williamsburg and encountered a man moving from table to table selling lottery tickets. On impulse, Washington got up from his chair, found the man across the noisy, candlelit room, and purchased

$3,000 (in today's currency) worth of them, stuffing the tickets into the pockets of his coat with his large hands. He often purchased tickets for lotteries held to raise money for friends and neighbors in debt. Washington was such an easy mark for lotteries that men who did not raise enough money to cover the prizes often sought him out, certain they could talk him into buying tickets for anything. He once bought $3,600 in lottery tickets from a friend, Lord Stirling, who traveled all the way from New Jersey to Virginia to sell them to him.

Martha knew that her husband loved to play cards before they were married, but she probably did not realize the extent of his passion for card games. He played for hours late at night at taverns in Williamsburg, especially at the Raleigh, where the legislators spent their leisure time, and at Christiana Campbell's. Card games were always organized at parties and balls, and Washington inevitably wound up at a table at one of them. He played against the governor, Lord Dunmore, often at the Royal Palace. There were always card tables set up at Mount Vernon when the Washingtons hosted parties there. His diaries showed that he sometimes played cards every night of the week, especially when in Williamsburg on business. The colonel was not a casual player; he was a high-stakes gambler. His diaries showed that he probably put at risk between $12,000 and $15,000 a year in today's money playing cards. He played well, though, and on most occasions, his diary showed, he broke even.

The Washingtons enjoyed attending county fairs, well-advertised outdoor extravaganzas offering some form of entertainment for everyone, such as horse racing, wrestling, competitions among fiddlers, foot races, puppet shows, rope dancing, choir singing, and even a beauty pageant with the prettiest girl in the county taking home a cash prize.

Another popular entertainment for the rich was fox hunting, one of George Washington's genuine pleasures. On many occasions in fall and spring, he gathered friends and neighbors for fox chases across the rolling hills of the farms of Mount Vernon and through nearby forests. He loved the hunts for the sport of chasing the sure-footed fox, like all participants did, but he also reveled in the hunt because it gave him the chance to gallop throughout the countryside as fast as his well-trained mounts—such as Ajax and Blue Skin, his treasured iron-gray hunter—could carry him. Washington and his horses would leap over fallen logs, splash through streams, and charge up and down slopes as shafts of early morning sunlight cut through the trees.

He enjoyed the chance to play host to his guests at the end of the day, inviting them for dinner and wine at Mount Vernon, bragging to them that his wine cellar made it "the best tavern in Virginia." Unlike most men, though, he was very serious about his hunts. His guests were expected to meet him at Mount Vernon shortly after daybreak, dressed in their finest riding outfits, and with their best horses.

Washington, the region's best horseman, was also its the best-dressed fox hunter. He sported a blue coat, scarlet waistcoat, buckskin breeches, top boots, a velvet cap, and carried a small whip to urge his mount to run faster. He kept a large kennel of dogs for the hunts (they sometimes scampered into the kitchen house and devoured any food that the servants had left out, driving Martha Washington crazy). He led the chase with his servant Billy Lee, who was almost as good a horseman as Washington, just behind him. Washington recorded the date and starting time of each hunt and whether or not they actually captured any foxes, and he wrote down the amount of time it took to corner the animal, expressing anger when they went home empty-handed. It was a competition, like just about everything else he did, and he wanted to win.

⚬⚭⚬

Women of the upper class in the eighteenth century dressed elegantly. So did Martha, but generally she preferred plainer gowns than the ostentatious styles favored by most other wealthy wives, especially as she grew older. Women of the era wore satin and silk gowns, elaborately quilted petticoats, different-colored stockings, numerous strands of beads, necklaces, bracelets, earrings, and scarves, and kept closets full of shoes. Dresses had whalebone stays to keep them tight, and overweight women like Martha wore corsets. Bodices on dresses were tight, and cut low to accentuate bosoms.

All women favored the cumbersome hoop skirt. These wide skirts were a vision to behold across a room, with designs in stripes, flowers, and even garden landscapes. The hoopskirt was very difficult to dance or walk in. They were so wide that staircases were sometimes built with curved banisters to accommodate them. When outdoors in winter, women wore a long coat with an attached hood. In milder weather, they favored a cloak with an attached hood. All women wore cloaks of some kind, usually red, when traveling.

Another mainstay was the bonnet, tied under the chin, to offer protection from the wind on a carriage or horseback ride. (Mrs. Washington always loved to ride in fast carriages and needed her bonnets to protect her from the wind.) Ladies favored a small, wide headress that supported frizzed hair piled high on their heads. (Many magazine writers lampooned the way most women felt compelled to dress.) Men's and women's fashions in the colonies replicated fashions in London that Americans read about in their newspapers and magazines. Mrs. Washington and Patsy purchased most of their dresses from London too, but bought some needed accouterments from clothing shops in Alexandria and Williamsburg

Martha purchased bottles of expensive perfume, scented waters, facial powder, and lip salves. There was a formula for barley water that would, newspapers assured wealthy women, prevent wrinkles when their face was washed with it. Another formula, which included egg whites, white rose petals, and wheat bread crumbs mixed together, assured eradication of acne. A third formula guaranteed brighter and whiter skin. Women also used imported lip salve from India, facial paints from China, and cold creams and soaps from all over the world.

Dressing in the most expensive gowns, and traveling with handsome cloaks and bonnets, was not done to simply look good or replicate high society in London. Women had no political or financial influence, so fashion became one of the few ways in which they could express their personal styles. It was a way to strike up friendships with other women and to establish a legitimate societal need to spend their husbands' money, money they could not have otherwise spent. Clothing gave women of the era the independence that, their husbands argued, all Americans so desperately needed from the king.

The women of the gentry dressed well when they spent time with each other at church, balls, barbecues, county fairs, or visits to each others' homes. These encounters helped women to create a fulfilling social world for themselves, full of relationships with other women and their children. They enjoyed these bonds, and their own busy, event-filled domestic lives, because it made up for being barred from participation in the man's world of politics, commerce, and the isolation of plantation life.

Women were generally the fashion plates in their homes, but not at Mount Vernon. George Washington loved fine clothes even more than his wife did. This enthusiasm, like his delight in discussing furniture, food, interior decorating, and his dancing, was yet another surprising passion for a husband whose other qualities were so manly. It was yet another interest that created strong bonds between the pair.

He took great pleasure in selecting the latest fashions through his shoppers in London and spent large sums of money on clothes for himself, his wife, and his children. He ordered specific apparel, but frowned on ostentation. In 1761, Washington ordered from the Carys in London "a handsome suit of cloth clothes for winter wear, a handsome suit of thin, ditto, for summer, a fashionable cloak for a man six feet high and proportionable, with best beaver hats, plain...I want neither lace nor embroidery. Plain clothes, with gold or silver buttons, if worn in genteel dress, are all that I desire."

Because of his gargantuan size, Washington's clothes rarely fit. He described his frame as accurately as he could to the tailors of London, reminding them that he was "six feet...slender rather than corpulent," but that did not help. He complained often, telling

Richard Washington, no relation, who worked for the Carys in London, "Whether it be the fault of the tailor or the measure sent I can't say, but certain is my clothes have never fitted me well."

They fit him well enough to permit him to cut quite a figure, though. Whether on political trips to Williamsburg; on business trips to Virginia, Maryland, and western lands; or entertaining at Mount Vernon, George Washington was one of the best-dressed men in America. People always commented on his expensive clothes, and how the combination of his clothes and erect carriage gave him an aura of importance. He reveled in the image he projected, but he never believed that fancy clothes meant much, always reminding friends, "Do not conceive that fine clothes make fine men, any more than fine feathers make fine birds."

⌇⊗⌇

The Washingtons traveled often and spared no expense when they made trips. The entire family would climb into their luxurious white carriage, which was drawn by six horses and driven by a servant dressed in a splendid livery outfit. It was one of the finest carriages in the colony, exceeded only by those of the Carters, who rode in carriages that had six wheels and a separate chair for the driver. Washington's cash accounts for a single month, October 1772, show how much money he spent on traveling. During the first week of that month, the family went to Annapolis for one week for the opening of the horse racing season and the accompanying balls. The family returned to Mount Vernon for ten days and then they were off to Williamsburg in their carriage, accompanied by more servants, for another week of festivities there. At the start of that trip, George gave ten pounds cash in "spending money" to his wife, four pounds to Jacky, and three pounds to Patsy. As always, their visit to Williamsburg was filled with legislative sessions, shopping, games for the children, and balls and parties for the Washingtons at night.

Then it was back to Mount Vernon for more dinners, parties, and visits from guests. That year brought a different kind of visitor: Charles Wilson Peale, the thirty-one-year-old Philadelphia artist, whom the Washingtons paid to paint George's first portrait. Peale asked Washington to pose in his militia uniform, with musket and sword, his hand casually placed in the waistcoat. Washington told the Rev. Jonathan Boucher, who ran the boarding school where his son Jack was a student, that he was in a sullen mood that day, but added, "I fancy the skill of this gentleman's pencil will be put to it, in describing to the world what manner of man I am." When finished, the portrait of Washington would be the first of thousands that would hang on walls throughout the world.

All of the parties, races, musical concerts, plays, fox hunts, and visits to friends meant little to the Washingtons when compared to the joy they found in their children. Jacky and Patsy brought them the same pleasure that other children brought their parents, but both were very troubled and needed much love and affection from their parents, who constantly worried about them.

CHAPTER SEVEN

GEORGE, MARTHA, AND THE CHILDREN

George Washington usually returned home to the main house after the day's work on his farms around 3 p.m. There, after handing his coat to a servant, he walked through the house to greet his wife and children, whom he had sorely missed while in the fields.

Washington's new family at Mount Vernon—his brand-new bride and her two children—brought him happiness, but also great responsibilities. He now had his own family, plus his mother, sister, and brothers scattered throughout Virginia.

George was always glad to see his brothers, sister Betty, and members of the Dandridge clan, but he had no interest in having his tart-tongued mother at Mount Vernon. He did not get along with Mary Washington and visited her infrequently. He had been glad, as a teenager, to move to Mount Vernon, far away from her, and enjoyed the distance between them. Washington saw his mother on his sporadic visits home from the army as a young man, but they were few. If Mary Washington had any dreams about living at Mount Vernon, or even spending much time there as "grandmama," he always dispelled them.

His adamant opposition to any desire she had to reside at Mount Vernon at any time was exemplified in a letter he later wrote to his mother. "I am sure, and candor requires me to say, [living here] will never answer your purposes in any shape whatsoever. For in truth it may be compared to a well-resorted tavern, as scarcely any strangers who are going from north to south, or from south to north, do not spend a day or two at it. This would, were you to be an inhabitant of it, oblige you to do one of three things: first, to be always dressing to appear in company; second, to come into [the room] in a dishabille; or third, to be as it were a prisoner of your own chamber. The first you'd not like, indeed, for a person at your time of life it would be too fatiguing. The second, I should not like, because those who resort here are, as I observed before, strangers and people of the first distinction. And the third, more than probably, would not be pleasing to either of us."

Washington tried to make up for his mother's disappointment by purchasing a small home for her in Fredericksburg, near her daughter Betty's large house. He rented out his mother's plantation, which he owned, and turned over the rent to her as income. Over the years, he would stop there to see her when he could.

George Washington was probably sterile. He did not believe that until near the end of his life, but all indications are that the father of this country could not father children. As president, he told friends that he and Martha never had children because Martha had suffered internal injuries during the difficult birth of her fourth child, Patsy, and could not bear any more children. He went so far as to imply in 1786, when he was fifty-four, that if Martha died and he remarried a very young woman, he might sire a family.

George's inability to have children might have created some tension in the marriage. Martha probably expected to become pregnant right after their marriage, and have several more children, as most women did in that era. Families of eight or nine children were not uncommon. Among the gentry, many children meant more male heirs, more males to oversee plantations, and more females to provide grandchildren. George had to be content as the stepfather of Martha's two small children. He agreed to let Martha make the major decisions in the upbringing of Jacky and Patsy because they were her offspring. As their stepfather, he went along with her decisions, although he did shower them with toys and clothes he ordered from London from the beginning of his marriage. This sometimes proved a prudent policy, but at other times it did not because Martha was often overly lenient in the discipline of her offspring.

Martha was obsessive with child care. Because she had lost two children, she constantly worried about the welfare of Jacky and Patsy, especially after 1763, when Martha's youngest sister Mary died at the age of seven. For several years after her marriage to George, Martha would not travel without her children, despite her husband's assurances that the nannies at Mount Vernon would take good care of them. Even when she found the strength to leave one or both alone for a period of time, she constantly worried. In 1762, Martha wrote to her sister Nancy that she was terrified about Jacky, left at home for two weeks while she took Patsy to visit George's relatives in Westmoreland County. "I carried my little Pat with me and left Jacky at home for a trial to see how well I could stay without him...I was quite impatient to get home. If at any time I heard the dogs bark or a noise out, I thought there was a person sent for me [about Jacky]." She worried about her son every day and her fears caused her imagination to run wild. She wrote to Nancy, "I often fancied he was sick or some accident had happened to him so that I think it is impossible for me to leave him."

In that same letter, one of the few of Martha's that exist, she admitted that the overprotection of her two children had probably hurt friendships and curtailed her own enjoyment. "Friends I am always thinking of and wish it was possible for me to spend more of my time amongst [them]," she noted. Martha told Nancy that she would love to visit her, but reminded her that her children came first. "Assure yourself nothing but my children's interest would prevent a visit," she told her.

Jacky and Patsy were brought up like other children of Virginia's upper class. They had slave nannies as toddlers and servants when they were teenagers. They played with both white neighbors and black slave children on the sprawling grounds of Mount Vernon; they often became friends. Their parents read children's books to Jacky and Patsy, fawned over them, played games with them, and bought them the best clothing and toys from the finest stores in London.

Most parents in the gentry of Virginia had very good relationships with their children. The reason was simple. The children of the rich were in the care of nannies and tutors throughout most of the day; if there were problems, they dealt with them. The disciplining of children was considered prudent among the middle and working classes throughout much of the century because a child had to work hard for his parents on their farm. Harshness eased up for those youngsters during the last quarter of the eighteenth century, but it had eased for rich families much earlier. The parents spent time with the children early in the morning, in late afternoon, at dinner, and in the early evening. Wealthy parents only saw their children under the best of circumstances. This gave children and parents happier relationships.

But Patsy and Jacky were different from most children, with genuine problems, and their parents had to be intimately involved in their care.

George and Martha wanted a normal life for their youngsters and outwardly provided a typical upbringing in entertainment, travel, and schooling. John Stedlar was hired to teach the children how to play musical instruments. He taught Patsy the harpsichord and flute, and Jacky learned to play the violin. Jacky and Patsy attended dancing school regularly, as did most of the children of the gentry. A dancing master, Mr. Christian, gave lessons at the homes of the planters on a rotating basis. Lessons might be one day each week at Mount Vernon and then one day each week the following month at neighbor George Mason's home.

The homes of the gentry in northern Virginia were too far

apart for any central school to be established and Alexandria was ten miles away, two hours by horse and longer by carriage. The Washingtons elected to hire a private tutor, Walter McGowan, who lived at Mount Vernon for several years, to educate their children. Jacky and Patsy learned how to read and write, and studied literature, Latin, and mathematics in a school day that lasted from just after breakfast until early afternoon. Their academic training was more advanced than that of most children of the upper class. In most regions, lessons in foreign languages or mathematics were not taught for seventy more years.

The Washingtons were different in their approach to their children. Martha coddled them and was overindulgent. Perhaps the best thumbnail sketch that described Martha was offered, not about her attitude towards her children, but her grandchildren, by Abigail Adams in 1789. "Mrs. Washington is a most friendly, good lady, always pleasant and easy, dotingly fond of her grandchildren, to whom she is quite the Grandmamma," she wrote.

On the other hand, George was a stern taskmaster to his stepchildren and, later, to his stepgrandchildren. One said that the grandchildren were "much in awe of him, although he was kind in his manner to them. They all felt they were in the presence of one who was not to be trifled with." Yet he continually felt that as a stepfather he had to give in to his wife's wishes. He once said of his reluctance to punish an irresponsible grandson, "Mrs. Washington's happiness is bound up in the boy...any rigidity used toward him would perhaps be productive of grievous effects on her."

George may have been strict in many ways, but in others he doted on his stepchildren. He felt great sympathy for Patsy, who began to have epileptic fits when she was just a toddler. He showered her with gifts whenever they traveled to a city or village in Virginia and bought her whatever dresses and shoes he could find. Her new stepfather sometimes went overboard.

Just after his marriage, George placed an expensive order for clothes for Martha, Jacky, and Patsy. For the girl, just two years old, he bought four pairs of leather, two pairs of silk, and four pairs of callimanco shoes; also eight pairs of kid mitts, and four of kid gloves. At age four, he bought her four pairs of callimanco, six pairs of leather, and two pairs of satin shoes; also twelve pairs of mitts, and six pairs of white kid gloves. He also purchased six pairs of fine thread and four of worsted stockings; two caps; two pairs of ruffles; two tuckers, bibs, and aprons; two fans; two bonnets; six pocket handkerchiefs; one cloth coat; one stiffened coat of fashionable silk made with packthread stays; six yards of ribbons; two necklaces; and one pair of silver sleeve buttons with stones.

When Patsy was six, George acquired for her a stiffened coat of fashionable silk; four fashionable dresses to be made of long lawn; two fine frocks; a satin capuchin hat; necklaces; a Persian quilted coat; laced aprons; six handsome egrettes of different sorts; and one pair of silver shoe buckles. He never stopped buying her clothes. At eleven, he ordered for Patsy ten pairs of pumps in leather, black callimanco, and satin.

Over the years George bought Patsy a harpsichord, books, winter coats, winter and summer dresses, an expensive Persian coat, hundreds of pairs of stockings, mittens (sometimes a dozen pair per order), silver and gold shoe buckles, dozens of egrettes (head ornaments), thousands of clothing and hair pins, boxes of gingerbread, dozens of toys, dolls, a child's tea set, a child's "grocery shop," wax baby dolls, and even a bound Bible with "Martha Parke Custis" inscribed on its front page.

Patsy's illness caused considerable concern to Martha in the first year of her marriage to George Washington. Sometimes the little girl improved and sometimes she relapsed. Any improvement thrilled her parents. In 1760, when Patsy was four years old, she went without fits for some time and her relieved mother sent an optimistic note full of emotion to her friend Margaret Green, the wife of the Rev. Charles Green, the pastor of Truro Church, where the Washingtons worshipped. Green was also a part-time doctor who had tended to Patsy.

Martha wrote, "I have the pleasure to tell you my dear little girl is much better. She has lost her fits & fevers both and seems to be getting well very fast. We carried her out yesterday in the chariot and the change of air refreshed her very much." Again, in April

1762, Martha was very hopeful for her daughter. Patsy had come down with several colds and fevers during the winter, which were easily cured, but her epilepsy was apparently better. Martha wrote her to sister, "I think Patsy has been heartier than ever."

George and Martha tried everything possible to cure their daughter of epilepsy. Doctors of the era knew little about the illness except that it was a nervous disorder of some kind. Various herbs, tree barks, and tonics were prescribed for it, as well as ether, "fits drops," "nervous drops," and other potions. The usual method of treatment was bleeding, the same primitive treatment that physicians used for just about any malady of the day. Without warning, victims of epilepsy would go into violent seizures that would shake their entire bodies; some seizures could be fatal.

In 1767, Dr. Rumney made the first of more than a dozen visits to Mount Vernon to treat Patsy. For a year, Patsy seemed better. The year 1768 was a poor one for her, though; Dr. Rumney visited more often. George also called in Dr. Hugh Mercer, who had studied at the University of Aberdeen in Scotland. They offered more and different pills and purges, but she grew worse. Rumney visited her often throughout the year, but there was no improvement and she continued to have fits. Additional doctors were called in. One physician even gave her an iron ring to wear that was supposed to ward off epileptic seizures and could be used to bite down on when the fits arrived. They took her to any physician they thought could help.

On March 25, 1771, George and Martha traveled with Patsy to Williamsburg for yet more visits to Dr. John Carter, one of the South's outstanding doctors. Carter again examined Patsy, who was then thirteen, and asked her and her parents about the fits and then prescribed medicine that probably did little good. The Washingtons and their daughter came back to Carter's office again on May 7 for another visit. This time George scribbled in his expense accounts that they purchased four more bottles of drops for "the fits" at the price of one pound sterling and five shillings from Carter. Two days later they were back at Dr. Carter's for yet another check up and more drugs. Two days after that they went once more, and this time

Carter gave Patsy ether to smell if another fit shook her frail body.

The Washingtons brought in doctors from other colonies, too. They asked doctors to visit Mount Vernon from great distances to see Patsy; they came often. On July 29 of 1771, a Dr. Johnson traveled from Maryland to see Patsy, giving her medicine for "the fits." He came again on November 12 and left them more medicine, charging them eleven pounds sterling.

The Washingtons talked about Patsy's illness liberally in order to solicit the names of friends or relatives who knew something about epilepsy and could help her. A man named Thomas Jackson met them and told them that his brother had treated epileptics and could procure medicine for Patsy; George and Martha jumped at the chance. Washington wrote to Jackson in 1770, "Your obliging offer we cheerfully embrace and Mrs. Washington would think herself much favored in receiving those samples and directions for the use of them, which your brother administers for the fits." Washington told him that Patsy's recent bouts had been frequent for nearly two years—in one eighty-six day period she had seizures on twenty-six days, and some of those days had more than one fit—and that the condition "rather increases than abates" and that the samples should be sent "as soon as possible." The Washingtons also implored the Rev. Jonathan Boucher, who ran a boarding school where Jack was enrolled, to buy vials of ether at apothecaries in Annapolis and send them via courier to Mount Vernon.

Another doctor suggested a special diet and different lifestyle, writing Martha that her daughter should engage in "moderate exercise, temperate living which she may think abstemiousness and her being attentive to keep her body cool and open which may, I hope, be effectually done and agreeably to herself by the use of barley water and light cooling food."

In the 1750s, entrepreneurs built cabins in small colonies at Warm Springs, in the mountainous western section of Virginia, and promoted the mineral water of the springs as nature's medicine for any affliction. Hundreds of people traveled there from all over the region to gain relief from whatever ailed them by bathing in the springs. The Washingtons took Patsy, who was then twelve, there in the summer of 1769 and remained for several weeks. They lived in a small, crude cabin, took meals in a tiny inn, and went to the infrequent entertainments available in the mountainous resort area. Patsy drank the mineral waters and bathed in them for hours, as did so many, but they did not help.

Their daughter's epilepsy dominated the lives of George and Martha Washington. When she was a small child they refused to leave Mount Vernon without her, severely disrupting travel and entertainment plans they might have had. If she became ill while traveling, they rushed home and canceled engagements. Washington noted of one trip that "we set out to go to Captain McCarty's but Patsy being taken with a fit on the road by the mill, we turned back." Martha spent an enormous amount of time watching over Patsy, and asked all the workers at Mount Vernon to keep an eye on her. George and Martha made numerous visits to her room at night to check on the little girl. There were often as many doctors as friends at their home for dinner and overnight stays; they worried about her constantly.

Her health affected the life of her brother, too. When he was fifteen, Jack had the opportunity to travel abroad with his headmaster, Rev. Boucher, but his parents rejected the offer because Martha was terrified that something might happen to him on such an extensive journey. George described her feelings in a letter to the headmaster that ended with the chilling line, "The unhappy situation of her daughter has in some degree fixed her eyes upon him [Jack] as her only hope," meaning that Martha did not expect Patsy to live very long.

Unable to cure her of epilepsy, the Washingtons smothered Patsy with love and gifts. They constantly purchased books and toys for her when she was a little girl and later, when she became a teenager, helped her turn into a sophisticated young lady. She learned to dance the minuet, the Irish jig, and the Virginia reel, and spent hours playing her small harpsichord.

George was always slipping Patsy considerable amounts of spending money whenever the family went on a trip. His diaries and expense accounts are full of incidents of his largesse to his daughter, such as in a note on May 12, 1772, when the family went to Alexandria to watch a new ship being launched, "by Miss Custis for pocket money, three pounds."

Martha and George were fussy over anything they ordered for their daughter. In the summer of 1772, Martha wrote to a woman who assisted the Carys, her buyers in London, with a detailed description of a suit of clothes for Patsy, reminding her they were for a sixteen-year-old girl so that the size would be right. She complained bitterly that the previous year they ordered a complete suit for Patsy, but all of it was not delivered. "I can't help adding that I think it necessary that the last year's suit (which ought to be returned if she could do without it in the meanwhile) should be completed with a tippet and cap, as it is scarce more than half a suit without [them]," she wrote.

Her mother pampered Patsy, but would not overindulge her when it came to clothes. Nothing irritated Martha more than high prices or pleased her more than bargains. She bought her daughter fine clothes from London, but reminded buyers to look for good prices. She did not want to spoil her daughter and disdained buying clothing that Patsy would outgrow in a short time. At one point in 1764, Martha sent a note to Mrs. Shelbury, a London milliner who worked for Cary, asking her to purchase "such things as misses of her age usually wear here." Then she told her to look for special clothes for her daughter, "those which may be more genteel and proper for her." They should not be too genteel, though, "provided it is done with frugality, for as she is only nine years old; a superfluity or expense in dress would be altogether unnecessary."

⚬⚬⚬

The problems the Washingtons faced with their son Jacky were entirely different. The rambunctious toddler grew into an absolute hellion as a teenager. He was stubborn, egocentric, and worse, to George, a child who had no interest in academics. Washington desired that his stepson follow in his footsteps. He wanted him to grow up into a refined and compassionate man, educated at the finest college, to marry well and take his place, like his stepfather, as an upstanding citizen of Virginia. Jacky had other plans.

Young Custis had little interest in schooling. He apparently did not open a book in the five months following the departure of Walter McGowan as the children's tutor in late 1767, when he was thirteen, angering his father. Upset at his behavior, and fearful that without an education he would become useless, Washington finally engaged his wife in a lengthy argument over the upbringing of their son.

Jacky's problem, he told her bluntly, was that his mother had coddled him from birth. The boy had been overprotected his entire life, spoiled worse than any child he knew, and had grown up believing that he did not have to learn anything or do anything because his mother and father would always take care of him. When it came to her children, George told her, Martha was afraid of her own shadow. His wife feared that Patsy would die of epilepsy, and that Jacky would drown. The Washingtons lived on the Potomac and her children swam in it, with black and white playmates, all the time. Martha's brother had drowned in the Rappahannock as a boy, and she was terrified that the impulsive Jacky would take too many risks as a swimmer and meet the same fate. She feared this catastrophe all of her life and even insisted that George order the headmaster of the school Jacky attended as a teenager to stop him from swimming too often or staying in the water too long.

Whenever George chided Martha on her obsessive behavior towards Jacky, she countered that it was George, not her, who had showered him with presents throughout his entire life and who constantly took him to the racetrack, of all places.

The solution, George insisted, was not another tutor, but a boarding school where Jack could receive a fine education that would permit him to be accepted at a college and succeed there. A boarding school, with a tough headmaster, would also provide the type of Spartan lifestyle and discipline that had been so lacking at Mount Vernon.

So, after inquiries, George sent his stepson off to Caroline County, Maryland, and the small boarding school of the Rev.

Boucher. The headmaster, born in England in 1738, was a highly respected Anglican minister and a tutor of gentry children in Virginia prior to establishing his school. In 1768, he gladly registered the headstrong fourteen-year-old Jacky Custis. George was confident that Boucher would make an upstanding young man out of his stepson. He told Boucher that young Jacky was a scholar in the making and, bending the truth a bit, wrote that his stepson was "a boy of good genius, untainted in his morals, and of innocent manners. Two years and upward he has been reading of Virgil and was [at the time McGowan left] entered upon a Greek testament, though I presume he has grown not a little rusty in both."

Boucher happily agreed to take young Custis under his wing, and for three turbulent years tried, as he told Washington, "to exert my best endeavours to render him worthy of yours and his family's expectations." He applauded Washington's love for his son and interest in his future, writing, "You, sir, seem so justly sensible of the vast importance of a good education that I cannot doubt of your heartily concurring in every plan that might be proposed for the advantage of your ward: and what I am more particularly pleased with is the ardent desire you express for the cultivation of his moral, as well as his intellectual powers, I mean that he may be made a good, as well as learned and a sensible man."

Boucher's early letters were full of optimism and hope for Jacky, even though Washington's son was no scholar. "He is far from being a brilliant genius," Boucher wrote, but he would work with him. The headmaster was eager to have the son of one of the wealthiest men in the country as his student. He could attract even more business by reminding prospective parents that his school was chosen by none other than George Washington. He fawned over Jack, telling Washington, "I have not seen a youth that I think promises fairer to be a good and useful man than John Custis!" The confident minister did not know what he was getting himself into.

Boucher had his hands full with Jack Custis at his school, which was later moved to bustling Annapolis to lure more students. He was soon complaining bitterly about Jack in several letters to Washington, forgetting that in Washington's initial letter

he had told Boucher that he wanted him "fit for more useful purposes than a horse racer." And, in another letter, Washington said
he wished Jack would lead "a life of as little indulgence and dissipation as should be thought necessary…restrained from the practice of those follies and vices which youth and inexperience are
but naturally led to [trouble]."

Sometimes the educator, as well as his stepfather, was ready to
give up on the teenager. Boucher wrote to Washington in 1770
that "the chief failings of his character are that he is constitution-
ally somewhat too warm-indolent and voluptuous. As yet, these
propensities are but in embryo. 'Ere long, however, they will discover themselves and if not duly and carefully regulated, it is easy
to see to what they will lead…sunk in unmanly sloth."

At times, Boucher saw some hope for the impulsive teenager.
In the summer of 1769, Washington wrote to Boucher that Jack's
attitude had not improved, but Boucher disagreed. "We now do
much better than formerly," he said, defending Jack and himself.
"You will remember my having complained of Jack's laziness
which, however, I now hope is not incurable. For I find he will
bear driving, which heretofore I used to fear he would not. He has
met with more rigor since I saw you than in all the time before and
he is the better for it."

And at other times he did not. Jack's schoolwork was so poor,
in fact, that Boucher wrote to George Washington in 1770 that his
future as a prominent man would be dim if "he appears illiterate
amongst men of letters, into whose company, in traveling, he will
often fall." In the spring of 1770, Boucher recommended that
young Jack join a tour of England and Europe that he planned to
conduct if he could convince a few parents to send their children
with him. He told Washington that in two years his stepson would
attend college and that a tour of Europe would help. "Traveling
will be of particular service to him," he said, and urged Washington to consider the idea.

Jack never went to Europe. Many members of the great families
of America, parents and children, traveled to Europe before and
after the Revolution, but, ironically, no one in the most prominent

family of all, the Washingtons, ever left the United States.

Perhaps he should have gone. His behavior became worse the following semester, when he was sixteen, and prompted a frustrated Boucher to send a lengthy letter to his father outlining his many faults. Boucher said Jack's "love of ease and love of pleasure, pleasure of the kind exceedingly uncommon in his years. I never did in my life know a youth so exceedingly indolent...one would suppose nature had intended him for some Asiatic prince."

Boucher told Washington in rather blunt language that Jack paid no attention to his studies and that he was more attracted to the social life than any student he had ever met. He told Washington that "he seldom goes [out] without learning something I could have wished him not to have learned." Jack had fallen in with bad company, too. Boucher told Washington that there was only one other boy with as much disregard for his studies, and a love of the good life, as Jack; that was the son of Samuel Galloway. Naturally, Boucher wrote, the two of them became fast friends. "He has done your ward more harm than he or his family can easily make amends for." He told Washington that there were probably more disreputable characters in Annapolis than in any other city, and that Jack managed to befriend every one of them. He was living a life "of idleness and dissipation among them." Jack "does not much like books," Boucher complained, and said he spent much of his time foxhunting and at the racetrack.

Then there were the girls. "Jack has a propensity to [women]," Boucher wrote, "that I am at a loss of how to judge of, much more how to describe." Young Jack had a particular propensity for his buddy Galloway's sister, whom Boucher said was "young and pretty" and that the two carried on in someone's house. The Galloway girl was just one of many. "This is no pleasing picture of his conduct here," wrote Boucher, who then told the Washingtons that he was often tempted to kick Jack out of his school. He always relented, though, because he feared that Jack would only get himself into more trouble if he lived somewhere else. "He will be in less [trouble] here than almost anywhere else," the frazzled headmaster said.

Washington could not have agreed more. In one letter he urged

Boucher to keep a close eye on his son and not "allow him to be rambling about nights in company with those who do not care how debauched and vicious his conduct may be." In another letter, on February 3, 1771, a clearly upset Washington wrote that he did not want Jack to fall in with a bad element, instructing the headmaster "to prevent as much as possible his connecting with store boys and that kind of low loose company who would not be displeased at the debauchery of his manners."

Washington was just as fed up with his son as his tutor was. He wrote to Boucher on December 6, 1770, that "his mind is a good deal released from study, and more than ever turned to dogs, horses, and guns." He had previously admitted to Boucher that he was certain that Jack would calm down under the eye of a strict headmaster, "but I may have asked too much."

And then there was the wedding incident. Washington sent Jack to Baltimore to be inoculated for smallpox (without telling Martha so as not to frighten her) because Boucher told him that he might take Jack with him on a trip to Europe, and a precautionary inoculation was advisable. Washington had had the pox as a teenager and knew how dangerous it was. He sent his stepson to a doctor for inoculation and the standard recovery period of several weeks.

Somewhere between his inoculation and recovery, Jack disappeared. He talked the Baltimore doctor into writing a note to his headmaster, telling him that Jack needed an extra week of rest because he was very ill. A friend of Boucher's told him that he saw Jack in the middle of that week, when he was so "ill," and he was the picture of health. Then it was learned that during his "recovery" from his "illness" Jack, who was allegedly "very sick," turned up at the two-day wedding of a friend in Baltimore. His severe "illness" did not prohibit him from eating, drinking, and dancing with as many pretty girls as he could find.

Boucher fumed. When Jack finally returned to school, he wrote to Washington with great sarcasm that "the season of suspense is now over" and that "Mrs. Washington will have the pleasure of learning from undoubted authority that her son is happily and easily released from a formidable disorder, without hardly a mark to tell that he ever had it. He is as well as ever he was in his life, indeed has such strong symptoms of health."

Washington was furious and angrier still that letters he received from his stepson that summer were full of spelling and grammatical errors. He sent him a sharp note chastising him for his troubles at school. Washington forgave him for the letters, though, deciding that he had probably made so many errors because he wrote them too quickly. Young Jack took that admonition as an opportunity to agree with him and defend himself as a scholar. "All therefore that I can now do is to promise to be more attentive and watchful for the future. Your gentle, yet very striking observations shall have their due weight with me."

Then, in the very next line, the seemingly repentant Jack wrote that he looked forward to the next visit of his mother and father to Annapolis so he could take them to the racetrack.

Sometime in the fall of 1771, Washington communicated with Dr. John Witherspoon, headmaster at Princeton, who was highly critical of Boucher's educational methods. He told Washington that Boucher should be spending more time with Jack and teaching him Greek. When Washington conveyed Witherspoon's opinion to Boucher, the Annapolis headmaster exploded. He told Washington that he did not need some other educator telling him how to run his school and that Jack could not handle Greek. He delicately wrote of Jack's scholarship that "his particular genius and complexion are not unknown to you and that they are of a kind requiring not the least judgment and delicacy to manage properly." He reminded him too that he had done a Herculean task of keeping young Custis out of trouble. "I have hitherto, I thank God, conducted him with tolerable safety through some pretty trying and perilous scenes."

The Washingtons visited the school as often as they could, sometimes bringing Patsy. George and the Rev. Boucher corresponded frequently about Jack's education, or what George often saw as the lack of it. Boucher went out of his way to spend more time with Jacky to please his important—and very rich—father.

This combination of hard work by all, if not by Jack himself, paid off, and Jack graduated from Boucher's academy in 1773 and seemed eager to continue his education at a college. Neither George nor Martha wanted him to attend William and Mary because, everyone told them, the professors seemed to be constantly involved in petty feuds with people in Williamsburg, the students were more interested in parties and girls than in their studies, the fabled taverns of Williamsburg were directly across the street from the campus, and the racetrack was less than a mile away. It was the worst possible place for their son to attend college. Boucher, by 1773 a staunch loyalist, advised them not to send their son to Witherspoon at Princeton because Boucher saw the New Jersey campus as a hotbed of patriotic fanaticism.

The choice was King's College in New York, run by Dr. Myles Cooper, a well-known educator and a loyalist. The school had a good reputation for academics, and would give Jack the chance to live in a big city, meeting students from all over the colonies. There, he could grow into the well-rounded, educated gentleman that his mother and father had always expected him to be.

There was one more reason that they selected King's College. In April, to the utter astonishment of his parents, Jacky announced that he was engaged to be married to fifteen-year-old Nelly Calvert, one of the daughters of the rich, influential Calvert family of Maryland. George and Martha had no idea that they were seeing each other; no one did. The harried headmaster, Boucher, who was supposed to be watching over Jack, was as surprised as the parents. He wrote, defensively, that "I beg leave to assure you on my word of honour, that, never til that moment, had I the most distant suspicion of any such thing being in agitation," and told Washington that he was "not to blame."

Jacky was head over heels in love with young Nelly, who was just as smitten with him. The Washingtons were thunderstruck; marriage was unthinkable. After all, Jacky was just eighteen and Nelly was only fifteen, barely into puberty. Faraway New York City, where Jack would be 250 miles away from Nelly, suddenly loomed as a superb place for their son to attend college.

Like any proud father, George Washington took his stepson to King's College in May 1773. Father and son traveled via Philadelphia, where they stayed at the Jockey Club for a few days, and George proudly introduced Jack to men of influence he knew in that city. They were then joined by Lord Stirling, who owned iron mines in New Jersey, for the trek to New York. They stayed with Stirling at his large stone mansion in Morris County and might have toured some of his ironworks there before going on to New York.

There, George turned Jacky over to Dr. Cooper, who assured him, as Rev. Boucher had, that he would take good care of his son. Before returning to Virginia, George went to a farewell dinner for General Thomas Gage, head of all British forces in the American colonies, who was returning to London. Washington had served with Gage in the French and Indian War and was happy to be invited to his farewell dinner.

General Gage would be back, and soon. He and George Washington would face each other again, but not under such pleasant circumstances.

CHAPTER EIGHT

TRAGEDY AND JOY

B y the time spring had arrived in 1773, Patsy Washington, just seventeen, felt much better. Her epileptic seizures had been shorter and the intervals between them greater. The Washingtons had told friends that their daughter's spirits were considerably improved, too. The dark-haired teenager had grown into an attractive young woman. Patsy dressed as a woman, not a girl, attended as many dances as possible, kept up with her music lessons, enjoyed picnics, and visited as many girlfriends in the region as she could. There had not been any boys in her life yet, but she was at an age when they would be calling.

George and Martha continually worried about Patsy. Their daughter still wore the iron ring on her finger to bite down on in case of a seizure. Her mother and stepfather, always fretful, tried to stay as close to her as they could during the days and nights, without seeming to be cloying. Still, as the years progressed, Patsy's health seemed to improve.

At the height of summer that year, on June 19, Patsy joined her parents, her Uncle Jack and his family, Nelly Calvert, and Nelly's governess for dinner at Mount Vernon. It had been a busy month in what appeared to be a beautiful summer and there was much to talk about. George Washington had returned on June 8 after accompanying Jacky to King's College. Friends from Fredericksburg had dined at Mount Vernon on June 11 and later that evening Nelly arrived, as did Dr. Rumney, one of the many doctors who had treated Patsy over the years, and another family friend. A ship's captain named Harper was there too, and presumably regaled them with tales of life on the high seas. George went to the church at Alexandria for a meeting on the thirteenth. Some family friends visited on the fifteenth. Several more guests had dinner at Mount Vernon on the sixteenth and stayed over night. Uncle Jack arrived with his family on the eighteenth.

Nothing special was planned for the 19th. George remained home with Uncle Jack and his family while Martha attended to the business of running the household. The dinner that began just after 3 p.m., was routine, just another family gathering. It was very pleasant, too, because, George remembered later, Patsy seemed in remarkably good health. Suddenly, around 4 p.m., without saying a word, Patsy started to go into convulsions. She slipped off her chair and slumped to the floor, her body heaving. The women shrieked. Servants raced into the room. A startled George leaped out of his chair and ran to her. He held Patsy in his arms and tried to soothe her trembling body, as he had done so often in the past when she had seizures. But there was nothing he could do to help her this time. After several frightening minutes, the shaking of her body stopped, and her head fell to one side; Patsy died in her father's arms.

George was crushed. He wrote to Burwell Bassett, his brother-in-law, "The sweet innocent girl entered into a more happy and peaceful abode than any she has met with in the afflicted path she hitherto has trod." The stoic Washington was too overcome to offer much detail on his daughter's sudden demise or his feelings, but described her death in emotional language: "She was seized with one of her usual fits and expired in less than two minutes without uttering a word, a groan, or scarce a sigh."

Earlier, in April 1773, Bassett's own young daughter had died. Washington sent him a consoling letter full of tender language that surely duplicated his own feelings at the loss of Patsy. He told Bassett how badly he and Martha felt about the girl's death, attributed it to the mysterious will of the Almighty, and told the Bassets to be strong. "Your own good sense will arm you with fortitude to withstand the stroke, great as it is, and enable you to console Mrs. Bassett, whose loss and feelings are much to be pitied," he counseled them.

Patsy was buried in a vault at Mount Vernon the next day, with the Rev. Massey of Pohick Church conducting a solemn funeral service. The small burial was attended only by the Washingtons, Uncle Jack's family, Nelly and her governess, George and Sally Fairfax, who were despondent over the death of the girl they had grown to know and love, and a number of grieving Mount Vernon slaves. Over the next few days, the Fairfaxes visited the Washingtons to help them get over their despondency, and George and Martha, in turn, visited them. Nelly Calvert stayed at Mount Vernon for several days to comfort the parents.

Patsy's sudden death astonished everyone. Her brother, Jacky, just settling in at King's College, was devastated by the news. He knew something was very wrong when he received an urgent letter from his father and noticed that it had a thick black seal on it. He could not bring himself to read it and rushed to the office of Doctor Cooper, who opened it and read it to him.

Jacky was so traumatized by the news that he waited two weeks to write to his mother and father. The college president warned the Washingtons that their son's letter might be delayed because he was so upset. "The shock, you may suppose, was severe," he declared.

Jacky explained to his mother that he did not return home because he could not have arrived until nearly a week after the burial and would have been so distraught that his appearance probably would have done his mother more harm than good.

Jacky had worried about his sick sister all of his life. Because of her epilepsy, he wrote to his mother that perhaps Patsy would happier in heaven than on Earth. "Her case is more to be envied than pitied, for if we mortals can distinguish between those who are deserving of grace and who are not, I am confident she enjoys that bliss prepared only for the good and virtuous...comfort yourself with reflecting that she now enjoys in substance what we in this world enjoy in imagination."

Condolences poured in from all over.

Many friends and relatives tried to comfort the parents by reminding them of how difficult Patsy's life had been. George's brother-in-law, Fielding Lewis, was one of them. He wrote, "Poor Patsy's death must have distressed Mrs. Washington very much, but when she considers the unhappy situation she was in and the little probability of ever getting well, she must conclude that it's better as it is, as there was little appearance of her ever being able to enjoy life with any satisfaction."

The royal governor, Lord Dunmore, was extremely upset. He had socialized with the Washingtons often and always felt badly about their daughter's epilepsy. He wrote to George that "I am now most exceedingly sorry" about the girl's death. He added that, "I do condole with you, and Mrs. Washington, for your loss, though as the poor young lady was so often afflicted with these fits, I dare say she thinks it a happy exchange." Dunmore even offered to travel to Mount Vernon to grieve with the parents, but the press of business prevented him from making the trip.

But no one could comfort Martha Washington. She was forty-two years old, and she had lost three of her four children. Not only was Patsy's death a shock, as the death of any teenaged child is, but she and her husband had honestly believed that Patsy was getting better. To think that her epilepsy was subsiding, and then to watch her collapse and die from it—right in front of her—was almost too much for Martha to bear.

Martha plunged into mourning. George ordered special mourning clothes and rings for her that she wore for a long time. Her husband did not know what he could do to comfort her, and he suffered himself.

A very distraught George stopped all business for three entire weeks, leaving the plantation work to his managers and completely neglecting the business paperwork that piled up in his office.

George had as many friends to the house for dinner as possible, trying to keep Martha's mind off her daughter's demise. He traveled to the Ferry Farm with Martha to visit his mother, Mary Washington, and took Martha with him on his rounds of the plantation each day, trying to fill up her days with activities of any kind. Jacky wrote his father a tender letter thanking him for the love he knew his father must have extended to his mother, telling him, "I am persuaded that your goodness left no stone unturned to render this shock as easy as possible."

His son had a suggestion. Jacky wrote to his stepfather that remaining at Mount Vernon would just make things worse for his mother; she would see Patsy everywhere she turned at the plantation. He wanted his parents to move to New York for a period of time, just to get away from Mount Vernon. He had discussed his idea with Dr. Cooper, who not only thought it was a good plan, but he assured the Washingtons that he would obtain comfortable lodgings for them in the city. Cooper even volunteered to visit the Washingtons when he traveled south in the fall.

Martha did not want to leave Mount Vernon, though. She understood Jacky's view, but she believed that her home, her loving husband, and her friends were what she needed most during this terrible time. And she loved Mount Vernon. The mansion and its grounds, plus the routine and familiarity of her home, could be enough to help her get through this tragic chapter in her life. Her husband agreed with her. Neither was in a hurry to move to New York, even for a few months. They would move there one day, however, when George Washington was elected the first president of the United States and Martha became the country's First Lady. But that was a long time in the future.

George asked Martha's mother if she wanted to move to Mount Vernon for a while to be with her daughter; she declined.

But there was a solution. Martha wanted her son Jacky back home. She would not listen to any of her husband's arguments that he needed an education to gain responsibility and maturity, that he needed to establish independence or identity. She was not interested in her husband's view that living away from home would substantially help her son, who had been so reckless for so long. She wanted her last child home with her so that she could be with him every day and protect him from what was becoming a very cruel world.

Jack Custis, nineteen, returned home in early December, completing one semester at King's College. He would never return, even though the college has always proudly listed him as one of its alumni. Young Jacky had done well, Dr. Cooper assured the Washingtons, and had made considerable progress as both a scholar and a man. Jack was happy to be home for several reasons. He had never been eager to go to New York in the first place. Jack wanted to help comfort his mother during her grieving. Most important, he was desperately in love with Nelly Calvert and intended to marry her as soon as possible.

His stepfather was adamantly against the wedding. He felt that the marriage was coming too soon, and that both young people, just teenagers, were not mature enough to enter such a union and begin a family. He had been married at twenty-six and did not understand why his stepson, nineteen, wanted to become a husband so early in life. He was also completely against marriage for Nelly Calvert, who was just fifteen. The squire of Mount Vernon believed both Jack and Nelly were barely out of childhood. Jacky's departure from college and marriage were "much against my wishes," George wrote before the wedding. He told friends that, in fact, his irresponsible son would not be fit for marriage "for some years" hence.

George had expressed his feelings to Benedict Calvert, Nelly's father, whom he had met on visits to Annapolis and Jack's school, in a letter in the spring of 1773. He told Calvert that he was afraid the pair were rushing into marriage and that their children should wait at least three years before they married. He assured Calvert that he admired his daughter and thought the two a fine couple, but he was convinced they were just too young. He wrote to

Calvert of his headstrong stepson, "His youth, inexperience, and unripened education is and will be insuperable obstacles, in my eye, to the completion of the marriage." He believed, too, that his stepson had given little thought to what he was about to do, complaining to one of his brothers-in-law that Jacky was getting into marriage "before, I am certain, he has ever bestowed a serious thought of the consequences."

Jacky and Nelly paid no attention to his feelings; they were in love and had made up their minds. They had Martha's support; she thought marriage and children would help mature her son. Martha was just nineteen when she married and did not think Nelly was too young for matrimony. Martha had quietly enlisted the support for the wedding of the two young lovebirds of just about every Dandridge and Washington in the entire colony of Virginia, in addition to every neighbor, friend, and acquaintance. Everybody loved Nelly.

Even the cranky Boucher, Jacky's teacher, was in love with her. He told George that Jacky "could nowhere have entered into a more prudent engagement. Miss Calvert has merit enough to fix him, if any woman can." Boucher simply gushed over Nelly, telling Washington that the marriage was "a most pleasing of all connections" and called Nelly "the most amiable young woman I have almost ever known" and a "darling child" and concluded by telling George that he and his wife were lucky to have her. All of the Fairfaxes seemed smitten by her, too. George found himself all alone against a wide-ranging army of family members, neighbors, and educators. It was no secret that he was also just as fond of Nelly Calvert as the rest of his family since the engagement and her frequent visits to Mount Vernon. He wrote that their campaign had left him the only person opposed to the union and that with "the desires of his mother and acquiescence of almost all of his relatives to encounter, I did not care...to push my opposition...I have yielded, contrary to my judgment."

Martha Washington wanted to attend the wedding, but she could only do so dressed in black mourning clothes. She communicated with a seamstress about making some clothes for her, but never purchased them. She acquired only the clothes her husband obtained for her. She did not want to ruin a joyous wedding by arriving in black, though, and commiserating with all on the death of Patsy. So, at the last moment, she decided not to attend. George Washington arranged to have Nancy Carlyle, a niece of Sally Fairfax, remain with Martha while he was gone. He attended the wedding alone at the Calvert plantation in the early evening of February 3, 1774, stayed over that night, and remained all of the next day and the following night as one of the guests at the extravagant reception the proud Calverts hosted at their large Maryland estate. George returned to Mount Vernon the next day.

Washington was not happy about the union, but he made certain that he included the news in just about all the letters he sent out during the weeks after the wedding. Friends and associates wished the young couple well. One of the most enthusiastic was from Dr. Cooper, who wrote to George, "I hope and earnestly wish the young adventurer may enjoy every pleasure in his new state…from every account of the young lady's disposition and qualifications, and from my own knowledge of his, I cannot but think that they bid very fair for happiness; I pray heaven they may attain it."

Cooper, an avowed loyalist who must have loathed Washington's emergence by then as one of Virginia's leading political radicals, then sent Washington a huge bill for Jack's education. He wrote that "the amount seems large" but reminded him that he had to charge Jack for a horse and carriage and for traveling expenses he gave him, and those charges "swell the bill exceedingly."

After the wedding, in a burst of affection expressed in a touching letter of gratitude for everything his father had done for him at the wedding, and in general for himself and his new bride, Jacky wrote that he "was at a great loss of words" in expressing his love for his father. He told him that he had nothing but "affection and regard, both of which did not I possess in the highest degree for you. I…shall strenuously endeavor by my future conduct to merit a continuance of your regard and esteem."

Soon afterwards, George Washington realized that in Nelly Calvert his son had found an exceptionally loving and lovable young woman. His wife Martha truly loved her and so did he. Perhaps marriage would make Jacky responsible, even though everything else his parents had tried did not. Within months, the Washingtons were constantly dining with Jacky and Nelly at Mount Vernon. The marriage turned out to be one of the best things that ever happened to the Washingtons and, in a small way, coming eight months after Patsy's demise, helped to dissolve the black fog of grief that had enveloped all of Mount Vernon.

Just five months later, George and Martha were jolted by yet another change in their lives; their best friends, the Fairfaxes, departed for England. Lord Fairfax, in England, had replaced George William Fairfax as his agent in America, cutting off all income except that derived from the Belvoir plantation. At the same time, George William inherited an estate in England. It was a period, too, when political tensions in America had heightened. The Boston Tea Party had taken place just a few months before, various embargoes were in effect, men were starting militias, and the colonies and the Crown seemed on a collision course. The Fairfaxes, staunch loyalists to king and empire, were appalled by what was going on in the Americas. All of these were reasons why they decided to leave, never to return.

George and Martha rode to Belvoir to see them off when they boarded a ship docked at their wooden wharf on the Potomac River. George had been his close friend for twenty-one years. He had known Sally just as long, and the infatuation he had had for her so long ago must have resurfaced, if only for a moment, when they said their good-byes at the wharf. Political events were happening quickly by then in America, but neither of the two sets of neighbors could know as they parted on the banks of the Potomac that one couple would rapidly fade into obscurity and the other would soon become the most famous in the world.

CHAPTER NINE

THE POOR WRETCHES: THE WASHINGTONS AND SLAVERY

"I can only say that there is not a man living who wishes more sincerely than I do to see a plan adopted for the abolition of [slavery]."
—*George Washington to Robert Morris, April 12, 1786*

A ll of the managers and overseers who worked on the different Washington plantations had direct orders to let him know of any problems on their farms. The troubles reported usually ranged from broken plows to misplaced shipments of tools, but in the spring of 1760 an ominous letter reached Washington's desk at Mount Vernon from overseer Christopher Hardwick—Winchester plantation had been hit by a smallpox epidemic.

The epidemic had swept through the central part of Virginia, bringing down farmers, planters, indentured servants, and slaves alike. Smallpox was deadly. In most cases 10 to 15 percent of those afflicted died, but in some villages the death toll climbed as high as 40 percent, the rate being higher on slave plantations where laborers lived in overcrowded cabins.

Instead of relying on the farm manager to tend to those who came down with the disease, George Washington rode there himself after consulting a doctor and obtaining written instructions for medical treatment. It was a grueling trip, but Washington was determined to take care of his sick slaves. Upon arrival, he found "everything in the utmost confusion, disorder, and backwardness." Hardwick had suffered a broken leg, was bedridden in his cabin, and was paying no attention to the smallpox infestation that was about to ravage the farm.

Washington swung into action. He sent another overseer to the town of Winchester to find a nurse to treat the ill workers. The pair brought back medicines and blankets and other items so that Washington could "settle things upon the best footing I could to prevent the smallpox from spreading...for the care of the Negroes." He then ordered that some of the stricken blacks be housed in an overseer's house and in Washington's own farmhouse there until they recovered. He paid the nurse to tend to his people. Washington visited those who had come down with smallpox and comforted them. He moved through the slave cabins, looking for early signs of the pox in others, and personally checking as many slaves as he could. Washington had had smallpox when he was a teenager and was immune to further attacks.

Several weeks later, back in Mount Vernon, he received the good news that all of the slaves at the Winchester plantation had lived.

His emergency visit to the farm to personally treat the slaves was an example of the feelings he had about the welfare of the several hundred slaves that he and his wife owned. It was also an example of the conflicted attitude he had towards his workers that he would not resolve until, on his deathbed in 1799, he freed the slaves that belonged to him.

American slavery was born in Virginia just a long carriage ride from Mount Vernon. In 1619, the first ship carrying a cargo of twenty Africans arrived, and the blacks were put to work on the plantations that had been developed by the first settlers, who had arrived ten years earlier. They worked alongside white indentured workers and their numbers grew. Over the next few generations, slavery took hold in Virginia and would remain intact for 175 years.

Profits were considerable within the tobacco empires of the Chesapeake Bay; by the 1770s there were more than 350,000 slaves in the southern colonies, or 22 percent of the population (the number would grow to four million by 1861). Colonies passed laws to forbid slaves to run away from their owners, sanctioned the beatings and murders of slaves, instituted curfews, and forbid their travel from plantation to plantation without written authorization.

The supporters of slavery in the 1760s did not have to state the obvious, that slaves enabled their owners to amass large fortunes, had done so for more than one hundred years, and would continue to do so for the owners' children. The arguments offered by supporters were: 1) owners provided necessary food, clothing, shelter, and medical care for slaves—workers would not find those guarantees elsewhere; 2) blacks were inherently lazy and, if free, could never find enough employment to subsist on their own; 3) the slaves were happy; 4) white women would be sexually assaulted by male slaves if the slaves were granted freedom; 5) freed slaves would work cheaper than poor whites and create massive white unemployment; 6) the Bible approved slavery; and 7) freed blacks would use firearms to take what they wanted by force and kill their former masters and their families. Some of the supporters of slavery even suggested that blacks were an ignorant race and better off in bondage or, as one white defender of slavery wrote in a newspaper, "he lives free of all anxiety...perplexing cares troubles and disappointments and these, I humbly conceive...make up the whole of our unhappiness."

And besides, slavery's supporters argued, America was surrounded by slavery. The institution was lawful in many South American nations, such as Venezuela and Brazil, and on Caribbean islands, such as Antigua, Haiti, and Cuba. If it was legal there, why not in the southern colonies?

Virginia was not only the largest slave colony in America in 1760, with 140,570 men and women in bondage, but its slave population was also more than twice that of the second-largest colony, South Carolina, with 57,334. The African Americans in Virginia represented just over 40 percent of all the slaves in the thirteen colonies. Virginia's black population was 40 percent of its total population of 339,726 in 1760. The number of slaves in Virginia grew dramatically in the next two decades, to 187,000 in 1770 and to 220,000 in 1780.

There were slaves in the northern colonies, too, although far fewer in number. New York led the northern colonies with sixteen thousand in 1760; New Jersey had six thousand and Massachusetts had forty-six hundred. The other northern colonies had far fewer.

Throughout those years, southern legislatures increased their support of slavery, but the institution grew increasingly unpopular in the northern colonies. Vermont would eliminate slavery in 1776, Pennsylvania in 1780, and Massachusetts in 1783. All of the northern colonies, and later states, would abolish the practice by 1804; some New England towns banned it on an individual basis prior to that year.

There was an antislavery movement in George Washington's Virginia, even though it certainly never achieved the prominence of those in northern colonies. The movement in Virginia began in the 1750s, when Quakers traveled throughout the colony in a crusade to convince planters to free their slaves; some did. In the 1760s, the Baptists made the elimination of slavery part of their evangelical crusade there. These religious groups even managed to persuade legislators in the House of Burgesses to introduce bills to abolish slavery in 1773 and 1779, although both efforts failed. A governor of Virginia, James Wood, in 1801 became the president of the Virginia Abolition Society. In 1782, antislavery proponents even managed to pass a short-lived bill that provided for easy private manumission of slaves; thousands were released.

Even prominent Virginians who did not free their workers still thought the institution wrong. One, Robert Beverley, wrote, "I am really ashamed of my country whenever I consider [slavery]."

Another governor, Francis Fauquier, asked his slaves to forgive him in his will. Thomas Jefferson, always ambivalent about the issue, had a slave mistress, and called slavery "a perpetual exercise of the most boisterous passions, the most unremitting despotism on the one part, and degrading submission on the other."

Virginia residents against slavery, such as Quaker planter Robert Pleasants, conducted letter-writing crusades urging prominent citizens who owned slaves to release them.

Washington's attitude on slavery and towards his own slaves shifted throughout his life. He thought nothing of selling a load of flour in order to raise money to buy slaves, and he once permitted farmers who owed him debts to use their slaves as collateral. He sold one slave for rum and sweetmeats. Throughout his life, Washington accused his slaves of being lazy and duplicitous, and told friends that they were dishonest and stole from him. When meat was taken from one of his warehouses, he scowled to his plantation manager, "I know of no black person about the house that is to be trusted." On one occasion, he wrote that he had "many workmen and little work" and on another he referred to "my Negro carpenter or any other bungler." He ran ads in newspapers, offering twenty-dollar rewards, in efforts to capture any of his slaves that ran away from Mount Vernon or his other farms. He often accused his slave laborers of being lazy when they worked in the field, and he spent an enormous amount of time watching over them to ensure their productivity.

Yet he was often gentle and beneficent with "his people," or "his family," as he called the slaves, and did far more than most slave owners to ensure their health and welfare. He ordered his managers to make certain that the slaves always had enough to eat and that their cabins were repaired if damaged by a storm. He gave his slaves extra food. Those who worked hard were given cash or food bonuses for themselves and their families; all received bonuses after a good harvest. They were permitted to visit friends and relatives on nearby plantations and visit towns such as Alexandria. Washington sometimes gave them cash "tips" when they worked at parties; he encouraged visitors to tip them, too. They were allowed to sell food, such as berries, chickens and eggs, or animals they killed, to neighbors or to him. His men and women were permitted to travel to an open-air slave produce market in Alexandria each Sunday morning to sell everything from food to brooms that they made.

Washington was one of the few slave owners to permit his slaves to carry muskets and hunt for additional game for their families and for sale. He also was one of the few who paid his slaves to keep poachers off his property.

Perhaps his most bizarre transactions with his slaves was the purchase of their teeth. During the 1780s, dentists began to market dentures of real teeth. They ran ads in newspapers offering to buy teeth from anyone so that they could make these dentures for Americans who had bad teeth, and there were many. Mount Vernon slaves, and others, sold teeth that had fallen out of their mouths or could be easily extracted. In 1784, Washington, who had terrible teeth, was being treated by a newly arrived French dentist, Jean John Pierre Le Moyer, who advertised for teeth. Washington purchased nine teeth from his slaves "on acct. of the French Dentist," he wrote in his diary. His slaves' teeth were surely meant for him, and he spent the next several years using them in custom-made dentures.

Despite this generosity, his conflict with slaves was never ending. He often accused his people of stealing goods from the plantation and selling at them same Sunday markets where he permitted them to set up their stalls. He paid them bonuses to use their well-trained dogs to track poachers, but he also charged that they used the dogs to conduct nighttime robberies of his possessions at Mount Vernon. At one point he ordered most of the dogs killed and told overseers, in a brutal order, to hang any dogs that returned or were hidden.

He was insistent on proper clothing for his people. Martha worked with more than a dozen domestic slaves to produce and mend slave shirts and breeches in a clothing factory they created in one of the outbuildings. George spent considerable sums of money on clothing for slaves, telling one manager that if he needed more money, "let me know without delay the quantity necessary that it may be sent in time." Children of slave families were not required to work until they were almost teenagers, and even then did light work, such as weeding. Washington spent large amounts of money for medicine and used numerous area doctors to treat his slaves, calling them as often for sick workers as he did for members of his immediate family who fell ill. Overseers and managers had to report sick slaves to him right away so that they could be treated; George sometimes cared for them himself.

He did not shout instructions at them when they were in the field; he labored with them for many hours each day, their coworker as well as their boss. Most overseers were hired whites, but Washington appointed some black slaves as overseers and wrote of one that he was "sober, honest, and industrious." He wrote of another black overseer, Davy, that he worked "as well as the white overseers, and with more quietness than any of them."

Washington disdained the whipping of slaves and only permitted flogging after an overseer had explained good reasons for it, and in writing. Any overseer who flogged a slave without Washington's permission risked being fired, and was referred to by Washington as "a worthless white man." Washington also fumed about other slave owners who routinely beat their slaves.

He acted as his own police chief, too, interceding in violent squabbles between slaves or within families. Two-thirds of the slaves at Mount Vernon were married, and from time to time men abused their wives. Washington took it upon himself to step into these situations. As an example, in 1795 he discovered that a husband from another plantation had beaten his wife, Fanny, one of Washington's female slaves, so badly that she was bedridden for an entire week. Washington promptly barred the husband from any more visits to his wife.

Washington always preferred a system of rewards instead of beatings to make slaves complete their work and wrote that a flogging "often produces evils which are worse than the disease." He offered more days off, less grueling jobs, and additional food to good workers, and he cut back rewards for those who were lazy.

He ordered his overseers to the field on time so that the slaves would be on time; overseers were forbidden to drink too much because they could not control their workers if they were inebriated. Small and large gangs of workers were ignored in favor of medium-sized, manageable crews. He advised his overseers that "the only way to keep [people]...at work without severity, or wrangling, is always to be with them."

In return for what he saw as fair treatment, he expected his slaves to work hard, and they did. They had to be in the fields just after sunup, ready to plant or harvest crops. They worked in groups in the fields under the close supervision of overseers. Generally, slaves at Mount Vernon and throughout Virginia worked from about 8 a.m. until 11 a.m. and then had some time off for lunch. They returned to their labors and worked through the afternoon, ending the day around 6 p.m., but later if tasks had not been completed. They returned to their cabins then and had dinner. Any or all could be called out after dinner for additional work; house slaves were on call twenty-four hours a day. Field hands toiled in brutal winters and hot summers without much relief.

They were expected to be sober (he fired drunken white workers and gave inebriated slaves harder tasks as punishment) and industrious. "I expect my people will work from day break until it is dusk in the evening," Washington wrote, adding that "every laborer, male or female, does as much in the twenty-four hours as their strength, without endangering their health or constitution, will allow of."

George and Martha had their favorites. Martha formed close relationships with several of the women house slaves who were there to help her throughout the day. George formed an especially close relationship with Billy Lee, a slave who was almost as expert a horseman as he. Lee accompanied Washington on many of his early morning rides and just about all of his foxhunting expeditions. Lee went with Washington as his valet when the Revolution began and served with him until it ended in 1783. He often went riding with Washington in the morning or afternoon when the general needed some form of recreation. Lee was near his side at all of the major battles of the war and lived with him at Mount Vernon until he died as a very old man.

His management of the slaves and white workers brought results. His schooners, mills, dairy barns, slaughterhouses, and granaries were well-run and his carefully laid-out farms were efficient. A visitor, Benjamin Latrobe, wrote that Mount Vernon had "good fences, clear grounds, and extensive cultivation [that] strike the eye as something uncommon in this part of the world." Latrobe added that the gardens were laid out in precise squares and tended with great care. Samuel Vaughn, who visited the farms, bragged that they were always "neat, kept perfectly clean & in prime order."

Washington's stepgrandson, George Washington Parke Custis, later wrote that "as a master of slaves, Washington was consistent...They were comfortably lodged, fed, and clothed...well cared for in sickness and old age and kept in strict and proper discipline."

Visitors who had been to numerous plantations throughout the South were impressed by his treatment of the workers. "General Washington treats his slaves far more humanely than do his fellow citizens of Virginia. Most of these gentlemen give their blacks only bread, water, and blows," wrote Julian Niemcewicz, a Polish count who toured America in 1798. Another traveler, Richard Parkinson, from England, said that George Washington's military background helped. "Washington managed his Negroes better than any other man, he being brought up in the army and by nature industrious beyond any description."

Throughout his life, George Washington always defended the institution of slavery. When he was president, he scoffed at the efforts of Quakers to introduce legislation to end slavery in 1790, writing that it was "very malapropos" and "an ill-judged piece of business that occasioned a great waste of time." He often told friends and dinner guests that there was no point in crusading to end slavery because it would probably cease over the years. Why worry? "Time, patience, and education and it will be overcome," he told one visiting diplomat after the war.

His support of the institution was based on an understanding of the traditional reasons for it and his friendships with the rich and powerful in Virginia, almost all of whom were slaveholders. They reminded Washington that because slaves were property, what their owners did with them was no business of anybody outside his household, particularly the religious agitators and the infernal antislavery groups. If a man's property could be taken away, then he had no liberty.

But, he argued just a few years after his marriage to Martha, how can unhappy Americans claim that they should not be "slaves" to England when they would not let go of their own slaves?

Washington always found himself on both sides of the issue. He not only told friends that the elimination of slavery was a good idea, but he often tried to take the lead in eradicating it. Ironically, in his very first session as a member of the House of Burgesses, in 1759, he was witness to a debate over whether or not new slaves imported from the Caribbean should be taxed in order to discourage the slave trade. In the late 1760s, after he became one of the leaders in the crusade against the Stamp Act, he became so enthused by the idea of liberty for all that he decided to introduce a bill into the House of Burgesses along with friend, neighbor, and staunch antislavery advocate George Mason, to eliminate the slave trade with Africa and the Caribbean. The two men offered an historical argument, charging that "one of the first signs of the decay and perhaps the primary destruction of the most flourishing government that ever existed [the Roman empire] was the introduction of great numbers of slaves."

His appalled friends in the legislature talked both men out of formally introducing it. Later, in 1774, as the long train of taxes and restrictions by the Crown brought the colonies closer to a call for a Continental Congress and rebellion, he and Mason again denounced the slave trade. This time he did so very publicly, writing a series of "resolves" on politics that were published in the *Virginia Gazette* and several other leading southern newspapers. One of them called for the elimination of the slave trade and the restriction of slavery to its current, domestic boundaries. He and Mason wrote, "We take this opportunity of declaring our most earnest wishes to see an entire stop forever put to such a wicked cruel and unnatural trade."

His remarks on slavery to friends paralleled later writings of Thomas Paine, who asked Americans, "If the [British] could carry off and enslave some thousand of us, would we think it just?" George's feelings also mirrored the speeches of the ministers and antislavery leaders in Virginia, and his views made the gentry uneasy. His conversations and letters to them echoed the best arguments of the antislavery leaders, that Americans could not keep slaves themselves while they cried out for liberty. He wrote to Bryan Fairfax in 1774 that colonists had to assert their political rights against England or they would become as "tame and abject slaves as the blacks we rule over with such arbitrary sway" and, to friends, often referred to his own men and women in bondage as "the poor wretches."

No one in Virginia paid much attention to him.

However, in 1772 the thinking of the gentry had changed and a bill very similar to Washington's did pass. It called slavery "a trade of great inhumanity" and barred all African and Caribbean slave ships from Virginia, but it did not outlaw slavery itself. The institution would not be buried on the grounds that it paralleled American slavery to England because slave owners had constructed a careful and brilliant defense stating that "liberty" meant the freedom to keep one's property, and slaves were property.

From time to time, liberal-thinking people like Washington would toy with the idea of ending slavery, but planters brought enormous pressure to bear on them. An example was Landon Carter, the nephew of Robert Carter, the South's largest slaveholder. The younger Carter determined that the fall in tobacco prices in the early 1770s would ruin his business and decided to invest heavily in ironworks instead. He also decided to free his five hundred slaves. Neighbors urged him not to do so because that many freed blacks would cause havoc throughout the region. Carter was adamant, but gave in and accepted a modified plan to release just thirty per year over a seventeen-year period. That plan collapsed after a few years when planters told him that his newly freed slaves incited their own slaves to press for freedom, too. The entire scheme was abandoned.

Washington's opposition to slavery was reinforced during the Revolution, when he found that his closest generals, aides, friends in politics, and ministers he met were staunch opponents of slavery.

His most trusted general in the war, Nathanael Greene of Rhode Island, was a Quaker who had opposed slavery all his life as a member of that church (ironically, he was forced to leave the nonviolent religion because he took up arms to fight the British). John Jay, a president of the Continental Congress and the son-in-law of his friend Governor William Livingston of New Jersey, was very much opposed to slavery, calling it "odious and disgraceful," as was Washington's chief of staff, Alexander Hamilton.

After the war, Jay became the president of the New York Manumission Society, and Hamilton served as the group's vice president. In 1799, when he was governor of New York, Jay signed a bill to free slaves in that state. Governor Livingston, who was against slavery for years, signed a law prohibiting the purchase of slaves in New Jersey when the war ended. Gouverneur Morris, a member of the Continental Congress and an antislavery leader, spent months living with Washington in a winter camp during the war and tried to convince him to change his mind about slavery.

Perhaps the most virulent opponent of slavery in Washington's wartime inner circle was the Marquis de Lafayette. He wrote, "I would never have drawn my sword in the cause of America if I could have conceived that thereby I was founding a land of slavery."

The men seemed to have persuaded Washington to abandon slavery. In 1779, in the middle of the war, when his Mount Vernon profits had decreased, he seriously considered selling off all of his slaves. He wrote to his cousin Lund Washington that he could not do so, though, because his slaves would then simply wind up on other plantations, probably run by owners far less humane than he; in the letter he again indicated his sympathy for "these poor wretches."

In 1783 and again in 1786, Lafayette was certain that he had talked Washington into a unique experiment. Lafayette planned to use freed blacks as laborers in the Caribbean and on a farm in

Virginia that he would oversee with Washington; they would prove that paid labor could be as productive as slave labor. Washington was enthusiastic about the experiment, writing to Lafayette that "your late purchase of an estate in the colony of [Guinea] with a view of emancipating the slaves on it is a generous and noble proof of your humanity. Would to God a like spirit would diffuse itself generally into the minds of the people of this country."

Yet again, Washington backed off and did not join Lafayette; the experiment was never carried out. That same year, Washington wrote to financier Robert Morris that "there is not a man living who wishes more sincerely than I do to see a plan adopted for the abolition of [slavery]," and told neighbor John Mercer, "I never mean (unless some particular circumstance should compel me to it) to possess another slave by purchase; it being among my first wishes to see some plan adopted by which slavery in this country may be abolished by slow, sure, and imperceptible degrees." Then, in another letter to Mercer just a month later, he told him he needed to buy six slaves to replace indentured workers whose terms would be up in three years, and tried to bargain with Mercer for a lower price per slave. Still, Washington would not free any of his own slaves.

Washington's ambivalence about slavery caused him severe labor problems. Over the years, as slave women gave birth to children, the size of his worker population became enormous, reaching more than three hundred at the time of his death. The slaves on his farms grew increasingly older, too; many could no longer work and had to be cared for at great cost in time and money. He would not sell individuals or break up families. He wrote of his dilemma, "What then is to be done? Something must or I shall be ruined."

Washington was always a mass of contradictions. He would not free his slaves, and would not join Lafayette in his experiment, yet he freed five thousand slaves who fought for him in the American Revolution. Desperate for troops and realizing that as commander of the army he had the power to do just about whatever he wanted, he convinced Congress to grant freedom to any slave who fought for the Continental Army for a term of at least one year of service. But then, when the war ended, he immediately reversed field and insisted that the British return to their Virginia owners all of the slaves who had fled their plantations to either join the British force or to seek British protection.

These contradictions would surface again when he became the new nation's first president.

This compassion for slaves extended to his stepson, Jacky, whom George asked to look for runaways during the war, in 1781, the year that a smallpox epidemic ravaged Virginia. Jacky did not find any of the runaways, but wrote to his mother with sadness that "the mortality that has taken place among the wretches is really incredible. I have seen numbers lying dead in the woods, and many so exhausted that they cannot walk."

Many of Virginia's slaveholders had the same conflicted feelings about slavery, and these feelings grew in the middle of the seventeenth century. Some believed slavery was immoral and felt queasy about their own slaves. Many feared slave insurrections as the slave population of some colonies, especially in Virginia and South Carolina, increased dramatically. One of the largest slave owners, William Byrd, was so fearful of an insurrection that he unsuccessfully lobbied Parliament to limit the number of slaves in Virginia. He wrote that "a man of desperate courage" would lead a rebellion that "would tinge our rivers as wide as they are with blood."

They had reason to fear, too, because in 1736 slaves had revolted on the Caribbean island of Antigua. In 1740, slaves on several plantations along the Stono River, in South Carolina, killed ten whites and burned down several homes; in the battle to capture the slaves, ten blacks and twenty whites were killed. In 1741, eleven slaves were executed and forty deported after they were found guilty on questionable charges of setting a series of fires that destroyed many homes in New York City.

Those opposed to slavery offered other arguments. One was that by embracing the profitable slave-driven agricultural economy, Virginia and the southern colonies were ignoring the industrialization that might one day overtake farming as the premier source of profit in America.

Others offered righteous indignation that Virginia whites were letting their love of the profits accrued by slave labor ruin their lives. Richard Henry Lee argued in a speech in the House of Burgesses in 1759 that other colonies, without slaves or with few, were providing better lives for their residents than Virginia. He asked, "To what sir, can we attribute this strange, unhappy truth? The reason seems to be this: that with their whites they import arts and agriculture, while we, with our blacks, exclude both."

Martha Washington supervised a large domestic staff in the main house. When she arrived in 1759, she brought several personal maids with her from White House. She inherited some of George's slaves and more were added over the years. Some of the most valued were Breechy, the butler; Mulatto Jack, another butler; Doll, the cook; Beck, the scullion; Jenny and Mima, who did the washing and ironing; Sally, Martha's assistant; seamstress Betty; and Julius and Rose, who worked for Jacky and Patsy. Martha also was in charge of seven more slaves who worked around the main house at Mount Vernon. Some two dozen worked in the Custis homes at other plantations.

Her grandson "Wash" remembered that she kept busy supervising these staff workers before breakfast until late at night, long after dinner had been served. That did not end the day, though, because on many nights following the meal Martha worked with a number of women in making breads. Her grandson recalled the "admirable management of her servants and household" and saw the dozens of women who were trained by her to sew transformed into "beautiful seamstresses."

Martha's great skill in working with the house slaves was due to experience and personality. She had overseen the domestics at the Custis plantation for seven years and knew what to do and what not to do to get the maximum work out of her laborers. She had to walk a fine line between cajoling her people and commanding them in order to get them to complete tasks. She also had to smooth over feuds between the slaves and members of her family.

Her friendliness enabled her to succeed at household management in an era when unhappy slaves were common and created
chaos on many plantations. In her diary, one woman echoed the
common planters' wives' complaint that their slaves were
unmanageable. She wrote, "Business negligently done and much
altogether neglected, some disobedience, much idleness, sullen-
ness, slovenliness."

The actual chores of the day and the management of slaves
made the running of the plantation household an intense job. The
inability of many wives to manage angry slaves unwilling to follow
instructions or determined not to work caused such great frustration that many wished they had no slaves at all. A generation later,
Mary Chestnut of South Carolina wrote of wives she knew, "They
have a swarm of blacks about them like children under their
care…and they hate slavery." Many southern planters' wives complained that they spent the entire day "following after and watching Negroes. It is a terrible life." Another wrote, "I sometimes think
I would not care if they all did go, they are so much trouble to me."

There were a few letters from Martha to friends on her feelings
about slavery, and in them she expressed little admiration for her
workers. Like George, she believed that they were lazy and inso-
lent and had to be constantly watched. She wrote to Elizabeth
Powel about a new slave she was trying to purchase. She wrote
that his abilities "to be trustworthy—careful of what is committed
to him—sober and attentive, are essential requisite in any large
family, but more so among blacks, many of whom will impose
when they can do it."

Her granddaughter Nelly may have reflected Martha's view.
In a letter, she referred to slaves as "these ignorant people" and
"the dark torments of our lives," and said that an antislavery
organization "creates discontent and foments insurrection and
murder." She was so fearful that her own slaves would flee that
she would not bring them on any trips she made to free states.

Martha left the chastising of slaves to George. Her husband
bristled at any laxity in work anywhere at Mount Vernon, espe-

cially when he was away. He threatened any woman who did not complete her assigned sewing tasks for Martha that she would be made a field hand and sent to toil in the hot sun. George wrote in anger during one of his absences, "It is observed by the weekly reports that the sewers make only six shirts a week and the last week Caroline (without being sick) made only five; Mrs. Washington says their usual task was to make nine with shoulder straps and good sewing; tell them therefore from me, that what *has* been done, *shall* be done by fair or foul means and they had better make choice of the first, for their own reputation and for the sake of peace and quietness; otherwise they will be sent to the several plantations and be placed as common laborers under the overseers there at." In leaving the discipline of slaves to her husband, Martha was able to create an image of herself among the workers as a helpful mistress, always eager to make their lives better.

No matter how good Washington may have been to them, his people always preferred freedom over slavery and often ran away. They began to flee Mount Vernon in 1761, when four escaped together, and they fled periodically over the years, even when he was president. Washington was enraged when any of his slaves fled and told family and friends; he wrote public ads to recapture them, saying that he had treated them well and that he was appalled by the ingratitude. He offered $20 rewards for their return. His physical description of the runaways indicated how well the men and women of Mount Vernon were dressed. He wrote of fugitive Peros, aged between thirty-five and forty, as wearing "a dark-colored cloth coat, a white linen waistcoat, white breeches, and white stockings." In another ad, he wrote that a runaway slave took with him "a coat, waistcoat, and breeches of light brown duffil, with black horn buttons, a light-colored cloth waistcoat, old leather breeches, check and oznabrig shirts, a pair of new milled yarn stockings, a pair of dold ribbed ditto, new oznabrig trousers, and a felt hat."

There were two runaways whose departure genuinely shocked George and Martha—chief cook Hercules and Oney Judge, a young seamstress who had worked for Martha since the age of ten and had grown close to her. The pair fled in the summer of 1796,

Hercules to live with friends in Philadelphia and Judge to live with a man in New Hampshire.

Martha was surprised, writing to her sister, "Am obliged to be my own housekeeper which takes up the greatest part of my time—our cook Hercules went away so that I am as much at a loss for a cook as for a housekeeper—altogether I am sadly plagued." George was furious. He first wrote of Oney, "She has been the particular attendant on Mrs. Washington…and was handy and useful to her being perfect mistress of her needle…the ingratitude of the girl, who was brought up and treated more like a child than a servant (and Mrs. Washington's desire to recover her) ought not to escape with impunity." And then George, president at the time, went to great lengths to get local officials in New Hampshire to find Judge and return her by boat to Mount Vernon. They refused.

Martha may have been angry when her slaves ran away, purposefully worked slowly, or made demands, but she always did what she could to make their lives tolerable within the hideous institution to which they were born. Toward the end of her life, in November 1800, an aging and tired Martha wrote a letter to a friend about the health of her people which symbolized her feelings for the slaves of Mount Vernon. She wrote, "We have had an uncommon sickly autumn; all my family, whites, and blacks, have been very sick, many ill—thank God they have all recovered again and I was so fortunate as not to lose any of them."

George Washington's years of overseeing a large force of slaves and white laborers on his Mount Vernon farms turned him into an efficient administrator who could react to adverse conditions, whether it was sick workers or bad weather, quickly. He laid out his fields by number and crop, charted the daily and even hourly progress of his workers, tried new ways of doing things when the old ones failed, and became a master of planning and precise detail in everything that he did. His success on his farms, and his mastery of his slave workforce, had turned him into a man who could run an army just as well as he could run a plantation. He himself noted he had all "the distinguishing characteristics of a good manager." He could have easily substituted general for manager.

It seems ironic that Washington would go on to lead a nation to freedom using the management skills he had learned overseeing his slaves, but that victory would not bring any freedom at all to those same people.

CHAPTER TEN

WAR CLOUDS: THE REVOLUTION

The Stamp Act was a levy placed on newspapers, broadsides, pamphlets, all legal documents, and playing cards to raise money to pay for British troops quartered in the colonies. It seemed necessary to Parliament and was passed with little debate and no fear that it would cause controversy in America. The Crown believed that it had to station troops in the Americas to guard against any other French activity following the end of the war in 1763 and to prevent Indian attacks. The cost would be about 350,000 pounds a year, and the colonists were assessed 60,000 of it.

The act came on the heels of the Sugar Act, which taxed molasses, other foodstuffs, and wines; the Iron Act, which curbed sales of American iron goods to the British Isles; and the Currency Act, which outlawed colonial paper money. These bills infuriated colonists from Georgia to Massachusetts. They claimed that it was "taxation without representation," a catchy slogan that would unify the colonists over the next ten years and lead to the Revolution.

It was the Stamp Act that not only drew George Washington, the quiet legislative representative from Frederick County, into the protests against the Crown, but also put him on the road to becoming one of America's leading radicals. By the time the Stamp Act was introduced in 1765, Washington had been in the House of Burgesses for six years. A reluctant public speaker, he sat quietly during public debates and admired the soaring oratory of others, particularly Patrick Henry, whose words Jefferson called "torrents of eloquence." He especially admired Henry's speaking superiority when he replied to charges that opposition to the Stamp Act was treason with his memorable rejoinder, "If this be treason, make the most of it."

Washington's real skill was his power of persuasion in one-on-one encounters and in small groups of men. It was there—at breakfasts, dinners, and social events—that he utilized these social gifts to convince others to vote with him on particular measures. His convincing demeanor extended to the royal governor's mansion, where his wealth and influence had enabled him to become friendly with Lord Dunmore, the governor, and his predecessors. He dined at the governor's palace frequently with his wife and family, danced at balls there, went hunting with Dunmore, and spent considerable time with him.

The Stamp Act led to a reexamination of the colonies' ties to England. Why did they need the mother country anymore? Over one hundred and fifty years, the American colonies had grown into their own country. Abundant crops and fruitful trading pacts with England, Europe, and the islands of the Caribbean had created a prosperous international trading economy. Good harvest at home meant that farmers were not only able to feed themselves and their families, but they were also able to earn some extra money selling their food at markets. The residents had developed efficient legislatures. More than forty newspapers flourished and provided readers with news and advertisements. The colonists, collectively and individually, honored all religions.

Most important, they believed that the cornerstone to civilization was virtue. They had plenty of it, they bragged, but found it lacking in England. There, crime was on the rise, women poisoned their husbands, prostitution flourished, cities had become congested, gangs of children lived in rancid hovels, and the government was corrupt. Parliament, they were convinced, was run by uncaring and unfeeling rulers and many of its members had been tainted by criminality, according to British newspapers.

Americans had come to believe that they had, over time, developed a reverence for, and legislative support of, personal liberties. These freedoms, tied to representative government in colonial assemblies and freedom of the press and religion, had created an American ideal.

The Stamp Act threatened to ruin that ideal.

George Washington seethed when he first heard of the act, authorized in March of 1765 and scheduled to go into effect one year later. Like many, he had paid higher taxes for the furniture and other goods he had purchased from England. And, like so many others, he and his wife continually complained that the goods he was being taxed so highly on were overpriced and shabby. The sale of second-rate goods to colonists was acceptable to Parliament, the Washingtons believed, because its members saw Americans as a second-rate people.

The American belief in ideals and virtue was so strong that they felt that civil disobedience, and even a war, to gain independence was not a radical severing of ties to England, but a necessary action to validate their ideals. That civil disobedience began with the Stamp Act. Several colonial courts, including Virginia's, declared the Stamp Act illegal and tax men in Virginia refused to collect it, fearful for their safety. The House of Burgesses passed a bill outlawing the new stamp tax, aided by ringing oratory from Henry, and the royal governor disbanded the legislature. Tax collectors were beaten up in several colonies, and their appointed successors refused to work. Men trying to collect the tax in Massachusetts were tarred and feathered, and a building thought to become a tax office was torn down; the home of Massachusetts lieutenant governor Thomas

Hutchinson was destroyed. New Jersey men told a collector that they would wreck any home he lived in. Stamp riots continued for several days in Newport, Rhode Island. In New York, flags were flown at half-mast to mourn the imposition of the tax, and a mob burned New York's royal governor in effigy.

The Stamp Act brought about an underground movement called the Sons of Liberty. The organization's members denounced the act, decrying the "wicked and treacherous ministry" that sponsored it. Colonial newspapers conducted a strident campaign against the new tax. Press opposition was summed up best in the scathing denunciation of it in Rhode Island's *Newport Mercury*. Its editor said the act "could deprive us of all our invaluable charter rights and privileges, drain us suddenly of our cash, occasion an entire stagnation of trade, discourage every kind of industry, and involve us in the most abject slavery."

Washington was appalled by the stamp tax, as he had been about the previous tax bills. He had written a scalding letter about the Currency Act in which he predicted that acts like it "will set the whole country in flames." Now he wrote to his mother-in-law that Virginians simply would not pay it, that it was "unconstitutional" and "a direful attack upon [our liberties] and [we] loudly exclaim against the violation."

The crusade against the act, so swift, powerful, and universal, succeeded, and within a year it was repealed.

Throughout those years, Washington supported all of the anti-Crown measures passed by the Virginia legislature and stood with his fellow legislators against the governor and Parliament. Yet he could not bring himself to become a radical, as so many of his friends had been for years. They were always frustrated with him for taking so long to see what they had seen so clearly right away. Washington always said that he had to think things through before coming to any decisions, but that when he made up his mind he would be unshakable. Patrick Henry said of Washington's thinking that it was "slow in operation, being little aided by invention or imagination, but sure in conclusion."

There were other considerations in Washington's slow move from loyal British citizen to angry consumer to unhappy British subject to armed radical. Few people in America had as little to gain and as much to lose as George and Martha Washington if an armed rebellion against the king took place. Most of Washington's business was with England. He owned hundreds of slaves who might have no value if the colonial economy came apart in a war or if he went bankrupt and there were no prospective buyers for slaves. He feared for his family. If war came, his son, Jacky, might enlist in an American army, or be drafted, thus putting his safety at risk. His nephews might put their lives at risk, too.

The Crown would arrest, try, imprison, and surely hang the leaders of any rebellion, as they had done to the leaders of the Scottish rebellion twenty years before. The government could seize all of his lands, money, and his precious Mount Vernon, and ruin his family. How could he leave Martha for extended periods of time? How could Martha cope without him? The rabble-rousing small farmers in Pennsylvania, the shopkeepers in Annapolis, the dock workers in Norfolk, and the ministers in Boston had very little to lose in a rebellion, but he did. He had dreamed since boyhood of the life that he had achieved by the 1770s—personal wealth, prominence, and a happy family. How could he give it all up?

Events pushed him, though, and so did the seemingly unending conversations with the radicals who were his friends: Edmund Randolph, Thomas Jefferson, Patrick Henry, and George Mason. It was after talks with Mason in 1769 that Washington took a long first step toward radicalism when he became one of the public leaders of the Non-Importation Agreement, the movement to halt the importing of goods from England in an effort to show Britain that boycotts could cripple business and would be used often if taxes continued to rise. He, Mason, and others formed the Virginia Association to boycott goods in their colony; it was Washington's list of targeted goods that was accepted by the legislature.

Unlike other Virginia leaders, Washington did not think the boycott would be embraced by all because "selfish designing men (ever attentive to their own gain and watchful of every turn that can assist their lucrative views in preference to any other consideration)" would not go along with it. The only way to overcome their reluctance, and make the boycott work despite them, was very public statewide politicking. Washington took the very visible role of riding throughout the state and personally talking to more than one thousand Virginians, asking each to join him in the mass boycott. The public crusade was a first for the reticent planter. For the first time, too, Washington also used the colonial press to win public support for the boycott, agreeing with Mason when he wrote to him that "it may be necessary to publish something preparatory to it in our Gazettes, to warn the people at least of the impending danger and induce them the more readily and cheerfully to concur in the proper measures to avert it."

Washington not only saw the boycotts as a political tool to halt taxation plans from the Crown, but as a way in which people's virtue could be improved upon. He and his wife, notorious spenders, had started to dress in plainer clothes; Martha was ordering ordinary clothes for her children. Giving up the things people enjoyed made them stronger people, he argued. In 1765, he wrote to his mother-in-law that the material goods were not critical, that "the necessities of life are mostly to be had within ourselves." In 1769 he wrote to Mason that the cutbacks would force wealthy planters to lead more moral lives and show the poor that virtue, and not wealth, was the most important ingredient in a good life. Virginia's leaders also wanted to help residents cut their debt to England by not buying more goods and encouraging the production of goods in America.

The Washingtons participated in the boycotts that covered the next few years like many other colonists. The Daughters of Liberty, a network of women's groups, which made homespun clothing, was founded and staunch female patriots such as Abigail Adams railed that if the British were not afraid of America's men, they certainly should be afraid of its women.

It was the boycott that really pulled Washington into the radical fold. The governor disbanded the assembly when it passed the boycott agreement, and a number of legislators defied him by meeting illegally at the Raleigh Tavern; George joined them. That week he also purchased a copy of John Dickinson's pamphlet, *Letters from a Pennsylvania Farmer,* which blasted the Crown's policies. His rides throughout Virginia to convince residents to join the boycott had not only put him in contact with large numbers of colonists for the first time, but they also made him a visible face of the rebellion that seemed to be growing.

In his letters, he adopted a more incendiary tone and talked of armed opposition for the first time, writing to George Mason that "no man should scruple to hesitate a moment to use arms in defense of so valuable a blessing on which the good and evil of life depends." He told his friends, too, that it seemed to him that the Crown "would be satisfied with nothing else than the deprivation of American freedom."

The British did feel the sting of the boycott, which lasted two years, and when it was dropped, Parliament repealed all of the Townshend Act taxes except the one on the popular tea. England insisted, too, that all tea in America had to be purchased from the East India Tea Company. In December 1773, fed up with the tea tax, the Sons of Liberty dressed as Mohawk Indians and boarded the merchant vessel *Dartmouth* in Boston. They dumped its cargo of more than three hundred crates of tea into the harbor and did the same to the tea shipment on another vessel in March.

England reacted brutally, issuing what colonists called the Intolerable Acts. They included the quartering of British soldiers in colonial homes, the deportation of "political prisoners" to London to stand trial, and the closing of Boston Harbor, which dealt a devastating blow to the economy of New England. The acts, denounced in most of the colonial newspapers, caused an uproar throughout America.

Washington was furious. He had been reluctant to become a full-blown radical because he wanted America to patch up its disputes with England. He sincerely believed that he was a loyal British subject and was loath to break that bond. Washington did not want a rupture between the two unless England exhibited tyrannical behavior and acted to directly take away American freedoms. Despite the long string of political threats, disbanded assemblies, and train of taxes, Washington, like most Americans, was sure that both sides could work things out.

His thinking had changed by the early 1770s, though, when he charged that the Intolerable Acts were "an unexampled testimony of the most despotic system of tyranny that was ever practiced in a free government." He told the House of Burgesses of Britain's abuses, in no uncertain terms, "Shall we after this, whine and cry for relief, when we have already tried it in vain? Or shall we supinely sit and see one province after another fall prey to despotism?"

He was not alone. The never-ending increase of taxes, restrictions, and disputes between the colonies and the Crown, over many years, pushed thousands into the radical fold. They argued with Washington that the oppression they suffered at the hands of the British was not just in taxes imposed by Parliament, but also in high prices for imports, low prices for exports, and, because England was America's chief trading partner, economic strangulation. Shortly after the Townshend Acts, George Washington— who had taken ten years to make up his mind about what to do, who had dined and hunted with the royal governor, who had called for a thousand toasts for the king's good health at parties and in taverns, who had wanted so badly to serve His Majesty in the British Army—took over the organization and training of an armed militia group near his home, paid for their uniforms, and boldly vowed to train one thousand soldiers and march them to war if it came.

Events moved rapidly. Washington and Mason organized another very publicized boycott at a public meeting in Alexandria, arguing in their document that America was now "a conquered country." Washington joined others in calling for a national day of fasting to protest the closing of Boston Harbor and with them signed a resolution that charged that the closing of the harbor was "a dangerous attempt to destroy the constitutional liberty and rights of all North Americans" and, in even more heated language, charged that all of England's actions were efforts "to reduce the inhabitants of British America to slavery."

The resolution was not announced at the House of Burgesses, but in a venue where the new political rabble-rousers knew they would gain far more attention—the *Virginia Gazette.* Over the previous decade, the *Gazette,* under two different editors, had become one of the best-written, most influential newspapers in America. Virginia had a high literacy rate, over 50 percent, and everybody read the *Gazette.* The newspaper was delivered to hundreds of residents throughout the state, sold in the cities, and was always found in shops and taverns where thousands gathered. The *Gazette* also reprinted stories from newspapers in other cities, especially Boston, keeping Virginians informed about the political disputes that were shaking the colonies. They were published on the morning of May 26, 1774, in the pages of the *Virginia Gazette* and reprinted in other colonial newspapers. Lord Dunmore promptly dissolved the assembly, again.

Others were just as unhappy with the seemingly endless taxes and political intimidations as George Washington. In Massachusetts, James Otis wrote that "the imposition of taxes, whether on trade, or on land, or houses, or ships, on real or personal fixed or floating property, in the colonies is absolutely irreconcilable with the rights of the colonists as British subjects and as men."

Throughout these years, leaders in Parliament argued that, even with the new taxes, the colonists were paying only about one-third the taxes of British citizens. The Americans countered that the way taxes were climbing, though, they would soon be paying far more. Neither side ever understood the viewpoint of the other on taxes, or on just about any other issue of the day.

The newspapers were full of news. Britain had sent more soldiers to Boston; the navy there had been strengthened, too. Parliament threatened to dissolve Massachusetts's charter. The British secretary of state reneged on a promise made after the French and Indian War to let hundreds of Americans who fought in it claim lands in western Virginia. The Virginians, like other colonists, formed a secret Committee of Correspondence that prepared for war if it came. The papers carried news that Massachusetts had called for a Continental Congress to meet in Philadelphia in September of 1774 to determine what to do in the national emergency. Virginia would select several delegates to travel to Philadelphia for the Congress; George Washington would be one of them.

He wrote to his friend Bryan Fairfax, "The crisis is arrived when we must assert our rights or submit to every imposition that can be heaped upon us." He argued that he and others in the country had done everything they could to cooperate with the Crown, but to no avail. "Have we not addressed the Lords, and remonstrated to the Commons? And to what end? Does it not appear, as clear as the sun in its meridian brightness, that there is a regular, systematic plan formed to fix the right and practice of taxation upon us? Does not the uniform conduct of Parliament for some years past confirm this? Do not all the debates in the House of Commons on the side of the government expressly declare that America must be taxed? Is there anything to be expected from petitioning after this?"

Just two months later, in September 1774, Washington and other Virginians rode to Philadelphia for the First Continental Congress. He wrote to Captain Robert Mackenzie, a British officer with whom he had served fifteen years earlier, that he foresaw trouble. He told Mackenzie that no one in America favored rebellion, but "none of them will ever submit to the loss of those valuable rights and privileges which are essential to the happiness of every free state, and with which life, liberty, and property are rendered totally insecure."

As a military man, he feared the consequences of war more than the civilians around him, telling his old friend with remarkable prescience that if it came, "More blood will be spilt on this occasion...than history has ever yet furnished instances of in the annals of North America."

Washington, as usual, spoke little at the congressional sessions, but made it a point to get to know as many delegates as he could after the meetings ended, in taverns and at dinners. It was the same kind of effort to befriend all those who made him an important member of the House of Burgesses. He took every possible opportunity to meet people. His diary showed that he dined at the homes of several Pennsylvanians who were delegates and dined with others at Philadelphia's City Tavern every evening. He attended a ball and several entertainments held for the delegates, and on one day, September 25, attended two church services for them at a Quaker Meeting House and at St. Peter's Episcopal Church.

His desire to befriend people and learn all he could from them was inexhaustible. He dined with Dr. William Shippen in Philadelphia the next day and then accompanied Shippen on a tour of Pennsylvania Hospital, the nation's first complete hospital. (Shippen's daughter Peggy would later marry Benedict Arnold.) On September 27, he spent the evening at dinner with the delegates from Virginia, and the next day he spent the entire afternoon talking to the delegates from Massachusetts. By the end of the First Continental Congress, the now very political George Washington was a familiar figure to every delegate; he had impressed them all.

When Patrick Henry arrived back in Virginia from the Congress, he was asked by many who the key players were. He replied, "If you speak of eloquence, Mr. Rutledge, of South Carolina, is the greatest orator; but if you speak of solid information and sound judgment, Colonel Washington is by far the greatest man on that floor."

In Washington they saw a determined man. As they talked again and again of armed conflict, most pleasing to them was Washington's experience as an officer with the British Army during the French and Indian War. It was an image he cultivated.

Washington's wife Martha was not a political woman prior to the war. She saw her role as that of the loving wife of a political figure who needed comfort when he returned home from legislative meetings or testy debates over the issues of the day at a tavern or at someone's home. There is no indication that she was involved in any of the protests against the Crown; she merely stood by her husband as he wrote his letters and persuaded others to denounce Parliament at dinner parties and meetings. She did read newspapers because George subscribed to a number of them, but that apparently did not lead her into a political role in the 1760s and early 1770s. She always scoffed at suggestions that she had to be political as the wife of George Washington. Typical was her rejoinder to such a suggestion in 1788 that "we have not a single article of news but politics, which I do not concern myself about."

She was not alone. Women were not permitted to participate in politics, and they understood their place in the political world of America. They could not hold elective office, serve on juries, or affect public life. That was not always so. Women were full partners with their husbands, or male friends, in the founding of the colonies and in defending their settlements against Indian attacks. Throughout the seventeenth century, women did just as much farm work as their mates and the indentured servants and slaves that worked on their land, as did their forebearers in England. Women participated in the controversial Bacon's Rebellion in 1676 and were involved in numerous disputes with public officials in recognizing religious groups, such as the Puritans.

Several events changed this. Newfound economic prosperity meant that wealthy women enjoyed more leisure time to devote to balls and visits, and their husbands had more money to buy them expensive clothing. Within a generation, they drifted out of any involvement in public life and devoted their time to family and personal leisure. Education changed too, emphasizing family, separation of the sexes, and dominance of males; the importance of the passive life for women; and an enjoyment of the good things life had to offer.

Women were told that their work was done. They had toiled for years alongside their husbands in fields and now they had raised large families who could replace them as laborers and permit them time to be mothers and assume their new roles as moral authorities in their households. Prosperity permitted husbands to hire indentured workers or paid laborers, or slaves in the South, freeing up women to devote themselves to domestic duties. Churches and teachers at schools in the colonies emphasized the women's role in the house and family and they were told, as were the men, that society now revered them as domestic authorities.

Their reliable books on marriage, magazines of the day, and countless columns and letters in the leading newspapers constantly reminded them that sewing and childrearing were their preserve and politics belonged to the menfolk. The *Spectator,* one of London's leading newspapers circulated widely in the colonies, scolded women that getting into political matters was "repugnant to the softness, the modesty, and those other endearing qualities…natural to the fair sex" and reminded women that they should "distinguish themselves as tender mothers and faithful wives rather than as furious partisans." In a behavior book written by a woman, ladies were told that politics "is a subject entirely above your sphere."

Women who did become involved in any facet of political life, such as signing or sending petitions to legislators, were seen as mavericks, and they even asked for forgiveness if they did so. One North Carolina woman wrote to the colony's governor about a family matter and preceded her complaint by stating, "It is not for me, unacquainted as I am with the politics and laws, to say with what propriety this was done." A group of women writing to a governor started their query by stating, "It is not the province of our sex to reason deeply upon the policy of the order."

Instead of public affairs, women like Martha Washington were encouraged to plunge into the affairs of their churches. It was a wing of the domestic sphere in which they could do much good for the virtue of the people and the good of the community, social arbiters believed, without interfering in the political affairs of their husbands and fathers. Women jumped at the chance to do so and many ran their church boards and founded church social organizations; some Quaker women even became ministers.

Women who did none of those things, such as Martha Washington, found great solace in just going to church regularly, reading their Bible every morning and evening, as Martha did, and raising their children to be God-fearing citizens. As a natural corollary to church service, women were urged to read newspapers, magazines, and books, and to create libraries in their homes so that they could sit down with a good book, discuss it with their husbands, or read to their children. Many did so. The Washingtons, as an example, had a library with approximately seven hundred volumes, a sizable collection for the era.

∽∾

The growing political rift with the Crown was the major source of upheaval in the colonies, especially Virginia, but there were other reasons why the Washingtons and their contemporaries were so worried.

The planters had made fortunes in tobacco, but by 1774 tobacco had begun to decline as a popular import both in England and in Europe. George Washington had diversified his crops by then, producing mostly wheat, but most planters had not and their profits began to shrink. Most still owed considerable sums of money to their buyers in London for all of the goods they had purchased over the years to support the lavish lifestyle that slave labor and tobacco profits had initially provided. The fading tobacco market made it impossible for them to pay their debts. The Crown also forbid colonial trade with European nations and curbed their ability to trade with Caribbean islands and South American countries, crippling trade that had anchored the market economy that had been so successful for so long.

The Great Awakening had caused some wealthy Virginians, the Washingtons especially, to take another look at their family's lifestyle, and they found pampered materialistic children, like their son, Jacky, who preferred parties and drinking to education and hard work. Their children did not defer to them as they had deferred to their parents, and young people in general had lost respect for their elders. Church attendance had started to drop and ministers could no longer provide the solace the rich had found so comforting. The new Baptist and Methodist churches that had been founded during the past twenty years threatened the supremacy of the established Anglican church that they revered. And yet, at the same time that religion, regardless of the sect, played a larger and larger role in Virginian, and American, life, the population explosion brought more crime in the ever-growing cities, and prostitution was prevalent in cities such as Williamsburg and Richmond and in seaports such as Norfolk.

The dozens of antislavery groups had not convinced many to free their slaves, but they had convinced some, and the question of the morality of slavery loomed ever larger. They discovered that more slaves were fleeing their plantations and heading north, to freedom. They feared slave insurrections.

Later, Washington wrote to Joseph Reed of the frustration that he and others felt at that time: "We had borne much; we had long and ardently sought for reconciliation upon honourable terms; that it had been denied us, that all our attempts after peace had proved abortive; and had been grossly misrepresented, that we had done everything which could be expected from the best of subjects, that the spirit of freedom beat too high in us to submit to slavery, and that if nothing else could satisfy a tyrant and his diabolical ministry, we are determined to shake off all connections with a state so unjust and unnatural."

By the time George returned to Mount Vernon after the concluding days of the First Continental Congress in November 1774, the Washingtons, their fellow Virginians, and many other Americans found themselves on the eve of a crisis that was not just political, but social and cultural as well. The events that had transpired since the end of the French and Indian War in 1763 and the first imposition of new and controversial taxes in 1764 seemed ready to bring about an explosion of some kind.

George's conversion to radicalism had the wholehearted support of his wife, but they must have agreed over the years that, if things proceeded too far, they would be forced to forfeit everything. Together they would lose their combined fortune, lands, and slaves, in addition to Mount Vernon. But Martha must have known that she had even more to lose because, if there was a war, George would insist on some role in the leadership of an American army, as he had military experience. They had much to lose together, but Martha had still more. She might lose her husband.

Her fears grew in the spring of 1775, as the Revolution began in earnest when Massachusetts militia companies engaged the British in two skirmishes at the villages on Lexington and Concord on April 19. The Americans killed and wounded 269 British soldiers in the skirmish; the Massachusetts militia suffered 90 dead and wounded. The British retreated into the city of Boston and were then bottled up there by a rapidly growing American militia force of nearly twenty thousand men. Three weeks later, on May 10, 1775, amid national chaos, the Second Continental Congress met. Washington was again elected as one of Virginia's delegates at a state session in Richmond.

Despite her fears, Martha supported whatever her husband would propose. Anyone who questioned her loyalty to him and the cause had only to listen to Edmund Pendleton's story of the morning that he and other Virginia delegates left Mount Vernon for Philadelphia and the first Congress a year earlier. Martha had hosted a lavish breakfast for the group in the dining room at Mount Vernon and then walked with them outside, where they mounted their horses.

"I was much pleased with Mrs. Washington and her spirit," Pendleton wrote. "She seemed ready to make any sacrifice and was cheerful, though I know she feels anxious. She talked like a Spartan mother to her son on going into battle [saying] 'I hope you will stand firm…I know George will.' When we set off she stood in the door and cheered us in the good words, 'God be with you gentlemen.'"

George Washington, like thousands of other Americans, had traveled a long road to that moment. The world had changed in that brief time and so had Washington. A cautious man, he had waited, hoping that the king and Parliament would change their minds about their American policy. They did not. By the spring of 1774, he had long moved past the point where he *wanted* to take bold steps to end British oppression. He was now at the point where he *had* to do so.

Washington rode away from his beloved Mount Vernon that morning in May of 1775 as a little-known Virginia businessman, and he would not return home for six long years. When he did, it would be as the most famous man in the world on the eve of a battle that would change the course of history.

CHAPTER ELEVEN

THE COMMANDER IN CHIEF AND LADY WASHINGTON

Just about all of the delegates gathered in Philadelphia in the spring of 1775 for the Second Continental Congress knew George Washington this time. There were several reasons for the new familiarity: he had befriended most of them at the first Congress the year before; by now everyone in the country had read of his defiant vow to march his militia to Boston to fight the Redcoats if necessary, and his name had appeared in the newspapers more often as his public opposition to the Crown grew.

Now he was not merely a congressional backbencher observing much and saying little. As war clouds enveloped America, Washington volunteered to serve on the brand-new and all-important congressional military committee that was charged with deciding how to fight the British and with the naming of a commander in chief of the American forces. Some may have overlooked the presence of Virginia's George Washington at the first Congress, but nobody did now.

How could they? Washington arrived in Philadelphia wearing his bright red and blue militia uniform, sword at his side, hat tilted cockily on his forehead, riding on one his favorite horses, a dazzling sight to all who saw him. There could be no doubt in any delegate's mind that George Washington was ready for war.

He and Martha had discussed his military participation as a possibility if a full-scale revolt followed the battles of Lexington and Concord. He would, of course, head up the Fairfax Regiment in any broader confrontation that might come. Since he was the only Virginian with substantial command experience in an army, he might be put in charge of all of Virginia's military forces. But was there more that he could do?

Everywhere he went, whether for formal Congressional hearings, or at dinners at the homes of Pennsylvania delegates, or at convivial gatherings at local taverns, where ale flowed freely and the worsening political situation was discussed until the bar closed, George Washington impressed everyone. A crisis was at hand and they all knew it. In addition to the battles at Lexington and Concord and the bottling up of the British Army in Boston, Benedict Arnold and Ethan Allen, with his Green Mountain Boys, had captured Fort Ticonderoga, the important British stronghold on the southern tip of Lake Champlain, and had also captured St. John's, a British port on the Richelieu River in Canada, sinking five British ships and capturing four others.

The first order of business was to raise an army if a full-scale war developed. The military force that surrounded the British at Boston consisted of nearly twenty thousand men, but they were hardly soldiers. The American troops there consisted of badly trained and poorly equipped militias from different colonies. The army needed an experienced commander in chief to whip the amateur troops into shape. They also faced a political necessity. Most of the Americans involved in the siege of Boston came from Massachusetts. If there was going to be a revolution, it had to be fought by an army of men and officers that represented all of the colonies, not just a single state.

There were several candidates for commander, but none were

popular. There was John Hancock, the Massachusetts shipping magnate and president of the Congress, but he was a politician with no military experience. There was Charles Lee, a transplanted British officer. Lee had experience, but would an American army follow a man with a thick British accent and, delegates complained, a rather abrasive personality?

As the days passed, George Washington became a more and more attractive candidate. He was from Virginia and his southern background would serve as a counterbalance to the New England officers at Boston. By 1775, he had become a true political radical, as ardent a champion of independence as any other national figure. Virginia was home to some of the ablest public figures and political thinkers in the country—Edmund Randolph, Patrick Henry, Thomas Jefferson, and Richard Henry Lee—and their help would be invaluable if a full-blown war erupted. Their friendship for Washington as the head of the army would provide him with support. The colonies would also need the resources of the vast and highly populated Virginia colony, such as troops, funds, food, and shipping.

Washington was a successful businessman who had developed exceptional leadership skills and an admirable and highly disciplined work ethic. He was an innovative farmer and paid obsessive attention to details on his lands, talents necessary in the head of an army who would often be inundated with paperwork. Washington was also a politician. He had been a member of the Virginia legislature for sixteen years and knew how to work with other politicians, something he would have to do as a commander who worked for Congress.

His greatest credential went beyond those attributes. George Washington was one of the few Americans who had military command experience from the French and Indian War. He had risen to the rank of colonel and, in several years as an American officer with the British Army, had been in heated battles, lengthy campaigns, and, for three years, served as the administrator of a chain of military outposts in Virginia. He was also a dignified, stoic, respected man who would lead the army as a wise and professional general and not a fiery rebel. Nobody else had that background. There was one drawback: he had never actually led a large military force.

No one was more impressed with the tall Virginian than John Adams, who added that nobody looked more like a general than Washington. Standing ramrod straight at an imposing six feet, three inches, the muscular Washington, in his immaculate, beautifully tailored red and blue uniform, looked like a storybook hero.

Even so, Washington was apprehensive about his selection. Who would not be? If a war came, it would pit an American collection of farmers, blacksmiths, and shopkeepers against the greatest army in the world. The British could put four hundred or more ships to sea at once; America had no navy. The British Crown could hire mercenary armies like the Hessians. The American had no allies. The British generals were the best in the world. America's generals were men who had little experience; many had never led men or fired a cannon in their lives. The British treasury seemed bottomless; the colonists had no money.

Washington made it a point to never ask for the position. He outlined the type of man that Congress needed. In doing so, he described himself. But he never acknowledged that. His humility impressed everyone, because Congress was full of overly ambitious men, such as Adams, who was bluntly told by his wife, "I long impatiently to have you on the stage of action."

When Congress offered him command of the army, George Washington was humble in accepting, telling the delegates, "I this day declare with the utmost sincerity that I do not think myself equal to the command I am honored with." He wrote to his Fairfax Company officers, "I have launched into a wide and extensive field, too boundless for my abilities and far, very far, beyond my experience. [It is] an honor I did not aspire to; an honor I was solicitous to avoid."

The new commander told the delegates, too, that since he was wealthy he would accept no pay, just expenses, no matter how long the war lasted. This offer to serve without compensation stunned the delegates, and then most Americans when it was announced in the newspapers. It was a magnanimous gesture that not only reminded everyone that the Washingtons were very wealthy, but also that they were willing to risk everything to win the war. No one in the room had any idea that the rebellion would last for eight long years. Never, in all that time, would George Washington ask for any salary.

"There is something charming to me in the conduct of Washington. A gentleman of one of the first fortunes upon the continent, leaving his delicious retirement, his family and friends, sacrificing his ease and hazarding all in the cause of his country!" said John Adams.

But the biggest reason that George Washington was reluctant to become the commander in chief of the Continental Army and ride off to Boston to engage the British was that the war would take him far away from his wife and his son. He loved them dearly and did not want to leave them for any length of time, especially to fight a war in which he might be killed.

On June 20, he wrote to his brother Jack that he was nervous about the appointment. "I am embarked on a wide ocean, boundless in its prospect, from whence, perhaps, no safe harbour is to be found," he told him, and implored his brother to visit his wife and family while he was gone. He thought of Martha, too, when he wrote to brother-in-law Burwell Basset that "it is an honor I wished to avoid, as well from an unwillingness to quit the peaceful enjoyment of my family as from a thorough conviction of my own incapacity and want of experience."

He wrote Martha two letters, once again expressing his incapacity for the post and asking for God's help in accomplishing it. Then he penned a tender passage describing how much he would miss her. He wrote, "I should enjoy more happiness and felicity in one month with you, at home, than I have the most distant prospect of reaping abroad, if my stay were to be seven times seven years."

He wrote that it was "destiny that has thrown me upon this service" and put his trust in God not just to win the war, but to bring him back to Mount Vernon and his wife.

He was terribly conflicted about leaving her and wrote a heart-felt letter to his stepson, Jacky, then twenty-one, asking him to look out for her while he was away with the army. "My great concern upon this occasion," he told his son, "is the thought of leaving your mother under the uneasiness which I fear this affair will throw her into. I therefore hope, expect, and indeed have no doubt, of your using every means in your power to keep up her spirits, by doing everything in your power to promote her quiet. I have, I must confess, very uneasy feelings on her account, but as it has been a kind of unavoidable necessity which has led me into this appointment I shall more readily hope that success will attend it."

He urged Jacky to visit his mother frequently because she would be lonely there without any family. The Washingtons had been apart before. George traveled alone to Williamsburg on business or for House of Burgesses sessions. He visited the Custis plantations alone. He and others had been gone for weeks on land speculation expeditions. Martha was used to his absences. Now, though, a war would take him away for a longer time than during any period in their marriage.

Confident that his son would take care of his wife, George Washington then made out his will. He left his wife everything and, in a macabre aside, asked her to remember him to family and friends if he were killed.

Washington always feared for Martha's well-being when away from her. Again, at the very end of 1776, just before the crossing of the Delaware, he wrote to his Mount Vernon manager and cousin, Lund Washington, that if he was killed or captured the cousin had to make certain that the British did not capture Martha. He told him to make sure she escaped and sent him two fast horses for that purpose. He knew that if the rebellion failed, its leaders would be executed, just as the heads of a Scottish rebellion had been thirty years earlier. He wrote Martha one more time, on June 23, promising to be home in the fall.

On July 2, 1775, the tall Virginian arrived in Cambridge, Mass-achusetts, on a rainy day just two weeks after the bloody battle of

Bunker Hill, where American casualties, killed and wounded, totaled 441 and British losses 1,150. He came prepared to assume command of the Continental Army, his wife and stepson far away in Virginia.

CHAPTER TWELVE

THE CAMBRIDGE CAMP

George Washington prayed for a short war. Just before he arrived in Cambridge, he wrote to the New York Legislature to "be assured that every exertion of my worthy colleagues and myself will be equally extended to the reestablishment of peace and harmony between the mother country and colonies." He wrote to Massachusetts lawmakers that he wanted "to see this devoted province again restored to peace, liberty, and safety."

The commander in chief missed his family and worried about them, because back in Virginia things were not going well for the Washingtons or their neighbors. There was personal tragedy. His stepson Jack's wife, Nelly, whom George and Martha loved like their own daughter, gave birth in September after a grueling pregnancy, but the child died. Following the baby's death, Nelly was sick and depressed. She and Jack slipped into a deep mourning that lasted for months.

The Washingtons' former friend John Murray, Lord Dunmore, the royal governor, had fled Williamsburg at the start of the war and lived on a vessel in Norfolk harbor, protected by a flotilla of British warships. He outraged Virginians when he decided to offer freedom to any slave that fought for the British. Virginians were afraid that a large, well-equipped slave army—two hundred thousand slaves lived in Virginia—would defeat the militia. They also feared the ruination of their plantation businesses with the loss of slave labor. Many who had treated their slaves badly were apprehensive that their workers—armed with muskets, pistols, and knives—would come after them in British uniforms and kill them.

The delegates in Congress were terrified by Dunmore's actions, fearing a widespread slave defection, and asked the Committee on Safety in Virginia to do all it could to halt the enlistment of slaves in the British Army. American generals, including Washington, told Congress that a slave army was a dismal prospect and had to be halted.

In the *Virginia Gazette,* writers told the slaves that they could be executed if captured in a British Army uniform and, if not, they would be separated from their families and sold to new owners in the dreaded West Indies.

These arguments made no impression. Eight hundred Virginia slaves—of all ages and from all sections of the colony—joined the British Army. They were given impressive bright-red uniforms, named the "Ethiopian Regiment," and trained and awarded their own motto: "Liberty for Slaves." Another twenty thousand unarmed slave men, women, and children fled from their owners to gain freedom under British protection.

Martha Washington and her neighbors along the Potomac feared that their own slaves would abandon them, but none did. Martha had something more immediate to worry about. Dunmore, struggling to save Virginia from the rebellion, ordered British warships to sail up the Potomac to capture Mrs. Washington and destroy Mount Vernon, along with Gunston Hall, the plantation of rebel George Mason, and the homes of other patriots. All were frightened.

Lund Washington wrote to George, "Alexandria is much alarmed and indeed the whole neighborhood. A report prevails that there are five large ships laying off the mouth of the Cone River...The women and children are leaving Alexandria and stowing themselves into every little hut they can [find], out of reach of the enemy's cannon as they think; every wagon, cart and pack horse that can be got are employed in moving the goods out of town."

Martha was at first determined to stay at Mount Vernon, but an emergency note from Mason, brought by a courier on horseback at full gallop, convinced her to flee. She stayed away from Mount Vernon for two days, until a another courier told her the British had sailed back to Norfolk. The feisty Martha was not afraid of Dunmore's troops, certain that she could always outrace them in her carriage or, if captured, talk them into releasing her and her family. Lund told George that the ingenious Martha had designed an escape plan in which she could flee Mount Vernon with others "in ten minutes."

George, nervous about her safety, asked her to join him at Cambridge. Her mind was not made up by pleas from her husband or relatives, but, it appears, from an article that was published in a pro-British newspaper. The article charged that Martha Washington was not with George because she was "a warm loyalist" and had, in fact, left her traitorous husband and was living by herself under the protection of the British Army in New York. This wild story followed a scandalous report about a letter, which turned out to be a forgery, that insinuated Washington had had an affair with a servant girl while in Philadelphia. The two newspaper articles made up Martha's mind—she was no traitor, and the best way to prove that was to be at her husband's side—war or no war.

She took Jack and Nelly, her nephew George Lewis, and several house slaves with her on the long journey to Massachusetts. Managers could run the plantation; George reminded them to continue giving money and food to the poor of the region, as he and Martha had for years. "Let no one go away hungry," he wrote.

Martha Washington had never been north of Alexandria, Virginia, in her entire life. Now she was going to journey halfway up the Atlantic Coast—in the middle of a war. Martha and Nelly wore plain, homespun dresses on the trip and Martha stopped powdering her hair. To protect Nelly's health, they rode covered in rather plain blankets. Martha and her family made the journey in their elegant white coach, pulled by four strong horses, driven by a livery man intent on getting to Boston as quickly as possible as winter set in. Back home, Washington's cousin Lund removed and stored some of the Washingtons' most valuable furniture in case the British attacked again.

Along the way, people who arranged for their stays at inns began referring to Martha as "Lady Washington," a title that connoted not just respect for Martha and her husband, but recognition that America now had a royalty, too—the Washingtons. She hated the title, but the press loved it and repeated it continually in stories. The nickname stuck.

Lady Washington was astonished at the welcome she received in Philadelphia on November 21, when her small entourage arrived. The patriots there greeted her as if she were a visiting queen from an important European country. Just outside the city, she was met by a company of finely dressed horsemen led by Joseph Reed, a friend of George's. (Her dutiful husband made all the arrangements for her trip, imploring those who provided lodging and food to give her plenty of rest as she made her way north because he was concerned about her health and that of the frail Nelly.) The local newspapers trumpeted her arrival as her carriage made its way through Maryland and Delaware. The prominent families of Philadelphia had arranged a grand ball in her honor. Martha had no idea that her husband's elevation to commander in chief of the army would make him, and her, national celebrities overnight. She was astonished, writing to friend Elizabeth Ramsey, "I don't doubt but you have seen the figure our arrival made in the Philadelphia papers—and I left it in as great pomp as if I had been a very great somebody."

She was impressed that a ball was being held in her honor, but the local patriots wanted it called off because it was precisely the type of ostentation the Revolution sought to avoid. Martha, who loved balls, but knew that her status had suddenly changed, told the organizers to cancel it. Her decision was widely reported in newspapers throughout the country and hailed as a sign of her devotion to the Revolution, to the relief of patriots everywhere.

When Martha and her loved ones left to continue on to Cambridge, they were given an escort out of town by nattily dressed soldiers on horseback and then, wherever they went, men accompanied them, both for protection and ceremony. The newspapers reported her general route and schedule, and when her carriage approached any town the bells of the churches there were rung to honor her. She had at once become a woman of importance, "a great somebody," and yet a woman who dressed, spoke, acted, and appeared to be quite ordinary—the regal but plain woman of the newly emerging democratic American nation.

What seemed to impress Martha Washington the most on her lengthy journey along the Atlantic seaboard was the land upon which she traveled, whether the city streets of Philadelphia, the Watchung Mountains in New Jersey, the river valleys of Connecticut, or the tiny villages that dotted Massachusetts. The woman who had never left Virginia was struck by the America that she saw, calling it a "beautiful country."

One month later, on December 11, 1775, Martha, Jack, and Nelly arrived in Cambridge unannounced. Martha was hailed as a true patriot for risking her safety on a five-hundred-mile trip over bumpy highways through British and Tory territory in a cold winter to be at George's side. Her willingness to travel so far from home to spend the winter with her husband, leaving the comforts of her plantation at Mount Vernon, impressed everyone.

When Martha arrived in Boston, the seaport of seventeen thousand residents was a city encircled by the Continental Army. General Thomas Gage and, later, General William Howe commanded some sixty-five hundred British troops that were quartered in local warehouses or in hundreds of tents pitched on the Boston Commons. The Redcoats were criticized by everyone and called cowards by newspaper writers throughout the country, such as the editor of the *Pennsylvania Journal,* who wrote, "There is no true courage to be observed among them."

Washington was appalled at his "army" when he arrived in Cambridge. Disorder was everywhere. No troops were being drilled. Men drank all day. Gambling was rampant. Men who had never fired a musket shot themselves while trying to do so. Soldiers relieved themselves on the streets. Tents and huts were flimsy and shabbily built. Garbage piled up outside the tents and no one collected it. Officers feuded with each other. Men from city militias did not want to be housed next to men from country militias. Ethnic groups fought with each other. The Virginians did not like the men of Massachusetts and the men from Massachusetts did not like the Virginians; nobody liked the Pennsylvanians.

A disgusted Washington wrote to his cousin Lund, "I come to this place the third instant and found a numerous army of Provincials under very little command, discipline, or order. I found an enemy who had drove our people from Bunker's Hill strongly entrenching."

He wrote to Richard Henry Lee that it took his bungling soldiers eight days to accomplish what could be done in one hour and that "between you and me, I think we are in an exceedingly dangerous situation." He told his brother Jack, "I found a very mixed multitude of people here, under very little discipline, order, or government," and complained to General Phillip Schuyler that when he inspected his army, "Confusion and disorder reigned in every department." He was particularly unhappy with the men from Massachusetts, writing to Lund that "the people of [Massachusetts] have obtained a character which they by no means deserved; their officers generally speaking are the most indifferent kind of people I ever saw...the [troops] are an exceedingly dirty and nasty people."

During those early years of the war, he saw the militia and their leaders as not only inexperienced, but incompetent. "To place any dependence upon militia is, assuredly, resting upon a broken staff. Men just dragged from the tender scenes of domestic life, unaccustomed to the din of arms, totally unacquainted with every kind of military skill, when opposed by troops regularly trained, disciplined, and appointed, makes them timid," he wrote to Continental Congress president John Hancock. The new commander had even less regard for the men who led them. "Their officers are generally of the lowest class of people and, instead of setting a good example to their men are leading them into every kind of mischief," he complained to New Jersey governor William Livingston. He began to think about asking Congress for a permanent army with one- to three-year terms in order to overcome the amateurish militia.

Washington immediately began to turn his collection of inexperienced troops into an army. Soldiers and officers were disciplined for any rules infractions. All were up at dawn and given work to keep them busy through late afternoon. They built barracks, repaired wagons, and took turns cooking food for their companies. They learned how to maintain and fire muskets. Inspections were held, and officers and the general roamed throughout the camp checking on huts, tents, and warehouses. Fortifications were built and maintained. Officers who found lodging in local homes were ordered to keep them in good order.

Martha settled into the headquarters and home of her husband, which had formerly belonged to Tory John Vasal (it would later be home to poet Henry Wadsworth Longfellow). There, Martha spent the next six months.

She was face-to-face with war for the first time and she did not like it, writing to her friend Elizabeth Ramsey, "I confess I shudder every time I hear the sound of a gun," and that the bombed-out ruins of Charlestown and occupied Boston saddened her. "I just took a look at poor Boston and Charlestown—from Prospect Hill. Charlestown has only a few chimneys standing in it; there seems to be a number of very fine buildings in Boston, but God knows how long they will stand; they are pulling up all the wharves for firewood." She lamented, "to me that never sees anything of war, the preparations are very terrible indeed, but I endeavor to keep my fears to myself as well as I can."

In Boston, Martha immediately befriended the wives of other officers, especially Lucy Knox, the wife of the portly General

Henry Knox, and the spunky Kitty Greene, the spouse of Nathanael Greene, the Quaker who became the youngest general in the army and one of Washington's closest advisors. She invited them to visit her and she visited them, as she did the wives of other officers. Martha, Lucy Knox, and Kitty Greene became fast friends and remained close throughout the war. Martha soon began arranging dinners at Vasal House for the officers and their wives at which she and the general presided as they had presided over so many similar dinners at Mount Vernon. These dinners, and other socials organized by Martha, would continue throughout the war and provide a much-needed escape from the pressures of conflict at all of the winter camps where Martha lived until 1783.

The officers' wives, and all of the women in Boston who met her, were taken aback by the general's wife. Lady Washington was not the pompous "royal" they expected. She was open, friendly, charming, and a conversationalist who could engage anybody, man or woman, in discussions about the ordinary events in life: deaths of loved ones, births of children, child care, cooking, sewing, horseback riding, ice skating, the difference in weather between New England and Virginia, friendships, shopping, and the latest fashions. She possessed none of the airs or pretensions of the wealthy women from Virginia they had heard about. Martha wore simple clothes, happily served and drank tea with anyone who stopped by, and talked endlessly about her family.

The first impression of everyone when they met her was that she was friendly. She was, one woman wrote, "a sociable, pretty kind of woman."

Mercy Otis Warren's immediate positive reaction to Martha, and her surprise at the commander in chief's wife's ordinary demeanor, was typical. Warren, a playwright, essayist, and ardent feminist, was the wife of James Warren, the president of the Massachusetts Provincial Congress. She was the sister of patriot and renowned orator James Otis. She wrote to Abigail Adams of Martha, "I will tell you I think the complacency of her manners speaks at once of the benevolence of her heart, and her affability, candor, and gentleness qualify her to soften the hours of private life or to sweeten the care of the hero and smooth the rugged paths of war."

Ordinary women who met her in Boston, and later in the war, were just as effusive about the general's wife. A well-dressed New Jersey woman who was a member of one of the many sewing circles Martha organized throughout the war seemed shocked when she met her in Morristown in 1777. "Her graceful and cheerful manners delighted us all," the woman wrote, "but we felt rebuked by the plainness of her apparel and her example of persistent industry, while we were extravagantly dressed idlers in these perilous times. She seems very wise in experience, kind hearted and winning in all her ways. She talked much of the sufferings of the poor soldiers, especially of the sick ones. Her heart seems to be full of compassion for them."

She also probably served as a sounding board for her husband, who found that venting to his wife eased the enormous tension he often felt as commander. He may have informed her of everything the army did as the siege of Boston droned on. Finally, Washington decided to put cannon on top of Dorchester Heights, a promontory that overlooked the city. The cannon could rake the British ships and buildings in town and force them to surrender or flee. Henry Knox, a former Boston bookseller who had become head of American artillery, procured cannon from Fort Ticonderoga in New York. And in a remarkable feat of transportation, he moved them three hundred miles to Boston in rain squalls and snowstorms. Three thousand men under the command of General John Thomas labored all night on March 4 to install the guns. In the morning, the astonished British looked up at a long line of cannon ready to fire upon them. General Howe had no choice. He decided to evacuate the city on March 17.

George Washington did not believe they had seen the last of the British. He was convinced that they evacuated Boston only to attack America somewhere else, probably near New York City. He began to move his troops towards New York in the early summer, and there he would meet the Redcoats head on.

The letters that Martha wrote to relatives and friends from the camp in Boston, and from other winter camps later in the war, show clearly that she completely understood not only the military war between the British and the Americans, but the political conflict between the patriots and Tories. Her husband kept her informed about all of the military and political movements that were swirling about them, although she never disclosed a single piece of information to anyone, even close friends. As an example of her deft knowledge of the situation in Boston, in a letter to her sister she described the evacuation of the British Army and then ventured a prediction that the British would move to New York, which was correct. She provided her sister with tiny details of the siege, too, such as the number and type of ships captured.

She wrote to Anna Maria, "Our navy has been very successful in taking their vessels. Two were taken last week loaded with coal and potatoes, wines, and several other articles for the use of the troops." She understood the problems the British sympathizers, the Tories created for the army and where the Tories were concentrated, writing to her of New York that "there are many Tories in that part of the world or at least many are suspected there to be unfriendly to our cause at this time."

As always, there was good news and bad news. The bad was that her brother William Dandridge had drowned, something she always feared for the men in her family and for her son ever since the death of her brother John. Far away in the middle of a war, she could not attend William's funeral.

There was good news, though. Nelly, who had been so sick and despondent when she lost her first child in the fall, was pregnant again. She was not well, though, and Martha urged Nelly and Jack to leave Boston in the spring and travel to the home of Nelly's parents in Maryland so that she could get better and give birth to a healthy baby. Martha remained at her husband's side as George ordered the army to New York to await the British.

CHAPTER THIRTEEN

THE DEATH OF GEORGE WASHINGTON...

The worst storm to hit the Atlantic Coast in thirty-five years arrived on the morning of February 24, 1777, covering the streets of New York City with more than a foot of snow and dropping fifteen inches on Morristown, the 1777 winter home of the Continental Army. It followed a previous storm, and soldiers in Morristown reported banks of snow three feet high from wind drifts; the storm paralyzed all of New Jersey.

It was still another headache for George Washington. He had arrived in Morristown after he crossed the Delaware River on Christmas night, 1776, and scored twin triumphs over the British at Trenton and Princeton, surprise victories that boosted the morale not only of his beleaguered troops, but of the entire nation. He chose the tiny village of two hundred and fifty people because it was close enough to New York City so that he could monitor British troop movements but far enough away to give him time to flee if the Redcoats launched a major attack against him.

Residents did all they could for the general. They housed soldiers in their homes, some taking in as many as a dozen men. Local farmers provided as much food as possible for the army, and public officials and ministers did all they could to encourage area residents to join the military. Washington turned Arnold's Tavern, located on the village green, into headquarters. He would live in two small rooms on the second floor. Here in Morristown, with the help of locals, the commander in chief hoped that his wounded men would heal from the New York battles and that he would be able to rebuild his decimated military forces.

Before the stunning victories during the last days of 1776 and the first days of 1777, the American Army had been repeatedly beaten in battles in and around New York City. At the same time, an American invasion of British-held Canada had failed. More than five hundred men had died of smallpox in the hasty retreat south into New York State.

At New York, Washington met the English force of thirty-two thousand soldiers with an army of nineteen thousand men, all from militia companies. He had not only misjudged the skills of the enemy, but badly misjudged the capacity of his own army. The British overwhelmed the Americans in Brooklyn in late August. The Americans suffered fifteen hundred killed and wounded; another eleven hundred were taken prisoner. In short order, the Americans were forced to abandon their defenses at Harlem Heights in Manhattan, and were routed at White Plains, with heavy losses. The British then attacked their encampment at Fort Washington in Manhattan, seized it, and captured three thousand men.

The later Christmas crossing of the Delaware kept the Revolution alive, but the shrunken army Washington took to Morristown was small and weak.

Martha had accompanied George to New York and lived with him in Manhattan as he planned the defense of the region, but had been sent home before the summer battles commenced. He did not want her, or any officers' wives, in danger. He had another reason to send her to Mount Vernon. Martha had never been inoculated for smallpox, which was again killing people throughout the Atlantic seaboard. He wanted Martha to travel home via Philadelphia so that doctors in that city could inoculate her and supervise her recovery. Martha suffered an outbreak of the pox, but the inoculation succeeded. When she felt better, she traveled on to Mount Vernon.

In Morristown, George Washington was worried. Even though the British seemed comfortable in New York that winter, he feared an attack, telling financier Robert Morris that "a storm will burst soon, somewhere, and the [British] aim will be at this army." He warned members of Congress that, despite his victories at Trenton and Princeton, the winter would prove critical.

Washington hoped he could rest his army in Morristown, but since his arrival he had encountered only trouble. Despite his pleas to remain, many troops left, having completed their enlistments. They were followed by deserters. His force had dwindled to just sixteen hundred men ready to fight, while the British had a well-rested army of thirty-two thousand soldiers stationed in different places in the colonies and on ships. He had to quarter his men in the homes of locals, who complained that the soldiers drank too much and cursed too often.

Upon his arrival, Washington found himself in the middle of a severe smallpox epidemic that threatened to wipe out his weakened army and at the same time decimate the people of New Jersey and other colonies. Townspeople in Morristown began to die from the pox one week after the army camped; everyone was alarmed. Panic spread throughout the colonies. John Adams warned his wife that "the smallpox is so thick in the country that there is no chance of escaping it."

General Washington was infected by smallpox himself as a teenager and knew the problems that it caused. The traditional solution was inoculation followed by a ten-day period of rest and strict diet, but he did not have ten days. He might lose a third of his men in that time. Telling doctors and aides that he would "shudder at the consequences" of not inoculating the army, he took the unprecedented step of ordering immediate inoculations (inserting the smallpox virus itself into the bloodstream through a small incision), with no rest or diet, for his three thousand men in Morristown and several thousand others in the colonies, from Virginia to Massachusetts. He also offered free inoculations to tens of thousands of civilians who lived near army camps and might be infected. He did so without approval from Congress because he knew it would take weeks for them to learn of his crisis and act upon it.

The bold step worked. The immediate inoculations saved the army in Morristown and a large civilian population, and his doctors managed to complete it without the British knowing until much later.

He was faced with other problems. The colonists had no reliable currency; the British had the pound sterling. The Americans issued paper scrip, not backed up by monetary funds, and few people relied upon it. In the winter of 1777, scrip-driven inflation began to eat away at the ability of everyone, especially officers in the army, to pay for needed goods. Recruiting new troops to replace those who had left turned out to be difficult. To battle the large British fleet, the Continental Congress had no navy and had to rely on a patchwork fleet of privateers and merchant ships turned into warships.

His staff had been reduced. Some of his aides had been sent to other cities on army business, some were sick, and his new aide, the brilliant Alexander Hamilton, would not report until March 1. Washington had to do their work in addition to his own. He had always been an ardent micromanager, both at Mount Vernon and in the army, and his need to intercede in many areas drained him. By the end of February 1777, he was exhausted.

A snowstorm on February 24 meant even more work. Unwilling to leave the job of snow removal to lower-ranking officers, the commander in chief took it upon himself to supervise the clearing of Morristown. He was outside in cold, windy weather for several days, overseeing the clearing of the roads and the shoveling of snow from homes, warehouses, and stables.

The outdoor labor in the inclement weather brought on yet another bad sore throat. The commander had suffered from brutal sore throats all of his life, but this was the worst ever. His throat was raw, his voice had turned into a rasp, and phlegm began to gather in his passages, making if difficult for him to talk, move, or even breathe. He was ordered to his bed in Arnold's Tavern to recover, but there, under the covers and attended by Dr. John Cochran, his condition worsened over the next two weeks. More phlegm filled his throat and he began to run a high fever.

Dr. Cochran employed all of the standard medical practices of the day, which were primitive. He bled Washington to remove tainted blood and applied rubber suction cups to his forehead to suck out sweat. He had him consume herbal concoctions. Nothing worked. The general, forty-five, feared he was going to die; his father and brother Lawrence had passed away in their forties, and the other men in his family had died young. Washington feared that the army would not stay together without him and that the Revolution would collapse. Most of all, he was furious that he was going to die without his wife at his side.

The desperately ill general took steps to hold the army together from his deathbed. He told the recently arrived Hamilton to oversee the army while he was bedridden. Washington asked Nathanael Greene to take over as commander in chief if he passed away, but Greene assured Washington that he would live. His condition became so poor that Hamilton summoned some of the important men in the army and in public life to Morristown to say their farewells to the chief. Hamilton and other aides made plans for his funeral and discussed the problems of digging his grave in frozen ground covered with snow.

Despite predictions by many that he would pass away, the general held on, day after day, hoping that his wife would arrive before he died. Washington probably told Cochran to make Martha's homemade sore throat remedy—molasses and onions—that had cured him so often in the past. Perhaps it would work this time, too, although the prospects, given the severity of his illness, seemed dim.

Martha left Mount Vernon in late February. Her husband needed her; she would go anywhere to be with him. She made it to Philadelphia and remained there as the town was immobilized by snowstorms. Mrs. Washington planned to stay with friends in that city before moving on to Morristown. Grim-faced soldiers arrived one night. Making certain they did not alert anyone to the general's condition, the troops took Martha aside in the town-house where she was staying and explained to her that the general's condition was very poor, that he might die, and that he wanted her to be with him.

Mrs. Washington made up a story for her friends, kept up as cheerful a disposition as possible, and left Philadelphia before dawn the next morning, telling the driver of her horse-drawn carriage, which had been turned into a sled, to take her to Morristown as fast as possible. The soldiers accompanied her the sixty miles to Morristown over snow-covered roads that ran through barren forests, the recently installed runners of the sled digging into the deep snow and the wind blowing it about. Bundled up with blankets, Mrs. Washington was terrified that she might not make it in time.

By the time her sled pulled into the village, Washington's health had improved slightly. Perhaps his health had improved because of his incredibly strong physical condition or maybe he had convinced Dr. Cochran to give him some of the molasses and onions. Martha promptly took over as his nurse, as she had done so often during their eighteen years of marriage. She administered her molasses and onion remedy, plus other Mount Vernon specialties, kept him warm, and added some generous doses of tender loving care. Her presence boosted his spirits and those of his aides.

Several days later, Washington was able to get out of bed and resume his duties as the head of the army. His aides were happy to have him in charge and very happy, as always, that Mrs. Washington was back.

⊂⊗⊃

The general was soon seen in camp, riding his horse throughout the town and taking recreational rides through the countryside, his servant Billy Lee nearby. He once again started to write letters to congressmen and other public figures. Most of all, he felt better because Martha was with him. He was able to vent all of his frustrations about the war, the army, and Congress to her as he could to no other person. Washington was always comforted by his wife, who listened to his complaints and shared his concerns.

But Martha's presence in Morristown in the winter of 1777 did not just make life easier for her husband; her good cheer improved morale throughout the camp. The Cambridge house was far smaller than their mansion at Mount Vernon, but at least it was a home. In Morristown, she moved into George's cramped two-room, second-floor apartment. Just outside their door was a ballroom that had been turned into offices where military clerks worked all day. Many of them slept in small rooms at Arnold's Tavern. Living in that tiny, crowded space above a tavern was a far cry from her palatial home at Mount Vernon, but Martha never complained.

She began to work feverishly to improve morale at Morristown. She tried to recreate life at Mount Vernon for her husband, certain that the relaxation that routine could bring would ease his troubles. Everyone, regardless of rank, smiled every time she referred to George, their eminent and internationally respected commander in chief, as her "old man." She urged other generals to bring their wives to Morristown to live with them in the homes where they had been quartered. Lucy Knox arrived shortly afterward, but Kitty Greene, about to give birth to a daughter she would name Martha Washington Greene, could not. Mrs. Washington turned the afternoon officers' meetings with her husband into dinner parties, inviting local officials and their wives.

She was pleased that Governor Livingston and his family had moved into the home of Lord Stirling in nearby Basking Ridge, because she knew that Livingston and her husband had become good friends (Washington wanted him near camp to protect the governor from the British, who had tried to kidnap him). Martha grew close to Mrs. Livingston and the governor's teenaged daughters. She told her husband to tell any governors, congressmen, or foreign dignitaries who planned to visit Morristown to bring their wives with them and some did.

"His worthy lady seems to be in perfect felicity while she is by the side of her 'old man,' as she calls him. We often make parties on horseback [with] the general and his lady, Miss Livingston, and his aides," wrote Mrs. Martha Bland, living in the Morristown camp with her husband.

Martha arranged sewing circles, as she did in Boston. She invited the wives of generals, along with women she met in the Morristown area, to join her in repairing the tattered uniforms of the soldiers who had survived the fierce battles at Trenton and Princeton and in manufacturing new shirts and stockings. One woman wrote, "As she was said to be so grand a lady, we thought we must put on our best bibs and bands. So we dressed ourselves in our most elegant ruffles and silks and were introduced to her ladyship. And don't you think, we found her knitting and with a speckled apron on! There we were without a stitch of work and sitting in state, but General Washington's lady with her own hands was knitting stockings…and this was not all. In the afternoon, her ladyship took occasion to say, in a way that we could not be offended at, that at this time it was very important that American ladies should be patterns of industry to their countrywomen, because separation from the mother country will dry up the sources where many of our comforts have been derived."

The paltry army, beset with troubles on all sides during the winter, grew slowly in the spring and by June had increased in size from just sixteen hundred men to nearly nine thousand. Washington had persuaded the ironworks owners in the area to turn their factories over to the production of cannons and shells, and now, as the summer began, the American artillery corps had grown.

Martha left Morristown in early June after three months in camp. The despondent commander in chief had been glad to have her at his side. Her effect on her husband was obvious to all, such as Nathanael Greene, who wrote, "Mrs. Washington is excessively fond of the general and he of her; they are very happy in each other."

Back at Mount Vernon, Mrs. Washington kept busy. Martha started yet another sewing circle, this one with her slaves and several paid women laborers, to make shirts and stockings for the army. She oversaw the running of the plantations at Mount Vernon and the Custis family farms elsewhere with assistance from managers.

Her personal life was active, too. Her son, Jack, had no interest in joining the army, much to the relief of Martha and George, and kept busy managing his plantations in Virginia. He planned to run for a seat in the House of Burgesses, following in his father's footsteps. Nelly was pregnant again (she would eventually have twenty children; ten survived). She and Jack spent most of their time at Mount Vernon, and Martha spent a considerable amount of time taking care of them, especially when her daughter-in-law's pregnancy advanced.

Martha visited her sister Anna Maria at her home in Eltham, Virginia, in August and convinced her to let her take her two sons, Burwell, thirteen, and John, eleven, back to Mount Vernon with her to be inoculated against smallpox when another epidemic began to sweep through Virginia. Sally Fairfax, the daughter of the Washingtons' friend Bryan Fairfax, wrote that everyone remained in their homes during the epidemic, afraid to venture into nearby villages. "Mother won't even go to Alexandria. The infection is never out of town," she told her father, and urged him to have her brother inoculated.

The inoculation and treatment of the Bassett boys went well, and Martha wrote to Anna Maria in late November, "Your boys are as well as they were when I brought them from Eltham...they have been such good boys that I shall love them a great deal more than I ever did."

She sent the boys home, but made certain that there was no danger of them taking the dreaded pox to Eltham with them. She wrote to Anna Maria, "I have had all their clothes washed and rinsed several days and do verily believe that they can bring no infection home with them. If you are afraid, let someone who has had the smallpox put out their clothes to air for a day or two in the sun."

Martha also had the boys' slave servant, a teenager named Thomas, inoculated, and made certain that all of his clothes were washed, rinsed, and dried out.

It was one of the last letters she would send her favorite sister. Anna Maria, thirty-eight, ill for several years, died on December 17. Now Martha only had her mother, brother Bartholomew, and sisters Betsy and Frances left. She wrote to Burwell Bassett that perhaps it was best that her sister had finally passed on because "for the last three or four years of her life could have very little pleasure, her health was such that must render her life a misery." She told her brother-in-law, "I do most sincerely lament and console with you on the loss of our dear departed friend," and told him she hoped to see Anna Maria again in heaven.

Anna Maria had once asked Martha to raise her daughter, nicknamed Fanny, if she died. Martha told Bassett that young Fanny could move to Mount Vernon. That did not happen, though, because that winter George once again asked her to join him at the army's winter camp. The American forces had achieved a major victory in October 1777, when General Horatio Gates, with Benedict Arnold, defeated a large British Army led by General John Burgoyne at Saratoga. However, Washington's army, the other Continental force, had not fared well. In the autumn, his soldiers had been defeated at Brandywine Creek and at Germantown, just outside of Philadelphia, permitting the British to seize and occupy the national capital. His friend the Marquis de Lafayette was shot at Brandywine, and Washington, riding back and forth in the line of fire to rally his troops, was almost hit in numerous volleys. Congress insisted that Washington set up winter camp near Philadelphia to protect the region from other British attacks.

A series of calamities befell the army as it arrived in winter camp on December 19: low provisions, poor medical supplies, overcrowded hospitals, runaway inflation, lack of clothing, disease, and a nefarious plot to unseat Washington as commander in chief. He was deeply troubled and needed his wife, who left Mount Vernon on January 26, 1778, upon receipt of his urgent letter.

He warned her that they had set up camp in "a dreary kind of place." It was somewhere twenty miles northwest of Philadelphia that she had never heard of—Valley Forge.

CHAPTER FOURTEEN

THE AWFUL VALLEY FORGE WINTER

H er husband had rented a two-story, six-room, gray stone house on the banks of the Schuylkill River from a local farmer, Isaac Potts, for his headquarters while the army was in winter camp at Valley Forge, a wide plain so named because it was near an ironworks called the valley forge. The tiny house overflowed with the general's staff. They were crowded into a fifteen-by-fifteen-foot office on the first floor of the building, over-looking the river. The aides all slept on narrow beds that folded up and served as desks during the day in two cramped rooms upstairs.

The general's office could be found in a similar fifteen by fifteen-foot room behind his aides' first-floor space. His room was lighted by two high windows on the southeast side of the building during the day and by candles at night. In it was a stone fireplace, a small wooden secretariat for the general, and a chair with a writing board for one of his aides.

George Washington slept upstairs in a bedroom that could barely hold a bed and small table near a window; his huge frame seemed to fill up the entire room when he entered it. There was no large room for staff meetings, so Washington ordered a wing built onto the house, with dining facilities. Outside his windows, the general could see the river and, some fifty yards away, a stable, where he mounted horses that he rode to and from the camp and the countryside for recreation.

Martha arrived at Valley Forge in a large sleigh on February 5, accompanied by Colonel Caleb Gibbs, one of her husband's most trusted aides, who had met her at an inn near Brandywine and had taken her to the camp. She had her servants, assisted by some army officers, carry her heavy trunks upstairs to the one room she would share with her husband for the rest of the winter. George often banged his head on the low ceiling over the staircase they climbed to transport the trunks.

Her journey to Pennsylvania had been an arduous one. It began auspiciously in Alexandria at the end of January. As Martha left the town and headed north in her carriage, she learned from a friend, James Bowdoin, a wealthy Boston merchant, that his partner, French merchant Emanuel de Pliarne, had drowned while trying to cross the Potomac. Bowdoin was distraught. As soon as Mrs. Washington left Maryland and crossed into Delaware, it started to snow—hard. She wrote to a friend, "The traveling was pretty rough." By the time she reached Brandywine, the scene of her husband's defeat just a few months before, the storm turned violent. "At an inn at Brandywine Creek, at a ford, where I lodged, the snow was so deep in the roads in some places that I had to leave the [carriage] behind with the innkeeper and hire a farm sleigh to bring me to [Valley Forge]."

Mrs. Washington had come at the height of yet more crises that confronted the general and the soldiers in the grueling winter of 1777–1778. She was shocked at the exhausted condition in which she found her usually vibrant husband. She wrote with concern that "the general is well, but much worn with fatigue and anxiety. I never knew him to be so anxious as now, for the poor soldiers are without sufficient clothing and food, and many of them are barefooted. Oh, how my heart pains for them."

The general had spent the entire month of January trying to resolve the medical, food, and clothing crises that had struck the army, troubles that would make the encampment at Valley Forge not only the most catastrophic for the army in the American Revolution, but perhaps in all of American history.

Problems began immediately. There was no shelter at Valley Forge for Washington's fourteen-thousand-man army so the men were put to work building hundreds of sixteen-by-fourteen-foot wooden huts to serve as barracks. There were not enough boards for the huts, however, because the creeks and rivers that powered area sawmills had frozen and the mills shut down. There were few tools for building anything. Weeks went by before the cabins could be completed. Soldiers slept in thin canvas tents or hastily constructed log lean-tos. Some slept in open, windswept fields; many fell ill from bronchitis and pneumonia. To get soldiers into huts quickly, officers permitted the completion of badly built cabins with porous roofs and spaces between boards. Water seeped in and stagnated, causing disease and sending hundreds to the hospital.

Men urinated in the streets of the camp, garbage was not collected, and horses that died were left where they fell; their carcasses rotted. The orders from General Washington to pick up garbage and cart off horses were delayed in their completion or ignored by lower-ranking officers.

Hundreds of sick and wounded men arrived jammed into wooden carts and carriages, but there was nowhere to house them. No one in the military had been paid in over two months. The promised "thousands" of soldiers from Pennsylvania never arrived. One army doctor snarled, "A pox on my bad luck."

The weather at Valley Forge was not severe that winter. It was the lack of food and clothing, and the burgeoning medical crisis, that took the lives of twenty-five hundred men, nearly one-quarter of the soldiers there.

The army's clothing supply had been low since the previous

summer, but it had declined to crisis proportions by winter. Congress ran the quartermaster's department, which was in charge of transporting uniforms, but had not replaced its director, who had resigned months before. The department was in chaos, and orders to ship clothes piled up on desks attended by no one. There was no production or shipments of shoes; footwear was so sparse that Washington created contests with prizes for men who could make the best footwear out of whatever materials they could find. One Rhode Island colonel, whose men had been barefoot for weeks, snapped that they had the look of "a ragged, lousy, naked army." A Massachusetts general said of his soldiers that "they are naked from the crowns of their heads to the soles of their feet."

What angered the soldiers was that the residents of Chester County, who lived around Valley Forge, claimed they had no spare clothing to give or sell the army. In truth, most did not. The British had ransacked the region prior to the American encampment, as they often did, looking for provisions and clothes. As an example, the Redcoats burst into the farmhouse of teenager Christina Leach, in the Philadelphia area, and arrested her father, brother-in-law, and his two sons and stole all of their cattle. "It is a sad and troublesome time," Christina wrote.

American soldiers refused to listen to people like the Leachs, accepted no excuses, and condemned everyone. "The inhabitants are only fit for pick horses," snapped Elias Boudinot, one of Washington's aides.

Other officers wrote that they only had one shirt for every ten men, or had companies in which three-quarters of the men did not have shoes, or companies where the men wrapped cartridge belts around their feet to cover them in snowfalls. To warm themselves, some men tore down their tents, cut up the canvasses, used them as blankets, and then had to sleep in the fields.

No clothing was forthcoming from the home states, either. In Virginia, an angry John Harvie complained to Governor Thomas Jefferson of his inability to gather clothing from the residents to send to Valley Forge. He wrote, "The avarice and disaffection of the people is so great that they refuse any price we can give for the necessary provisions for the army. The supporters of the [Revolution] are weak men without any character."

There was little food. When the army arrived, it was discovered that the supply clerks had misled Washington when they assured him they had 7.6 million pounds of flour; there were just twenty-five barrels of flour for fourteen thousand men. A check showed that the beef guaranteed to last seven months was only enough to last eight days. Local farmers did not have all of the cattle that the Pennsylvania politicians had promised. It was true that they had raised 1.4 million pounds of beef *per year* before the war, but no one remembered that an army consumed nearly that amount of beef *per month*. The locals needed the beef they possessed for themselves and would not sell to the army. And many of the residents of Chester County were Quakers, who opposed all wars and all armies and would not help them either.

It was problematic to deliver any food that could be procured. There was a shortage of both wagons and drivers, and the wagons could not travel over bad roads or flooded highways. The quartermaster's department was mismanaged. Many of its supervisors were corrupt and several wound up in prison.

The soldiers at Valley Forge were often forced to go three or four days without food and began to starve. Jedediah Huntington wrote to his brother back home that the troops "live from hand to mouth," and another officer wrote of the food shortage that "we have been driven almost to destruction."

Washington exploded in a long and strident letter to the president of Congress, Henry Laurens. He told him that the soldiers felt abandoned by their country. He informed Laurens that within days the army would "starve, dissolve, or disperse."

In that same searing note, he reprimanded congressmen whom he thought did nothing to help the army and Pennsylvanians whom he accused of sitting by and letting his soldiers die. He wrote, "I can assure those gentlemen that it is a much easier and less distressing thing to draw remonstrances in a comfortable room by a good fire side than to occupy a cold, bleak hill and sleep under frost and snow without clothes or blankets...although they seem to have little feeling for the naked and distressed soldier. I feel super-abundantly for them and from my soul pity those miseries."

The food and clothing problems paled in comparison to the medical woes that faced George Washington and his men by early February, when Martha arrived. The only real "hospital" in the area was in Philadelphia, and it was occupied by the British. Washington had to commandeer every large building he could find and have his doctors turn them into hospitals overnight. These included barns, warehouses, churches, courthouses, and linen mills. Even general stores, taverns, and pottery shops were turned into medical facilities. Still short on space, Washington ordered the speedy construction of a three-story wooden hospital with room for three hundred beds, which was promptly named "Washington Hall" by the soldiers, that was, upon completion in just three weeks, one of the largest hospitals in America.

Hospitals were at first occupied with the wounded from Germantown and Brandywine, but they quickly filled up with men who fell sick at Valley Forge. Many came down with scabies, a condition that brings on the constant itching of scabs that cover most of the body. It is caused by lice and unsanitary living conditions, such as those in the winter camp. The unpredictable weather and badly designed huts brought on other sicknesses. Others had severe cases of typhus, dysentery, diarrhea, the flu, rheumatism, and pleurisy. Almost all of the soldiers who developed gangrene in their arms or legs lost their limbs; many died.

The newly renovated hospitals were hopelessly overcrowded, and it was not unusual to find five hundred men in a facility designed to house half that many. Men with one disease were placed in wide-open rooms alongside men with other diseases. Soldiers caught each other's illnesses and died. Medical care was poor because, in an organizational mix-up, a dozen of the sixty doctors in the army had been given unauthorized furloughs to go home. A dozen more fell ill from treating their patients; some quit and left. Medical supplies remained low throughout the war.

Ninety percent of the soldiers in a Virginia regiment died in one hospital. One-third of all the soldiers sent to the hospital at

Bethlehem perished. Half the soldiers in wards in a hospital at Lititz died. One-fifth of all the troops from the state of North Carolina at Valley Forge passed away. By March 2, doctors told Washington that just 30 percent of the men in his army were fit for duty.

Dr. Benjamin Rush, the army's chief physician, wrote a savage note to Patrick Henry in which he said of the hospitals that "more are dying in them in one month than perished in the field during the whole of the last campaign." Conditions were so bad that Rush joked to others that the worst thing that could happen to a sick soldier was to be put into an army hospital.

No one was angrier than George Washington. He wrote to Governor Livingston, "I sincerely feel for the unhappy conditions of our poor fellows in the hospitals, and wish my powers to relieve them were equal to my inclinations. Our difficulties and distresses…wound the feelings of humanity"

As if all this suffering was not enough, the colonies were hit with yet another smallpox epidemic that winter that the general's speedy inoculations rendered harmless. And on top of all that, Washington had to fight off a conspiracy to unseat him as head of the army, to be replaced by General Gates. The cabal was headed by a disgruntled general, Thomas Conway, an Irishman, whom Washington loathed. Thanks to some deft politicking with Congress by Washington, and considerable help from his aides, the plot fell apart.

Martha had been as depressed as her husband when that awful winter began. When she left Virginia, the smallpox epidemic had started, and she feared it would reach Mount Vernon and put her immediate family and slave family in jeopardy. Anna Maria's death, while not from smallpox, had made Martha despondent.

She knew that her husband's spirits were lower than they had been at any point during his life as he struggled to keep the army together at Valley Forge. When he asked her to join him in what must have been a morose letter, she told Burwell Bassett, "I must go."

Martha's arrival was welcomed by the officers and men, as it had been at the previous camp at Morristown, and would be during each winter of the war (remarked one officer: "Mrs. Washington had the courage to follow her husband to that dismal abode [Valley Forge]"). Another wrote that to end the stress, all the general needed was "a visit from Mrs. Washington, a generous glass of wine, or riding on horseback almost every dry day."

The general was pressed by crises daily, and he soon realized that he was spending little time with his wife, so he determined to create time each day that was needed by the couple. He decided that every morning the two would enjoy a one-hour breakfast together in the one room they shared on the second floor of the Potts' House, and that they could not be interrupted by anyone or for any reason. It was here, on those quiet mornings at Valley Forge, whether talking about the war, the farms back home, or the family, that Martha gave her husband the emotional sustenance that he needed and it was there that the bonds between them grew even deeper. And it was there, out of the earshot of anyone, that he could complain to her about his woes. It was there that she also served as his sounding board for all of the ideas he had to win the war. In that one room where no one could interrupt them, she could comfort him.

At Valley Forge, Martha recreated her role as the genial hostess that she had carried out with such success in Morristown the previous winter and in Boston in 1775. Her mere presence took much of the stress off Washington's aides Alexander Hamilton, Robert Harrison, and Tench Tilghman. She once again organized numerous sewing circles that included generals' and officers' wives and local women. The women walked past the busy first- floor office of the Potts' House and climbed the stairs to the second-floor bedroom of the Washingtons on the narrow staircase. There, in cramped quarters, sipping tea as they worked, the women produced hundreds of shirts and other pieces of clothing and mended coats and breeches that had been torn in battles. They could not manufacture shoes, but they could, and did, make hundreds of needed stockings for the barefoot men in camp. At these frequent meetings, Martha discussed the war, the soldiers, families, the occupation of Philadelphia, Pennsylvania's loyalists and, of course, her family. The others talked about their own families. All of them hoped for a quick and favorable end to the Revolution.

Mrs. Washington again began dinner parties for the officers and their wives that one visitor described as "elegant." She was reunited with Lucy Knox at Valley Forge, and this winter Kitty Greene had come from her home in Rhode Island, too. Lord Stirling's wife, whom she had visited so often the previous winter, also accompanied her husband to camp. The ladies helped her organize the dinner parties and nighttime receptions that were added to ease some of the tension of the brutal winter camp. The evening parties featured coffee and cakes and sometimes group singing. Even George, who could not carry a tune, joined in with the choral singing of the officers and their wives on those winter nights.

On February 22, on his forty-sixth birthday, Martha hosted a party for her husband. She had the band of the Second Continental Artillery Company entertain and tipped them fifteen shillings, much to the delight of the musicians. Throughout the terrible winter, everyone could see the fondness between the Washingtons. Lafayette wrote to his wife that Martha "loves her husband madly."

Martha spent many days making sure that her husband allowed himself time to pose for portraits by Charles Willson Peale, the lieutenant-artist who kept asking him to sit for him. Washington disdained all artists, but liked Peale because he was in the army. Martha continually asked artists to paint her husband because she was never satisfied with any of the hundreds of portraits of him, always telling the artists that the paintings did not show him off as the very handsome man she found him to be. Worst of all, she told them, they all made him look old.

Martha continually kept busy with sewing circles, dinners, receptions, choral singing, hospital visits, Sunday prayer services, attending the plays the troops staged, and watching some of the athletic events in which they participated. One woman said of her industry, "I never in my life knew a woman so busy from early morning until late at night as was Lady Washington, providing comforts for the sick soldiers."

Some men, especially the Frenchmen, were disappointed that America's most famous man was married to such an ordinary-looking woman. They expected her to be a beauty, dressed in frilly gowns. "She is small and fat," sniped Chevalier Chastellux, a French diplomat who met her. "She was dressed very plainly and her manners were simple in all respects."

Women who tried to intercede with General Washington on their husbands' behalf, particularly women whose spouses had been imprisoned, often went to Martha first. They hoped that, as a woman and wife, she would understand their plight and convince the general to free their husbands. Elizabeth Drinker, a Quaker, was one of them. On April 6, 1778, she arrived at the Potts' House with a friend, Isabel Morris, to plead with Martha to persuade the general to release her husband, who was in jail for selling goods to the British Army. Martha talked to her for quite a while and then sent her to see George. He dismissed her after just a few moments. Martha invited Mrs. Drinker and Mrs. Morris to the daily 3 p.m. dinner that day. Afterwards, Martha brought Drinker upstairs to her room and, with great sympathy, told her that the general could not free her husband because, as she put it delicately, Americans should not be selling goods to the enemy. The man remained in prison.

Mrs. Washington regretted her meetings with women like Elizabeth Drinker and the others who pleaded for their husbands, sons, or neighbors. She understood their worry, but she also understood her husband's position as head of the army.

Mrs. Washington continually worried about the soldiers. She visited many of the wooden huts to serve as an amateur nurse and might have made rounds in the hospitals near camp, too, as her husband did. During her eight winters in camp during the Revolution she met thousands of soldiers. All of them admired her. Dr. James Thacher wrote, "Mrs. Washington combines an uncommon degree of great dignity of manner with the most pleasing affability. I learn from the Virginia officers that Mrs. Washington has ever been honored as a lady of distinguished goodness, possessing all the virtues which adorn her sex, amiable in her temper and deportment, full of benignity, benevolence, and charity. These surely are the attributes which reveal a heart replete with those virtues which are so appropriate and estimable in the female character."

A member of the life guard, who protected the Washingtons and saw her every day, wrote, "I am at present enjoying myself incomparably well in the family of Mrs. Washington…I am happy in the importance of my charge, as well as the presence of the most amiable woman upon Earth, whose character should I attempt to describe I could not do justice to."

Many of the men who served at Valley Forge remembered her worries over the sick and starving soldiers, and many added that just her presence there gave everyone a feeling that things would turn out well. One French officer, Colonel Pierre Duponceau, wrote that Mrs. Washington "undauntedly followed the fortunes of her husband and of her country." He recalled, "I still see her at the head of the table, with her mild but dignified countenance, which often reminded me of the matrons of ancient Rome. [She was] grave, yet cheerful. Her presence inspired fortitude, and those who came to her with almost desponding hearts, retired full of hope and confidence."

Others with the army marveled at the way that everybody felt the same way about the General's wife. Chastellux, the French diplomat, wrote that Martha was "beloved by all about her." And many noted that when George was with Martha he seemed very much at home. George Benet, who visited the camp at Newburgh, New York, later wrote that "Mrs. W was as plain easy and affable as he was and one would have thought from the familiarity which prevailed there that he saw a respectable private gentleman dining at the head of his own family."

And every winter, and in every camp, Martha told anyone she met how much she loved the army and worshipped the soldiers in it. One visitor to Mount Vernon just after the war wrote that it was "astonishing with what raptures Mrs. Washington spoke about the discipline of the army, the excellent order they were in, superior to any troops she said upon the face of the earth; even the English acknowledged it, she said. What pleasure she took in the sound of fifes and drums, preferring it to any music that was ever heard; and then to see the [troops] reviewed a week or two before the men disbanded, when they were all well clothed [finally] was, she said, a most heavenly sight."

She worried about her husband's emotional state as he struggled each day to keep the army alive and worked feverishly with members of Congress, colonial governors, and ministers—and continued a voluminous correspondence with public officials as well as army generals.

Martha fretted about troubling news from Mount Vernon. There, Sally Fairfax, the daughter of Bryan Fairfax, who had so worried about her brother getting inoculated to avoid yet another smallpox epidemic, died of it herself. A friend of Martha's, Nancy Whiting, died in childbirth. The pox threatened the Washingtons at Mount Vernon. Her son, Jack, wrote that he and Nelly had doctors try to inoculate their daughter Patsy three times, but none of the inoculations worked and they were terrified that she would be stricken. Jacky's fears were evident in a mournful letter to his mother. "This leaves us in very disagreeable suspense, as we shall be very uneasy lest she should get the disorder. I sincerely hope no accident will happen to the dear child. She has grown into the finest girl I ever saw and the most good natured quiet little creature in the world."

Patsy survived smallpox, though, and so did most of the men at Valley Forge, thanks to the commander in chief. Washington battled the crises that confronted his army every day, never believing that the fates and elements would overwhelm him.

Early on, he ordered all doctors who had gone home to return, under threat of arrest. Newly arrived food and clothing was sent directly to the hospitals. Dozens of pits were dug to bury garbage and dead horses. Urination anywhere except a latrine was made punishable by death. Medical supplies were sent from all over the country, windows were cut in cabins to provide ventilation, and men were ordered to bathe and wash their clothes daily to reduce the risk of sickness. A dozen small hospitals were built right in the

camp to get sick men immediate care. Officers were told to visit the hospitals to cheer up their men. Washington himself made the rounds to see bedridden soldiers at hospitals. "[It] pleased the sick exceedingly," wrote one doctor.

To obtain more food, he sent his men nearly one hundred miles from the camp on foraging missions to buy cattle, corn, and other foods, and invited local merchants to set up a produce market just outside of Valley Forge. When all of that was finished, he organized massive cattle drives as far away as Maryland and Massachusetts and had soldiers bring thousands of head of cattle halfway across the country to feed his men. Washington also won permission from Congress to completely reorganize the quartermaster department, putting his own trusted officers in charge. They streamlined its operations, ended most corruption, and made food delivery quicker.

He was never able to completely solve the clothing shortage, so he asked more women to become involved in sewing circles, and they did. He told the poorly clad soldiers to write home and ask their mothers and wives to make and/or send new clothes. Men mailed home long lists of clothing. William Gifford of New Jersey wrote to his militia captain back home to send him the "warmest breeches and stockings" he could find. William Weeks of New Hampshire asked a friend for homespun breeches, stockings, and "a shirt or two," explaining that "clothing of every kind being excessive dear and scarce here." Another asked his mother to mend torn shirts already at home and send them to him. This remedy helped.

Through it all, the deaths of some 2,500 men and 1,500 horses, the starvation, clothing crisis, and atrocious medical care, the men never lost their devotion to the cause. Elias Boudinot wrote of them, "We have a severe time of it, nothing but suffering for our poor fellows, but they do it without complaint."

Nor did they ever lose their admiration for their commander in chief. In January, at the height of the Valley Forge woes, John Crane, a surgeon in a Massachusetts company, wrote to a friend, "His Excellency, George Washington, is much beloved

by all ranks."

And the commander never lost his devotion to them. Isaac Gibbs of New Hampshire wrote to his brother that "remarkable that our troops amidst all their hardship which they suffer still keep a steady solid fortitude of mind, so much that General Washington a few days past returned his public thanks to the whole of General Poor's Brigade for their peaceable and manlike behavior."

When the various crises eased, Washington hired Baron Frederich von Steuben, a Prussian drillmaster, to turn his ragtag army into a professional fighting force. In May, the French government finally agreed to enter the war on the American side, pledging troops, cannon, muskets, ships, and money. That same month hundreds of new recruits arrived from all over the Atlantic seaboard to swell the size of the army.

George Washington and his men had somehow survived Valley Forge, to the astonishment of everyone. Artillery Lieutenant George Fleming may have put the feelings of the commander and the men best when he wrote to another officer with great pride that "our men are in good health and high spirits. Joy sparkles in the eyes of our whole army."

On June 8, confident that her husband was in much better spirits, Martha Washington left Valley Forge and once again returned to Mount Vernon. She was greatly relieved later in the month when she received word that the Continental Army had defeated the British at Monmouth, New Jersey, in what turned out to be one of the major battles of the war. She was happy for the victory, but was not pleased when she learned that, once again, her husband had thrown caution to the wind and, at the point where it appeared the Americans would lose the battle, rode back and forth in front of the lines to successfully rally his troops; he was an easy target for British cannon and hundreds of muskets that opened up on him. Amazingly, he emerged unscathed.

Across the country, women saw themselves in Martha Washington in the first stages of the rather extraordinary transformation of Mrs. Washington from Virginia housewife to

Revolutionary War heroine to the beloved First Lady of the United States. It was a transformation created by the mixture of the circumstances of women's and families' lives of the era, the Washingtons' lives, and the Revolution itself.

George Washington worked tirelessly on his image as a leader throughout the war, beginning on the day he took over the army in June of 1775 dressed immaculately in his uniform and sitting very impressively astride one of his handsome horses. He understood that people did not see a Revolution in the tens of thousands of men who fought in the army, but in the one man who was the commander in chief. Stunning victories at Trenton, and then Princeton, had given him an enormous popularity with the people that continued for the rest of his life. He used that popularity, and his image as a destiny-driven leader of men, to persuade thousands of people to help him win the war, whether they were governors, ministers, newspaper editors, or common farmers. His image of the citizen-soldier who served without pay and sought nothing but the gratitude of the people had made him an icon by the spring of 1777 and would later make him president and a revered historical figure.

Martha Washington never worked on her image and had no goals or ambition except to keep her family together through one of the great crises in American history and provide whatever comfort she could to her constantly embattled husband. The simple way that she lived her life throughout the war, the only way she could, impressed everyone.

Martha was startled by the reaction of the press and the people to her decision to leave Mount Vernon and live with George in winter camp in faraway Boston in 1775. To her, it was natural to be with her husband, no matter where he was. She never expressed any fear of injury or kidnapping and never believed that harm would come to her. To the general public, leaving her palatial estate at Mount Vernon, with all its comforts, to reside in winter camps with the army for eight long years was an enormous sacrifice for the cause. For a woman who had never been outside of Virginia to ride five hundred miles to Boston to live in the first winter camp was extraordinary. To continue to leave Mount Vernon and spend each winter with her husband, sometimes living in just one or two rooms in bitterly cold weather, was considered a great sacrifice.

Mrs. Washington thought nothing of visiting sick soldiers in camp hospitals each winter of the war, especially at Valley Forge, where so many had fallen ill. After her smallpox inoculation in 1776, she felt no risk of being in a camp infested with smallpox, typhus, or other fatal diseases. The men and women of the country were astonished that a woman could be so brave. There were constant rumors that British soldiers planned to kidnap the Washingtons and bring them to London as prisoners of war (there were two failed attempts). Martha not only paid little attention to the possibility, but frequently joked about it. This, too, impressed the public.

No other woman did these things. Neither Lucy Knox nor Kitty Greene, or any officers' wives, lived with the army every winter, and none of them put in anywhere near as much work for the soldiers as Martha.

And, in addition to all of that, Mrs. Washington and her home at Mount Vernon were vulnerable to British attacks. Every day, she woke up at Mount Vernon, or in winter camp, wondering if today would be the day that British warships would shell her house.

She chose to risk her own life to be with her husband and his soldiers. In fact, she thought nothing of it and maintained her amiable attitude through every calamity that befell them. As a good wife, she believed that she had to do these things. She was a traditional wife of the period whose job was to aid and comfort her spouse and care for their children. Yet, because she was the wife of the commander of the army, what she saw as routine wifely activities assumed huge significance to the public. All women wanted to help the cause like Martha, in their own small ways, the only ways permitted by the patriarchal society they lived in, to show that even though women had little power in America, they could do much in their own fashion. In Martha, they saw themselves.

The attachment of women to Martha was best symbolized in a

1780 drive, led by the women of Philadelphia, to collect money to buy shirts for soldiers. Martha, who was very distressed, told friends in Philadelphia about the tattered clothing the soldiers wore in the brutal winter of 1779–1780 and suggested a fund-raising campaign to aid the soldiers. Esther Reed, wife of Pennsylvania's governor and former Washington military aide Joseph Reed, organized the campaign. Martha herself contributed $20,000. The insistent women went house to house to collect money, even getting contributions from known Tories who contributed "to get rid of them," according to one. They nailed printed broadsides to trees, fences, and buildings to advertise the fund drive. In the first paragraph of the broadside, the women expressed their feelings about both their role in American life and patriotism: "Our ambition is kindled by the fame of those heroines of antiquity, who have rendered their sex illustrious, and have proved to the universe that…if opinion and manners did not forbid us to march to glory by the same paths as the men, we should at least equal, and sometimes surpass them in our love for the public good."

The women raised an impressive $300,000 and insisted on giving the money to Martha Washington, not the general, to make certain that it would be used specifically for shirts and also because the women of the country had come to see Martha as their heroine. Hundreds of women participated in the production of shirts for the soldiers and, in a human touch, each sewed her own name into the shirts, so that when their soldier was firing away at the enemy, they'd be there in spirit.

The sewing circles that Martha led in the war were among many that sprung up throughout the states. They were the successors of hundreds of similar sewing circles that were founded in 1769 by women determined to manufacture homespun garments during one of the boycotts of British goods ordered by the colonies' non-importation bills.

These circles were successful beyond anyone's dreams. Individual women—North and South—organized a dozen or so ladies in their neighborhood into a group to produce wool and then shirts, breeches, and jackets. The women would meet once a week, sometimes twice. Churches organized spinning and sewing groups, as did entire towns. Women not only spun wool and made clothing at their meetings, but they also produced clothing at home, too. Southern women with slaves who lived some distance from each other, such as Mrs. Washington, headed up sewing circles in their homes made up of slaves, hired women, the wives of plantation overseers, and their daughters. Some towns had as many as three dozen spinning circles. Some had more than fifty women; some were so large that half the women worked indoors and half outside the house or church. Some towns staged outdoor spinning circles and sewing-circle festivals in which residents could watch the women and work, eat, drink, listen to bands, and play games in nearby fields. The women kept track of who was working for the cause in their neighborhoods, churches, and towns, and remembered Martha Washington and others they read about doing the same thing elsewhere.

These circles were seen as part of the effort to win the war by the mothers, wives, and sisters of soldiers—it made women and their daughters feel that they were part of the war effort. Anne Terel, the wife of an American soldier, described this unique feeling in a letter published in the *Virginia Gazette.* She wrote of what women could do for "the glorious cause." She said women were part of "another branch of American politics which comes more immediately under our province, namely, in frugality and industry." She urged women "to raise their crops, make clothing, run their husbands' farms and stores, and secure the home front so that their husbands could continue to fight in the fields," proud that their women were just as patriotic as they, but in another way.

Terel was one of thousands of women whose husbands were away from home in the war. In his absence, she had to run their farm. Many women had to run small farms and shops when their spouses were gone; wives in the South who owned slaves had to maintain their family plantations on their own. Some southern women had their farms ruined by the British Army in the last few years of the war, and all women feared an attack by the British.

They did not have the same skills as farmers, or merchants, as their absent husbands and their businesses lost money—for years. In this, wives connected directly to Martha Washington, who ran Mount Vernon for eight years, suffering huge financial losses in uncertain markets.

The women heralded their support of the Revolution wherever they could. Newspapers served as useful vehicles to air their feelings. Many papers published letters from women who argued that if they were men they would be in the army, but as women they would do all they could on the home front to help the cause, emulating Martha Washington. Single women used the newspapers to let everyone know that not only did they support the troops and the cause, but they also would not be courted by any man who did not support the Revolution; papers even ran lists of names of these patriotic women.

The newspapers also covered the journeys of Mrs. Washington to and from the winter camps, sometimes foolishly printing the names of the villages where she would stay overnight and the highways her carriage would travel. These stories constantly referred to her as Lady Washington and reminded readers how revered the general's wife had become. The people felt a close connection to George and Martha Washington and, in the spring of 1776, many parents of newborn infants began to proudly name their boys George and girls Martha. The "Lady Washington" references and laudatory coverage helped to turn Martha into royalty; this happened in much the same way later, as the Washingtons established a unique institution—the American presidency.

CHAPTER FIFTEEN

SNOWED IN: MORRISTOWN, 1779–1780

Christmas had always been a special time for the Washingtons. In 1779, George Washington knew that his army would be in camp for the entire winter, and wanted his wife to be with him for Christmas. He had sent for her just after his arrival in Morristown, New Jersey, on December 1, when he rode into the village with hundreds of soldiers and a train of wagons and cannon from his autumn headquarters in Newburgh, New York, in the middle of the fifth snowstorm of the season. There was nearly two feet of snow on the ground in Morristown when the army arrived, and the very next day, December 2, another storm hit, this one dropping over six more inches. Another storm on December 6 dropped nine more inches. It was one of twenty-six storms that pounded the Atlantic seaboard states in the winter of 1779–1780, six of them of blizzard proportions.

Eager to be with her husband, Martha left Mount Vernon in

mid-November and headed for Morristown, by way of Philadelphia, as always. She was trapped in Philadelphia by yet another snowstorm that arrived on December 18. That storm followed a severe cold front that gripped the region on December 14, causing temperatures to drop below freezing and remain there for weeks (it was sixteen degrees below zero on January 16). The December 6 storm paralyzed every community in the New York–Philadelphia corridor and shut down travel. Herbert Muhlenberg, an amateur meteorologist in Philadelphia, wrote in his journal that day that "it began to snow hard early in the morning and continued thus all day." The storm wreaked havoc in General Washington's winter camp, where the weather prevented men from building their cabins nearby in a valley called Jockey Hollow, just two miles outside of the village and its large green. Washington had again decided upon Morristown as winter camp for the same reasons he had selected it in 1777.

"The snow on the ground is about two feet deep, and the weather extremely cold; the soldiers are destitute of both tents and blankets and some of them are actually barefooted and almost naked. Our only defense against the inclemency of the weather consists of brushwood thrown together. Our lodging last night was on the frozen ground. Having removed the snow, we wrapped ourselves in great coats, spread our blankets on the ground, and lay down by the side of each other, five or six together, with large fires at our feet," Dr. James Thacher wrote.

The snowstorms would continue in what was the worst winter in the history of North America. In addition to the twenty-six storms, a succession of cold fronts kept the East Coast in a deep freeze. The Delaware River froze over at the end of December and remained frozen until March 4, 1780; men in sleighs and on horseback rode over it. Baltimore's harbor remained frozen, closed to all shipping, for months. For the only time in recorded history, the wide and deep New York harbor froze over. British officers traveled back and forth across the Hudson on horseback.

The storms and ice kept Martha Washington in Philadelphia for the Christmas holiday, and she did not arrive in Morristown until the first week of January. Fearful for her safety on the treacherous roads, her husband had sent aides with a huge sleigh to transport her from Philadelphia. He was eager to see her for several reasons. He had been given the large two-story home of Mrs. Theodosia Ford as his winter headquarters. Mrs. Ford's husband, an army officer, had died during the general's last stay in Morristown in 1777. It was a large and spacious home that sat on a small knoll on the northeastern part of town, but Washington had more aides now than he had brought in 1777, and they filled up the entire house.

As always, Washington kept just one room for himself, an eighteen-square-foot bedroom on the second floor, and used a twelve-square-foot room at the rear of the first floor of the home for his office. The tiny room could only hold one large desk—the general's—a smaller one for an aide, and one or two wooden chairs. His aides slept in the other bedrooms upstairs, and Mrs. Ford and her family lived in the parlor downstairs. It was a madhouse of people who continually found themselves in each other's way.

George needed Martha to restore some order to the living conditions in the house, and he wanted her to take Mrs. Ford under her wing. His gracious hostess was trying to raise an entire family in one room. The Ford mansion was one of very few in the country that had a kitchen housed in the residence. The Ford kitchen took up nearly the entire back third of the house, but it was jammed with yet more aides using its tables and counters as desks. Meetings were held there too; decisions were made as morning eggs cooked.

Most of all, the general needed his wife to listen to him as he agonized over his numerous problems, troubles that had plagued him throughout the war but reached a crescendo in snow-covered Morristown. He had little administrative help because six of his eleven generals were either sick or had gone home on furloughs. The work of the missing generals fell upon him. Inflation had threatened to strangle the army. It now took $30 in American scrip to equal one British pound sterling or Spanish dollar, triple the exchange rate of just three months earlier. The people did not trust the shrinking Continental scrip, and its value was further reduced when the British began counterfeiting it. Yet another food and clothing shortage crippled the army.

The troubles were so great that on December 15, a glum Washington wrote to Congress that "our prospects are infinitely worse than they have been at any period of the war. And that unless some expedient can be instantly adopted a dissolution of the army for want of subsistence is unavoidable." General Greene wrote to a friend that the relations with the residents in Morristown were so bad that he was afraid that "the people will pull us to pieces."

For the Washingtons, the winter in Morristown was a far cry from the previous winter in Middle Brook (today Bound Brook), New Jersey, in 1778–1779, just twenty miles south of Morristown.

The weather during the 1778–1779 winter had been exceptionally mild. Martha was apprehensive about leaving Nelly, pregnant again, but her son Jack, recently elected to the state legislature, assured her that he could take care of his wife (their third child, Eleanor, was born on March 31, 1779) and that his mother's place, as always, was at her husband's side.

The winter of 1778–1779 was so pleasant that Washington and his wife accepted an invitation from Congress to visit Philadelphia for seven weeks. The delegates wanted to hear his assessment of the war, listen to his plans for the future, and form closer bonds with him. He had never left camp for long periods of time before and was eager to accept the invitation. In Philadelphia, he and Martha were feted at numerous balls and parties. The Virginians, he in his resplendent uniform and she in her simple but elegant dresses, were the center of attention wherever they went.

In Middle Brook, Martha again organized her sewing circles, arranged dinner parties for the officers and their wives, visited the sick, and did whatever she could as the general's wife to help the cause. She had attended a dance that became legendary when a boisterous Kitty Greene challenged any young man at the dance to best her in a dance marathon. Martha was stunned, and very pleased, when the only man who could match the energetic and fleet-footed Kitty was her husband, George. Not only did the commander in chief outdance all the younger men, he outdanced Kitty. She quit after three hours of nonstop dancing while Washington continued.

At Middle Brook, Washington continued his voluminous correspondence with Lund, his manager at Mount Vernon. The upkeep of his plantations worried him throughout the war because sales to Britain had halted and trade with the West Indies and other American cities had been reduced. Without Washington to oversee all work, the plantation might have fallen into ruin. George depended on Lund to keep it running. He sent Lund numerous letters throughout the war, with specific instructions on harvesting and rotating crops. Business did decline, but in Lund he knew he had a loyal manager, as he told him in 1775, "It is the greatest, indeed it is the only comfortable reflexion I enjoy on this score, to think that my business is in the hands of a person in whose integrity I have not a doubt and on whose care I can rely."

He grumbled about the plantations, declining business, and unsatisfactory output by slaves, but, in an odd way, his constant attention to Mount Vernon served as a much-needed escape from the worries of the war. He wrote about Mount Vernon, discussed it with other generals and public figures, and yearned to return to his beloved farms when the war ended.

Much of Martha's time during that winter was taken up by fretting about Jack and Nelly and the upcoming birth. She pleaded with them to send her more letters with news of their family, friends, and neighbors, and to tell her what they knew about the British in the South. She demanded to know where Jack and Nelly were spending the winter, whether at Mount Vernon or their plantation at Abingdon.

"[In] the last letter from Nelly she says both children have been very ill; they were she hoped getting better. If you do not write to me I will not write to you again 'til I get letters from you. Let me know how all friends below are; they have forgot to write to me, I believe. Remember me to all inquiring friends," she wrote her son, adding with a snide remark that she purchased presents for Jack's children but did not know where to send them because Jack never told her where he lived.

George was angry at Jack, too. He had insisted that his son get as much education as possible, which he did not, in order to avoid poorly advised business dealings. Back in Virginia, Jack was making bad investments, paying little attention to the wildly fluctuating Continental currency, and selling his land for far less than it was worth. George chastised him for that, snapping about his "unfortunate sale of the York estate to Colonel Braxton for twenty thousand pounds which, I suppose, would now fetch one hundred thousand pounds."

⁓

In Morristown in the winter of 1779–1780, Washington pleaded for help from the locals, New Jersey legislators, and the governors of all the states, especially Thomas Jefferson in Virginia, who pledged "every last shilling" to the army. Individual governors sent him food, as did state officials. Congress ordered some states to increase their cattle and flour shipments. Every emergency was met with assistance, but every emergency seemed to be succeeded by another. A severe food shortage hit again at the end of December. Regional food administrators howled to Washington that they had no food and one officer, James Wadsworth, scoffed, "Like the Israelites, I have been ordered to make bricks out of straw." Washington was so desperate for food that he sent hundreds of horses to Pennsylvania for the rest of the winter and gave the men the animals' corn to eat.

Baron von Steuben arrived several weeks after most of the troops and was startled. He wrote to Governor George Clinton of New York, "I was extremely shocked. [It was] the greatest picture of misery that was ever seen, scarce a soldier among them who has sufficient [clothes] to cover his nakedness in this severe season."

Men began to sneak out of camp to steal food, kitchen utensils, clothing, and anything they could find from area farmers. Washington ordered a halt to this behavior, writing that that his men were "becoming a band of robbers [rather] than disciplined troops." But he looked the other way and let them do it. They had to keep themselves alive because the army could not. Finally, on January 3, the commander was told by Nathanael Greene that there was no more money left to purchase supplies and that the army had run out of food. The money for clothing had been depleted, too. Then, in the first week of January, a double blizzard hit New Jersey, dumping over four feet of snow on the ground. Accompanying winds created ten-foot-high drifts. Washington watched it fall from his headquarters windows and wrote in a weather diary he kept: "January 6: Snowing and sunshine alternately. Cold with the wind west and northwest and increasing. Night very stormy. The snow, which is general in eighteen inches deep, is much drifted. Roads almost impassable."

When the double storm ended, all of the highways leading in and out of Morristown were covered with between four- and ten-foot deep snow drifts. Even if food could somehow be found, it could never be transported through the drifts the blizzard had left. Everything seemed hopeless. General Greene wrote, "God have mercy upon us. We have little to hope for and everything to fear."

Undaunted, Washington had Greene call in the Morris County Freeholders, the county's governing body, and gave them an ultimatum. They had to convince farmers to sell the army all the cattle and food that they had or he would seize it at gunpoint and perhaps even declare martial law, something he did not want to do. He also asked the Freeholders to call out everyone, from the local militia to small children, to somehow clear the roads.

The Freeholders reacted quickly. Finally realizing the plight of the soldiers, they convinced hundreds of people to sell the army cattle and food. They persuaded hundreds more to get out their sleds and carriages to clear eight miles of highway so that the cattle herds could be driven to Morristown. Washington's ability to persuade the lawmakers, and the admiration of the residents for the general despite their continuing squabbles with the army and Congress, saved the army.

Martha went to work immediately upon her arrival in Morristown. She was aghast at the office kitchen. She told her husband that far more room was needed and, at her direction, he ordered the construction of three outbuildings. One held a large kitchen and dining room with a stone fireplace, the second was for offices, and the third was a stable for his horses and those of his officers.

Washington, at his wife's urging, pressured men to complete construction as soon as possible, despite the weather, and they did.

Next, she spent much of her time at the home loaned to Nathanael and Kitty Greene for the winter. Kitty was about to give birth to her fourth child following a difficult pregnancy, and Martha surely comforted her and was there at the birth of the baby. Kitty was ill and bedridden for weeks afterwards, and Martha certainly helped take care of her. Later in the winter she consoled Theodosia Ford when she learned that her son Jacob had been wounded in a skirmish with the British. Jacob came back to Morristown to recover; Martha helped Mrs. Ford nurse her injured son in her one-room apartment.

Mrs. Washington then went to work contacting the women who had been part of her sewing circle in the winter of 1777 and asked them to join her once again. They asked friends to join them, and the women met at the Ford mansion on a regular basis in their own small clothing factory.

She again helped organize dinner parties and receptions for the officers and their wives, resuming her cordial relations with women who lived in the area. Her parties—and her sparkling personality—cheered up everyone. Invitations to local couples for these parties were treasured and women sometimes sold their cattle to raise money to buy a new dress for the once-in-a-lifetime chance to meet George and Martha Washington. Those who did not attend were eager to get information about the Washingtons from those who did. David Thompson wrote that his mother "kept asking how Mrs. Washington carried herself and the color of the dress she wore—also, did she powder her hair—was her dress too short—did her petticoat show—what men were there."

Nothing seemed to bring Martha's husband out of the doldrums, though. He had never had to contend with so many problems at the same time, and they had taken their toll on him. He had always been stoic and grim, but in the winter of 1779–1780 he had become morose. Not only had his army nearly starved to death, but the single military campaign of the winter, an attack on Staten Island, New York, had failed badly.

Benedict Arnold, who would later betray his country, was found guilty of malfeasance during his one-year appointment as military governor of Philadelphia the previous year because he used army wagons to transport goods from ships he allowed to dock illegally. He was reprimanded by Washington in Morristown at the direction of a court-martial board. He reminded Arnold, whom he trusted, that "our profession is the character of all. Even the shadow of a fault tarnishes the luster of our finest achievements...You should have been guarded and temperate in your deportment." It was a letter that infuriated Arnold.

The general was faced with a string of small mutinies at his other army camps that winter and with a serious one in Morristown that he had to put down with force. He had always told close associates, and his wife, that he trembled at the news of mutiny among his starving and beleaguered troops because just one could trigger a long chain of them and bring about the dissolution of the army.

Washington had no recreational outlets for his despondency, either. The snow prevented him from taking his customary afternoon horseback rides through the countryside with Billy Lee and bodyguards. All he did was listen to aides tell him about more problems and stare out the window as yet more snow fell.

Martha knew that what her husband liked to do best was dance, and she decided that if she could get her husband back on the dance floor, it would raise his spirits. She remembered how much enjoyment he had received from dances in Middle Brook the previous winter, especially his three-hour marathon with Kitty Greene. There was nowhere to hold a dance, though. Morristown had no large public buildings whose chambers could be used for a dance floor. The parlor at the Ford's mansion had been turned into a tiny apartment for Mrs. Ford and her children. None of the local taverns were large enough.

Ever as inventive as her husband, Martha decided to use one of the large wooden food warehouses as a dance hall. The oversized building, erected recently to store food, had high ceilings, a flat dirt floor, and plenty of room. Men joked privately that there was plenty of room because there was no food. She found a local band that she invited to play, and officers were asked to buy tickets to the dance to pay for the musicians. She invited all the officers' wives who were in camp or who lived nearby, the local militia officers and their wives, and dozens of single women for unattached officers.

There were a half dozen dances that winter and they were great successes, even though some held following snowstorms drew small crowds. The highlight of the evening, of course, was watching the commander in chief dance. Even those who had seen him doing the Virginia reel and the Irish jig before still marveled at the agility and phenomenal endurance he displayed for such a large man. He could literally dance all night. As always, Martha did marches and minuets, and perhaps a reel or a jig, then sat down to chat with those in attendance while her husband continued to dance. He danced with Kitty Greene, Lucy Knox, and the wives of other officers, and then danced with the local women who had been invited. Their stories of the night they danced with George Washington were passed down through their families for generations.

The dances did pick up the spirits of the general, and the other men in camp were infected with toe tapping, too. Local militia members invited soldiers to their homes for parties that included meals, drinking, and dancing. Soldiers held dances in their huts, and did the jig to music provided by a single energetic fiddler. These dances improved the spirits of everyone, such as Lieutenant Erkuries Beatty, who wrote of himself and his friends, "We kicked up a hell of a dust."

Veterans of the war venerated George Washington, but they were just as admiring of Martha, who all people remembered fondly. "Greatly was she beloved in the army," wrote her grandson of his talks with soldiers who had met her. "Her many interecessions with the chief for the pardon of offenders, and her kindness to the sick and wounded, caused her annual arrival in camp to be hailed as an event that would serve to dissipate the gloom of the winter quarters."

Two people at all of the officers' dances were Alexander Hamilton and Betsy Schuyler, the winter camp's lovebirds. Betsy was the attractive daughter of General Phillip Schuyler, a wealthy New Yorker. She went to the Morristown camp to spend the winter, and there, after just a few days, met Hamilton, who had just turned twenty-two, and who was smitten with her. What followed was a courtship that was observed with great amusement by George and Martha Washington, who did all they could to spur the romance.

Martha was amused at Morristown, as she was throughout the war and in the years just after it, at the attempts of people to guess her age. She was certainly unhappy with English philosopher Charles Varlo after he wrote that she was "some few years older" than George. Frenchman Claude Blanchard was one of the few who guessed it correctly, writing in 1782, when she was fifty, that she was "about fifty years old." She was very pleased with the Marquis de Chastellux's estimate in 1783, when she was fifty-one, that she was "about forty or forty-five," and with John Hunter, who put her age at fifty in 1785, when she had just turned fifty-four. She was thrilled by Olney Winsor, who visited her in 1788, when she was fifty-seven, and wrote to his wife that she was "perhaps forty-five."

One thing that Martha despised at Morristown, as she had at all of the winter camps, were the constant drills that were held to practice the security guard's defense of George and Martha in a kidnapping attempt. George was not worried about being seized, and Martha was so unconcerned that she treated the drills as a joke.

In the winter of 1777, guards began the drills for the first time. At an alarm, dozens burst into the second floor of Arnold's Tavern to secure it. The Washingtons were taken to the middle of the room and surrounded. A closet full of muskets in that room was opened and the weapons handed to aides, who assisted in guarding the commander and his wife. Dozens of other soldiers surrounded the building and still more jammed their bodies into every available window to fire at kidnappers or act as shields to protect the Washingtons.

In the winter of 1779–1780, more drills were held. The security guard's nervousness about an abduction was so great that all of the one hundred and fifty life guards were ordered to camp in tents in front of Ford's mansion. More remained inside, so many that there was usually not a room Washington entered, besides his bedchamber, that did not have armed soldiers in it. The new drills called for the Washingtons to be removed from the house, surrounded by soldiers, and taken away on horseback to a home several miles away. Martha thought the whole process was ridiculous and when guards entered her bedchamber to begin the drills she would, local lore had it, toss the bedcovers over her head and scream in feigned fear. George would go through the house with a lantern and a smile to tell everyone there was a drill going on.

But there was a kidnapping attempt, a very serious one. General John Simcoe, head of the Queen's Rangers, took five hundred rangers and sneaked out of New York at night at the end of January. His plan was to use little-known roads to arrive unseen at Morristown and then simply overwhelm Washington's protectors, seize the general and his wife, and bring them back to London as prisoners of war.

The precautions that the Washingtons scoffed at saved them. Sentinels miles from Morristown spotted the rangers and sent word back to Ford's mansion. The guards immediately spirited the Washingtons away, probably to the home of an ironworks owner in Rockaway, seven miles west. Simcoe and his men were engaged at several points on their route and turned back, never getting within ten miles of Morristown. The Washingtons remained in Rockaway for several days and then returned to Morristown.

Thanks to the efforts of Washington, Greene, and help from Congress, governors, and local New Jersey farmers, the army made it through the winter of 1779–1780. There were severe setbacks, such as the fall of Charleston, South Carolina, in the spring. But there were triumphs, too. The Continental Army was attacked twice at Morristown by the British in early June, at the battles of Springfield, and, assisted by a huge militia turnout of nearly five thousand men, Washington's army was victorious in both.

Still, there was no end in sight for the Revolution. Every winter Washington dealt with the same food and clothing shortages. Each winter the American economy worsened. The British continued to be relentless in their determination to crush the Continental army.

As spring arrived in 1780, the commander was grim. He wrote his brother Jack a very personal letter and in it unloaded all of his frustrations. He told his brother that he could not get new recruits, that food was always scarce, and that the spirit of the people was weak. He charged that they "slumber and sleep" instead of assisting the troops of his army. He wound up on a sour note, telling his brother that America was bringing itself "to the brink of destruction."

Upon her return to Mount Vernon, Martha told others how distraught her husband seemed. "The poor general was so unhappy that it distressed me exceedingly," she wrote to her brother-in-law just after the battles of Springfield.

And the war droned on.

CHAPTER SIXTEEN

THE WORLD TURNED UPSIDE DOWN: YORKTOWN AND THE END OF THE REVOLUTION

W ord spread quickly through the farms, slave quarters, and overseers' cabins at Mount Vernon on the night of September 9, 1781—General Washington, along with a small group of men on horseback, had suddenly arrived in the darkness, without advance notice. Mrs. Washington had been told that her husband was on his way, but she never anticipated how quickly he and Billy Lee, with aide David Humphreys and a few soldiers trailing them, would get there. Martha must have raced down the staircase when she heard shouts of joy and the sound of men at the front door.

Much had changed since the last time the general had seen his beloved Mount Vernon. Nearly six years ago, on May 4, 1775, he rode off to join the delegates at the Second Continental Congress in Philadelphia. He had left Mount Vernon as just another delegate and a little-known businessman. Now, he returned as commander in chief of the American Army and one of the most famous men in the world. If all went right, he would soon make history by trapping Lord Cornwallis at Yorktown, a small community on the southern bank of Virginia's York River, defeat him, and take a major step toward triumph in the Revolution.

He was exhausted, but glad to be home, even if for just a few days. He needed all of the comfort that both his wife and Mount Vernon could provide; 1781 had been a difficult year. It was the first year that he had to run the army without Benedict Arnold, who had betrayed his country. (Throughout the rest of his life Washington always referred to him as "that traitor Arnold.") Another mutiny erupted at the Morristown winter camp in January of 1781. The violent uprising of fifteen hundred Pennsylvania troops, protesting the lack of food, clothing, and pay, was the most troublesome of the war. The mutineers, with cannon, traveled all the way to Princeton, seized the town, and threatened to march on Congress. Washington brokered a deal in which almost all the men were honorably discharged, received back pay, and were given needed clothing. A second mutiny a few weeks later was put down quickly, and the leaders were shot by a firing squad. The American dollar was still weak, recruiting troops was still difficult, and British commander Henry Clinton had just asked his home office for ten thousand more troops and yet more warships in his determination to put down the rebellion.

The British had solidified their hold on the southern states. Following the occupation of Charleston in the spring of 1780, the British captured Savannah, Georgia, and other smaller towns, aided by nearly five thousand armed and zealous loyalists from Virginia and the Carolinas. Against Washington's wishes, Congress named Horatio Gates as head of the southern wing of the Continental Army, and he was promptly defeated by British forces at Camden, South Carolina. Washington's choice, Nathanael Greene, then replaced Gates, rebuilt the army, and conducted a masterful cat-and-mouse campaign in which he sometimes defeated Cornwallis's forces, sometimes lost, and always retreated to fight another day, luring Cornwallis into trailing after him at enormous cost in supplies and men (the British lost one-quarter of their soldiers in the battle of Eutaw Springs alone). Cornwallis's raids, carried out by his callous cavalry leader, Colonel Banastre Tarleton, and Benedict Arnold, terrified the farmers of the South.

Groups of British soldiers and their newfound Indian allies often rushed into farmhouses and threatened the inhabitants at gunpoint. One South Carolina woman wrote of an invasion by the Redcoats and their Indians, "I expected nothing but death, to live or die, but could not bear the thought of being murdered by savages."

. Tired of Greene's game, Cornwallis occupied Williamsburg in the summer of 1781 and then moved his army of six thousand men and a small fleet of ships to Yorktown, where he remained in September.

Washington feigned an attack on New York, tricking the British into heavily fortifying the city. Then, with a combined French and American force of eighteen thousand men and one hundred cannons, his largest army of the war, he moved south to face Cornwallis. His forces surrounded the British general by land at the same time that the French fleet under Admiral Comte Francois de Grasse cordoned off the York River where it entered Chesapeake Bay, making it impossible for the Redcoats to escape.

Washington was joined at Mount Vernon the following day by Viscount Donatien Marie Rochambeau, the head of the French forces in America, and another French general, Chastellux, who spent most of September 10 and 11 planning the attack on Yorktown with him. They were all joined by Jack Custis, his wife, Nelly, and their four children, whom George had never met, along with cousin Lund Washington, his estate manager, and some workers. The soldiers were hungry and exhausted and slumped into chairs in the new, high-ceilinged dining room, built in George's absence. The two-story south wing, where their new upstairs bedroom was located, and his new office downstairs were also new. The general and his aides scattered their food plates, bowls of fruit, and glasses of wine, and looked at the maps they had spread out upon the wide dining room table.

Living at Mount Vernon with the general for a few days was a thrilling experience for the soldiers. They wrote home of the elegance of the commander's home, the friendliness of his wife, and the ease with which the Washingtons housed, fed, and entertained a houseful of strangers. As the officers discussed Yorktown in the dining room on the evening of September 10, thousands of French and American troops were arriving or on their way to Williamsburg, near Yorktown, and Admiral de Grasse's navy was sailing into the Chesapeake. Henry Knox and his artillerists were collecting cannon. Washington and Rochambeau left in a hurry on September 12 and headed south towards Williamsburg. A grinning Washington sent Lafayette, already there, a humorous note just before they departed Mount Vernon: "I hope you will keep Lord Cornwallis safe…until we arrive."

When the soldiers left, they took Jack Custis with them, much against the wishes of his mother and wife. Jack had shown little interest in the Revolution and, as the father of four small children, was needed at home. Now, after seeing his stepfather again and being surrounded by generals and soldiers talking eagerly about the campaign against Cornwallis, he decided to join the army once more as a "civilian aide" to his stepfather. No one could talk him out of it. His mother and wife were afraid he would be killed or wounded, of course, but the general apparently told them that he would make sure that Jack would not be in harm's way. George appointed him as one of his aides, kissed his wife good-bye, and took Jack and the rest of his small entourage to Yorktown.

His wife prayed that her husband could win a great victory there and that it would finally end the war. She was as tired of the Revolution as every wife and mother who sent their loved ones into the army. These last few years had been long and hard on both George and Martha—and frustrating because the British showed no signs of letting up in the crusade to subdue the Americans.

The prayers of Martha, and many other Americans, were answered at Yorktown. Following a heavy cannon bombardment by French and American gunners, Cornwallis agreed to surrender on October 17, and on October 20 the British Army marched out of Yorktown between two long lines of French and American troops. Ironically, the tune the British military band played was

"The World's Turned Upside Down." Cornwallis, astounded that his army had been defeated and that the loss might mean the end of the war, refused to come out with his troops and remained at his headquarters, "sick."

Throughout the siege of Yorktown, General Washington and his officers made certain that Jack felt useful, riding about delivering messages and attending meetings far from the front lines. George had protected Jack from enemy fire, as he had promised Jack's mother, but he could not protect Jack from the diseases that infested all army camps. His son came down with "camp fever," probably typhoid, a week or so before the final surrender and became very ill. Jack was afraid he was going to die and told friends in camp that he had to hang on until the British surrendered. He was carried to the parade route and planned to sit on a horse to watch with the other officers, but he could not summon enough energy to do so. Soldiers placed him in a carriage on the roadside and there, half sitting up, half slouching, very ill, he watched the British Army surrender to his stepfather.

Custis faded fast, and the next day soldiers moved him to the home of his uncle, Burwell Bassett, in Eltham, thirty miles west, where he had visited so often throughout his life. He was cared for by Dr. James Craik, who had cared for George Washington and his family for a quarter of a century.

At Mount Vernon, Martha had prayed for her husband and son and for the safety of Henry Knox, whose very pregnant wife, Lucy, was staying with her. Letters arrived nearly daily reporting the progress of the Yorktown siege. Mrs. Washington was not told until much later that a cannonball had exploded within yards of her husband; miraculously, he was not killed. It was yet another of the many brushes with death he endured throughout the Revolution.

Then came the terrible news that Jack, her last child, was dying. Martha and Nelly rode to Eltham in a carriage. Nelly was distraught, and a composed Martha ordered the driver to travel as quickly as possible. Upon arrival, Martha was shaken by how ill Jack appeared in his bed. She prayed for him at his bedside. For days, Martha kept telling Nelly that their prayers would save his life. Jack's condition deteriorated quickly. Finally, certain he was going to pass away, Martha sent an express courier to Williamsburg to find her husband and bring him to Eltham.

Washington opened the letter and was shaken. His diary for that day stopped in mid-sentence; that might have been when he received word of his son's condition. He terminated all army business and summoned his aide Humphreys and Billy Lee. The three mounted right away and galloped as quickly as they could to Eltham, the general hoping that he would be in time to say farewell to his stepson, whom he had come to love so dearly ever since the day he first met him when little Jacky was three years old.

The general, riding hard all night, did make it in time. He arrived after midnight, several hours before Jack passed on, and had his chance to say good-bye, along with Martha, who was despondent over the death of her son. Nelly was now a widow with four small children to care for. George and Martha, who summoned up great courage to keep her composure, comforted Nelly on the following morning when Jack Custis was laid to rest at Eltham.

Several days later, after sending word to camp that he was detained because of the death of his son, General Washington accompanied Nelly and Martha back to Mount Vernon. Death haunted the Washingtons that terrible autumn and winter. George's brother Sam died that fall. Within months, George's brother-in-law, Fielding Lewis, a patriot who had nearly gone bankrupt operating a small arms factory for the army, died, too.

There was mourning at Mount Vernon, Abingdon, Eltham, and at the homes of all the relatives of the Washingtons and the Calverts in the days after Jack's death, but joy swept the nation as Americans celebrated the capture of Cornwallis. The Liberty Bell was rung continuously all night in Philadelphia, and thousands emerged from their homes to form a candlelight vigil. Bells tolled in nearly every church in the country the entire day that the news was received. Boston was illuminated by huge bonfires. Businesses closed and farms were shut down when couriers galloping down highways shouted as loudly as they could, "Cornwallis is taken!

Cornwallis is taken!"

In London, Prime Minister North could barely contain his anger when news of the historic defeat reached him. "Oh God, it is over!" he yelled loudly when he received word of the Yorktown defeat. "It is all over."

⁓

Yorktown did not end the war, though. There were no more major battles, but it took two long years for the Americans and British to finally conclude a peace treaty that gave America independence. Martha spent each of those winters in New Windsor, Ramapo, and Rocky Hill, in New Jersey, with George, waiting for the end; she also spent several months with him in Philadelphia in the winter of 1781–1782.

Martha and George worried about the safety of Mount Vernon and the slave community there. In 1780 there was another attempt by the British to shell their home. This time, Lund Washington met officers from the ship and talked them out of it, offering them wine, food, and other gifts. George and Martha were furious with Lund, and George sharply reprimanded him, telling him with real bitterness that he would rather have the enemy burn Mount Vernon to the ground than to have anyone at his home grovel before the Crown.

Finally, in 1783, word came that the peace treaty to formally end the American Revolution was about to be signed. Certain that the end was truly at hand, Washington made a decision that would stun the entire world—he would resign from the army, leave public life, and go back to Mount Vernon and his farming. Few could believe that the popular leader of the Revolution, whom so many had insisted be crowned a king, would walk away from power. King George III told friends that if Washington did indeed retire, he would be "the greatest man in the world."

Washington assured friends that he would resign, telling Lafayette in a tender letter that he was finished with public life and looked forward to days under "my own vine and my own fig tree, free from the bustle of camp," adding, "I will move gently down the stream of life until I sleep with my fathers."

He wrote a soaring farewell to the troops, who had borne so much with him:

"The glorious task for which we first flew to arms being thus accomplished, the liberties of our country being fully acknowledged and firmly secured by the smiles of Heaven on the purity of our cause, and the honest exertions of a feeble people determined to be free, against a powerful nation disposed to oppress them, and the character of those who have persevered through every extremity of hardship, suffering, and danger, being immortalized by the illustrious appellations of the *Patriot Army,* nothing now remains but for the actors of this mighty scene to preserve a perfect unvarying consistency of character through the very last act, to close the drama with applause, and to retire from the military theater with the same approbation of angels and men which has crowned all of their former virtuous actions."

When announcement of the formal signing of the treaty arrived in November, he made plans, along with New York governor George Clinton, to march into New York on the day the British left as a very visible gesture that the Americans had won the war. It would be a parade attended by thousands of New Yorkers and people from nearby New Jersey, with bands, banners, and ceremonies. A few days later, thousands thronged to the shores of the Hudson to watch a spectacular fireworks display in the general's honor. Washington's retirement schedule called for an emotional farewell dinner with his closest officers at Fraunce's Tavern in lower Manhattan, and then a long ride to Annapolis, Maryland, the latest home of the Continental Congress, where he would formally resign from the army.

The people would not let the commander proceed with his plans. His carriage was stopped at nearly every town it passed through as residents insisted on holding dinners for him. His passage through any small village was slowed and then stopped when thousands of people filled the streets, some having traveled a hundred miles or more just to see him. What was supposed to have been a quiet ride through Philadelphia turned into one of the largest celebrations in the city's history. Units of Light Horse cavalry accompanied his small entourage into and out of the city. Washington was given a nighttime torchlight parade attended by nearly all of the city's residents. As his carriage drove down the streets, all the bells in the city peeled, and hundreds of cannon—on land and on ships anchored in the Delaware River—boomed. Wilmington, Delaware, was shut down for two days so that people could attend a party and parade for the general; dozens of bonfires were kept burning all night. At Annapolis, a huge dinner and ball was thrown the night before his resignation, where the general danced with just about all of the more than three hundred women present.

The handsome new brick Maryland statehouse was packed for the resignation itself the following day, December 23, 1783. He stood in the well of the large assembly hall and faced the hundreds wedged into it, including many of his old soldiers, who were in uniform. He told the crowd, "Having now finished the work assigned me, I retire from the great theater of action; and bidding an affectionate farewell to this august body under whose orders I have so long acted, I here offer my commission and take my leave of all the employment of public life."

It was an emotional moment. Most of those present wept. Army aide James McHenry, as emotionally overwrought as the others, said that "the past, the present, the future, the manner, the occasion, all conspired to render it a spectacle inexpressibly solemn and affecting." Then, when Washington ended his short speech, everyone stood and roared their approval of him.

These were memorable moments for George Washington, and historical moments for the new nation, moments that everyone assumed would be shared by his wife, who perhaps might be attended by the special unit formed to protect her in the war, Lady Washington's Dragoons. But Martha wanted no part of the journey south and the parades, ceremonies, and balls at Annapolis. She was as disdainful of public life at the end of the war as she had been at its beginning. Mrs. Washington had left the army camp in Rocky Hill in the spring of 1783, as she always did, and returned to Mount Vernon by way of Philadelphia. It is not known whether or not George asked her to meet him in New York for the triumphant ride to Annapolis, or whether she wanted him to bask in the glory by himself, but she remained in Virginia.

Washington wanted to hurry home from Annapolis to his wife and Mount Vernon, where he planned to live out his days as a farmer. He mounted his horse and, with Billy Lee and one other rider, headed south for Mount Vernon, eager to be home for Christmas. The men rode as fast as they could to the Potomac River, crossed on a ferry at Alexandria, and then traveled on to his plantation.

George Washington arrived late on Christmas Eve, in time for the holiday. He was greeted by Martha, Lund, overseers, and dozens of his people on the front lawn as he rode up the long driveway. They cheered his arrival, just as thousands had greeted him throughout America on his way to Annapolis. He surely appreciated this reception just as much as he had that of the people jamming the streets of New York and Philadelphia.

The next morning George Washington rose just before dawn, as he always did, and walked down the staircase to his new office, where he plunged into the business books and ledgers he had not seen in years. He and Martha were now officially retired from public life and were certain that they would live out their years with friends and family at Mount Vernon as others ran the brand-new United States.

They were wrong.

CHAPTER SEVENTEEN

A LONG-AWAITED RETIREMENT TO MOUNT VERNON AND A SECOND FAMILY

s soon as he put his blue-and-buff-colored military uniform into his closet, George Washington plunged into the business affairs of Mount Vernon and its farms. He imagined their management would consume the rest of his life. Little had been done to complete the work that he had begun on the plantations before he was named the commander in chief of the army eight long years ago. His wife Martha and cousin Lund had certainly tried to follow his frequent and detailed instructions for the development of the farms, which were conveyed to them by couriers from his army camps throughout the war, but they were simply unable to do so. They had run out of money and many workers had left.

Mount Vernon's prewar agricultural success had collapsed during George's absence. The war ended any chances of profit for the land the Washingtons owned, and neither George nor Martha would raise money by selling their slaves because they did not want to break up the families of their workers.

The main house did have a south wing, containing George's library, because workers finished construction on it just before the Revolution commenced in 1775. The exterior of the north wing, but not its interior, had been finished after four years of labor, but the walls needed painting and the remainder of the flooring had to be laid down. The high, white cupola that sat on top of the old roof leaked, and a brand-new one had to be installed. This infuriated Washington. Calling the worker in charge of it "a rascal," he asked Lund how the man, "after one experiment could not tell what kind of shingles were necessary to prevent a common roof from leaking?...Besides ruining the plaster within, I shall have the furniture all spoiled; and remain in a scene of continual vexation and trouble till it is done."

Work was started on the large, columned portico that stretched the length of the rear of the mansion facing the Potomac, a dazzling architectural accomplishment by Washington, but not completed. Other rooms in the ever-growing home were in shambles. Work had yet to be completed on the interior walls in the lovely high-ceilinged banquet room. The recently returned Washington suspected he would have to accommodate the numerous guests who would come to visit each year. In fact, the banquet room was in such bad shape that the wide windows were covered by huge planks of wood nailed over the frames to keep out the wind. The icehouse, whose construction the general had overseen by letters mailed from three hundred miles away, was badly built and had to be torn down. The greenhouse was constructed according to his exact specifications, but when Washington saw it he realized that the facility was too small.

Throughout Mount Vernon and at the Washingtons' other farms, many buildings, such as stables and woodsheds, were in disrepair. Fences had fallen down over the years and needed to be replaced. The wooden gutters on the main house leaked and had to be removed in favor of copper ones. Hundreds of the tiny stones in his majestic front driveway had come undone and were scattered from eight years of neglect, and sturdier stones had to be found.

The completion of the old architectural plan was enhanced by additional designs for the mansion and grounds by George himself. He was determined to put his personal stamp on the new plans for the plantation, just as he had on the original ones.

He knew the renovations would be costly, so he tried to save money wherever he could. He wanted to plant hundreds of new trees around the mansion to improve its look, but he did not want to buy or import them. Instead, he rode throughout his farms to find the trees he desired and had workers uproot them and replant them near the main house. Neighbor George Mason allowed him to take some of his guelder rose and Persian jasmine trees as a gift. New York's Governor Clinton sent some New York linden trees (lime) and General Benjamin Lincoln gave him three spruce pines and two fir trees; willow trees were moved from Jack's plantation. Bushes were grown in a garden at Mount Vernon and moved elsewhere on the estate. Everything was planted with precision, such as the linden trees, which were put in the ground as the third tree in each row to give the grounds a symmetrical look. Berry trees, too, were planted in perfectly straight rows. Large lawns were seeded and reseeded. Instead of building new garden houses near the mansion, he worked with laborers to move two existing buildings there.

The newly retired general found that many of the things he was certain would bring him great joy in his twilight years brought him endless headaches instead. He spent an enormous amount of time on three commercial land projects close to his heart that went nowhere. The first was turning central Virginia's Dismal Swamp, thousands of acres of soggy marshland, into salable land. It was a glorious reclamation dream that he had nurtured for twenty years; it failed. The second was the construction of a lengthy canal connecting the Potomac River with the Ohio Territory that he was certain would become a busy commercial waterway for trade, just as the Erie Canal did much later. He spent several years and thousands of hours of work on the canal, but the waterway never materialized. His third great scheme was to sell tens of thousands of acres of land in the Ohio area that he had purchased to a wave of settlers he was convinced would leave the crowded Atlantic coast and flood the region right after the war. They did not, and the land sat for years.

The general looked forward to success for the Society of Cincinnati, an organization of Continental Army officers formed at the end of the war to honor Washington and themselves, with membership extended to their firstborn sons and, in years to come, to the first son of each firstborn son. The rather charming generational membership was not embraced by the public and, in fact, most Americans saw the society as a snobbish, effete group of officers who had nothing better to do with their time. Realizing how unpopular the Society had become in just its first year, Washington talked the officers out of the firstborn membership plan and then practically disavowed the group.

Upon his return from the army, he realized that Mount Vernon had not only never turned a profit during the years he was away, but that the worth of his assets in homes, buildings, animals, ships, and funds had been practically cut in half. Worse yet, he owed money to many people. He had borrowed cash from several lenders to buy land tracts and had not paid back any of it. He had been loaned several thousand dollars by New York's Governor Clinton at the end of the war. He owed his cousin Lund Washington eight years in back wages (he settled his account with Lund by giving him several hundred acres of land, along with some money), and he owed dozens of workers thousands of dollars in back pay. He groaned to a friend in 1785, "The fact is that I am really in want of money."

And while his efforts to raise and breed some exotic animals succeeded, others failed because Mount Vernon was not a suitable habitat for them. Several rare pheasants and partridges given to him as gifts died. His dream of breeding buffalo collapsed, too, when he could not procure enough to start a herd.

The Washingtons were deluged with visitors when they moved back to Virginia. Lafayette made a pilgrimage to America and spent several weeks living at Mount Vernon, rehashing the war and fretting about the political trouble in his native France that would soon lead to the French Revolution. Former congressmen and army officers made the trip to see their old commander. Political writers from the U.S. and Europe visited him seeking his advice. Painters, such as Charles Willson Peale, and sculptors, such as the Frenchman Jean Antoine Houdon, spent time there working on paintings and busts of him. (Houdon postponed the chance to work with Russian empress Catherine the Great for far more money.) At times, the plantation seemed overrun with princes, counts, and dukes from every European country, all eager to meet America's national hero.

Most visitors, though, were ordinary citizens. The general had become one of the most famous men in the world, and people from all over America drove wagons or rode horses to Mount Vernon to see him. Prior to the war, the couple received just over four hundred guests a year, but after his resignation from the army, that number increased to over four hundred a year; in one twelve-month period they entertained over six hundred guests.

Supervising the feeding and entertainment for all of these guests became such a great burden that Martha could not handle the responsibility and was forced to hire a house manager to assist her. The members of the domestic staff soon found themselves overworked, too. The costs of food and drink for these hundreds of guests was prodigious and the Washingtons, already strapped for money, could barely afford it.

Newly arrived guests thought nothing of riding off into the fields to find the general. They would discover him in his wide-brimmed hat or under an umbrella attached to his saddle in warm weather for protection, usually working with the slaves. They would then introduce themselves, constantly interrupting work.

George often returned home from the fields in midafternoon to find unannounced guests waiting for him. Many men who fought for him in the Revolution stopped in, sometimes bringing their families. All of his visitors acted as if they were making a pilgrimage to Mecca to see the Great Man. He was usually friendly, but sometimes he was so tired from work, and equally tired of guests, that he offered visitors a brief hello and then closeted himself in his study, declining to join them at dinner or for drinks. Many people thought that the overburdened Great Man was rather aloof. One 1788 visitor, Francis Vander Kemp, wrote that "there seemed to me to skulk somewhat of a repulsive coldness [about Washington]—not congenial with my mind, under a courteous demeanor." But the man's disappointment in the commander in chief was quickly alleviated by his wife, who often took on George's duty as host. Vander Kemp happily continued, "I was infinitely better pleased by the unassuming modest gentleness of the Lady [Martha] than with the conscious superiority of her consort."

Public officials and politicians were engaged by Washington in long discussions on the problems of the new United States, but general visitors were not and that disappointed them. Some, in fact, recalled that the general was often rather boring in his dinner conversations, drifting off into long explanations of why it took so long to travel on particular roadways or assessing the total length of the Potomac River. His mind would sometimes drift off, and he would stare vacantly across the room while he and Martha were talking to people. His wife had to grab him by his coat buttons, pull on them, and say "George!" to bring him back into the conversation.

But there was no doubt in anyone's mind that the general loved Mount Vernon and thoroughly enjoyed rebuilding and expanding his home and grounds there. He loved his afternoon riding and his fox hunts. He was once again enjoying his sprawling lands and his magnificent home.

Perhaps the biggest reason that George and Martha were so happy in retirement was their brand-new family. The Washingtons had made a bold decision to care for their grandchildren, Nelly and George Washington Parke Custis, or "Wash," and brought them to Mount Vernon to live. When Jack died in 1781, their daughter-in-law, Nelly, was left a single mother to four children:

Elizabeth, born in 1776; Martha, '77; Eleanor (Nelly), '79; and Wash, '81. The decision to take in grandchildren was not unusual at that time. Americans died young and many women died in childbirth, leaving a single parent to raise a number of children. The surviving parents often could not care for many offspring, especially if they did not remarry. Some parents found that they had so many children that they could not cope with the responsibility and asked their parents, or other relatives, to raise some of them. In addition to giving them a good home, it became the practice for grandparents to raise some of their grandchildren if the mother was willing. This made it possible for the grandchildren to become direct legal heirs of the grandparents, which secured their financial future.

Nelly was agreeable to the arrangement because she loved her in-laws, and knew that her children would be raised properly and inherit a small fortune. She must have understood, too, that as George Washington's children they would, as adults, gain entry to many social and educational institutions barred to most Americans. Besides, the two children had practically grown up at Mount Vernon during the war, and Nelly lived close enough to see them often.

Nelly, a beautiful young woman, remarried a rather dour local doctor, David Stuart, in 1783, two years after the death of her husband. She moved to his modest plantation at Hope Park, ten miles west of Alexandria. The Washingtons and Nelly maintained a close friendship all of their lives; she and her husband visited Mount Vernon, and their children, often. Nelly and Wash visited their mother at her home frequently and sometimes, when they were reluctant to go, were forced to visit by Martha, who never wanted Nelly to think that she had somehow lost her children.

Martha smothered Wash, whom she sometimes called "Tub," with love. She frequently wrote to friends about his health and well-being and often referred to him in affectionate terms, as she did in a letter to her niece Fanny Bassett, to whom she wrote, "My dear children have all been very well, til today my pretty little dear boy complains of a pain in his stomach."

Martha bragged about him constantly, telling her niece Fanny when she was away that "Tub is the same clever boy you left him. He sometimes says why don't you send for Cousin—you know he makes himself unhappy about absent friends." Her friends bragged to Mrs. Washington about how smart young Wash seemed to be. Elizabeth Powel wrote to her of "our little favorite, Master Custis," and told her she was sending the boy a book she bought for him. "I shall distrust my skill if he is not a child of penetration and genius. He has conciliating manners like your charming little Eleanor."

Throughout her life, Nelly complained that Martha fawned over her brother. "Grandmamma always spoiled Washington," she wrote to a friend. Nelly had to meet different standards. Just as Martha had at first been strict with her daughter Patsy, and lenient with Jacky, now, with her second family, she was hard on Nelly and easy on Wash.

The children loved Martha as if she were their natural mother. As she grew up, Nelly always told visitors and friends how much she loved her grandparents, especially Martha. She put it best in 1795, when she was sixteen, and had to leave them for the first time in her life (they sent her home early to Mount Vernon while they stayed in Philadelphia). She wrote to Elizabeth Bordley Gibson, a friend, of Martha that "it is impossible to love anyone more than I love her." In another letter a week later, she wrote, "I have gone through the greatest trial I ever experienced—parting with my beloved Grandmamma. This is the first separation for any time, since I was two years old. Since my father's death, she has been more than a mother to me and the president the most affectionate of fathers. I love them more than anyone."

Both Nelly and Wash liked Mount Vernon. They enjoyed the company of a whole new generation of children that lived in the Alexandria area, just as their parents had thirty years before. They, too, played with the children of slaves, as their parents had, and each had a slave to attend them as they grew up.

By the time Nelly was a teenager, Mount Vernon had been pretty much completed by her grandfather. She loved to walk and ride about it in spring and summer, but as a teenager and a young woman she found winters there hauntingly beautiful and full of romance. She wrote to a friend of one winter that "the trees, grass, houses [are] all covered with ice...the ecstasy from seeing all nature dressed in snow and ice...The appearance is beautiful and the river looks so wide and desolate—the Maryland shore so bleak and sublimely horrifying that I am quite delighted and in better trim than ever to enjoy the beauty of *Ossians Poems* and *The Mysteries of Udolpho* [a romantic novel]."

In another letter, Nelly remembered her childhood at Mount Vernon with deep nostalgic yearning, writing of "the dear scenes of our youth...where the sun always appears to shine as it did in our hearts in those happy days," and wrote of her grandmother Martha, "I had the most perfect model of female excellence ever with me, who acted the part of a tender and devoted parent, loving me as only a mother can love, and never approving in me what she disapproved in others."

That youth was full of play, but it was also full of education. Patsy had died at seventeen and Jack had never enjoyed school, and now George was once again determined that his new "children" benefit from a superior education. Tutors were brought in to live at Mount Vernon to teach Wash and Nelly (the girl was very attentive but Wash was not) in both academics and the finer things in life. They learned writing, reading, mathematics, and geography; music, dancing, and drawing; plus a foreign language. As Nelly grew into a teenager and traveled with George and Martha when Washington was elected president, she also received lengthy training at select girls' schools in manners, dress, sewing, singing, and playing the harpsichord. She grew into a lovely, educated, and refined woman.

From the day he arrived at Mount Vernon, young, headstrong Wash was the source of constant agitation to the general. Wash was an impulsive child who, at an early age, showed a disdain for books and education and a love of playing and later, as a young man, horses, gambling, and women—just like his father. Washington had him work with tutors and later, just as he did with

Jack, sent him off to the best boarding schools, hoping for the best and expecting the worst.

This second family not only gave new life to Martha, who loved children dearly, but also to George. They had been once again given the responsibilities of raising small children—at an advanced age—and, despite the difficulties, that helped to make the bonds between them even stronger. Washington enjoyed serving as a father and always referred lovingly to his various families throughout his life. There was his personal family of Martha, Patsy, and Jacky. He always referred to his slaves as "his family" and called his staff in the army "my family." It was natural then, when Jacky died, that he wanted to start yet another family with Wash and Nelly.

This constant need to be a father, the head of a family, may have led him to overcome his reluctance to become the first president so that he could view the nation as yet another of his families. In fact, when Henry Knox asked him to chair the Constitutional Convention, he told him that his work at the convention, and in the army, would "doubly entitle you to the glorious Republican epithet, 'the Father of Your Country.'" He was happy in all of his families, but very, very happy as the grandfather to Wash and Nelly, as was Martha. When Nelly was older she wrote of those years that one of the clearest memories she had was of the "perfect harmony" that existed between George and Martha.

The commander in chief told everyone that he was a tough disciplinarian as a new father to his grandchildren. Some agreed and some did not. Wash wrote that his grandfather was tough and that as a child he and Nelly were "much in awe of him, although he was kind in his manner. [We] felt [we] were in the presence of one who was not be trifled with." Yet visitors saw the general as an easy mark for his grandchildren. Lafayette wrote of Wash at age three that he was "a very little gentleman with a feather in his hat, holding fast to one finger of the good general's hand, which (so large that hand!) was all the little fellow could manage."

There was an extended family at Mount Vernon, too. Several other people lived with the Washingtons for long periods of time, at their insistence, perhaps to make up for the losses of Patsy and Jack. Martha's niece Fanny, the daughter of Anna Maria Bassett, resided with them for over a year and then married George's nephew, George Augustine Washington, whom she met there. Harriet Washington, the daughter of George's late brother Sam, stayed there for more than four years. George and Martha took her in, and paid for her two brothers' education, because their father died nearly broke. Patty Dandridge, the daughter of Martha's brother, moved in when her father died and remained for over a year. On and off, other nieces and nephews stayed for weeks at a time (the Washingtons helped to fund educations for various nieces and nephews and, when they were older, gave them money for land and homes). In addition, there was William Shaw, hired as Washington's secretary. He was replaced in 1786 by Tobias Lear, twenty-three, the son of a sea captain. He lived at Mount Vernon and worked for the general for years, earning his trust and confidence. The general said he was "a genteel, well-behaved young man."

Despite appearing bored to some, and overly interested in public affairs to others, George Washington was determined to remain in retirement. He also remembered that his brother, father, grandfather, and most other men in his family had died in their forties. Just after the Revolution ended, two of his best friends from the war, Pennsylvania governor Joseph Reed and General Nathanael Greene, passed away at a relatively young age. The general had escaped death on several occasions during the war and now, in his mid-fifties, felt he was living on borrowed time. He wanted to make the most of the few leisure years he believed he had left.

A letter to Lafayette reflected these feelings. He wrote to his wartime friend, "I called to mind the days of my youth and found they had long since fled to return no more; that I was now descending the hill I had been fifty-two years climbing and that tho' I was blessed with a good constitution, I was of a short-lived family and might soon expect to be entombed in the dreary mansions of my fathers...I have had my day."

Despite his repeated plea that he had retired from public life, Washington kept a close eye on the events that unfolded after his resignation from the army. He read ten newspapers a week, kept up a busy correspondence with many key public figures, and invited dozens of governors, congressmen, and state legislators to Mount Vernon.

All of them worried about the rule by the Continental Congress, operating under the Articles of Confederation, that had been in place since the last few years of the Revolution. Under the Articles, Congress ran the country with a figurehead president, elected by members of Congress, without a judiciary. Congress could pass laws, but not enforce them, and it had no power to levy taxes. It depended on the states to do so. In short, Congress was powerless.

On the banks of the Potomac, the general fretted with leaders about the wobbly new government which seemed assaulted daily by troubling events. The navies of foreign countries took advantage of the weak government and seized American merchant ships and seamen. Britain refused to evacuate the northwest territories, as it had agreed to do in the 1783 peace treaty. For a time, Spain closed the Mississippi River to American shipping in a political dispute. The United States was charged inordinately high rates on loans by European banks. State governments ignored the federal government, county governments ignored state legislatures, and cities ignored them all. Huge and often divided state assemblies, some with over four hundred members, accomplished little. Individual states feuded with each other.

The most worrisome event was Shays's Rebellion, a 1786 uprising led by Daniel Shays of Massachusetts, a former Revolutionary War officer. With one thousand men, he protested state taxes by seizing a federal arsenal. The rebellion had to be put down with force. Shays's Rebellion shook the general. "Good God!" he exclaimed in a letter to John Jay, "we are fast verging to anarchy and confusion." He sent out numerous letters on the rebellion, telling everyone what he wrote to Henry Knox, that "if there exists not a power to check" people like Shays, whom he called a "desperate character," what "security has a man for life liberty or property?" He told Knox that "we are far gone in everything ignoble and bad," and that the political situation was "combustible in every state, which a spark might set fire to." He complained bitterly to former army aide David Humphreys that mob rule had taken over and that the "federal government is nearly, if not quite at a stand [and] no one will deny [it]."

The tax uprising was probably the final nudge that Washington needed to return to public life, but he had been very worried about the struggling republic for years. As early as 1784, he had written to John Jay that "our affairs are drawing rapidly to a crisis," and told him in blunt language "to be fearful in investing in Congress, constituted as that body is with ample authorities for national purposes, appears to me the very climax of popular absurdity and madness." He had warned people during the last months of the war that America was becoming a country "directed by thirteen heads," for the thirteen colonies, and worried that without a strong federal government it might collapse.

Washington was under unrelenting pressure from his wartime friends to become involved in politics. John Jay had been urging him to become a public leader of some kind since 1786, when he wrote to him of events, "I am persuaded that you cannot view them with the eye of an unconcerned spectator."

The general finally relented. He rode from Mount Vernon to Philadelphia in 1787 to serve as the president of the Constitutional Convention. His welcome to Philadelphia in early May, in bad weather, would have delighted a European monarch. The general was met several miles from the city by a cavalry that escorted him into town. As they entered Philadelphia, batteries of artillery opened fire to provide an appropriate reception, and thousands of people lined the streets; hundreds jammed themselves into doorways and sat in open windows. As the general and his escorts trotted on their horses down Second and Market Streets towards City Tavern, the crowds cheered and waved in jubilation, and all of the church bells throughout the city tolled repeatedly. Wrote a newspaper editor who witnessed his arrival, "The joy of the people on the coming of this great and good man was shown by their acclamations." Another wrote that the joy was "upon finding our old and faithful commander in the full enjoyment of his health and fame."

George Washington saw his role as ceremonial, but all of the people recognized that his mere presence gave the convention legitimacy and strength. A newspaper editor wrote that the "future happiness and prosperity of the country" rested in the hands of the delegates and that "if there lives a man equal to so arduous a task, it is Washington!"

The general assumed command of the convention, just as he had of the army, in that same city twelve years before, with supreme modesty. James Madison wrote that Washington "lamented his want [of better qualifications] and claimed the indulgence of the House towards the involuntary errors which his inexperience might occasion."

The general said little during the debates, but in private he worked diligently to help create a new federal government with an executive, legislative, and judicial branch. Those in attendance listened carefully to everything he had to say. Madison wrote to Jefferson, who did not attend, that he should "be assured that [George Washington's] influence carried this government."

Washington favored a strong national government with an active president who would work with Congress to pass legislation, a court to oversee the work of both Congress and the president, and a strong centralized federal government that could overrule states in disputes. He also argued that the president should be the commander in chief of the army.

Those who saw him at the convention, and just after, were pleased that four years after his retirement from the army he looked robust. Many felt like Alexander Donald, a Richmond merchant who dined with Washington when he returned from the convention. He wrote, "He is in perfect good health and looks almost as well as he did twenty years ago. I never saw him so keen for anything in my life, as he is the adoption of the new form of government."

The description of the office of president was vague, but everyone there assumed that Washington would be president and fill it with the same success he had as the commander in chief during the war. The one great fear all might have had, but did not, was that the president of a brand-new country might turn the office into a dictatorship, ruling with the army. Washington had been urged to do just that by Congress and individuals during the worst moments of the war, but he had rejected the idea. Then, when he could have seized power at the end of the Revolution, with the happy consent of the entire country, he resigned from the army. Throughout the war, he assiduously bowed to the wishes of Congress, constantly reminding everyone that he was just a soldier who worked for the government. People admired him for that. Later, Jefferson wrote that that was his greatest asset as a leader, that "his was the singular destiny and merit...of scrupulously obeying the laws through the whole of his career, civil and military, of which the history of the world furnishes no other example."

He was also the beneficiary of a centuries-old dictum that in a crisis, whether military or political, a country's population prefers to put its fate into the hands of one man it can trust, rather than associations or committees. And in Washington, they had what British philosopher Henry St. John, Viscount Bolingbroke, called "the patriot king": the much-admired common citizen who was given royal stature by the people but who always remained one of the people, the extraordinary ordinary man.

George Washington would be neither a king nor dictator. British historian Archibald Alison wrote of Washington that "he was a Cromwell without ambition, a Sulla [Roman Emperor] without his crimes; and after having raised his country, by his exertions, to the rank of an independent state, he closed his career by a voluntary relinquishment of the power which a grateful people had bestowed."

Washington genuinely did not want the presidency. The general told everyone that he had no interest in leaving Mount Vernon to accept a job that might turn into one of the most powerful in the world. He was content in his born-again role of farmer, he loathed politics and politicians, and, with Wash and Nelly, he once again had responsibilities as the head of his family. Yet he remained acutely interested in public affairs.

He could not have expressed his disdain for the position more emphatically than he did to his old wartime friend Knox. He wrote to him, "My movement to the chair of government will be accompanied by feelings not unlike those of a culprit who is going to his place of execution."

In the end, though, George Washington's return to public life as the first president of his country was inevitable. The new country that he had fought so hard to create was coming apart. The people, so united in war, were now divided in peace. George Washington knew that he was the one individual everyone admired. All of the other leaders were merely politicians; he was the man who had won the war. The others were regional office-holders, or men who prided themselves on being Massachusetts men or Virginia men. As the head of the army, Washington had become the one man who was loyal to all the states and, at the same time, the new country as a whole. He was a national hero and the most famous man in the world. People would overlook all the shortcomings of the new government, and there would be many, because they trusted him to run it properly.

His friends insisted he become president. Elias Boudinot wrote to him that "there is no place for a refusal. The sacrifice is required and the offering must be made...you have no choice." General Anthony Wayne told him that the country was in trouble and that it was "a crisis that requires a Washington." Richard Henry Lee wrote that not only would Washington's life be unfulfilled if he did not take the office, but that "the public happiness will be very insecure" without him. Some, such as Governor Morris, were blunter, telling him that he *had* to be the president.

There was a groundswell for Washington's election by just about every newspaper in the United States, regardless of city, state, or region. The editor of the *Pennsylvania Gazette* wrote that the general was "the deliverer" of America and "will be called by the suffrages of three millions of people to govern the country by his wisdom." Another writer said that the general was "an able and tried friend of the people" but, more important, "a man who really loves the people, of a candid generous temper, and of an observing and reflecting turn of mind."

But what of his much-publicized retirement? How could he reenter public life when he had so vociferously vowed to finish his days as a farmer? An answer to that question came from Hamilton, to whom Washington had posed the question, probably certain the brilliant and loyal Hamilton could come up with a resolution. He did: "The absolute retreat [from public life] which you meditated at the close of the late war was natural and proper," Hamilton wrote, and told Washington that under almost all circumstances he should remain at home. But, his former chief of staff hastened to add, the nation now found itself in a crisis and Washington had to return to lead it once again. In fact, he would break his trust to the public if he *did not*.

No one understood this more than Martha, who hated politics. She initially wrote to her nephew John Dandridge that she strongly preferred to remain at Mount Vernon, like her husband. She told Dandridge that the presidency seemed to be something preordained for the general, though, and that "I think it was much too late for him to go into public life again, but it was not to be avoided." She told others that it was "inevitable," that "though the general's feelings and my own were perfectly in unison with respect to our predilection for public life, yet I cannot blame him for having acted according to his duties in obeying the voice of his country."

The phrase was used often by Washington, too. When he accepted his election, he wrote to Congress, "I promise that my endeavors shall be strenuously exerted to promote the welfare and glory of the United States," and then he told the head of the electoral college that he had "to obey the important and flattering call of my country." The general thought so much of the phrase that he even began his first inaugural address by stating, "Fellow citizens, I am again called upon by the voice of my country."

And, too, there was destiny. When Washington was elected commander in chief in 1775, he wrote to his wife, "It has been a kind of destiny that has thrown me upon this service," and that now, once again, destiny was reaching out to him, and to her.

History had summoned him to lead the American Army and now history had called him once more to become the first civilian leader of his country, a brand-new democracy that needed all the help it could get in its infancy. His wife, too, heard the voice of history and knew that her husband would become the president.

CHAPTER EIGHTEEN

THE FIRST
COUPLE

"I stood…before the door of the hall, elevated by a few steps from the pavement, when the carriage of the president drew up. As President Washington alighted, ascending the steps, [he] paused upon the platform, looking over his shoulder, in an attitude that would have furnished an admirable subject for the pencil; he was preceded by two gentlemen bearing long white wands who kept back the eager crowd that pressed on every side to get a nearer view. At that moment, I stood so near that I might have touched his clothes; but I should as soon have thought of touching an electric battery. I was penetrated with a veneration amounting to the deepest awe. Nor was this the feeling of a school boy only; it pervaded, I believe, every human being that approached Washington…. I saw him a hundred times afterward, but never with any other than that same feeling."

—*A young boy in a crowd that greeted President Washington as he arrived to address Congress in 179*

George Washington could not realize when he was sworn in that the people saw far more in the president, and in his wife, than anyone anticipated. That was evident to him when he left Mount Vernon at 10 a.m. on April 16, 1789, "with a mind oppressed with more anxious and painful sensations than I have words to express" and began what he thought would be an uneventful ride to New York for his inauguration. He rode off with just one aide, leaving Martha behind. His wife, reticent to live in the public spotlight, had no desire to do so now. She had not accompanied him on his triumphant trip from New York to Annapolis to resign from the army, and she had no wish to join him for the celebrations that accompanied his departure from Virginia. Now, on the eve of his greatest moment, she stayed home again, uninterested in the pomp that was sure to surround his inauguration. She would be along shortly, she told him, beside him now in the good times, just as she had been there in the bad.

Washington had hoped to travel to New York in "as quiet and peaceable manner as possible." The general was startled at the reception he received on his journey. It began at the ferry stop in nearby Alexandria. Hundreds of people, many of whom had traveled over one hundred miles in wagons, coaches, and on horseback, greeted him with loud cheers. It was there, at Alexandria, at a dinner in his honor, that he said good-bye to the men and women who had been his close personal friends since he had arrived at Mount Vernon as a teenager long ago. "Unutterable sensations must then be left to more expressive silence," he told them, "while, from an aching heart, I bid you all, my affectionate friends, and kind neighbors, farewell."

Newspapers throughout the country had published his travel itinerary and everyone knew his route. Crowds jammed every ferry stop he arrived at and lined the dirt highways that his carriage rolled down. Hundreds of cheering men, women, and children packed the village greens of tiny hamlets he traveled through, and tens of thousands filled the streets of cities. People shouted out his name with great joy and many just held their hands in the air, simply trying to touch the first president, the hero of the revolution, the great man.

Thousands in Baltimore jammed a parade route, and he was feted at a dinner at Grant's Fountain Inn. It was in Baltimore that he first outlined his general, uncomplicated view of the presidency. He told the crowd that his intentions were pure and that he sought no personal glory; his job was to simply unite the country. "It appears to me," he said, "that little more than common sense and common honesty, in the transactions of the community at large, would be necessary to make us a great and happy nation," and that he would govern well as long as he had the confidence of the people. And, too, he hoped people had faith in him in the trying times ahead, reminding one group, "I entertain a consolatory hope that the purity of my intentions, and the perseverance of my endeavors to promote the happiness of my country, will atone for any of the slighter defects which may be discovered in my administration."

And, wherever he went, he was as modest as always, reminding people in Philadelphia, "Heaven alone can foretell whether any, or what, advantages are to be derived by my countrymen from my holding the office."

Dozens of young girls spread flowers on the highway before him as he approached Trenton, where he had defeated the Hessians after crossing the Delaware on Christmas 1776, the turning point of the war. An eyewitness to his entry into Philadelphia said that over twenty thousand people "lined every fence, field, and avenue between the [Delaware] bridge and city," as well as Second and Market Streets, to welcome him. As he crossed the bridge, joined by hundreds of smiling war veterans in their old uniforms, thousands more joined the parade that then slowly made its way through the streets. Large choirs assembled on platforms in other towns and sang songs written to commemorate his life. He was hailed by mayors, governors, and ministers. The famous patriotic wartime drinking song, "War and Washington," rang out in taverns up and down the East coast.

He was greeted by a gigantic navy of ships when he finally reached the Hudson River and prepared to sail to Manhattan for the inauguration. He crossed in a long wooden barge rowed by thirteen men representing the thirteen colonies. One accompanying barge carried smartly dressed soldiers and a beaming General Henry Knox, thrilled to see his old friend again. A second barge carried a choir that sang to the new president as his vessel traversed slowly across the river. The water was cluttered with boats of all shapes and sizes, from small schooners filled with people shouting and waving at him to a large Spanish galleon that fired a thirteen-gun salute.

On the other side of the river he was greeted by several thousand more well-wishers. Soldiers had to hold them back as the president's barge approached a wharf, and Washington disembarked to yet more throaty cheers and boarded a carriage that took him to a temporary residence to await the inauguration. The carriage passed public buildings, taverns, and private homes that were adorned with enormous flags and posters carrying his name.

Wrote Elizabeth Quincy, an eyewitness, "[the president] frequently bowed to the multitudes and took off his hat to the ladies at the windows, who waved their handkerchiefs and threw flowers before him, and shed tears of joy and congratulations. The whole city was one scene of triumphal rejoicing."

As much as the dapper Washington loved London clothes, that inauguration day he wore a handsome brown suit made in Connecticut to promote patriotism, with white stockings and gold shoe buckles. Standing ramrod straight, rising to his full six feet, three inches, George Washington was sworn in as the first president of the United States on the balcony of the new Federal Hall in front of a large crowd in lower Manhattan. He repeated the oath of office in a clear and confident voice.

To the people, the president and Mrs. Washington were not merely the national hero and his wife. To them, the Washingtons represented all that was best in every American. They were visible symbols not just of victory in the war and the establishment of an independent nation, but also the achievement of a new moral order.

The government George Washington had decided to run was a good one, he told all, stating proudly that "the new Congress…will not be inferior to any assembly in the world," and even bragging to Catherine Macauley Graham, a British women's rights leader, that "the government, though not absolutely perfect, is one of the best in the world."

As president, he decided to take small steps and make it a simple office. The first president would work with Congress and the courts on the federal level, and governors and assembly leaders on the state level, to get the new government underway. He was determined, too, that the president had to serve as the representative of all the people, regardless of region, class, or political persuasion. The new president recognized that America was divided into three distinct sections—New England, the middle Atlantic, and the South—but saw all three as one large United States. He saw the western territories, from the Great Lakes all the way south to New Orleans, as part of the U.S., too. Washington had complained that during the Articles of Confederation the country was sinking into "anarchy and confusion" because it was directed by thirteen heads of the thirteen colonies. Now he saw all of the colonies as one nation.

He envisioned the presidency as a position in which the man who held it represented the people in a very personal way. He understood from the beginning, as his successors discovered, that the people saw the president as a unique individual and that their relationship to him was special.

Washington had been the one man the people trusted to get them through the war and now, as president, he was the one man the people trusted to get them through the peace. He had to do it in a way that enabled democratic government to flourish for the benefit of all, not just the few. He knew that if he could accomplish that one goal, while working with Congress to build a functioning government, he would be successful. He would keep politics simple and not become bogged down by the political theorists who besieged him daily with their deep, perplexing plans.

One great advantage he had was that everyone saw him as a war hero, and no one saw him as a politician. During the war, he had carefully constructed an image of himself as a servant of the people, above politics, working only for "the public good," as he often said. Washington had started burnishing this nonpolitical image long ago. He refused to personally campaign in his elections to the House of Burgesses in the 1760s and disdained any overt political role in the legislature, telling a writer, "I deal little in politics."

Washington was faced with the arduous task of not only filling a position only vaguely outlined in the Constitution, but also a job in which everything he did was watched by millions around the world and would be studied for centuries. Uncertain of what to do, the first president, like anyone, relied on what had worked for him in the past. First and most important, he decided not to fit the office, but to make the office fit him. He would simply be himself and in doing that he would be a good president, just as he had been a superior general by being himself. He determined that he would succeed as a civilian leader in much the same fashion that he had as the commander in chief of the army. Then, he had worked well with congressmen, governors, newspaper editors, and businessmen; he had listened to all of them and tried to do his best for the unimportant and the poor, as well as the rich and the powerful.

He enjoyed great success in the army with a council of war. Washington met with them regularly, solicited their advice, and then made his decisions. He did so because he considered them experts and he trusted them completely. As president, he replicated that council with the cabinet. He chose as his first cabinet secretaries men whom he trusted and with whom he had worked in the war. Alexander Hamilton, his chief of staff in the army, became secretary of the treasury. Thomas Jefferson, governor of Virginia during the conflict, who raised so many troops and provided so much money for the army, became secretary of state. General Henry Knox was named secretary of war, and Edmund Randolph, a longtime friend from Virginia, became the attorney general.

Washington, ever the micromanager, assumed most of the responsibility in hiring administrators for the new federal government. He took great care in selecting cabinet undersecretaries and other federal appointees, especially federal judges, asking his aide, Tobias Lear, and others to conduct investigations to make certain the appointees were men of good character. He told them to investigate "with every means in your power." He ran the federal government just as he had the army and his farms, plunging into the work of his own office as well as that of each department.

He maintained close ties to state governors and the leaders of state legislatures, just as he had in the war. All of them were urged to see him whenever they were in New York or, later, in Philadelphia. He corresponded with many men. During most of his first term, his relationships with senators and congressmen were excellent.

President Washington was able to govern not simply because he was looked upon as a national hero. He could do so because for eight long years during the Revolution he had befriended hundreds of governors, state legislators, and newspapers editors, whose help he always needed to keep the army together and win the war. These men also helped him in every way they could when he became the nation's first chief executive.

The president was determined to move slowly during his first term to establish the three branches of the new government so that they would function smoothly. He also was determined to create a strong executive branch and make the country financially sound. He did that in several ways. In 1790, at the urging of Hamilton, his secretary of the treasury, he convinced Congress to assume all of the wartime debts from the states and permit the state legislatures to flourish unencumbered by debt. He blunted southern criticism of that proposal by shrewdly making the establishment of the permanent national capital in the South, in what is now Washington, D.C., as part of the arrangement.

To pay for the assumption of debts and earn money to run the federal government, Washington and Congress devised a series of import taxes on goods brought in from Europe, particularly England. These taxes were substantial and gave the federal government more than enough money to meet its budget.

Again at Hamilton's urging, Washington established the National Bank in 1791. The bank, whose stocks were purchased by companies and individuals, became an immediate success and helped the U.S. to back its currency—in coin—quickly. Everyone now used the same currency; states had issued their own money prior to the Constitution. The establishment of the bank was an important step in the first presidency because, at the urging of Hamilton and James Madison, Washington insisted that he had "implied powers" that were not directly defined in the Constitution. This assumption, accepted by Congress, gave the presidency enormous power.

He urged a national manufacturing effort to minimize American reliance on imported European goods. He supported the expenditure of federal money to establish a national university so that America's brightest young people would no longer have to travel to Europe for their education.

During his first year in office, the Bill of Rights, which guaranteed freedom of press, speech, and speedy trials, was passed. The president, unwilling to become entangled in a debate during his first term, did not participate in discussions on the amendments, but seemed happy that they became law. He was pleased, too, that the new government recognized freedom of religion and that the sects respected each other.

Some of the things he wanted, and lobbied for, never came to pass. Washington was defeated on his attempts to build a large standing army and so whenever he needed troops he had to recruit them. He had long championed very small congressional districts to give more people a say in the government. Politicians from the large states always thwarted these efforts.

Jefferson, who worked closely with him and was often critical, wrote, "His mind was great and powerful, without being of the very first order; his penetration strong, though not so acute as that of a Newton, Bacon, or Locke; and, as far as he saw, no judgment was ever sounder. It was slow in operation, being little aided by invention or imagination, but sure in conclusion." This deliberate style, Jefferson maintained, was Washington's great strength. Washington never acted, Jefferson said, "Until every   circumstance,   every   consideration,   was   maturely weighted; refraining, if he saw a doubt; but, when once decided, going through with his purpose."

A French diplomat, Francois Guizot, agreed. He wrote, "Thus, when he had examined, reflected, and made up his mind, nothing disturbed him; he did not permit himself to be thrown into, and kept in, a state of perpetual doubt and irresolution, either by the opinions of others or by love of applause, or by fear of opposition."

He kept his famous temper in check most of the time, restrained his criticism of political enemies, and was not a gossip. This restraint helped him to govern well. Wrote one of his first biographers, "Perhaps self-control was the most remarkable trait of his character. It was in part the effect of discipline, yet he seems by nature to have possessed this power to a degree which has been denied to other men."

Those first few months were busy for Washington, Congress, the courts, his cabinet, the officers of the new federal government, and Washington's secretaries. An entirely new government had to be hurriedly put together and a country had to be run. "There was not a moment unemployed," wrote a weary Lear, Washington's chief secretary.

George Washington could not walk the streets or ride by on horseback or in his carriage without causing a crowd to gather that brought a complete halt to traffic and business. One man wrote of his sojourns through New York that "his presence inspired a veneration, and a feeling of awe, rarely experienced in the presence of any man." Wrote a French army chaplain, "Through all the land he appears to be a benevolent God. Old men, women, and children all flock eagerly to catch a glimpse of him when he travels and congratulate themselves because they have seen him. People carrying torches follow him through cities; his arrival is marked by public illuminations; the Americans…have waxed enthusiastic about him and their first songs inspired by spontaneous sentiments have been consecrated to the glorification of Washington."

Sometimes he was embarrassed by the fawning people. While walking in a parade in Salem, Massachusetts, the president seemed eager to flee the spotlight. "He looked oppressed by the attention that was paid him and as he cast his eye around, I thought it seemed to sink at the notice he attracted," wrote one observer, who added that Washington left the following celebration as quickly as he could. The president was even afraid to visit old friends because he knew people would surround the house. He begged off on an invitation to visit wartime aide James McHenry, telling him that "the party that may possibly attend me, the crowd that always gathers...all contributed to render a public house the fittest place for scenes of bustle and trouble."

Publicly and in private, people gushed over the new chief executive. Robert Morris, a friend, wrote to him that he was "an instrument in the hands of Providence to dispense happiness to the people, who have received Liberty at your hands."

Americans saw him as more than a president. They saw him as Bolingbroke envisioned his mythical patriot king—the popular patriarchal head of a people, the father of his country. Artist Edward Savage emphatically underscored that image of Washington when he produced a family portrait of the Washingtons with the two Custis children and a male slave around a table on which was spread the map of the plans for the city of Washington, D.C. It shows the president as both a strong leader and a tender family head, and, positioning him sitting next to the capital map, as the father of his country. Savage had numerous engravings made that were printed throughout the Republic, and the portrait solidified Washington's father image. He was called that wherever he went, such as on his southern tour in the spring of 1791, when the mayor of Petersburg, Virginia, referred to him as "the friend of mankind, the father of your country." Visiting foreign dignitaries picked up the phrase right away, too. In 1791, following his visit to the U.S., Frenchman Jean Pierre Brissot de Warville wrote that "the Americans seem to consider him as their father." And historian Henry Tuckerman wrote, "Providence left him childless, that his country might call him—Father."

Many who met him for the first time as president remarked that he appeared just as they had read about him. British architect Benjamin Latrobe's description was a good example. He wrote, "Washington had something uncommonly majestic and commanding in his walk, his address, his figure, and his countenance." He added that his face was highlighted "more by intensive thought than by quick and fiery conception. There is a mildness about its expression, an air of reserve in his manner lowers its tone still more."

French Comte de Segur wrote, "Simplicity, grandeur, dignity, calm, kindness, firmness were stamped upon his face and upon his countenance as well as his character."

Another Frenchman, Claude Victor, Prince de Broglie, writing about Washington's skills to govern, said: "Never was there a man better fitted to command the Americans, and his conduct throughout developed the greatest foresight, steadiness and wisdom."

If Washington was amazed at the public reaction to him when he became president, Martha was absolutely astonished at the way the people embraced her.

Her own journey to New York to join her husband began in late May, after she had packed for herself and the two grandchildren. She made arrangements for several slaves and one of her husband's nephews to accompany her to New York and left Mount Vernon in the hands of Lund Washington. She anticipated a quiet coach ride to Baltimore, Philadelphia, and New York.

Quiet it was not. Alerted by newspapers as to her route and timetable, crowds gathered to cheer her wherever she went. Her trip was halted in Baltimore when residents insisted that she attend a fireworks display in her honor. She did not reach Philadelphia on her own; Philadelphia reached out to her. Governor Joseph Reed, state officials, and a troop of horsemen met her several miles outside of the city and accompanied her to a ferry stop, where a sizable crowd of people waited to join her in a reception. Then it was on to the city itself by ferry in the presence of yet more well-wishers. In what she called "an agreeable journey," she was met by her husband and a dozen or more dignitaries, and even larger crowds when she reached Elizabeth to cross the Hudson in a barge. Again in Manhattan noisy throngs of people greeted a surprised First Lady.

The press and public once again called her Lady Washington, the name given to her during the Revolution. The title First Lady did not originate until the 1840s, and the first few wives of the president's were called Lady or the President's Lady. She settled into the presidents mansion with the grandchildren and began to set up yet another household for her husband and family, as she had done so often during the war.

Her first new home on Cherry Street was a handsome three-story building. The first floor featured a large dining room for state dinners and receptions. There was a fireplace outlined with blue and white tiles. The Washingtons' bedroom was on the second floor, and there were additional rooms on the third floor where aides and the domestic staff slept.

The first couple only lived there for a short time. In February 1790, Washington moved to Alexander Macomb's lavish mansion at 39 Broadway that overlooked the Hudson River. He talked Congress into spending $2,000 ($200,000 in today's money) to renovate it. The president paid for the construction of stables for his coach and horses. The Macomb house, made of honey-colored stone, was four stories high, fifty-six feet wide, elegantly appointed inside, and much larger than the Cherry Street home.

Horse stalls were needed at his residences because the president loved to ride. In good weather, he rode two or three hours each day, heading out into the countryside north of New York City. He enjoyed carriages and coaches, too, because they were yet another means of traveling about. Coaches also gave him more time to spend with his wife and grandchildren, who went with him. The sight of the Washington family riding through town, or on the highways, and later around the city of Philadelphia, became common. Those who knew the Washingtons always commented on their strong family ties. David Ramsey wrote that "for more than forty years of happy wedded love, his high example whole, and joins to the qualities of an excellent house-wife, that simple dignity which ought to characterize a woman whose husband has acted the greatest part on the theater of human affairs...[she] manifests that attention to strangers, which render hospitality so charming."

Martha did not know what a president's wife was supposed to do, so she simply replicated her role as hostess at Mount Vernon, treating the president's guests like they were old friends back in Virginia, supervising dinners and parties, traveling to see people, and inviting New Yorkers to the mansion. It had worked at Mount Vernon and she was certain it would work in the presidency. She was right.

The Washingtons wanted to be accessible to the people, so they hosted weekly dinners and parties. The president met anyone who wanted to socialize with him from 3 until 4 p.m. every Tuesday afternoon. These receptions were generally reserved for prominent residents, old friends, merchants, and visitors from other cities, but Washington sometimes invited unimportant people he had met that day or waved in people that he saw on the street, or he invited soldiers from near his home.

Late Thursday afternoon was reserved for state dinners, attended by visiting foreign dignitaries, cabinet executives, congressmen, and their wives. At the end of the dinner, the men remained, drinking port wine, while the ladies retired to another room to chat. The president usually stayed with the men for fifteen minutes, drinking wine and devouring as many nuts as he could scoop into his enormous hands, and he then retired to talk to the ladies and be with his wife.

The president was always very formal and stoic at these receptions that he presided over, dressed in a suit of black velvet, with gloves and a dress sword. He bowed in greeting, not shaking hands, smiled little, and refrained from humorous stories. Some guests said that he was so glum that they were afraid to speak and that for moments no one talked at all, to him or to one another. He was so rigid that his granddaughter said he actually scared her friends when they were at receptions with the Washingtons. It strengthened the tone of public manners. He had more real enjoyment in the bosom of his family, than in the pride of military command or in the pomp of sovereign power."

These excursions with his wife, grandchildren, and friends, along with his personal horseback rides, were designed to give the people a chance to see the president and first lady, but there was another reason. The landscapes he rode through reminded him of the wondrous beauty of the nation he led. The president wrote of Connecticut during a New England horseback excursion that "the country hereabouts is beautiful and the lands good." He wrote of Long Island that "the road is very fine and the country in a higher state of cultivation and vegetation of grass and grain...than any place."

The Washingtons were constantly asked to visit someone's home or farm. The president always thanked his hosts, but the numerous visits often wore him out and he was sometimes curt in his diary about them. After a stay at the much-publicized fruit gardens of William Prince, on Long Island, he scribbled in his journal that the gardens "did not answer my expectations; the shrubs were trifling and the flowers not numerous." He complained, too, that the locals' efforts to salute him upon arrival with a single cannon were rather comical. Later that day, his friend Governor Morris showed the president his brand-new barn, with much pride, but in his diary Washington derided it, writing that "it was not of a construction to strike my fancy" and chortled that his friend had paid far too much for it.

Visitors to Mount Vernon had always praised the way M Washington ran her household, which was constantly o crowded with guests in the years between the end of the war her husband's election. One man who summed up the Was tons' life well was French diplomat Jacques Pierre Bris Warville. He was struck by the way that the Washington aged to achieve ordinariness and elegance at the same t wrote, "Everything has an air of simplicity in his house; is good, but not ostentatious and no deviation is seen f larity and domestic economy. Mrs. Washington superi whole, and joins to the qualities of an excellent house-wife, that simple dignity which ought to characterize a woman whose husband has acted the greatest part on the theater of human affairs…[she] manifests that attention to strangers, which render hospitality so charming."

Martha did not know what a president's wife was supposed to do, so she simply replicated her role as hostess at Mount Vernon, treating the president's guests like they were old friends back in Virginia, supervising dinners and parties, traveling to see people, and inviting New Yorkers to the mansion. It had worked at Mount Vernon and she was certain it would work in the presidency. She was right.

The Washingtons wanted to be accessible to the people, so they hosted weekly dinners and parties. The president met anyone who wanted to socialize with him from 3 until 4 p.m. every Tuesday afternoon. These receptions were generally reserved for prominent residents, old friends, merchants, and visitors from other cities, but Washington sometimes invited unimportant people he had met that day or waved in people that he saw on the street, or he invited soldiers from near his home.

Late Thursday afternoon was reserved for state dinners, attended by visiting foreign dignitaries, cabinet executives, congressmen, and their wives. At the end of the dinner, the men remained, drinking port wine, while the ladies retired to another room to chat. The president usually stayed with the men for fifteen minutes, drinking wine and devouring as many nuts as he could scoop into his enormous hands, and he then retired to talk to the ladies and be with his wife.

The president was always very formal and stoic at these receptions that he presided over, dressed in a suit of black velvet, with gloves and a dress sword. He bowed in greeting, not shaking hands, smiled little, and refrained from humorous stories. Some guests said that he was so glum that they were afraid to speak and that for moments no one talked at all, to him or to one another. He was so rigid that his granddaughter said he actually scared her friends when they were at receptions with the Washingtons. It strengthened the tone of public manners. He had more real enjoyment in the bosom of his family, than in the pride of military command or in the pomp of sovereign power."

These excursions with his wife, grandchildren, and friends, along with his personal horseback rides, were designed to give the people a chance to see the president and first lady, but there was another reason. The landscapes he rode through reminded him of the wondrous beauty of the nation he led. The president wrote of Connecticut during a New England horseback excursion that "the country hereabouts is beautiful and the lands good." He wrote of Long Island that "the road is very fine and the country in a higher state of cultivation and vegetation of grass and grain…than any place."

The Washingtons were constantly asked to visit someone's home or farm. The president always thanked his hosts, but the numerous visits often wore him out and he was sometimes curt in his diary about them. After a stay at the much-publicized fruit gardens of William Prince, on Long Island, he scribbled in his journal that the gardens "did not answer my expectations; the shrubs were trifling and the flowers not numerous." He complained, too, that the locals' efforts to salute him upon arrival with a single cannon were rather comical. Later that day, his friend Governor Morris showed the president his brand-new barn, with much pride, but in his diary Washington derided it, writing that "it was not of a construction to strike my fancy" and chortled that his friend had paid far too much for it.

Visitors to Mount Vernon had always praised the way Mrs. Washington ran her household, which was constantly overcrowded with guests in the years between the end of the war and her husband's election. One man who summed up the Washingtons' life well was French diplomat Jacques Pierre Brissot de Warville. He was struck by the way that the Washingtons managed to achieve ordinariness and elegance at the same time. He wrote, "Everything has an air of simplicity in his house; his table is good, but not ostentatious and no deviation is seen from regularity and domestic economy. Mrs. Washington superintends the was never clear whether he was being overly official or taking the advice of aides to avoid developing friendships with people in government (he made it a policy not to attend any weddings or funerals for that reason, too).

The president's forced conversation with those he just met, and the periods of silence, were well-known. An architect who visited him wrote that "he did not speak at any time with remarkable fluency. Perhaps the extreme correctness of his language, which almost seemed studied, prevented that effect." Others said that he was careful to say the right thing and his searches for the words "well adapted to his meaning," according to a visitor, caused long gaps in conversations. British visitor Henry Wansey had breakfast with Washington at the presidential mansion in Philadelphia in 1794. He, too, found Washington's conversation halting, writing that "he is slow in delivering himself, which occasions some to conclude him reserved, but it is rather, I apprehend, the effect of much thinking and reflection, but there is great appearance to me of affability."

Yet many others remarked that when he was out of the public spotlight, especially when he was at Mount Vernon, he was a genial conversationalist. Jedidiah Morse wrote of his visit with Washington at Mount Vernon just before he became president that "General Washington is more cheerful than he was in the army. Although his temper is rather of a serious cast and his countenance commonly carries the impression of thoughtfulness, yet he perfectly relishes a pleasant story, an unaffected sally of wit, or a burlesque description which surprises by its suddenness."

And, too, visitors to Mount Vernon said, he was always charming when around his wife and family. One wrote, "I found him kind and benignant in the [family] domestic circle, revered and beloved by all around him; agreeably social, without ostentation, delighting in anecdote and adventures."

The Washingtons were especially animated when they met someone from a village or county that they had visited during the Revolution. "And if they had been through any remarkable places, his conversation is free and particular interesting, as he is intimately acquainted with every part of the country," wrote Isaac Weld of the president.

And some were convinced that the general could turn his somber demeanor on and off as he pleased to fit the image he was trying to create at the moment. William Carey said that he could pretend to be aloof with a man until he came to know him.

Jeffersonian Republican newspapers had great merriment criticizing the presidential receptions for federal officials. Wrote one editor, "It appears...that a new order of citizens has been created....consisting only of the officers of the federal government. The privileges of this order...consist exclusively in the profits of the $25,000 allowed for the president's table and in the honor of gazing upon him once a week at his levees."

The president ignored the criticism. If he did not enjoy his Thursday dinners, friends said, he certainly was much more animated at the weekly Friday night receptions hosted by his wife. These were parties, attended mostly by women, at which the Washingtons were far more informal. Here, in this relaxed setting, people had a chance to know the first couple better.

It was not the receptions themselves that helped to define the social and cultural life of the first presidency, but the atmosphere that the Washingtons created. "Hospitality, indeed, seems to have spread over the whole place its happiest, kindest influence," wrote Thomas Shippen. "The president exercises it in a superlative degree, from the greatest of his duties to the most trifling minutiae, and Mrs. Washington is the very essence of kindness. Her soul seems to overflow with it like the most abundant fountain, and her happiness is in exact proportion to the number of objects upon which she can dispense her benefits."

The nation admired George Washington because he had become a national hero through his triumph over the British in the war. He was a man of great character and unquestioned integrity, and superb leadership shown throughout the Revolution and as president of the Constitutional Convention. He was a man devoted to his wife and grandchildren, well-dressed, religious, and who had always done whatever he could for the poor. He had never been involved in a scandal, always treated his slaves well, and had given up the ease of retirement to lead the nation.

But what impressed Americans the most about the first couple was that there was nothing ostentatious about them. They dressed well, but no one could mistake them for foreign diplomats, who paraded about in their gaudy attire. The difference between the Washingtons, especially the first lady, and other prominent people was most obvious at their receptions. Charlotte Chambers outlined them in a letter to her mother just after she returned from one of the president's birthday parties:

"[Mrs. Washington] was dressed in a rich silk, but entirely without ornament. Next to her were seated the wives of the foreign ambassadors, glittering from the floor to the summit of their headdresses. One of the ladies wore three large ostrich feathers. Her brow was encircled by a sparkling fillet of diamonds, her neck and arms were almost covered with jewels, and two watches were suspended from her girdle, and all reflecting the light from a hundred directions. Such superabundance of ornament struck me as injudicious."

Even the fashionable Abigail Adams could not bear some of the overdressed women. She wrote that many of the receptions were "as much crowded as a Birth Night at St. James, and with company as brilliantly dressed, diamonds and great hoops excepted." Sometimes the ostrich-plumed women at the president's mansion became the target of much humor, such as the woman whose feathers were so high that they brushed against a lamp and set her headdress on fire.

Martha liked to poke fun at the fashionistas of New York. When she bought her niece a new watch with an elegant chain, she joked to her that the chain "is of Mrs. [Tobias] Lear's choosing and such as Mrs. Adams and those in the polite circle wear," and laughed that "it will last as long as the fashion [does], and by that time you can get another of the fashionable kind."

A story told by Jefferson illustrated the simplicity of the first couple. A prominent New England man called on Washington when he became president, and on the way up the stairs to the president's office passed Martha walking down them. He asked her, "Is his majesty home?"

Martha shrugged her shoulders. "No," she said, "but Mr. Washington is."

One of the women most eager to see Martha in New York was Abigail Adams. Abigail had met Martha several times during the siege of Boston in 1775–1776 and was immediately attracted to her cheerful personality. Now the Massachusetts woman was even more impressed with the way that her old friend carried herself as the first lady of America. She visited Martha right after the latter's arrival in the city. Nothing had changed in the more than a decade since they last met. "She received me with great ease and politeness," Abigail wrote her sister. "Her hair white [now], her teeth beautiful, her person rather short…Her manners are modest and unassuming, dignified and feminine."

Adams, like all the women who knew the first lady, remarked how ordinary she appeared, but impressively so. "She is plain in her dress, but that plainness is the best of every article," Adams wrote to her sister just after the inauguration and her husband's swearing in as vice president.

Everyone in New York enjoyed the company of the first lady. Mrs. Washington was always missed when she made her annual return to Mount Vernon with her husband and grandchildren. Life was empty and cold without her effervescent personality to add warmth to the occasion. Abigail Adams missed her more than most people. After their first year as wives of the president and vice president, Abigail wrote to her sister of Martha's departure for Virginia that "I shall part with her, I hope, only for a short time, with much regret. No lady can be more deservedly beloved and esteemed than she is, and we have lived in habits of intimacy and friendship. In short, the removal of the principal connections I have here serves to render the place delightful as it is, much less pleasant than it has been."

Perhaps Martha's greatest skill as the president's wife was her oldest one, the ability to befriend everyone and engage in lengthy conversations with anybody about anything. People who met her for the first time marveled at the way that she found some common ground between them. She even charmed people whom no one believed she could ever get along with. Once she met with Judith Sargent Murray, the strident feminist, whose cultural views of men and women and the world they shared were completely opposite her own. Murray found herself sitting at a reception, eyed coldly and suspiciously by all for her radical views, when Mrs. Washington approached.

Murray wrote, "Taking my hand, she seated me down beside her and addressing herself particularly to me, as the only stranger present, she engaged me in the most familiar and agreeable chat— she interrogated me respecting my journey, asked if my acquaintance in New York was extensive, and in what part of the city I abode. She informed me that she had the pleasure of being acquainted with my brother and she spoke of his late marriage, and the death of his companion, as events which had interested her feelings."

The two strangers from the opposite ends of the cultural rainbow continued talking for two hours, at times laughing and at times commiserating in whispers. They talked about their families and husbands, and Murray grieved with a still-distraught Martha over the death of her son Jack. Murray wrote to her parents of the gap between the two women that, "so much friendship did her salutations connect, so interesting and animated was our conversation, that a bystander would not have entertained an idea of the distance between us."

Martha was older than people remembered her from the war and it showed. Henry Wansey of Philadelphia noted that her hair was completely gray. Julian Niemcewicz, a Polish diplomat who met her in 1797, admired her "bonnet of white gauze, ribbons of the same color, encircled her head tightly, leaving the forehead completely uncovered and hiding only half of her white hair which in back was done up in a little pigtail."

City life also brought clothing shops, shoe stores, and beauty treatments that Martha never enjoyed before. She gushed in a letter to her niece like a little girl sent to live with rich relatives in the big city, "My hair is set and dressed every day and I have put on white muslin habits for the summer. You would, I fear, think me a good deal in the fashion if you could but see me."

The Washingtons traveled in expensive coaches, but were never accompanied by more than a handful of people. That, too, pleased the public that had tired of reading about the processions of hundreds of people that traveled with European monarchs. Congressman Thomas Rodney wrote after passing Martha in her coach on a highway with only a driver and three riders accompanying her that "in old countries a lady of her rank would not be seen without a retinue of twenty persons." He wrote proudly that "the motions of the president and his lady is the public talk of all ranks at and near New York."

And there was Martha's simple American elegance. Mrs. Adams put it best when she wrote, "Mrs. Washington is one of those unassuming characters which create love and esteem. I found myself much more deeply impressed than I ever did before their majesties of Britain."

The reign of the Washingtons as the first couple was nearly cut short in both June of 1789 and in May 1790, when George nearly died. In 1789 he developed a malignant cancerous carbuncle on his leg that doctors cut out. The president became quite ill following surgery, and many in the capital thought he would die. Senators, congressmen, justices, and foreign dignitaries went to see him to pay what might be their final respects. Abigail Adams, with her daughter, rushed down from Massachusetts as soon as they read the news and comforted Martha.

The crowds that gathered outside his window each day to await news of his condition became so large that Martha asked the constables to cordon off the street so that the excessive noise would not bother her husband as he rested. It took him eight long weeks to recover. He battled his way through another bout of quinsy, the bad sore throats that had nagged him all of his life. The ailment rapidly developed into pneumonia in the spring of 1790. The president, fifty-eight, fell ill on May 10 and sank so quickly that by May 15, his four doctors, along with his wife, feared that he had little time left. One visitor, William MacLay, wrote that he saw "every eye full of tears, his life despaired of. Dr. McKnight told me…his danger was imminent and every reason to expect that the event of his disorder would be [death]."

Large crowds again gathered outside the president's mansion each day to pray for him, as did Americans across the country. Finally, on May 20, his fever broke and he began to improve. After a few weeks, the president, his strong constitution once again fighting off death, recovered. He coughed, wheezed, and hobbled about, but he recovered.

Washington paid little attention to his brush with death, writing briefly in his diary of "a severe illness with which I was seized the 10th of this month and which left me in a convalescent state for several weeks." His illnesses shook Martha, though. The first lady and members of her family, in New York and back at Mount Vernon, tried not to show their worry, but it was evident to all. Her granddaughter Eliza wrote that "the general was so ill that his life was despaired of and we felt much distressed 'til assured of his safety."

Following his recovery, Washington's relieved wife reiterated her belief that the bad comes along as frequently as the good in life, and that, despite their tragedies, people have to carry on.

⁂

Martha Washington was not affected by high praise, as were most women. Thomas Jefferson said of Martha that "it is singular that she is incapable of being injured by flattery, for she received more of it from the ladies of Philadelphia than any woman had before, but it did not affect her. I attribute this to the goodness of her heart. No woman could be more idolized or have more incense paid her than she had, yet she had not the least degree of pride of affectation."

Those with no connection to the government felt the same way. Latrobe, an architect and naturalist, was just as surprised at Mrs. Washington's lack of vanity as every other stranger who met her. He wrote, "She has no affectation of superiority in the slightest degree."

Much of Martha's popularity emanated from her years living with the army in the winters of the Revolution. Americans placed a high value on participation in the Revolution because so many men—nearly two hundred and forty thousand, or 40 percent of the able-bodied men in the country—had taken part in it. That meant that, adding in soldiers' parents, wives, and children, most of the people in the country had been connected to the war in some way. The heroes of the Revolution that the people so admired, people like Washington, Hamilton, Jefferson, Adams, Madison, and Knox, became the idols of post-Revolutionary America. Martha, as the hardworking and long-suffering commander's wife, was one of them. The women who gave their husbands to the army to fight for the cause saw themselves in Martha, who had also sent her husband off to war.

There was a more important Revolutionary connection that made Martha Washington beloved as the first lady. Many families had not only sent their husbands, sons, and brothers off to war—they lost them to muskets, bayonets, cannonballs, and diseases. Thousands of women had lost sons, many their only son, and now lived on in the new republic as older and sadder mothers. Perhaps a South Carolina official put it best when describing the pension plea of a mother whose son was killed in the Revolution. He wrote, "The petitioner is old, infirm, and in poor and low circumstances…that her only son, upon whom all her hopes depended, was killed in the services of his country." Those women all connected to Martha, who had also lost her son, Jacky, in the war.

Men and women appreciated Martha's sacrifice. She had spent every winter visiting sick soldiers, comforting wounded ones, and cheering up all. The sewing circles she organized to make clothing for the boys in the army were legendary. She gave tens of thousands of dollars to the army out of her savings. Many men and women had given money to the army for shirts for the soldiers, as she did. Hundreds of women, too, had formed sewing circles and worked tirelessly to mend clothes for the army. Virginians in Norfolk were wounded in a British attack in 1776, had their homes shelled, and lived in fear of that happening again throughout the war, just as Martha did when Mount Vernon was nearly bombarded on two occasions. Southern women had run their farms and slave plantations, managing free or indentured white workers and slaves, sometimes hundreds of them, with their husbands away at war for years, just like Martha. Women had to avoid British patrols while riding to safety in their carriages, just like Martha. They had lost loved ones in the smallpox epidemics, just like Martha. They had raised grandchildren when their children died, just like Martha.

America's women felt that they were as much a part of the Revolution as their men, and that they had given just as much for freedom. General William Moultrie of South Carolina wrote in his memoirs that he admired "the patriotic fair...for their heroism and virtue in such dreadful and dangerous times" and added that "their conduct during the war contributed much to the independence of America." David Ramsey, a physician and early historian of the war, wrote of the women that "there was scarcely an inhabitant of the state, however obscure in character or remote in situation...who did not partake of the general distress" of the conflict.

Both George and Martha had met tens of thousands of soldiers, public figures, newspaper editors, merchants, farmers, ministers, and ordinary residents of the states where the army moved or camped. All of these men went home after the war and told their friends and family how hard both the Washingtons had worked for the cause. Just like her husband, Martha Washington was the symbol of the American Revolution.

Martha also fit perfectly into the "new woman" that the war had spawned. The American woman had little power in politics when the Revolution began and little power when it ended. However, the women had played an important part in the Revolution. They had worked hard for their country during the war, making clothes, donating money, writing heated letters denouncing the British to newspapers, and running their family farms and businesses while their men were away. They decided to take the power that they did have as wives and mothers and extend it. They became "Republican mothers," or politically savvy women who, barred from public life because of their sex, were determined to influence the nation through their husbands and sons. They would train and educate sons to go out into the world and always champion the ideals of the Revolution that their mothers had upheld for so long. Through them, they would influence the country in a way that they had been unable to do prior to the conflict.

On the personal side, they would continue to be the moral leaders of their families and the loving wives whose tender care would soothe their husbands, home from the vigors of work. This combination was heralded by feminist writers such as Murray in America and Mary Wollstonecraft in England, whose *Vindication of the Rights of Woman* sold thousands of copies in Britain and the U.S. (Abigail Adams was one of the first women to buy the book when it was published in Boston). Sargent and Wollstonecraft argued that women could no longer be seen as mere sexual objects and domestic toilers, but had to be the intellectual and political equals of their men, in the home, even if they could not be outside of it. "[Men] have been more anxious to make them alluring mistresses than affectionate wives and rational mothers," wrote Wollstonecraft. Women had to insist upon this relationship, they wrote, because in this manner they would gain an equality with men that would enable them to serve their families and their country better.

Even the ardent feminists, though, looked up to Martha Washington because, in her unassuming way, she was living the life of their new ideal woman, exerting great influence without any power of her own. Wollstonecraft argued that most women merely wanted love, "when they ought to cherish a nobler ambition, and by their abilities and virtues exact respect," and that was surely Martha Washington.

Murray, of Boston, wrote several volumes of poetry and a number of essays about women's rights, titled *Constantia,* in which she argued for full domestic equality for wives and, more important, equal education for girls. The essays were compiled into three book-length volumes in 1798. Most American men were appalled at her theories, but among the first people to buy the books were George and Martha Washington, paying $5 for them.

Many other women's rights advocates championed Wollstonecraft, including Philadelphia's Elizabeth Powel, one of Martha Washington's closest friends, who saw the first lady regularly in 1792, when Wollstonecraft's book was published. Powel also praised Reverend Enos Hitchcock's pro-women's rights book *Bloomsgrove Family,* buying one of the first copies issued and writing to him that "upon the mother the first impressions chiefly, if not entirely, depend." Powel and Mrs. Washington must have discussed these authors and their views.

Most of the men in America and England not only saw women's rights advocates such as Wollstonecraft and Murray as radicals, but as a real threat to their power in the household. Most male views of the feminists were similar to those of Ralph Izard, who called Wollstonecraft "a vulgar, impudent hussy." The Washingtons' reaction was to invite Murray and her husband to the president's mansion as their honored guests.

In postwar America, widows were no longer looked down upon because most of them were now running the farms and businesses of men who died in the Revolution. Numerous war widows opened up their homes as boarding houses to earn money for their remaining families; other widows ran their own stores. And then there were thousands of women who had learned how to conduct their husband's businesses during the war and continued to help them run them, as partners, after it ended.

Most of these women enjoyed working, especially since now many in society did not object to it. Eliza Pinckney ran her father's farms in South Carolina in the early 1800s and wrote, "[I] assure you I think myself happy that I can be useful to so good a father."

Most of all, the Revolution promised a new era in American life, as all revolutions do. The Revolution was not merely a war to gain independence from an oppressive mother country, but also a conflict to bring about a new democratic social order in which everyone would eventually become a full participant, women as well as men, and in which wives were honored just as husbands were. Benjamin Rush put it best when he said that "there is nothing more common than to confound the terms of the *American Revolution* with those of *the late American war.*"

The men and women of America had just lived through an evangelical movement—the Great Awakening—and had easily connected religion to the Revolution. Christian women, especially, had become more devout as they prayed not only for victory in the war, but for the safety of their husbands and sons. They read their Bibles and said their prayers, just as Martha Washington did each morning at Mount Vernon and in the army camps of the war.

No one fit this collective vision of the new woman better than Martha. She was the archetypal eighteenth-century spouse—a devoted wife, mother, and grandmother who enjoyed supervising her household. Yet now, after the war, and her eight years of living with the men who ran it, and hundreds of political dinner-table conversations after it, she had become, if not a political woman, a woman who lived in a political world. She was a grandmother and housewife, but she was also a woman who had the president's ear. She had achieved what the new women wanted so badly, and yet she remained the obedient housewife that every one of them still had to be. In her they saw not only themselves, but a better version of themselves.

Perhaps it was too simplistic to say that behind every great man was a good woman, but people in the 1790s strongly believed that men owed much of their success to their wives. Nowhere was this more obvious to the American public than in the Washingtons, where a gracious and nurturing wife helped her husband to see his own best virtues and create a new nation in the process.

Women and men both argued that the only way that the new Republican women could uphold the virtues and tradition of the Revolution was through education. Mothers of future citizens had to be trained to realize that they had a great responsibility to properly raise their children, especially daughters.

This women's education movement began in earnest with a

lecture by Dr. Benjamin Rush, "Thoughts Upon Female Education," to the graduating class of a Philadelphia academy in 1787. In that same year, Reverend Enos Hitchcock, the prominent Rhode Island educator, urged more schooling for females. He dedicated his bestselling book to Martha Washington.

These men urged the dismantling of the expensive boarding schools, where only the rich could attend, in favor of day schools for girls. Noah Webster disdained music and favored practical subjects, as well as politics, which was once taboo for girls. He wrote, "In America, female education should have for its object what is *useful.*"

Women's education thus improved in some regions in the postwar era. Records are difficult to find, but one book that traced the lives of important women who had biographies written about them showed that just 22 percent of these women born prior to the Revolution received an education beyond grade school but that 63 percent of them born after the inauguration of George Washington did. Some were reluctant to promote women's education. Ironically, while Martha and George provided advanced schooling for their granddaughter Nelly in New York and Philadelphia, her sister Eliza, living with Nelly and David Stuart in Virginia, had her education cut short by her tutors. "They would not teach me Greek and Latin because I was a girl," she complained. Her stepfather scoffed that she was "an extraordinary child and would, if a boy, make a brilliant figure."

Even so, in 1805, Murray, who complained so bitterly that there were not enough women's schools in the U.S. in the 1780s, wrote happily that "female academies are everywhere establishing, and right pleasant is the appellation to my ear."

Mrs. Washington spent a considerable amount of time placing her granddaughter in a good school in New York precisely because she did not want her to obtain a traditional prewar finishing school education. She wanted Nelly to learn what men learned. Nelly did, too, as an examination of her courses shows. Nelly studied embroidery, clothwork, drawing, painting, japanning, filigree, music, and dancing, but she also studied reading, English, spelling, grammar, writing, arithmetic, geography, and the French language. Martha was pleased that she did well in her studies and appreciated remarks such those of a friend on "the soul beaming through her [Nelly's] countenance and glowing in her smile, is as superior to her face, as mind is to matter."

Nelly was always still a distant second to Wash in Martha's affections, though. She usually brought up Wash, and not Nelly, when writing to friends, as she did in a letter to Fanny Bassett in the second year of her husband's presidency. "Dear little Wash is quite well and has a very good appetite and gains flesh and strength every day," she told her. "He is now well enough to go to school."

⚬⚬⚬

The years after the formation of the new government had brought substantial change to American life: shipping to Europe and the Caribbean resumed after the war and was profitable. The end of the war meant new and expanded trade with Britain and other countries. The development of lands in the western sectors of the states meant more agricultural success. A new federal banking system stabilized the U.S. economy, and cities grew and prospered. The 1790s saw more public schools, the first factories, expanded courts, many more elected public officials, new state assemblies, and yet another influx of immigrants.

George Washington wanted people throughout the growing United States to have a direct connection to their federal officials, so the president decided to take national tours to gather opinions about the government from ordinary citizens and give the people a chance to see the man they had elected to lead them. He went on these lengthy excursions, some as long as eighteen hundred miles, nearly every year and was pleased not just at the parades and wild celebrations in every village through which he passed, but also at the confidence of the people in the government. He wrote to the governor of North Carolina, Alexander Martin, that the purpose "was not be to received with parade and an ostentatious display of opulence. It was for a nobler purpose, to see with my own eyes the situation of the country and to learn on the spot the condition and disposition of our citizens. In these respects I have been highly gratified...The effusions of affection and personal regard which were expressed on so many occasions is no less [gratifying]."

Some of these effusions of affection were carefully orchestrated. Dragoons with trumpets often met the president and his escort five or six miles from town to accompany him into the community, where a celebration had been planned for days. Washington, who continually proclaimed his modesty, often alighted from his carriage as the men approached, mounted one of his beautiful white horses, and then led his own parade into the town.

When Washington left Annapolis, Maryland, after a forty-eight-hour visit on his 1791 tour, an editor wrote, "It is no exaggeration to declare that during two days all care seemed suspended; and the inhabitants of a whole town were made happy in contemplating him whom they consider as their safest friend, as well as the most exalted of their fellow citizens and the first of men."

Enormous crowds, with families that had come from one hundred miles away just to see him, met him at every town he entered. The entire adult population of New Bern, North Carolina, greeted him when he arrived in the spring of 1791. The town fathers hosted a three-hour public dinner in his honor, followed by a four-hour ball at which the president, a renowned dancer, glided across the floor with numerous ladies to widespread applause. Three days later he was greeted with a fifteen-cannon, forty-five-shot salute when he arrived at Wilmington, North Carolina, and thousands of people jammed the town square and streets, nearly blocking his route.

He wrote of his reception in 1789 at Portsmouth, Maine, that "the streets, doors, and windows were crowded here, as at all the other places." Wherever he went, choirs sang newly written songs to him, choruses of "War and Washington" were sung loudly, and hours of poems about the president were read from hastily erected wooden speakers' platforms. In Boston, he stood among dignitaries on a balcony on the second floor of the state house to view a parade in his honor that took hours to end and that included so many thousands of people that they had to be organized into categories, such as "mechanics."

He remained humble on all of these travels. The president could do that, contemporaries wrote, because he never had to refer to his fame—everybody else did it for him. "He had no need to seek a false glory...everyone surrounds him, in imagination, with his victories, his triumphs, his glorious toils, his public services," wrote Samuel Smith, president of Princeton University, who had known Washington for years.

These trips were a great success for the president. He found newspapers gushing over his arrival and streets adorned with enormous banners proclaiming his popularity. One banner in Cambridge read: "TO THE MAN WHO UNITES ALL HEARTS." On a later tour of the southern states in 1791, a Virginia newspaper editor wrote with near glee that "on Monday the second at two o'clock p.m., the beloved and excellent GEORGE WASHINGTON, Esq., the President of the United States of America, arrived in this city with his suite, to the inexpressible satisfaction as well of the citizens as of strangers. Never, it may be truly said, was joy, love, affection, and esteem more universal upon any one occasion—and never did these amiable passions of the human heart animate or more brilliantly display themselves than upon this occasion."

And, too, Washington greeted thousands of his soldiers from the army whenever they visited his homes in New York or Philadelphia or went to see him on his national tours. Mrs. Washington, too, loved to meet with veterans of the war at the president's mansion and often entertained them with drinks and cakes when her husband was too busy to see them. Many of the soldiers she welcomed were no strangers; they had met her during the winters of the war.

Whenever he met with visitors, the president asked them how they thought the government was performing. Washington was always interested in what people thought of the federal government, and him. He corresponded with dozens of friends from around America and asked them the same questions. He asked it of any public figure he met with, from governors of large states to town councilmen of little villages. In his quest for feedback, he read as many newspapers as he could and even sent aides into taverns to discreetly listen to the discussions about the government.

Most citizens agreed at the end of President Washington's first term that the new democratic government was working well. "If ever any government might be characterized, in a rationally republican sense, the government of the people, it is indubitably that government," wrote a friend."

John Jay, the first chief justice, wrote of Washington's first term, "It can be said with truth that his administration raised the nation out of confusion into order, out of degradation and distress into reputation and prosperity...and left us flourishing."

Martha's first six months as the first lady were not happy ones. She had trouble adjusting to both her new role, with the eyes of the entire nation on her, and to the transition from Mount Vernon to New York. She constantly asked her niece to remember her and George to friends and neighbors in Virginia and to tell them that she missed them intensely. The quiet shores of the Potomac were a far cry from the noise of New York that she could hear roaring through every window of her new home. All of her friends and associates in New York were new. Her husband poured out his frustrations to her in trying to run the new government while dealing with various factions in the House and Senate. Additionally, both Washingtons were plunged into grief when George's mother, Mary, died in 1789 after a yearlong bout with breast cancer. Mother and son never got along, but George was saddened by her passing.

Martha discovered quickly that since most of the congressmen and senators in the new government could only afford single rooms in Manhattan boarding houses while Congress was in session, they left their wives at home. Martha had hoped to meet and befriend many of those women, but there were few.

Then, much to the sociable Martha's chagrin, George decided that the president could not be just another public figure who traveled from house to house night after night as a much-welcomed dinner guest. He decreed that no one should ask the Washingtons to their home for dinners or even afternoon visits.

On the personal side, she discovered that she did not care for most of the women that she met in New York. She only had a few close friends, such as Lucy Knox and Abigail Adams, and missed them when they were not around. She wrote a mournful letter to Abigail Adams that year after bad weather forced Adams to cancel a visit to the Washingtons' home. "I should have been very happy to have seen you yesterday," she wrote, "and am truly sorry the bad day disappointed me of the pleasure."

And then, in the fall, George went away on a tour of New England. Martha, as always, stayed home. While George dined sumptuously in town after town, and was praised and toasted throughout the night, bored Martha sat home in New York.

Fed up with just about everyone and everything, she wrote a letter full of complaints to her niece that fall, telling Fanny, "I live a very dull life here and know nothing that passes in the town. I never go to the public place...there are certain bounds set for me which I must not depart from and as I cannot do as I like I am obstinate and stay at home a great deal. Indeed, I think I am more like a state prisoner than anything else." Just over a year later, she complained to Janet Montgomery, "I have been so long accustomed to conform to events which are governed by the public voice that I hardly dare indulge any personal wishes."

Her life did get better, though. She complained bitterly to her husband that she was too restricted, and he relented on most of the boundaries he had set for them in his attempt to create an image for the country's first couple. She and the children went outside more, and she and George went shopping, took carriage rides through the city together, and invited friends to their home more frequently. Martha ignored George's embargo on presidential social calls and simply "dropped in" on women she wanted to see. Martha also became close to the president's secretary, Tobias Lear, and his young wife, Polly, twenty-three.

One thing George and Martha had loved and given up during the hectic first six months of the first presidency was the theater. They started to see plays again, much to their satisfaction. They brought many of their friends; a theater party of a dozen people in addition to the first couple was not uncommon. Theaters were delighted to have them in attendance, taking out ads in newspapers to promote their appearance at the play. Theater managers even set aside sections of the best seats for them and a happy musical conductor composed a song called "The President's March," the forerunner to "Hail to the Chief," and orchestras at theaters played it when the Washingtons entered, as did all musical groups at any affair the Washingtons attended.

And, importantly, George promised his wife that for as long as he was the president, at least once a year, perhaps more often, they would return to Mount Vernon for an extended vacation. That pleased Martha greatly. "From that expectation I derive much comfort," she wrote with satisfaction to a friend.

Upon George's recovery from surgery and his return from his triumphant journey through New England, he seemed a changed man to Martha. He was happier, looser, and less worried. He sensed that the people were behind him and the new government. This cheery demeanor enabled him to enjoy life more, and Martha did, too.

So, by the end of 1789, the first year of American democracy and the first presidency, Martha was considerably happier as the first lady. That was evident in a long letter she wrote to friend Mercy Otis Warren the day after Christmas. She told her that she did not want George to become the first president and that she did not want to leave Mount Vernon, but now, after nine months in office, she saw the great love that the people had for her husband. She saw, too, that he had accomplished a great deal in his first year in office and established the presidency, and the country, as something special in the world. The Washingtons had made many friends in that year and now, despite her earlier gloom, the first lady appreciated all of them. She wrote, "This kindness of our numerous friends in all quarters that my new and unwished for situation is not indeed a burden to me."

She went on to say that "when I was much younger I should probably have enjoyed the innocent gayeties of life," but she had become resolute to spending her last years in front of "the fireside at Mount Vernon." She was now comfortable with the upheaval in their lives. She told Mercy Warren that she felt a bit out of place as the first lady, that "the arrangement is not quite as it ought to have been," and that a younger woman, very interested in parties and politics, should have been given the role. But, Martha added, she no longer felt "dissatisfied" with her situation. "No, God forbid, for everybody and everything conspire to make me as contented as possible in it."

She did not like the political life, but Martha, more than any other woman in America, knew that the rivers of fate moved in unusual directions and those rivers had brought her to the presidential mansion and made her husband a historic figure. She was going to make the very best of her lot. She told Warren: "I am still determined to be cheerful and to be happy in whatever situation I may be, for I have also learned from experience that the greater part of our happiness or misery depends upon our dispositions, and not upon our circumstances."

That ability to adapt to changes was one of her great strengths. Jared Sparks, one of the Washingtons' biographers, wrote, "Affable and courteous, exemplary in her deportment, remarkable for her deeds of charity and piety, unostentatious and without vanity, she adorned by her domestic virtues the sphere of private life, and filled with dignity every station in which she was placed."

The Washingtons were not pleased that New York had become the country's capital, and neither were the members of Congress. A decision was made to move the federal government to Philadelphia. The city on the Delaware was the largest in the United States and was considered much more genteel than New York. Massachusetts delegate Fisher Ames wrote of Manhattan, "While I am shut up here in this pigsty, smelling perfumes from wharves and the rakings of gutters, I long for the air and company of Springfield." Virginia congressman John Page added, "[New York] is not half so large as Philadelphia, nor in any way to be compared to it for beauty and elegance…. The [New York] streets are badly paved, dirty, and narrow as well as crooked."

The Washingtons enjoyed their lives in Philadelphia far more than their days in New York. It was more sophisticated than New York and its residents more refined. The Washingtons had friends in Philadelphia from their visits there during the war and George's time there for the Continental Congresses and Constitutional Convention, so the couple was feted at numerous teas and parties. The president continued his Thursday dinners, but Mrs. Washington added a Wednesday reception to her weekly Friday parties, providing even more entertainment at the president's mansion. They enjoyed the city's nightlife, especially the theaters. The Custis grandchildren were enrolled in good schools, the president had miles of open country roads for his horseback riding, and his wife was embraced by the women of Philadelphia and made many friends.

There was tragedy in Philadelphia, though. The Yellow Fever epidemic that swept through Pennsylvania in 1793 killed hundreds of residents of the city, including young Polly Lear, twenty-three, the wife of Washington's secretary Tobias. The entire cabinet, several federal judges, and numerous governmental workers attended her funeral. President Washington had maintained a strict policy of never attending a funeral but, distraught, he broke it to go to the funeral of the wife of his aide and friend. Martha, who had become a close friend of the vivacious young woman, mourned for weeks.

CHAPTER NINETEEN

THE MUCH-ADMIRED WASHINGTONS

G eorge Washington had to do little to establish his image as a popular president and revered national leader; his victory in the war had done that. As president, he met hundreds of foreign diplomats and their wives, and their appreciation of him as both war hero and national leader enhanced his reputation even more.

The French especially were enamored of the new president. Throughout the war, French leaders such as Lafayette, Chastellux, and Rochambeau had written laudatory letters home about him. His portraits hung in the capitals of Europe, even England, his birthday was celebrated as a national holiday in America, and throughout the United States hotels and inns began to display large silhouettes of his face on their front porches.

The presidency became more complex when Washington's second term commenced in the spring of 1793. He was confronted with three major crises that tested his skills as a statesman while, at the same time, rekindled those skills he had shown as a military leader in the Revolution. All three crises were revolutions of their own kind. One was in Europe, one in the territories, and one in the backyard of the federal government—western Pennsylvania.

Controversy accompanied the bloody French Revolution that began in 1789. The government soon fell, King Louis XVI and his wife, Marie Antoinette, were beheaded along with hundreds of others, and in 1793 the new government in Paris declared war on England, Holland, and Spain. The French asked America to come into the war on their side, fulfilling their obligations under the 1780 treaty under which the French had assisted the Americans and helped them win their own Revolution. Washington, however, had no desire to take his struggling young country into a world war in Europe. After weeks of heated cabinet meetings, he decided on a proclamation of neutrality in April 1793 to keep America out of the European conflict. As the cabinet debated, many in America wondered how the country could ignore its clear, legal treaty obligations to France. Washington, pondering at length, decided that even though the treaty was still legal, he just chose to ignore it because the war was not in America's best interests. This proclamation kept America out of the fierce European brawl.

Washington always defended his decision to remain neutral and said of other countries, "I trust we shall never so far lose sight of our own interest and happiness as to become, necessarily, a party in their political disputes...it is among nations as with individuals, the party taking advantage of the distresses of another will lose infinitely more in the opinion of mankind and in subsequent events than he will gain by the stroke of the moment."

He also argued that the U.S. had grown so speedily into a world power since the end of the Revolution that it had the political clout to withstand the insistence of *any* other world power to become its ally in a foreign war. He wrote to a merchants group in Baltimore that "caution must be united with firmness to preserve for the United States the blessings of peace." And he reminded everyone that the U.S. had just finished a terrible war and did not need another. "We have experienced enough of its evils in this country to know that it should not be wantonly or unnecessarily entered upon," he wrote to a business association in Philadelphia.

The president bluntly told a friend that his policy was simple: "meddling as little as possible in their affairs where our own are not involved."

His stand was greeted with sharp criticism. Hundreds of citizens began walking about New York and Philadelphia with tricolored French cockades on their hats. Politicians accused him of breaking his word, and some newspapers thought entry into a world war would benefit the U.S. Washington not only stood firm, but he refused to turn over any of his documents concerning the treaty to the Senate, thereby establishing the historic right of executive privilege for the chief executive.

Shortly afterwards, though, the British Navy, arguing that the ships of neutrals could still be seized, began to halt and board American merchant ships, confiscating goods and imprisoning seaman. Washington sent John Jay to London to negotiate a treaty in 1794 that ended that practice, restored commercial shipping between Britain and the U.S., and, importantly, once again permitted America to collect taxes on British imports.

The treaty stirred controversy in France, where it was seen as prejudicial, and in America, too. Critics charged that the U.S. was now taking great pains to befriend England, the very country it had gone to war against just a decade ago. The treaty did have unintended consequences, though. It shored up American and British trade. It also made the Spanish nervous about their own role in America now that the Americans had both a treaty with France and this new one with England. Two years later, the Spanish signed another treaty in which they guaranteed Americans unimpeded passage of the Mississippi River, the use of the port of New Orleans, and a pledge from the Spanish government to help the Americans defend the Mississippi against any raids by Indians.

It was the Indian problem that confronted Washington with the next crisis of his second term. He had sent the army to put down Indian attacks on settlers in 1779, during the Revolution, and was angered that the same problem resurfaced in 1790. Shawnee and Miami tribes in the western areas of Pennsylvania, Ohio, and what is now Indiana began to harass settlers who flocked to the west, and its cheap lands, after the war. They refused Washington's pleas to become assimilated into the increasingly white population. The president sent General Josiah Harmar with several thousand men to quell the Indian attacks in December of 1790, but Harmar's forces were defeated, with a loss of two hundred men. He then sent a seasoned Revolutionary general, Arthur St. Clair, but his army was routed, too, with a loss of eight hundred men.

Angry at both his failed policy of assimilation and at the loss of so many men, Washington sent another army in 1794, under his old wartime comrade Anthony Wayne. This time Wayne trained and prepared his men for battle and was better equipped. His forces met their Indian opponents at a place called Fallen Timbers, in what is now northern Indiana, and crushed them. The battle ended the Indian wars of the eighteenth century, and new treaties helped to achieve a fragile peace.

The final insurrection came from the irascible Pennsylvania farmers who distilled whiskey in barns. In his continuing effort to raise tax money, Washington imposed a tax on whiskey producers and drinkers, annoying both groups. The farmers who made whiskey refused to pay the tax, drove off tax collectors, and stood firm against the president's policy. Furious, Washington decided to assume the role of commander in chief, put on his old uniform (quite tight now), mount his horse, and ride toward Pittsburgh. There he would assume command of an army directed by Hamilton to attack the recalcitrant farmers. Fortunately, the farmers ended their opposition before Washington arrived. The tempest ended and the farmers paid their taxes.

As first lady, Martha maintained her persona of a nonpolitical woman, but in fact she read the ten newspapers a week that the president received and certainly discussed the important events of his administration with him, just as she had during the war. She commented on some foreign and domestic policy at private parties (she thought the treaty with France should have been declared illegal because it had been made with the king and now he was dead and his monarchy disbanded). Publicly, though, she said nothing. The first lady was probably much like Abigail Adams, discussing events with her spouse in private while making no comments for newspapers. A friend of Mrs. Adams's remarked of her that she "had a distinct view of our public men and measures and had her own opinions which she was free to disclose but not eager to defend in public circles." He might have said the same thing about Mrs. Washington.

Toward the end of his first term, Washington was tired of politics, irritated by the press, and annoyed at threatening foreign governments. He was displeased that the nearly unanimous support he had enjoyed in Congress had begun to unravel. One of his favored projects in the Constitutional Convention in 1787, which already seemed long ago, was to not only carve the country into small congressional districts to give people more of an influence in Congress, but to apportion congressional seats fairly so that no one region gained dominance in voting. Yet in the spring of 1791, just two years into his first term, northern congressional leaders tried to pass a bill that would give top-heavy representation to the northern states. Washington was so angry that he exercised his very first veto, forcing Congress to draw up a fairer districting map. Just a few months later, the Anti-Federalist struck hard, trying to push through legislation that would make their leader, Secretary of State Jefferson, next in line for the presidency if something happened to both the president and vice president. Washington worked with Federalist congressional groups to defeat that motion, but the vote was close. During the final two years of his first term, he encountered yet more resistance from Congress, eroding his tight control of governmental policy. Anti-Federalist newspapers had begun what would later become a series of attacks on his administration.

He had served as president and unified the country. Four years had passed since his election in 1789, and he wanted to leave, but could not. Hundreds begged him to stay, reminding him that while the government had stabilized, there was still turmoil within and without that threatened it and the country still needed him. Hamilton knew how to play to Washington's love of the American people, writing to him that "on patriotic and prudential considerations, the clear path to be pursued by you will be again to obey the voice of your country...I pray God that you will determine to make a further sacrifice of your tranquility and happiness to the public good." Jefferson, too, appealed to Washington's vanity, telling him that the regional disputes and political factions could not be resolved by anyone else.

But there was another reason to stay. Leaving the presidency after four years might bring about the loss of his cherished place in history that he had cultivated so zestfully throughout his life. Martha's friend Elizabeth Powel, the wife of Samuel Powel, a Philadelphia merchant who became the first president of the University of Pennsylvania, put it bluntly, warning him about "quitting a trust upon the proper execution of which the repose of millions might be eventually depending."

Washington then decided to run again, and was again unanimously elected in the electoral college, made up of men chosen for the post by their respective state legislatures. Why did he decide to remain? He agreed with the reasoning of both Hamilton and Jefferson, but he felt the cleavage in the country went beyond their limited political vision. Once again, with the arrival of political parties, disputes with foreign powers, troubles with the Indian tribes, and newspaper criticism, Washington felt, as he felt in 1789, that only he could keep the country together. Sacrifices had to be made—again.

The president, now sixty-two, wrote to an aide, David Humphreys, that spending the rest of his days at Mount Vernon was enticing. "Perhaps in no instance of my life have I been more sensible of the sacrifice than in the present. For at my age, the love of retirement grows every day more and more powerful." Yet, he continued, there was work to be done, to "sink the roots of constitutional government in the virgin soil of America."

He prepared for his second term amid much criticism from his political opponents and opposition newspapers. In some quarters, the public was disappointed in Washington, but there was enormous respect for him. Aaron Bancroft of Massachusetts, who fought at Bunker Hill, wrote, "The first years of his civil administration were attended with the extraordinary fact that, while a great proportion of his countrymen reprobated his measures, they universally venerated his character, and relied implicitly on his integrity."

The president and Mrs. Washington found that no matter how important they became they could not resolve one of the great moral problems of their lives—slavery. The president had gone back and forth on freedom for his slaves many times during his life, even conjuring up a scheme with Lafayette after the war to make a hundred or more slaves paid laborers. He had sent letters to plantation managers, relatives, friends, and public figures asserting his hatred of slavery and his desire for an end to it. Yet he could not bring himself to simply release his workers.

He felt honor-bound to care for his people all of their lives. This resulted in dozens of elderly slaves who could no longer work but had to be housed and fed. As an elderly couple, the Washingtons now had several generations of slave women in their charge who grew up to be mothers and then grandmothers, ever increasing the slave population of Mount Vernon during the Washington presidency.

There was just one movement to eliminate slavery during his presidency. Quakers handed him a petition to abolish the institution in 1790. It was a rare chance for Washington to free his slaves, as he had wanted to do and could have done by using the Quakers as a pretext to save face with his southern slaveholding friends. He would not do it, though. Inexplicably, he scoffed at the resolution, charging that it was "very malapropos" and an "ill-judged piece of business [that] occasioned a great waste of time."

He remained conflicted as president. In 1791, he was warned that under Pennsylvania law, the slaves who lived with him in the presidential mansion in Philadelphia might be ruled freedmen and women after several months residency in that state and taken from him. A nervous Washington, fearing the loss of five or six of his best servants, asked Tobias Lear to devise a scheme, with Martha, to send his servants back to Virginia secretly in a plan he admitted "deceive[ed] the public."

He once again changed his mind about slavery in 1794, at the beginning of his second term. Disheartened that his farm business had slipped while he was away during his presidency, just as it had during the war years, he told Lear that he would sell off several hundred acres of farmland to other planters with instructions for the slaves living on the land to be freed. He followed that up with a letter to friend and former Virginia governor Alexander Spotswood that he might free all three hundred of his slaves. "I would not, in twelve months from this date, be possessed of one slave," he told Spotswood, but the land could not be sold and the plan died.

Then, two years later, he changed his mind yet again. When his wife's closest attendant, Oney Judge, fled the president's mansion with her boyfriend in 1796 and found freedom in New Hampshire, Washington used the powers of his office to try to get her back. An antislavery New Hampshire judge rebuffed him. As president, he also ran ads in newspapers to retrieve any slave that fled Mount Vernon.

All of his efforts to free his slaves were hindered, too, as he noted bitterly in his will, by the legal ownership of the workers. About half belonged to George and the other half were owned by the Custis estate—Martha and her children and grandchildren. Many slaves had intermarried. George could not free his one hundred and fifty without worrying that in so doing he would be breaking up families, something he did not want to do. These conflicted views on slavery would not be resolved until George Washington drew his last breath.

☙❧

Two of the real disappointments of Washington's second term were the growth of political parties and the press attacks on him by newspapers controlled by the Anti-Federalist. Some began during his first term.

He knew that political factions had existed from the time he resigned from the army through his inauguration, but he was blindsided by the emergence of formal, national parties—his Federalist and the Anti-Federalist, or Jeffersonian Republicans, who favored more rights for states in the new government. The president feared that parties would undo everything he had worked for in building a successful government. Washington told friends, "[parties] may now and then answer popular ends, [but] they are likely in the course of time and things, to become potent engines by which cunning, ambitious, and unprincipled men will be enabled to subvert the power of the people and to usurp for themselves the reins of government; destroying afterwards the very engines which have lifted them to unjust dominion." He said that parties were the "worst enemy" of popular government.

The opposition press charged Washington with keeping the "seclusion of a monk and the supercilious distance of a tyrant" and of "harboring dark schemes of ambition." He was accused of "political degeneracy." Critics wrote of his gambling prior to the Revolution, published reports of his love of drinking wine, and called him "a swearer and blasphemer." He was chastised for encouraging people to celebrate his birthday as a national holiday, for acting like a monarch, and for secretly planning to take over the government as an American Cromwell. Even Thomas Paine, whose works he had read to the troops during the war, turned on him, calling him a "hypocrite" and "imposter." One virulent editor wrote that Washington had "debauched" the nation and urged that the day he left office be celebrated as a national holiday.

Publicly, Washington said he was not hurt by the media attacks. Of the critics he said, "I care not; for I have consolation within that no earthly ambitions nor interested motives have influenced my conduct. The arrows of malevolence, therefore, however barbed and well pointed, never can reach the most vulnerable part of me."

Privately, he seethed. Exasperated by the press, he protested to Jefferson that some editors had put him in the same class as "the common pickpocket." Near the end of his first term, he warned Attorney General Edmund Randolph that no one could stop the press from exaggerating and fabricating information and that constant media attacks would bring the entire government to a standstill.

Despite his unhappiness with the media, the president refused suggestions by friends to either shut down critical newspapers or raise postal rates to hurt their circulation. His wife was not so forgiving. Martha was just as angry with the press as her husband. A British diplomat's wife who knew the initial two first ladies wrote that "Mrs. Adams…has spirit enough to laugh at [press] abuse of her husband, which poor Mrs. Washington could not."

Martha constantly complained that the press was unfair to her husband, charging that most reports printed as fact were wild rumors. She was still bitter after George's retirement, writing to her friend Elizabeth Powel that, in just the three months that they had been back in Virginia, the press had turned two minor incidents into major news stories: the overturning of granddaughter Nelly's carriage and serious injuries caused by the accident, and a life-threatening fever that put Washington in bed for weeks and nearly killed him.

Martha wrote that there was "no foundation at all" to either story. On the carriage accident, "no such event ever happened nor has she [Nelly] even received the least hurt by any other accident. She is as well as she ever was in any period of her life." She added that the story about the general's fever was "equally groundless." She said that "in a hot day in May he threw off his flannel; and a sudden change in the weather at night gave him a cold, which disordered but never confined him. This is all the foundation for *that* report."

George Washington complained to Knox, too, that he was exasperated by the members of the new political parties who frequently attacked him. "To misrepresent my motives, to reprobate my politics, and to weaken the confidence which has been reposed in my administration are objects which cannot be relinquished by those who will be satisfied with nothing short of a change in our political system," he told Knox. Then, after some thought, he added that his enemies had failed, that his popularity upon leaving office "deprives their sting of its poison."

Tired and frustrated by the growing complexities of the presidency, George Washington decided to leave office and return to Mount Vernon at the end of his second term. He was physically exhausted. Washington felt that the duties and responsibility of the presidency had become far more arduous as the years went by and the new American republic became a major participant on the world stage. While pleased with his success as president, the public work he had completed, and his foreign policy decisions, he was saddened that his two terms brought about rifts between his friends. Hamilton and Jefferson never got along as he had hoped, and both resigned their offices because of their animosity toward each other. Washington no longer saw his old Virginia friend Edmund Randolph when the latter became involved in unethical conduct with foreign officials during the president's second term.

He explained at great lengths his desire to retire to anyone in the capital who asked him but, oddly, he put it best in a simple statement to a delegation of visiting Cherokee Indians. He told them that they should stop their constant roaming, stay in one place, and become farmers. He added, "What I have recommended to you I am myself going to do. After a few moons are passed, I shall leave the great town and retire to my farms. There, I shall attend to the means of increasing my cattle, sheep, and other useful animals, to the growing of corn, wheat, and other grain and to the employing of women spinning and weaving."

His last duty, as he saw it, was to write a farewell address to the people. What he penned, with the help of James Madison and Alexander Hamilton, was published in September 1796 in all of the newspapers in the United States. It was an extraordinary address that not only summed up his success as the country's first president, but also outlined his hopes for the American nation in the centuries to come.

"The name American, which belongs to you in your national capacity, must always exalt the just pride of patriotism more than any appellation derived from local discriminations," he wrote, reminding the people that they were a united nation and not a collection of colonies or states any longer, that they lived in "a common country" and that in a real sense, as Americans, they had, with slight shades of difference, "the same religion, manners, habits and political principals." He told them that they had fought hard to earn their liberty in a bloody war against England and that they deserved what they had. They had a responsibility, too, to maintain their liberty now and assure that it would flourish in the future.

The president declared that the Constitution was a noble document and, since it could be amended, would always serve as a sturdy framework for liberty. Americans had to be loyal to their country and liberty because both went hand in hand. He urged them to always see the United States as a whole, and to fear any political party that might emerge to endanger that because of self-interest. Parties, he warned, could "serve always to distract the public councils and enfeeble the public administration. It agitates the community with ill-founded jealousies and false claims, kindles the animosity of one part against another, foments occasional riot and insurrection...it opens the door to foreign influence and corruption."

And it was foreign influence that worried Washington the most. "'Tis our true policy to steer clear of permanent alliances," he wrote of foreign entanglements. He said the Republic could only remain strong if it kept out of the affairs of other countries. "The nation," he wrote, "which indulges towards another an habitual hatred, or an habitual fondness, is in some degree a slave. It is a slave to its animosity or to its affection, either of which is sufficient to lead it astray from its duty and its interest...there can be no greater error than to expect or calculate upon real favors from nation to nation."

He reported that despite the problems the country faced, it was doing well and that, after just eight years, the United States was a stable democracy of which the people could be proud. He summed up his presidency with some satisfaction:

"The situation in which I now stand for the last time, in the midst of the representatives of the people of the United States, naturally recalls the period when the administration of the present form of government commenced; and I cannot omit the occasion to congratulate you and my country on the success of the experiment; nor to repeat my fervent supplications to the Supreme Ruler of the universe, and Sovereign arbiter of nations, that His providential care may be extended to the United States; that the virtue and happiness of the people may be preserved, and that the government, which they have instituted for the protection of their liberties, may be perpetual."

George Washington had accomplished just what he set out to do: he had achieved unity and stability. Wrote Samuel Smucker, an early nineteenth-century historian, "He left the Republic in a compact and united condition; the community at large flourishing and prosperous; and their reputations among foreign nations as a young and vigorous empire, unspotted. Greatly respected and destined to achieve with the lapse of time, a high and glorious position among the oldest communities on the globe."

Even though some of the opposition newspapers grumbled that they were glad he had left, the reaction of the press and the people to the presidency of George Washington was overwhelmingly positive. Most citizens agreed that he studied issues of the day and the bills before him for some time before deciding how he stood, that he kept close tabs on his federal departments and always knew what their administrators were doing, and that he was honest and never duplicitous with people. Chief Justice John Marshall wrote that he admired Washington for always adhering to the Constitution and for risking his reputation with decisions that were often controversial. He said that Washington's greatest skill was in spending much time soliciting and listening to different opinions on a matter that required presidential action and then, after substantial advice, acting. "His decisions, thus maturely made, were seldom if ever to be shaken."

John Jay wrote of the presidency that Washington always enjoyed the support of the people. "When at a subsequent and alarming period, the nation found that their affairs had gone into confusion, and that clouds portending danger and distress were rising over them, in every quarter, they instituted under his auspices a more efficient government, and unanimously committed the administration of it to him. Would they have done this without the highest confidence in his political talents and wisdom?"

Massachusetts congressman Fisher Ames reminded people that almost all generals who became the heads of their country, usually in bloody coups, made poor chief executives. Washington was a great one. Ames wrote that the entire Revolutionary and colonial era would be called "the age of Washington."

It was not in his lengthy and much-quoted grandiose farewell address, printed in just about every newspaper in the world, that Washington really explained his satisfaction in serving eight years as America's first president. He put it bluntly, and best, in a short note to the people of tiny Shepherdstown, Virginia (now in West Virginia). He wrote to them that "if it has been my good fortune, through the course of my civil and military employment, to have met the approbation of my countrymen, my wishes will be consummated; and I shall have found the only reward I ever had in view."

Upon Washington's selection as the commander in chief of the Continental Army in 1775, John Adams had told friends that the new general would become "one of the great characters of the world." In 1797, Adams succeeded him as president following a heated election against Thomas Jefferson, who became vice president. Washington had been feted lavishly on his final birthday in office on February 22 at a large party that signaled the end of his public life. Those there said that the president was barely able to speak when asked for a toast and that Mrs. Washington sobbed. Still, the nation's first president was glad to leave office. He told Adams at his inaugural that he was glad to be going. "I am fairly out and you are fairly in! See which of us will be happiest!"

CHAPTER TWENTY

FIRST IN THE HEARTS OF THEIR COUNTRY- MEN: THE FINAL RETIREMENT

The Washingtons headed home to Virginia shortly after Adams's inauguration. The trip back to Mount Vernon took seven days because many towns insisted on hosting the new ex-president. The Delaware Light Horse military regiment accompanied the Washingtons through their state and then turned the honor over to the Light Horse troop from Maryland, which rode with them to Baltimore. Thousands of people in Baltimore filled the streets to welcome the him on his way south to Virginia. They arrived home exhausted, and went to sleep. The next morning George Washington happily began his retirement. "Grandpapa is very well and has already turned farmer again," wrote his granddaughter of his return.

Over the past few years, the Washingtons had carted numerous purchases and gifts from Philadelphia to Mount Vernon. These included a plow manufactured in New England, new lightning rods made for them by Benjamin Franklin, a carpet, glass lamps, packages of chocolates, a set of china, pineapples for preservation, goats for breeding, combs, children's furniture, guitars, and a striking new blue cape, flame-red on the inside, for the president. On his final trip, the president made certain that his aides packed all of the Washingtons' remaining clothes and boots, and that they remembered, above all, to bring with them the president's dog and Mrs. Washington's bird, a beautiful cockatoo.

On his very first day back at Mount Vernon, a very cloudy March 16, ex-president Washington rose at dawn, as he always did, washed, shaved, and sat down at his desk in the office below their bedroom to begin sorting out plantation paperwork. His public life was over. He wrote in his diary of that day, "At home all day alone."

The president was once again called the general by everyone and he set about inspecting his home and property and was appalled at the disrepair, as he had been upon his last return in 1783, fifteen years earlier. He lost no time in donning the clothes of a farmer, perhaps his most beloved role in his long life, and plunging into the supervision of repair crews in the main house and throughout his lands. "I have scarcely a room to put a friend into or set in myself without the music of hammers or the odoriferous smell of paint," he happily wrote to his former aide and the new secretary of war, James McHenry.

George and Martha received numerous letters thanking both of them for their friendship over the years. Artist John Trumbull was thankful that Washington had sat for the many portraits which made Trumbull world-famous, and he added, "I have viewed with that gratitude which is due to him from all his countrymen, the great and continued service which he has not ceased to render to America and have admired in common with the world, that great example which his life has offered to mankind."

Press and political criticism subsided once he was out of office. Wrote a minister: "Although his opponents eventually deemed it expedient to vilify his character, that they might diminish his political influence, yet the moment that he retired from public life, they returned to their expressions of veneration and esteem."

Ever the inventive farmer, the former president quickly began working on a new and improved wheat threshing machine, reorganized his lands, rotated his crops, and even built a large whiskey distillery, one of the first in the South. He hired a full-time housekeeper to give Martha free time after eight years as the first lady, and added Albio Rawlins to serve as his personal clerk.

He let everybody know that his political life had ended and that he was glad of it, writing to the new treasury secretary Oliver Wolcott that "to make and sell a little flour annually; to repair houses...and to amuse myself in agricultural and rural pursuits will constitute employment for the few years I have to remain on this terrestrial globe."

Mount Vernon was a busy place. In 1795, two years after his wife's death, Tobias Lear had married Martha's niece, Fanny Bassett, which delighted the Washingtons. Then, tragically, Fanny died nine months later. In a romantic twist, the grieving Lear was consoled by another niece, Frances Dandridge Henley. The two soon married and moved to Mount Vernon with the president and first lady. Lear's mother, Mary, would visit at Mount Vernon for months at a time. Harriet, Washington's late brother Sam's daughter, had been in residence with her husband Andrew Parks when the Washingtons retired and had made herself very much at home (they later moved to Betty Washington's home in Fredericksburg). Another addition was Lawrence Lewis, his sister Betty's favorite son. Washington was looking for someone, preferably family, to help with his responsibilities and to assist in the never-ending entertainment. Lewis moved in and was liked by everyone. He was especially liked by George and Martha's granddaughter, Nelly, who married him eighteen months later on her grandfather's final birthday in a small but elegant ceremony at Mount Vernon. The general and his wife hosted the wedding and reception and were very pleased with the marriage (though, as the years passed, Nelly missed the glamorous life around George Washington and found her marriage to the quiet Lewis rather dull).

George's grandson, George Washington Parke Custis, "Wash," was not much of a scholar. The irresponsible Wash had been spoiled by his grandmother just as she had spoiled Jacky. Lear wrote when the grandchildren were young that Martha "will experience many sorrowful hours on their accounts when the effects of her blind indulgence of them comes to display itself more fully—every day produces sad proofs of its evil tendency." Yet George did not step in to stop Martha's coddling because he understood that Wash was a replacement for Jacky. He told Lear, "Mrs. Washington's happiness is bound up in the boy. Any rigidity towards him would perhaps be productive of grievous effects on her."

Wash drifted through tutoring during his early years, with little interest in learning, just like his father, but the Washingtons used their influence to get their grandson admitted to Philadelphia College (later the University of Pennsylvania). There, Wash floundered. Martha wrote to her niece Fanny that "my dear little Wash is not doing half so well as I could wish. We are mortified that we cannot do better for him."

Wash wrote to his overly concerned grandfather that he was applying himself to education. At first, George's return letters were full of encouragement and useful advice. He told him to work hard, put aside time for his studies each day, respect his professors, and try to get along with fellow students. He advised Wash to establish good habits because they would help him succeed after graduation, that a good student made a good citizen. He urged him to be kind to everyone he met and to give any indigent person he passed money if he had some in his pocket.

He wrote to his grandson, "The assurances you give me of applying diligently to your studies and fulfilling those obligations which are enjoined by your Creator and due to his creatures are highly pleasing and satisfactory to me. I rejoice in it on two accounts. First, as it is the sure means of laying the foundation of your own happiness and rendering you...a useful member of society hereafter. Secondly, that I may if I live to enjoy the pleasure, reflect that I have been, in some degree, instrumental in effecting these purposes."

Wash assured Washington that he was studying hard and making progress. "The translating of French has become quite familiar," he told his grandfather, and added that his penmanship had improved, along with his study of classic literature, geography, and even arithmetic. The officials at the school painted a different picture, though, telling the president that not only was Wash not studying, he was spending much of his time with disreputable characters. George wrote to them that he was at wit's end over his grandson's education and view of the world. "I could say nothing to him now by way of admonition, encouragement or advice that has not been repeated over and over again," he wrote to Dr. Samuel Smith, president of Princeton, where he enrolled after being expelled from Philadelphia College.

But every time that Wash was criticized by George or some college official, he would write the president a letter of deep remorse and promise to hit the books. He answered one scathing letter from his grandfather by telling him, "Dearest sir, did you but know the effect your letter had produced, it would give you as consummate pleasure as my former one did pain. My very soul, tortured with the strains of conscience at length called reason to its aid and happily for me triumphed. That I shall ever recompense you for the trouble I have occasioned is beyond my hopes...could you see how happy I now am, you would soon forget all that is past...that I have abused such goodness is shocking, that I shall ever do so again, I will risk my life."

The gullible president was relieved but reminded his grandson, yet again, to keep away from bawdy characters, that he should not "mistake ribaldry for wit and rioting, or swearing, intoxication and gambling for manliness."

In another letter, his grandfather scolded Wash for extravagances when it came to his clothes, but the boy answered, as always, that he was innocent of those charges and that "I am not fond of such things, and have not spent money in that way." And then there were Wash's many women. His grandfather reprimanded him for paying too much attention to girls at college and not enough to his books and wrote to him that "the hours that might be more profitably employed at your studies are misspent in this manner."

Wash, as always, pledged to reform and he constantly told his grandfather how much he loved him. In April 1798, he wrote to the ex-president and apologized for all of his shortcomings and then expressed his "gratitude and obligations to you...they are indelibly ingrained on my mind and can never be erased."

In a series of letters, Wash told his grandfather exactly what he wanted to hear, taking great pains to remind him that on the Fourth of July, the national holiday, he had joined others in the annual independence celebrations at Princeton, firing off cannons all day and attending a ball at night to celebrate the day that America declared an independence that his grandfather then won on the battlefield.

Wash bounced from school to school—Philadelphia, Princeton, and St. John's College, in Annapolis, ejected from all three—and at each his grandfather reminded the college president that his son needed all the help they could give him. When he went to St. John's, Washington wrote to the head of the institution that "there seems to be in this youth an unconquerable indolence of temper and a dereliction to all study." He reminded them all too, as he did the president of St. John's, that his son had spent far more time chasing women than studying and implored them to keep the young ladies of the town far away from his handsome grandson.

Wash's expulsions from schools did not surprise George, who had been through it all before with Jacky. He wrote to Samuel Smith, the president of Princeton, that "from his infancy I have discovered an almost unconquerable disposition to indolence in everything he did that did not tend to his amusements" and added that he would not even attempt to beg Smith to let his grandson back in.

His grandfather knew Wash's intellectual limitations, telling family friends, "I believe Washington means well, but has not resolution to act well."

But his grandmother always downplayed the young man's academic failures, writing to friends that he "is at Princeton doing well," or that Wash's education had, in fact, somehow been enhanced by attending three colleges.

George had more family woes. He had promised to care for his late brother Sam's two sons, and to put them through college, and he fumed at Mount Vernon that the boys were now charging him for music lessons, music stands, French lessons, fancy shoe buckles, expensive silk stockings, and even a hairdresser that coifed them in their rooms three times a week.

Death had claimed all of his brothers and sisters except Charles and also many of his wartime comrades, such as Nathanael Greene, dead at just forty-six, and Robert Harrison, only forty-five. He had even survived many members of the First Continental Congresses and the governors he worked with so closely during the war. George was not maudlin about their passing, but Martha was. She wrote about her own and George's death to a friend, trying to make it comical, that they might both die in fits of laughter. She wrote to her old best friend and neighbor Sally Fairfax, who fled America with her husband just before the Revolution, and forlornly told her that the Potomac neighborhood they knew as young women no longer existed.

She wrote to Sally, "The changes which have taken place in this county since you left it (and it is pretty much the case in all other parts of this state) are, in one word, total. In Alexandria, I do not believe there lives at this day a single family with whom you had the smallest acquaintance. In our neighborhood, Colonel Mason, Colonel McCarthy and wife, Mr. Chichester, Mr. Lund Washington, and all of the Wageners have left the stage of human life: and our visitors on the Maryland side are gone, and going likewise."

Even as an old man, Washington cut an impressive figure back in Virginia. A passerby who saw him step out of a boat at a dock in Alexandria to march in a parade in his honor when he was sixty-six, just a year before his death, described him this way: "He was six foot, one inches high, athletic, with very large limbs, entirely erect, and without the slightest tendency to stooping; his hair was white and tied with a silk string, his countenance lofty, masculine, and contemplative; his eye light gray. He was dressed in the clothes of a citizen and over these a blue suit out of the finest cloth. His weight must have been two hundred and thirty pounds, with no superfluous flesh, all was bone and sinew and he walked like a soldier."

Then, as the parade began, Washington's eyes were attracted to something beyond the crowd and, the man noted, as so many who met Washington did during his life, his whole face changed. He wrote that "his eye was instantaneously lighted up with the lightning's flash. At this moment I see its marvelous animation, its glowing fire, exhibiting strong passion." Others remembered too, that, even in his sixties, his eyes and face took on a sudden animation and passion when he seemed intrigued by something.

That passion did not last much longer. On December 12, 1799, two years after his retirement from the presidency, Washington went riding, as he always did, but stayed out far too long on a day when it was difficult to travel because of intermittent sleet storms and light snowfalls. The president returned to his home at Mount Vernon late in the afternoon and was quite hungry. He dismissed pleas from his wife and Tobias Lear that he change his wet clothes before dining. The president remained in his damp clothes most of the night and awoke the following morning at 5 a.m. as usual, and went out to make morning inspections of the farms. He returned home that afternoon tired and drawn and had a very bad sore throat. In the early hours of the next morning he awoke in bed with a start, hardly able to breathe, phlegm building in his throat, a fever raging through him.

Martha summoned everyone in the household and sent a rider to Alexandria to fetch Dr. James Craik. An alarmed Craik brought two other doctors and, worried at Washington's condition, they began the standard practice of bleeding the patient. Martha had no faith in bleeding and told them so, but the bleedings continued throughout the day and night. Her homemade remedy of molasses and onions, which had chased away his sore throat on so many occasions in the past, did no good now and he began to sink.

Washington's condition deteriorated rapidly, and within twenty-four hours he was gravely ill and hardly able to breathe. In words that were barely audible, the president asked Martha and Tobias Lear to burn old wills and to save a new will he had recently written in a drawer. In the new will, in addition to bequeathing possessions to members of his family, he made arrangements to free all of the more than one hundred slaves that he owned and set aside money for their care.

Washington started to fade. He whispered to Lear and Martha, "Have me decently buried and do not let my body be put in the vault in less than three days after I am dead. Do you understand?" he said, looking at Lear, who shook his head in agreement.

"'Tis well," the president whispered, and then he died.

"Is he gone?" Martha asked Lear as the general's hand went limp. Lear nodded.

"I shall soon follow," Martha said quietly, and rose to tell the members of the household that the general had passed away.

Eulogies were delivered all over the globe. Perhaps the most famous one in America was given by Henry Lee, highlighted by his remembrance of his friend as "first in war, first in peace, first in the hearts of his countrymen." John Marshall was just as gracious, telling the U.S. House of Representatives that "more than any other individual, and as much as to one individual was possible, has he contributed to found this our wide-spreading empire, and to give to the Western world its independence and its freedom." Jefferson, a longtime friend and later a political enemy, said George Washington was not just a leader for his times, but for all time. "His was the singular destiny and merit, of leading the armies of his country successfully through an arduous war for the establishment of its independence; of conducting its councils through the birth of a government, new in its form and principles, until it had settled down into a quiet and orderly train; and of scrupulously obeying the laws through the whole of his career, civil and military, of which the history of the world furnishes no other example."

Memorialists were just as effusive in England. The editor of the *London Courier* wrote of Washington, "The whole range of history does not present to our view a character upon which we can dwell with such entire and unmixed admiration." The editor of the *British Register* wrote, "No one ever passed through the ordeal of power and influence more free from the remotest suspicion of selfish and ambitious designs. To have passed so unsullied through a career of glory and usefulness is so high and rare a blessing."

Perhaps the greatest eulogy was silent. Upon hearing of his death, the king of England ordered the flags on all of the ships in the British Navy, Washington's fierce enemies so long ago, to be lowered to half-mast.

Most of the people who visited after George's passing found Martha a shattered woman. She moved out of the bedroom she shared with George and turned a small room on the third floor into a chamber where she spent most of her time. Every morning, she walked slowly down a narrow path to George's tomb to pray. She told Manasseh Cutler that she had "become a stranger among her friends" and "welcomed the time she should be called to follow her deceased friend." Everyone noted that she had lost the "cheerful disposition" that was her hallmark since those first days that people met her at dances in the springtime at Williamsburg when she was a giddy teenaged girl looking for boys.

Oliver Wolcott visited her in the summer of 1800, seven months after George died, and found her an emotional wreck. He wrote to his wife that "the decay of strength, the increasing marks of age and occasional suffusion of countenance plainly show that the zest of life has departed."

Mrs. Henrietta Liston, wife of the British ambassador, saw her twice that same summer and was saddened. "I listened with tender interest to [her] sorrow, which she said was truly breaking her heart," Mrs. Liston wrote, adding that she was "grieving incessantly. She repeatedly told me that…all comfort had fled with her husband and that she awaited anxiously her [death]. It was evident that her health was fast declining and her heart breaking." Mrs. William Thornton wrote, "Mrs. Washington is much broke since I saw her last."

In Martha's last months, those who lived at Mount Vernon were upset at her decline. Dr. Craik, the family physician for over forty years, described the demeanor of everyone when he told the story of Martha's pet parrot. The bird had lived in Philadelphia and at Mount Vernon for many years, spending much time on the veranda overlooking the Potomac, where he flew in and out of his cage at will. On May 20, 1802, Thomas Cope, his family, and a friend of his daughter's visited Martha, but could not see her because she was bedridden. Dr. Craik entertained them on the porch that overlooked the Potomac. Suddenly, the parrot flew out of his cage and, chattering away, flapping his wings and scratching, attempted to perch himself on the shoulder of Cope's daughter's friend. The girl, startled, chased him away, jumped out of the chair, and fled. The parrot, rebuffed and disheartened, returned to his cage and sulked. Craik explained that the bird had been fed, caressed, and played with daily by Martha for years and loved Mrs. Washington dearly. Without her, "he seems quite lost and dejected."

Martha was very disturbed by what might have been an attempt to burn down her home in the winter of 1800 by slaves who knew they would be freed upon her death. Extremely upset, and anxious to avoid further trouble, she then freed the slaves in January 1801. Martha Washington was ready for death, which came on May 22, 1802, as another spring was underway at her beloved Mount Vernon, the home her new husband had brought her to in the long-ago spring of 1759. She gave instructions for her funeral to her grandchildren and laid out a white gown as her last dress. Then Martha Washington died, displaying "fortitude and resignation throughout," according to Thomas Law, who was there at the end.

Letters of condolences poured in. Granddaughter Eliza Custis wrote that "the first of men chose her as his wife—the companion of a life of glory—and well did she repay his confidence and attachment." A slave who worked for her remembered the famous Mrs. Washington as a woman who "didn't suppose she was so much better than anyone else." President Jefferson, who was detested by Martha late in life, was saddened at her passing. He wrote that she was "benevolent and virtuous in life...in my judgment as one of the most estimable of women, and had inspired me with an affectionate and respectful attachment to her."

There were hundreds of newspaper tributes around the world. The editor of the *Alexandria Advertiser and Commercial Intelligencer* may have been closer than anyone in assessing the

Washingtons' remarkable union when he wrote, "She was the worthy partner of the worthiest of men, and those who witnessed their conduct could not determine which excelled in their different characters, both were so well sustained on every occasion."

Martha Washington was buried next to the young colonel she had met at a friend's house one blustery late winter afternoon in 1758, a man who had gone on, with her always at his side, through numerous personal tragedies and public crises, to, more than anyone else, create the United States of America.

BIBLIOGRAPHY

PAPERS

Arnold-Screven Papers. University of North Carolina.

Beatty Brothers. Papers. Morristown National Historical Park.

Boudinot, Elias. Simon-Boudinot Papers. Princeton University Library.

Gates, Horatio. Papers. New York Historical Society.

Knox, Henry. Papers. Morristown National Historical Park.

Langdon, John. Papers. Lilly Library, Indiana University.

Mount Vernon Library Papers.

Southern Historical Collection, University of North Carolina.

Stewart, Charles. Papers. New York Historical Society.

Valley Forge Historical Park Papers.

Washington, George. Papers. Library of Congress.

Washington, Martha. Papers. Mount Vernon Library Collection.

Wayne, Anthony. Papers. Huntington Library, San Marino, California.

Wild, Ebenezer. Papers. Massachusetts Historical Society.

JOURNALS

"Letters of George Washington Bearing on the Negro." *Journal of Negro History,* October, 1917.

"Quartermaster's Receipt Book in the Revolution." *Proceedings of the New Jersey Historical Society,* July, 1920.

Abraham, Mildred. "The Library of Lady Jean Skipwith: A Book Collection from the Age of Jefferson." *Virginia Magazine of History and Biography* 91, July, 1983.

Beale, Richard, ed. "The Colonial Virginia Satirist: Mid-Eighteenth Century Commentaries on Politics, Religion and Society." American Philosophical Society, *Transactions* VII, 1967.

Bradford, S. Sydney. "Hunger Menaces the Revolution." *Maryland Historical Magazine,* March, 1966.

Breen, T.H. "The Culture of Agriculture: The Symbolic World of the Tidewater Planter, 1760–1790." David Murrin, John Hall and Tad Thate, eds. *Saints and Revolutionaries: Essays on Early American History.* New York: W.W. Norton, 1984.

Corry, John. "Sketch of the Life of the Late General Washington." *British Magazine,* February—June, 1800.

Humphrey, Carol Sue. "George Washington and the Press," in Mark Rozell, William Pederson, Frank Williams, eds. *George Washington and the Origins of the American Presidency.* Westport, Conn.: Praeger Press, 2000.

Hunter, John. "Diary of John Hunter." *Pennsylvania Magazine of History and Biography* 17 (1893).

Latrobe, Benjamin. "Through Virginia to Mount Vernon: Extracts from the Journal of Benjamin Henry Latrobe." *Appleton's Booklovers Magazine* 6, 1905.

Longworth, Polly. "Portrait of Martha Washington." *Journal of the Colonial Williamsburg Foundation.* Summer, 1998.

Macauley, Alexander. "Alexander Macauley's Journal." *William & Mary Quarterly,* First Series, XI, 1902–3.

Mitros, David. "Shepard Kollock and the New Jersey Journal." *Morris County Circular,* 2001.

Norton, Paul and F.M. Halliday, eds. "Latrobe's America." *American Heritage,* August, 1962.

Nutting, P. Bradley. "Tobias Lear, S.P.U.S., First Secretary to the President." *Presidential Studies Quarterly,* XXIV, Fall, 1994.

Parker, Robert. "Robert Parker Diary." *Pennsylvania Magazine of History and Biography* 28 (1904).

Smelser, Marshall. "George Washington and the Alien and Sedition Acts." *American History Review,* January, 1954.

Thompson, Mary. "First Father: George Washington as a Parent." Mount Vernon Ladies Association Paper, April, 2000.

Tilden, Robert, trans. Johann Doehla. "The Doehla Journal." *William and Mary Quarterly,* 2d Series, 1942.

Torrence, Clayton, ed. "Arlington and Mount Vernon, 1856: As Described in a Letter of Augusta Berard." *Virginia Magazine of History and Biography* (April, 1949).

Vail, R.W.G. "A Dinner at Mount Vernon : Form the Unpublished Journal of Joshua Brooks (1773–1859)." *New York Historical Society Quarterly,* April 1947.

Wordham, George. "A Physical Description of George Washington." *Daughters of the American Revolution Magazine,* February, 1974.

PAMPHLETS

Torres-Reyes, R. *A Study of Medical Services in the 1779–1780 Winter Encampment.* National Park Service, Washington Association, 1971.

BOOKS

200 Years Ago Today at Valley Forge. Valley Forge Historical Park, 1979.

Abbot, W.W. Ed. *The Papers of George Washington.* 45 vols. Charlottesville: University of Virginia Press, 1987–2005.

Adams, Charles. ed. *The Letters of Mrs. Adams, the Wife of John Adams,* 3rd ed. 2 vols. Boston, 1841.

Alden, John. *George Washington: A Biography.* Baton Rouge: Louisiana State University Press, 1984.

Alison, Archibald. *History of Europe from the Commencement of the French Revolution to the Restoration of the Bourbons.* 10 vols. London, 1829–1642.

Andrews, Charles. *Colonial Folkways, Chronicle of America.* New Haven: Yale University Press, 1921.

Andrews, Garnett. *Reminiscences of an Old Georgia Lawyer.* Atlanta: Franklin Stearns Printing House, 1870.

Bain, Chester. *A Body Incorporate: The Evolution of City and County Separation in Virginia.* Charlottesville: University of Virginia Press, 1967.

Baker, W.S. Ed. *Character Portraits of Washington, as Delineated by Historians, Orators and Divines, Selected and Arranged in Chronological Order, With Biographical Notes and References.* Philadelphia: Robert Lindsay, 1887.

Baker, William. *Washington After the Revolution, 1789–1799.* Philadelphia: J.P. Lippincott Company, 1898.

Bancroft, Aaron. *The Life of George Washington: Commander-in-Chief of the American Army, through the Revolutionary War; and the first President of the United States.* London: Stockdale, 1808.

Benson, Mary. *Women in Eighteenth Century America: A Study of Opinion and Social Usage.* Port Washington, NY: Kennikat Press, 1935.

Berlin, Ira and Philip Morgan, eds. *Cultivation and Culture: The Shaping of Slave Life in the Americas.* Charlottesville: University of Virginia Press, 1993.

Bernard, John. *Retrospectives of America, 1797–1811.* New York: Harper Brothers, 1887.

Billings, Warren, John Selby and Tad Thate, eds. *Colonial Virginia: A History.* White Plains: KTO Press, 1996.

Binger, Carl. *Revolutionary Doctor: Benjamin Rush, 1746–1813.* New York: W.W. Norton, 1966.

Blanton, Wyndham. *Medicine in Virginia in the Eighteenth Century.* Richmond, 1931.

Blumenthal, Walter. *Brides from Bridewell: Female Felons Sent to Colonial America.* Westport: Greenwood Press, 1972.

Boatner, Mark. *Encyclopedia of the American Revolution.* Mechanicsburg, PA.: Stackpole Books, 1994.

Bourne, Miriam. *First Family: George Washington and His Intimate Relations.* New York: W.W. Norton, 1982.

Boyd, George. *Elias Boudinot, Patriot and Statesman, 1740–1821.* Princeton: Princeton University Press, 1952.

Boyd, Julian. *The Papers of Thomas Jefferson.* 31 vols. Princeton:Princeton University Press, 1950.

Boyle, Lee. *Writings from the Valley Forge Encampment of the Continental Army, December 1777-June 19, 1778.* 5 vols. Bowie, MD: Heritage Books, 2001–2005.

Brady, Patricia. *George Washington's Beautiful Nelly: The Letters of Eleanor Parke Custis Lewis to Elizabeth Bordley Gibson, 1794–1853.* Columbia: University of South Carolina Press, 1991.

Brown, Kathleen. *Good Wives, Nasty Wenches and Anxious Patriarchs: Gender, Race and Power in Colonial Virginia.* Chapel Hill: University of North Carolina Press, 1996.

Bryan, Helen. *Martha Washington: First Lady of Liberty.* New York: John Wiley and Sons, 2003.

Bryant, Arthur. *The American Ideal.* Freeport: Books for Libraries Press, 1969.

Butterfield, L.H., ed. *Adams Family Correspondence.* 6 vols. Cambridge: Harvard University Press, 1963.

Cary, Virginia. *Letters on Female Character.* 2d ed. Philadelphia, 1830.

Chandler, J.A.C. and T. B. Thames. *Colonial Virginia.* Richmond: Times-Dispatch Company, 1907.

Chinard, Gilbert. *George Washington as the French Knew Him: A Collection of Texts.* Princeton: Princeton University Press, 1940.

Clinton, Catherine. *Plantation Mistress: Woman's World in the Old South.* New York: Pantheon Books, 1982.

Cometti, Elizabeth, ed. *The American Journals of Lt. John Enys.* Syracuse: Syracuse University Press, 1976.

Conway, George. *George Washington and Mount Vernon, A Collection of Washington's Unpublished Agricultural and Personal Letters Edited with Historical and Genealogical Introduction.* New York: Long Island Historical Society, 1889.

Cooley, Henry. *A Study of Slavery in New Jersey: Johns Hopkins University Studies in Historical and Political Science.* 14th Series. New York: Johnson Reprint, 1973.

Cornwell, Alfred and John Meyer. *The Economics of Slavery and Other Studies in Economic History.* Chicago: Aldine Co., 1964.

Cott, Nancy. *The Bonds of Womanhood: "Woman's Sphere" in New England, 1780–1835.* New Haven: Yale University Press, 1997.

Dalzell, Robert and Lee Baldwin Dalzell. *George Washington's Mount Vernon: A Home in Revolutionary America.* New York: Oxford University Press, 1998.

Darlington, William, ed. Christopher Gist. *Christopher Gist's Journals, With Historical Geographical and Ethnological Notes.* Pittsburgh: J.R. Weldon and Co., 1893.

Davis, David Brion. *The Problem of Slavery in the Age of Revolution, 1770–1823.* Ithaca: Cornell University Press, 1975.

Depauw, Linda, Conover Hunt, and Mariam Schneir. *Remember the Ladies: Women in America, 1750–1815.* New York: Viking Press, 1976.

Desmond, Alice. *Martha Washington: Our First Lady.* New York: Dodd, Mead & Co., 1943.

Diamant, Lincoln, ed. *Revolutionary Women in the War for American Independence, a One Volume Revised Edition of Elizabeth Ellet's 1848 Landmark Series.* Westport: Praeger, 1998. *Diary of a Little Colonial Girl.* Richmond, Virginia, 1903.

Dowdy, Clifford. *A Climate for Greatness: Virginia, 1732–1775.* Boston: Little, Brown and Company, 1970.

Dunlap, John. *Sentiments of an Americana Woman.* Philadelphia, 1780.

Eddis, William. *Letters from America: Historical and Descriptive, Comprising Occurrences from 1769 to 1777, Inclusive.* London, 1792.

Ewing, William. *The Sports of Williamsburg.* Richmond: Dietz Press, 1937.

Familiar Letters of Public Men of the Revolution. Philadelphia, 1847.

Farish, Hunter, ed. *Journal and Letters of Reverend Phillip Fithian, 1773 1774, a Plantation Tutor of the Old Dominion.* Williamsburg, VA.: Colonial Williamsburg Press, 1943.

Ferling, John. *First of Men: A Life of George Washington.* Knoxville: University of Tennessee Press, 1988.

Fields, Edward Jr. ed. *Diary of Colonel Israel Angell, Commanding the Second Rhode Island Continental Regiment during the American Revolution, 1776–1781.* Providence, 1899.

Fields, Joseph, ed. *Worthy Partner: The Papers of Martha Washington.* Westport: Greenwood Press, 1994.

Fitzpatrick, John. *Diaries of George Washington, 1748–1799.* Mount Vernon Ladies Association. Boston: Houghton-Mifflin, 1925.

———. *Writings of George Washington.* 38 vols. Washington, D.C.: U.S. Government Printing Office, 1932.

Fleming, Thomas, *Beat the Last Drum.* New York: St. Martin's Press, 1963.

————. *First in Their Hearts: A Biography of George Washington.* New York: W.W. Norton, 1984.

Flexner, James. *George Washington: The Forget of Experience, 1732—1775.* Boston: Little, Brown and Co., 1965.

————. *George Washington: Indispensable Man.* Boston: Little, Brown and Company, 1969.

Ford, Paul. *The True George Washington.* Philadelphia, 1898.

Ford, Worthington, ed. *Journals of the Continental Congress, 1774–1789.* 24 vols. Washington, D.C.: U.S. Government Printing Office, 1904.

Fordyce, Rev. James. *Sermon to Young Women.* Philadelphia, 1787.

Floyd, Nicholas. *Biographical Genealogies of the Virginia-Kentucky Floyd Families.* Baltimore: Williams and Wilkins, 1912.

Franklin, Benjamin. *Reflections on Courtship and Marriage.* Philadelphia, 1746.

Freeman, Douglas Southall. *George Washington: A Biography.* 6 vols. New York: Charles Scribner's Sons, 1954.

Freneau, Philip, Trans. Abbe Robin. *New Travels Through North America in a Series of Letters...in the Year 1781.* Philadelphia, 1783.

Gaines, Hugh. *The Journal of Hugh Gaines.* New York: Dodd, Meads & Co., 1902.

George Washington Parke Custis. *Recollections and Private Memoirs of Washington by His Adopted Son George Washington Parke Custis, with a Memoir of the Author by His Daughter; and Illustrative and Explanatory Notes, by Benson J. Lossing.* New York: Derby & Jackson, 1860.

Greene, Evarts. *Revolutionary Generation, 1763–1790.* New York: Macmillan, 1943.

Greene, George Washington. *The Life of Nathanael Greene.* New York: George Putnam and Sons, 1867.

Greene, Jack, ed. *The Diary of Landon Carter of Sabine Hall, 1752–1778.* Charlottesville: University Press of Virginia, 1965.

————. *The Ambiguity of the American Revolution.* New York: Harper and Row, 1968.

Grob, Gerry and George Billias, eds. *Interpretation of American Historical Patterns.* 2 vols. New York: Free Press, 1967.

Guerard, Mary. *A Woman's Letters in 1779 and 1782.* Charleston: South Carolina Historical Society, 1909.

Hamilton, Stanislaus, ed. *Letters to Washington and Accompanying Papers.* 5 vols. Boston, 1898–1902.

Harris, Barbara. *Beyond Her Sphere: Women and the Professions in American History.* Westport: Greenwood Press, 1978.

Harwell, Richard, ed. Douglas Southall Freeman. *George Washington* (abridged). New

York: Collier Books, 1968.

Hervey, Nathaniel. *The Memory of Washington*. Boston: Munro, 1862.

Hinckley, Robert, ed. Christina Leach. *Diary of Christina Young Leach of Kingssessing, 1765–1796*. Philadelphia: Historical Society of Pennsylvania, 1911.

Hirschfield, Fritz. *George Washington and Slavery: A Documentary Portrayal*. Columbia, MO.: University of Missouri Press, 1997.

Historical Sketches of the Town of Leicester, Massachusetts. Boston, 1860.

Hopkins, Barbara, Caroline Force, Dorothea Roberts, and Gladys Foster. *Washington Valley: An Informal History*. Ann Arbor, 1960.

Hughes, Rupert. *George Washington*. 3 vols. New York: William Morrow, 1926.

Johnson, Henry, ed. *Correspondence and Public Papers of John Jay*. 4 vols. New York: G. P. Putnam's Sons, 1893.

Kaminski, John and Jill Adair McCoughan, eds. *A Great and Good Man: George Washington in the Eyes of His Contemporaries*. Madison, WI: Madison House, 1789.

Kaminsky, John and Gaspare Saladino, eds. *The Documentary History of the Ratification of the Constitution*. Madison, WI · State Historical Society of Wisconsin, 1988.

Kdzerda, Stanley, ed. *Lafayette in the Age of the American Revolution: Selected Letters and Papers, 1776–1790*. Ithaca: Cornell University Press, 1977.

Kerber, Linda and Jane Hart. *Women's America: Refocusing the Past*. New York: Oxford University Press, 2000.

Kibler, Luther J. *Washington in Williamsburg*. Rockefeller Library, 1933.

Knollenberg, Bernard. *George Washington: The Virginia Period, 1732–1775*. Durham: Duke University Press, 1964.

Koch, Arlene. *Power, Morals and the Founding Fathers: Essays in the Interpretation of the American Enlightenment*. Ithaca: Great Seal Books, 1961.

Koontz, Louis. *Robert Dinwiddie: His Career in American Colonial Government and Westward Expansion*. New York: Books for Libraries Press, 1970.

Lauber, Almon, ed. *Orderly Books of the Fourth New York Regiment, With the Diaries of Samuel Tallmadge, 1780–1782, and John Barr, 1779–1782*. Albany, 1932.

Lebsock, Suzanne. *Virginia Women, 1600–1945, "A Share of Honour."* Richmond: Virginia State Library, 1987.

Leckie, Robert. *George Washington's War*. New York: Harper Collins, 1992.

Lee, R.H. *Memoir of the Life of Richard Henry Lee*. Philadelphia, 1825.

Lipscomb, Andrew and Albert Bergh. *The Writings of Thomas Jefferson*. 20 vols. Washington, D.C.: 1903.

Longman, Paul. *The Invention of George Washington*. Los Angeles: University of California

Press, 1988.

Lossing, Benson. *Mary and Martha: The Mother and Wife of George Washington*. New York: Harper and Brothers, 1886.

———. *Mount Vernon and Its Associations*. W.A. Townsend and Company, 1859.

Ludlum, David. *Early American Winters*. Boston: American Meteorological Society, 1966.

Maier, Pauline. *From Resistance to Revolution: Colonial Radicals and the Development of American Opposition to Britain, 1765–1776*. New York: Alfred Knopf, 1972.

Marshall, John. *Life of George Washington, Commander in Chief*. 5 vols. Philadelphia: 1804–1807.

Martin, Isabella and Mary Avary, eds. *Mary Chestnut. Diary from Dixie*. New York, 1922.

Mays, David, ed. *The Papers and Letters of Edmund Pendleton, 1774–1803*. 2 vols. Charlottesville: University of Virginia Press, 1967.

McDonald, Forrest. *We the People: The Economic Origins of Our Constitution*. New Brunswick, NJ: Transaction Publishers, 1992.

McVeigh, Lincoln, ed. Nicholas Cresswell, *Journal of Nicholas Cresswell, 1774–1777*. New York: Dial Press, 1924.

Mellwaine, H.R. and J.P. Kennedy, eds. *Journals of the House of Burgesses*. 13 vols. Richmond: Colonial Press, E. Waddy Co., 1905–1915.

Memoirs of Long Island: George Washington and Mount Vernon. New York, 1899.

Mereness, N.D., ed. Lord Adam Gordon. *Travels in the American Colonies*. New York: Antiquarian Press, 1961.

Methie Budka, trans. Julian Niemcewicz. *Under the Vine and Fig Tree: Travels Through America, 1797–1799, 1805, With Some Further Account of Life in New Jersey*. Elizabeth, NJ: Grassman, 1965.

Mitchell, Stewart, ed. *The New Letters of Abigail Adams, 1788–1801*. Boston: Houghton-Mifflin Company, 1947.

Morgan, Edmund. *Virginians at Home*. Charlottesville: Dominion Books, 1968.

Morse, Jedidiah. *American Geography, or a view of the present situation of the United States of America*. Elizabethtown, NJ, 1789.

Nell, William. *The Colored Patriots of the American Revolution*. Boston: Robert Eallot, 1855.

North, Mary Beth. *Liberty's Daughters: The Revolutionary Experience of American Women, 1750–1800*. Boston: Little, Brown and Company, 1980.

Page, Thomas Nelson. *Social Life of Old Virginia*. New York: Charles Scribner's Sons, 1897.

Paine, Lauren. *Benedict Arnold: Hero and Traitor*. London: Robert Hale, 1963.

Parkinson, Richard. *A Tour in America in 1798, 1799 and 1800*. 2 vols. London, 1805.

Paulding and Washington Irving. *The Life of Washington*. 2 vols. New York, 1835.

Porter, Albert. *County Government in Virginia: A Legislative History.* New York: Columbia University Press, 1947.

Pucas, Stephen. *The Quotable George Washington: The Wisdom of an American Patriot.* Madison, WI.: Madison House Press, 1999.

Quarles, Benjamin. *The Negro in the American Revolution.* Chapel Hill: University of North Carolina Press, 1961.

Randall, Willard. *George Washington: A Life.* New York: Henry Holt, 1997.

Rankin, Hugh, ed. "Albigence Waldo." *Narratives of the American Revolution, as Told by a Young Soldier, a Home-Sick Surgeon, a French Volunteer and a German General's Wife.* Chicago: R.R. Donnelly and Sons, 1976.

Read, D.B. *The Life and Times of General John Graves Simcoe.* Toronto: Virtue Publishing, 1890.

Rice, Howard, ed. Marquis de Chastellux, *Travels in North America.* 2 vols. Chapel Hill: University of North Carolina Press, 1963.

Rothman, David, ed. *The Colonial American Family: Collected Essays.* New York: Arno Press and *The New York Times,* 1972.

Ryan, Dennis. *A Salute to Courage: The American Revolution as Seen through Wartime Writings of Officers of the Continental Army and Navy.* New York: Columbia University Press, 1979.

Saffron, Morris. *Surgeon General to Washington: Dr. John Cochran, 1730–1817.* New York: Columbia University Press, 1977.

Scheer, George and Hugh Rankin. *Rebels and Redcoats.* New York: World Publishing Company, 1957

Schroeder, John, ed. *Maxims of George Washington: Military, Political, Social, Moral and Religious.* Mount Vernon: Mount Vernon Ladies Association, 1989.

Schwarz, Philip, ed. *Slavery at the Home of George Washington.* Mount Vernon Ladies Association, 2001.

Scott, Anne Firor. *The Southern Lady: From Pedestal to Politics, 1830–1930.* Chicago: University of Chicago Press, 1970.

Selby, John. *The Revolution in Virginia, 1755–1783.* Williamsburg, VA: Colonial Williamsburg Foundation, 1988.

Showman, Richard, ed. *The Papers of Nathanael Greene.* 6 vols. Chapel Hill: University of North Carolina Press, 1989.

Sipe, C. Hale. *Mount Vernon and the Washington Family: A Concise Handbook on the Ancestry, Youth and Family of George Washington, and History of His Home.* 4th ed. Butler, PA: Ziegler Printing, 1927.

Sklar, Katherine and Thomas Dublin. *Women and Power in American History.* Englewood Cliffs: Prentice Hall, 1991.

Smith, Bonnie Hurd, ed. *From Gloucester to Philadelphia in 1790: Observations, Anecdotes and Thoughts from the 18th Century Letters of Judith Sargent Murray.* Cambridge: Judith Sargent Murray Society, 1998.

Smith, Richard Norton. *Patriarch: George Washington and the New American Nation.* Boston: Houghton-Mifflin, 1993.

Sociology for the South. Richmond, Morris, 1854.

Sparks, Jared. *The Life of George Washington.* 4 vols. Boston: Ferdinand Andrews, 1830.

Sprigg, June. *Domestick Beings.* New York: Alfred Knopf, 1984.

Spruill, Julia. *Women's Life and Work in the Southern Colonies.* New York: W.W. Norton and Co., 1972.

Syrett, Harold. *The Papers of Alexander Hamilton.* 27 vols. New York: Columbia University Press, 1961.

William Tappert and John Doberstein. *Journals of Henry Melchior Muhlenberg.* 6 vols. Philadelphia: Muhlenberg Press, 1959.

Tate, Thad. *The Negro in Eighteenth Century Williamsburg.* Williamsburg: Colonial Williamsburg Foundation, 1965.

Thacher, James. *Military Journal of the American Revolution, from the commencement to the disbanding of the army, Comprising a detailed account of the Principal events and battles of the revolution with their exact dates and a biographical sketch of the most Prominent Generals.* Hartford: Hurlbut, William and Co., 1862.

Thane, Elswyth. *Potomac Squire.* New York: Duell, Sloane and Pearce, 1963.

———. *Washington's Lady.* New York: Dodd Mead & Co., 1960.

Thayer, Theodore. *Colonial and Revolutionary Morris County.* Morris County Heritage Commission, 1975.

Trussel, John Jr. *Birthplace of an Army: A Study of the Valley Forge Encampment.* Harrisburg: Pennsylvania Historical and Museum Commission, 1998.

Van Doren, Carl. *Benjamin Franklin,* New York, 1938. Reprint: Westport, CT.: Greenwood Press, 1973.

Vander Kemp, Francis and William Spohn Baker, eds. *Washington After the Revolution, 1784–1799.* Philadelphia: J.B. Lippincott Company, 1898.

Wallace, Willard. *Traitor and Hero: The Life and Fortunes of Benedict Arnold.* New York: Harper Bros., 1954.

Ward, Christopher. *War of the Revolution.* 2 vols. New York: Macmillan Co., 1952.

Warville, Jean Pierre Brissot. *Nouveau voyage dans les Etats-Unis de L'Amerique Septen-*

trianale, fait en 1788. Paris, 1791.

Weeks, Stephen. *Southern Quakers and Slavery: A Study in Institutional History.* Baltimore: Johns Hopkins University Press, 1896.

Wertenbaker, Thomas. *Patrician and Plebian in Virginia: Or the Origin and Development of the Social Clashes of the Old Dominion.* New York: Russell & Russell, 1959.

Wharton, Anne. *Martha Washington.* New York: Charles Scribner's Sons, 1897.

Williams, William. *America Confronts a Revolutionary World.* New York: William Morrow Company, 1976.

Wills, Gary. *Cincinnatus: George Washington and the Enlightenment.* Garden City, NY: Doubleday, 1984.

Wilson, Woodrow. *George Washington.* New York: Harper & Brothers, 1897.

Wood, Gordon. *The Creation of the American Republic, 1776–1787.* New York: W.W. Norton, 1969.

Wright, Louis and Marion Tinling, eds. *William Byrd's Secret Diary.* Richmond: Dietz Press, 1941.

Zagari, Rosemary, ed. David Humphreys, *The Life of George Washington, with General Washington's 'Remarks.'* Athens, GA: University of Georgia Press, 1991.

Zupan, Josephine. *The Letter Book of John Custis IV, of Williamsburg, 1717–1742.* New York: Roman and Littlefield, 2005.

NEWSPAPERS

Dunlop's Daily American Advertiser, 1791.

Gazette of the United States, 1789.

Maryland Gazette, 1791.

National Gazette, 1792, 1793.

National Intelligencer, 1847.

New York Daily Advertiser, 1789.

New York Gazette, 1789.

Pennsylvania Evening Post, 1775.

Pennsylvania Herald, 1787.

Pennsylvania Journal, 1775.

Pennsylvania Packet, 1787.

Petersburg (Va.) Gazette, 1787.

Philadelphia Federal Gazette, 1789.

Raleigh (N.C.) Register, 1808.

Republican Star and General Advertiser, 1828.

South Carolina Gazette, 1749.

Star Gazette of North Carolina, 1790.

The Aurora, 1795.

Virginia Gazette, 1777.

Virginia Herald and Fredericksburg Advertiser, 1789, 1791.

NOTES

Abbreviations for frequently used sources

GWW ....The Writings of George Washington

PGW ....The Papers of George Washington

CONG ....Letters of Delegates to Congress

GREENE ....The Papers of Nathanael Greene

JOHB....................................Journals of the House of Burgesses

JCC....................................Journals of the Continental Congress

CHAPTER ONE

2   Was, by all accounts, rather plain looking: Polly Longworth, "Portrait of Martha Washington," *Journal of the Colonial Williamsburg Foundation*, (Summer, 1988), 6. Martha always ordered gloves for "small hands"; "Invoice of Goods to Be Shipped by Robert Cary Co., for the use of George Washington," GWW III:141; Willard Randall, *George Washington: A Life*, New York: Henry Holt, 1997, 171.

3   Always seemed to know somebody acquainted with a guest: Judith Sargent Murray to her parents, August 14, 1790, Bonnie Hurd Smith, ed., *From Gloucester to Philadelphia in 1790: Observations, Anecdotes and Thoughts from the 18th Century Letters of Judith Sargent Murray*, Cambridge: Judith Sargent Murray Society, 1998, 254.

3   Caused her to be distinguished: Elizabeth Cometti, ed., *The American Journals of Lt. John Enys*, Syracuse: Syracuse University Press, 1976, 251–252; George Washington Parke Custis, *Recollections and Private Memoirs of Washington by His Adopted Son George Washington Parke Custis, with a Memoir of the Author by His Daughter; and Illustrative and Explanatory Notes, by Benson J. Lossing*, New York: Derby & Jackson, 1860, 406.

4   Reined in his horse: Willard Randall, *George Washington: A Life*, 173–175.

4   In conversation they become animated: George Washington Parke Custis, *Recollections and Private Memoirs of Washington by his Adopted Son*, 484–485; George Wordham, "A Physical Description of George Washington," the *Daughters of the American Revolution* Magazine, February, 1974, 85–88; John Corry, "Sketch of the Life of the Late General Washington," *British Magazine*, February to June, 1800, in W. S. Baker, ed., *Character Portraits of Washington as Delineated by Historians, Orators and Divines, selected and arranged in chronological order with biographical notes and references*, Philadelphia, Robert Lindsay, 1887, 131; Jean Pierre Brissot de Warville, *Nouveau Voyage dans les Etats-Unis de L'Amerique Septentrianale, fait en 1788*, Paris, 1791.

5   On great occasions remarkably lively: Jedidiah Morse's eulogy on Washington, delivered on December 31, 1799, Charlestown, Massachusetts.

5   His general appearance never failed: George Mercer, in Douglas Southall Freeman, *George Washington, a Biography*, 6 vols., New York: Charles Scribner's Sons, 1954, III: 141; Aaron Bancroft, "Essay on George Washington, Commander in Chief of the American Army; Through the Revolution; and the First President of the United States," London, Stockdale, 1808, in Baker, 155.

5   His personal appearance is truly noble: James Thacher, *Military Journal of the American revolution, from the commencement to the disbanding of the army, Comprising a detailed account of the Principal events and battles of the revolution with their exact dates and a biographical sketch of the most Prominent Generals*, Hartford: Hurlbut, William and Co., 1862, 30.

6   March 5 afternoon: Anne Hollingsworth Wharton, *Martha Washington*, New York: Charles Scribner's Sons, 1897, 34–35.

7   George and Martha talked long into the night: Benson Lossing, *Mary and Martha: The Mother and Wife of George Washington*, New York: Harper and Brothers, 1886, 94–98; Lincoln Diamant, ed., *Revolutionary Women in the War for American Independence, a One Volume Revised Edition of Elizabeth Ellet's 1848 Landmark Series*, Westport, Conn.: Praeger, 1998, 144; Alice Curtis Desmond, *Martha Washington: Our First Lady*, New York: Dodd, Mead and Company, 1942, 77–83.

9   There was something dashing: R.W.G.Vail, ed. "A Dinner at Mount Vernon: From the Unpublished Journal of Joshua Brookes (1773–1859)," *New York Historical Society Quarterly*, April, 1947, 81; Rupert Hughes, *George Washington*, 3 vols. New York: William Morrow, 1926, I:354–360.

10   A pleased Washington: *Pennsylvania Magazine of History and Biography*, LXVI (1932), 115.

10   He wrote Martha a tender letter: GW to Martha Custis, July 20, 1758, GWW II: 242.

11   To guarantee the landslide: J.A.C. Chandler and T.B.

Thames, *Colonial Virginia*, Richmond: Times-Dispatch Company, 1907, 282–283.

11   According to family lore: John Ferling, *The First of Men: A Life of George Washington*, Knoxville: University of Tennessee Press, 1988, 62–63; Martha's handkerchief remained as a family heirloom for years, but was then given away by her granddaughter as a gift. Martha gave away many of her and her husband's keepsakes after the president died, Eleanor Lewis to Elizabeth Gibson, March 22, 1821, Patricia Brady, Ed., *George Washington's Beautiful Nelly: The Letters of Eleanor Parke Custis Lewis to Elizabeth Bordley Gibson, 1794–1851*, Columbia: University of South Carolina Press, 1991, 103–107.

12   Guests filled every bedroom: Helen Bryan, *Martha Washington: First Lady of Liberty*, New York: John Wiley and Sons, 2003, 121–123; Lossing, *Mary and Martha: The Mother and Wife of George Washington*, 99–103.

12   The soul of the corps: Address from the Officers of the Virginia Regiment, December 31, 1758, PGW Col. Ser. VI: 179–180.

13   It was a letter: To the Officers of the Virginia Regiment, January 10, 1759, PGW, Col. Ser. VI: 186–187.

CHAPTER TWO

16   Augustine Washington moved his family: Randall, 21–23.

17   An apprentice to a tinker: Benson Lossing, *Mount Vernon and Its Associations*, W. A. Townsend and Company, 1859, 45–46.

18   Only the veteran express couriers: Howard Rice, ed., trans., quoting the Marquis de Chastellux, Chastellux, *Travels in North America*, 2 vols. Chapel Hill: University of North Carolina Press, 1963, I: 111; Freeman, *George Washington, A Biography,* 6 vols., New York, II: 383.

18   He also surveyed: Chester Bain, *A Body Incorporate: The Evolution of City and County Separation in Virginia*, Charlottesville: University of Virginia Press, 1967, 10–11.

18   Described as "a giant": James Paulding and Washington Irving, *The Life of Washington*, New York, 2 vols., 1835, in Baker, 188–189.

18   Belvoir, the neighboring plantation: Robert Dalzell Jr. and Lee Baldwin Dalzell, *George Washington's Mount Vernon: A Home in Revolutionary America*, New York: Oxford University Press, 1998, 30–32.

19   He wrote to a friend: Thomas Flexner, *George Washington: Indispensable Man*, Boston: Little, Brown & Company, 1969, 7–8.

20   Speak seldom: George Washington to Bushrod Washington, November 10, 1787, GWW XXIX. 309–313; George Washington to David Stuart, November 30, 1787, GWW XXIX: 323–324.

20   To the young women of Virginia: Freeman, George Washington, Biography, II: 386–387.

20   This stoic persona: Freeman, III: 141; Carl Van Doren, Benjamin Franklin, New York, 1938, 529; *Virginia Magazine of History and Biography* (15), 1908, 356.

21   "Live in harmony and good fellowship": George Washington to John Augustine Washington, May 28, 1755, PGW Col. Series I: 289–293.

21   "If I can gain any credit": George Washington to William Byrd, April 20, 1755, GWW I: 114.

22   He was direct: George Washington to John Washington, May 14, 1755, GWW I:124.

23   Belonged to the Indians: John Fitzpatrick, ed., *The Diaries of George Washington*, 6 vols., New York: Houghton Mifflin Company, 1925, hereafter DGW, I: 144–151, French commander; I: 136–140, Half King.

23   "I can't say that ever in my life": Purchase list, GWW I: 27.

23   Gist wrote: William Darlington, ed., Christopher Gist, *Christopher Gist's Journals, with Historical Geographical and Ethnological Notes*, Pittsburgh: J.R. Weldon and Co., 1893, 83–84.

23   He nearly drowned: DGW, I: 62–65.

23   Fashioned snowshoes and walked: Darlington, *Christopher Gist's Journals*, 84–86.

24   Washington found the notoriety: DGW I: 43–102.

24   King George II was annoyed: George Washington to John Augustine Washington, May 31, 1754, in PGW, Col. Ser. I: 118–119.; King George's remark from Diaries I: 197.

25   He wrote to a friend: George Washington to William Fitzhugh, November 15, 1754, PGW, Col. Ser. I: 351–352.

27   "You have behaved yourself": Miriam Anne Bourne, *First Family: George Washington and His Intimate Relations*, New York, W.W. Norton, 1982, 30–31.

28   Dinwiddie wrote to the state legislature: Louis Koontz, *Robert Dinwiddie: His Career in American Colonial Government and Westward Expansion*, New York, 1941, reprinted, New York: Books for Libraries Press, 1970, 334.

28   These were all skills: Freeman, II: 386–387.

29   He was appalled: Flexner, *Washington: The Indispensable Man*, 32.

29   He complained that the soldiers: George Washington to Robert Dinwiddie, June 27, 1757, GWW II: 77–80.

29   "No man that was ever employed": George Washington to Robert Dinwiddie, September 17, 1757, PGW, Col. Ser. IV: 411–412.

29   He had been an American officer: Koontz, *Robert Dinwiddie: His Career in American Colonial Government and Westward Expansion*, 346–347.

29   He vented his frustrations: George Washington to the Earl of Loudon, January, 1757, GWW II: 6–20.

29   His half brother Augustine wrote: Quoted in Bourne, *First Family: George Washington and His Intimate Relations*, 30–31.

30   Washington had ordered: Invoice of sundry goods to be shipped by Mr. Washington of London for the use of George Washington, April 15, 1757, GWW II: 23.

30   They needed decisions from him: William Fairfax to George Washington, August 5, 1758, Stanislaus Hamilton, ed., *Letters to Washington and Accompanying Papers*, 5 vols., Boston, 1898–1902, III: 17–18.

30   Washington became gravely ill: Robert Leckie, *George Washington's War*, New York: HarperCollins, 1992, 138–142.

30   He told the colonel to go home: Hamilton, II: 231, 242.

30   Plenty of rest: Hamilton, II, 243.

30   Writing an army friend: George Washington to Rev. Charles Green, November 13, 1757, GWW II: 159; GW to Colonel John Stanwix, March 4, 1758, GWW II: 165–167.

31   In her lovely handwriting: Hamilton, I: 74.

32   Sally visited him frequently: John E. Ferling, *The First of Men: A Life of George Washington*, 50–51.

32   Sometimes he was welcomed at Belvoir: James Flexner, *George Washington: The Forge of Experience*, 1732—1775, Boston: Little, Brown and Company, 202–205.

32   Washington's only two existing letters: George Washington to Sally Fairfax, September 12, September 25, 1757, PGW, Col. Ser., VI: 10–13, 41–43.

33   Washington wrote Sally one last letter: George Washington to Sally Fairfax, May 16, 1798, GWW XXXVI: 162–264.

34   "I could not trace": Ferling, 341.

34   The doctor gave Washington: Helen Bryan, *Martha Washington: First Lady of Liberty*, 88, 112.

34   Realized that he was close: Elswyth Thane, *Washington's Lady*, New York: Dodd, Mead & Company, 1960, 1–8.

CHAPTER THREE

35   The home on the plantation: From a description in a "for sale" ad in the *Virginia Gazette*, December 24, 1768.

36   Dandridge used his income: Albert Porter, *County Government in Virginia: A Legislative History*, New York: Columbia University Press, 1947, 46–47, 76–77.

37   They assessed and collected: Porter, 90–91.

37   The invitation that he accepted: Bryan, 16–24.

38   The tutor was paid a salary: Hunter Farish, ed., *Journal and Letters of Reverend Phillip Fithian, 1773–1774, A Plantation Tutor of the Old Dominion*, Williamsburg, VA: Colonial Williamsburg Press, 1943, xxiv-xxv.

38   From time to time the wealthy: Porter, 98–99.

38   Dancing classes: Farish, *Journal and Letters of Reverend*

Phillip Fithian, 1773–1774, A Plantation Tutor of the Old Dominion, 42–43.

39   There were so few women: Walter Blumenthal, *Brides from Bridewell: Female Felons Sent to Colonial America*, Westport: Greenwood Press, 1972, 18, 37.

41   He was accused of fathering: Freman, II: 281–283.

42   Not missing a beat: Joseph Fields, ed. *Worthy Partner: The Papers of Martha Washington*, Westport: Greenwood Press, 1994, 423.

42   Under his name: Lossing, *Mary and Martha: The Mother and Wife of George Washington*, 86.

42   The tangled legal claims: Freeman II: 285–287.

43   She told a court: Freeman, II: 296–297.

43   Daniel rejected that idea: Josephine Little Zuppan, *The Letter Book of John Custis IV, of Williamsburg, 1717–1742*, New York: Rowman and Littlefield, 2005, 15.

44   No one noted what conversation: Lossing, 88.

45   His odd death: Bryan, 67–68.

47   She plunged into mourning: Alice Curtis Desmond, *Martha Washington: Our First Lady*, 70–72.

47   "What will become of me?": Eliza Carrington to Ann Fisher, November, 1810, Eliza Ambler Papers, Colonial Williamsburg Foundation, in Sauzanne Lebsock, *Virginia Women, 1600–1945, "A Share of Honour,"* Richmond: Virginia State Library, 1987, 47.

48   To avoid that custom: Catherine Clinton, *Plantation Mistress: Woman's World in the Old South*, New York: Pantheon Books, 1982, 78–79; Sklar and Dublin, 59.

48   Mrs. Martha Richardson wrote: Martha Richardson to James Screven, November 29, 1819, April 16, 1819, in Arnold-Screven Papers, Southern Historical Collection, Chapel Hill: University of North Carolina, in Catherine Clinton, *Plantation Mistress: Woman's World in the Old South*, 77.

49   Nocholas assured her: Robert Carter Nicholas to Martha Custis, August 7, 1757, Custis, *Recollections and Private Memoirs of Washington*, 497–498.

49   "I now enclose the bill": Martha Custis to John Hanbury, August 20, 1757, Fields, 6.

50   "He must not only": George Mercer to Martha Custis, April 24, 1758, Fields, 39–40.

51   Throughout all of her problems: Martha Washington to Mercy Otis Warren, December 26, 1789, Fields, 224.

51   "I wish a suitable offer": Diary of Meta Morris Brimball, December 10, 1860, Southern Historical Collection, University of North Carolina archives.

51   "If there was a prospect": Judge Garnett Andrews, *Reminiscences of an Old Georgia Lawyer*, Atlanta: Franklin Stearns Printing House, 1870, notes.

51   "When a young man": *Raleigh Register*, October 12, 1808.

51   One story that ran: *South Carolina Gazette*, November 6, 1749.

52   "She is as thick": Hamilton, IV: 64.

52   All widows and old maids: *Virginia Gazette*, November 19, 1772; *Star Gazette of North Carolina*, January 16, 1790.

52   Her first husband had died: Kathryn Kish Sklar and Thomas Dublin, *Women and Power in American History*, Englewood Cliffs; Prentice Hall, 1991, 2 vols, I: 51.

CHAPTER FOUR

55   He thought it majestic: C. Hale Sipe, *Mount Vernon and the Washington Family: A Concise Handbook on the Ancestry, Youth and Family of George Washington, and History of His Home*, 4th ed., Butler, Pa: Ziegler Printing, 1927, 61.

55   Reverend Andrew Burnaby: George Washington Parke Custis, *Recollections*, 166–167n.

56   He did not want the Custis clan: George Washington to John Alton, April 1, 1759, GWW II: 318–319.

58   Washington as her future: Hughes, I: 479; Flexner, *George Washington: The Forge of Experience*, 234–235.

58   Mount Vernon was actually: Bernhard Knollenberg, *George Washington: The Virginia Period, 1732–1775*, Durham: Duke University Press, 1964, 82–83.

59   The Virginia estates: Isaacs, 42.

60   The horrified squire: "Journey Over the Mountains, 1748," March 15, 1748, GWW I: 7; Spruill, 41.

60   Englishman William Grove: *Virginia Magazine of History and Biography, LXXXV (1977),* 26–28; Philip Freneau, trans., Abbe Robin, *New Travels Through North America*; in a Series of Letters...in the Year 1781, Philadelphia, 1783, 50–51.

61   Arrived in a kingdom: Brown, 25; Thomas Wertenbaker, *Patrician and Plebian in Virginia: Or the Origin and Development of the Social Clashes of the Old Dominion*, New York: Russell & Russell, 1959, iii-v, 118–119; Morgan, 53–54.

62   He wrote to Cary: George Washington to Robert Cary & Company, September 20, 1759, GWW II: 327–330.

62   "Even in the freest countries": Abigail Adams to John Adams, June 17, 1782, L. H. Butterfield, ed., *Adams Family Correspondence*, 6 vols., Cambridge: Harvard University Press, 1963, IV: 328.

62   They told friends: Benson Lossing Jr., *The Home of Washington, or Mount Vernon and Its Associations*, Hartford, CT: A .S. Hale & Company, 1871, 67.

64   Martha's tastes were elegant: Invoice, George Washington to Robert Cary, July 15, 1772, GWW III: 89–94.

64   Cost-wary Marth often complained: George and Martha Washington to Mrs. S. Thorpe, July 15, 1772, GWW III: 88.

65   "She was dressed very plainly": Claude Blanchard, July 20, 1782, in Gilbert Chinard, *George Washington as the French Knew Him: A Collections of Texts,* Princeton: Princeton University Press, 1949, reprint, New York: Greenwood Press, 1969, 67.

65   "Very neat, but not gaudy": Olney Winsor to Mrs. Winsor, March 31, 1788, John F. Kaminsky and Gaspare Saladino, eds. *The Documentary History of the Ratification of the Constitution, Vol. VIII, Madison*: State Historical Society of Wisconsin, 1988, 523.

65   "Received me with great ease": Abigail Adams to her sister, June 28, 1789, Stewart Mitchell, ed., *New Letters of Abigail Adams, 1788–1801*, Boston: Houghton Mifflin Company, 1947, 13.

65   Washington fumed at this treatment: George Washington

to Robert Cary & Company, February 13, 1764, GWW II: 413–417; "Invoice of Sundrys," GWW II: 370.

66   Despite his efforts: T H. Breen, "The Culture of Agriculture: The Symbolic World of the Tidewater Planter, 1760–1790," in David Murrin, John Hall, and Tad Thate, eds., *Saints and Revolutionaries: Essays on Early American History*, New York, 1984, 255–261, in Ferling, 66.

66   He wrote to Robert Cary: George Washington to Robert Cary, April 3, 1761, GWW II: 357.

67   The resourceful planter: Notes on wheat sales in Europe in DGW I: 303; John Selby, *The Revolution in Virginia, 1775–1783*, Williamsburg, VA: Colonial Williamsburg Foundation, 1988, 32; breeding sheep and buffalo, DGW I: 216; George Washington to James Cleveland, January 10, 1775, GWW III: 260–261.

67   Over the years: Lorena Walsh, "Slavery and Agriculture at Mount Vernon," Philip Schwarz, *Slavery at the Home of George Washington*, Mount Vernon Ladies Association, 2001, 60–61.

68   He accused the man: George Washington to George Muse, January 29, 1774, GWW III: 179–180.

68   The fifteen-foot-square room: DGW I: 107.

69   As he wrote in hid diary: DGW I: 124.

69   Describing a smallpox epidemic: DGW I: 115–116.

69   Two days later: DGW I: 117–118.

69   "My rascally overseer": DGW I: 138.

69   Washington had to be careful: DGW II: 28; Morgan, 55–56.

70   Washington had spent an entire day: DGW I: 122.

70   He was an obsessive micromanager: George Washington to Bryan Fairfax, July 4, 1774, GWW III: 227.

70   His weather notes: DGW I: 124.

71   So he built two more: George Washington to Robert Stewart, June 3, 1760, Hamilton, III: 183–184.

72   It provided the Washingtons: Dalzell and Dalzell, George Washington's Mount Vernon: *At Home in Revolutionary America*, 57–60.

CHAPTER FIVE

73   In Virginia, she lived in a patriarchal society: Clinton, *The Plantation Mistress*, 6–7; Barbara Harris, *Beyond Her Sphere: Women and the Professions in American History*, Westport: Greenwood Press, 1978, 19–22.

74   A woman was expected to obey her husband: Nancy Cott, *The Bonds of Womanhood: "Woman's Sphere" in New England, 1780–1835*, 2nd edition, New Haven: Yale University Press, 82–83.

74   Another famed Philadelphian: DePauw, Conover, Schneir, 12; Benjamin Franklin, *Reflections on Courtship and Marriage*, 1746, 43–45.

74   In a popular pamphlet: David Rothman, ed., *The Colonial American Family, Collected Essays*, New York: Arno Press and the New York Times, 1972, 35.

74   In his bestselling book: Rev. James Fordyce, *Sermon to Young Women*, Philadelphia, 1787, 161–162.

75   Ironically, given the future lives: Clinton, 8; Anne Firor Scott, *The Southern Lady*, 16–17; Nancy Cott, *The Bonds of Womanhood: "Woman's Sphere" in New England, 1780–1835*, 66–67; Virginia Cary, *Letters on Female Character*, 2d edition, Philadelphia, 1830, 47.

75   Thomas Nelson Page, an antebellum: Thomas Nelson Page, *Social Life in Old Virginia*, New York: Charles Scribner's Sons, 1897, 38–42.

75   "Woman naturally shrinks from public gaze…: *Sociology for the South*, Richmond: Morris, 1854, 214–215.

75   The women, and their men: Clinton, 14.

75   Many wives did so: Morgan, 44–48.

76   …wherein I was placed by him.: Morgan, 49.

76   Martha Washington was not one of those: Abigail Adams to John Adams,
    March 31, 1776, Butterfield, I: 369–370.

76   Like all wives of wealthy planters: DGW II: 183.

77   …prevented him from gaining too much weight.: Bryan, 131–134.

77   The entire meal might be topped off: Brown, 273; Leb-

sock, *Virginia Women, 1600–1945: A Share of Honour*, 41.

77   The cookbooks not only had hundreds of recipes: Mildred Abraham, "The Library of Lady Jean Skipwith: A Book Collection from the Age of Jefferson," VMHB 91 (July 1983), 319, in Lebsock, 41.

78   "My mind dwells upon the one subject…: Anonymous woman to Mary Houston, February 20, 1837, Houston Collection, Duke University; Mary Telfair to Mary Few, January 4, 1833, Few Collection, Georgia State Archives, in Clinton, 26–28.

78   One woman lamented of housework: Sprigg, 18–19.

80   Washington also asked overseers' wives: Julia Spruill, *Women's Life and Work in the Southern Colonies*, New York: W.W. Norton, 1972, 76–78; George Conway, *George Washington and Mount Vernon, A Collection of Washington's Unpublished Agricultural and Personal Letters Edited with Historical and Genealogical Introduction*, Brooklyn, NY: Long Island Historical Society, 1889, vol. 4, 273.

80   Most women put their daughters: Mary Beth Norton, *Liberty's Daughters: The Revolutionary Experience of American Women, 1750–1800*, Boston: Little, Brown and Company, 1980, 28–29.

80   Girls often formed early attachments: Morgan, 63–64.

81   Their mothers and grandmothers: Julia Spruill, "Housewives and Their Helpers," Kerber and Mathews, *Women's America: Refocusing the Past*, 35n.

82   Later, in the Revolution: DePauw, Conover, Schneir, 36.

82   Martha, George, and: Desmond, *Martha Washington, Our First Lady*, 109.

84   No one truly knows: George Washington to George Fairfax, September 29, 1763, PGW, Col. Ser. VII: 60–61.

84   Landon Carter, who had very little: Jack Greene, ed. *The Diary of Landon Carter of Sabine Hall, 1752–1778*, Charlottesville: University of Virginia Press, 2 vols., I: 16.

84   One of George's jobs: Robert Stewart to George Washington, December 14, 1762, PGW, Col. Ser. VII: 168–172; Thomas Fleming, *First in Their Hearts: A Biography of George Washing-*

ton, New York: W.W. Norton Co., 1984, 35–36.

86   Martha, with the help of two doctors: DGW I: 107–110.

86   He told her: James Flexner, *Washington: The Indispensable Man*, 41–42.

87   George was so pleased: George Washington to Richard Washington, September 20, 1759, GWW II: 336–337.

87   As a visitor to Mount Vernon: Lincoln McVeigh, ed., Nicholas Cresswell, *Journal of Nicholas Cresswell, 1774–1777*, New York: Dial Press, 1924, 255.

CHAPTER SIX

90   At these affairs: DGW II: 108.

90   The Jockey Club's gala: Cash Accounts, PGW, Col. Ser. IX: 110–111.

91   ...an elegant white carriage.: Ferling, 73–74.

91   An order that arrived in 1772: "Invoice of Goods," George Washington to Robert Cary, July 15, 1772, GWW III: 89–94.

92   As an example, Washington wrote: Kathleen Brown, *Good Wives, Nasty Wenches and Anxious Patriarchs: Gender, Race and Power in Colonial Virginia*, Chapel Hill: University of North Carolina Press, 1996, 268; DGW II: 3.

92   They usually hosted two or three: DGW II: 46, 71.

93   ... "at home all day without company.": DGW II: 20.

93   On another occasion: George Washington to Fielding Lewis, December 4, 1786, GWW XXIX: 101.

93   George ordered: May 1759 order to Cary & Company in London, GWW II: 320–321.

93   A London buyer: May 1759 order to Cary & Company in London, GWW II: 320–321; Hill, Lamar & Hill to George Washington, March 28, 1760, Hamilton, III: 177–178.

93   She was so busy: Fithian Diary, in Edmund Morgan, *Virginians at Home*, Charlottesville: Dominion Books, 1968, 43.

93   Some men and women were so eager: Brown, 270; Louis Wright and Marion Tinling, eds., *William Byrd's Secret Diary*, Richmond, VA: Dietz Press, 1941, 318; J.A.C. Chandler and Thomas, *Colonial Virginia*, 290–291.

94   One Swiss man traveling: Francis Lous Michel, in Edmund Morgan, 83.

94   One host cringed when a guest: Brown, 271.

95   Others complained that: Julia Spruill, *Women's Life and Work in the Southern Colonies*, New York: W. W. Norton and Co., 1972, 71.

95   One British visitor: Lincoln McVeigh, ed. Nicholas Cresswell, *Journal of Nicholas Cresswell*, 1774–1779, 251–255.

95   Elizabeth Powel, a friend of Martha's: Fields, *Worthy Partner*, 198.

96   Joshua Brookes, an English visitor: Benjamin Latrobe, "Through Virginia to Mount Vernon, Extracts from the Journal of Benjamin Henry Latrobe," *Appleton's Booklovers Magazine* 6, (1905) I: 15.; Julian Niemcewicz, *Under Their Vine and Fig Tree*, 85; Vail, "A Dinner at Mount Vernon: From the Unpublished Journal of Joshua Brookes (1773–1859)," 74.

96   "Hamilton told us: John London, quoted in Charles Andrews, *Colonial Folkways, Chronicle of America*, New Haven: Yale University Press, 1921, IX: 108, 116.

96   Chastellux, who dined at Mount Vernon: Chastellux, Travels in North America, I: 112.

96   Lord Adam Gordon, who visited Virginia: Thomas Wertenbaker, *Patrician and Plebian in Virginia: Or the Origin and Development of the Social Classes of the Old Dominion*, New York: Russell & Russell, 1959, v-vi.

97   ...their husbands' refinement.": John Bernard, *Retrospectives of America, 1797–1811*, New York: Harper Brothers, 1887, 150, in Wertenbaker, 88–89.

97   The chastised child was mad: Nicholas Floyd, *Biographical Genealogies of the Virginia-Kentucky Floyd Families*, Baltimore: Williams and Wilkins, 1912, 147–148; Bryan, 142.

97   It was enjoyed by all: Molly Tilghman to Polly Pearce, *Maryland Magazine*, VI, 233.

98   Molly Tilghman wrote of the marriage: Molly Tilghman to Polly Pearce, *Maryland Magazine*, VI, 141.

99   Whores rented rooms: Clifford Dowdy, *The Golden Age:*

A Climate for Greatness: Virginia, 1732–1775, Boston: Little Brown and Company, 1970, 62.

99 The street was lined with shops: Alexander Macauley, "Alexander Macauley's Journal," *William and Mary Quarterly*, 1st series, XI (1902–1903), 186–188.

99 The public buildings and larger homes: Warren Billings, John Selby, and Thad Tate, *Colonial Virginia: A History*, White Plains, NY: KTO Press, 1996.

99 Visitors to the town: Robert Tilden, trans., Johann Doehla, "The Doehla Journal," *William and Mary Quarterly*, 2nd series (1942), XXII (1942),
229–274.

100 Sometimes when rooms: Scott, 299.

100 When he traveled to Annapolis: DGW II: 35.

101 The lower classes: DGW II, 168–169.

101 A tutor, James Reid: Richard Beale, ed., "The Colonial Virginia Satirist: Mid-Eighteenth Century Commentaries on Politics, Religion and Society," American Philosophical Society, *Transactions*, N.S. LVII, Pt. 1 (1967), 48.

101 Washington was one of the many: DGW II: 154.

101 One claimed that a man: Ewing, *The Sports of Williamsburg*, 12–13.

101 Vaudeville shows: Ewing, 31–33.

102 ...an indoor fireworks.: *Virginia Gazette*, November, 1772.

102 He had attended plays: Kibler, *Washington in Williamsburg*; DGW II: 57–62.

102 They went alone: DGW II: 17, 39.

102 Martha Washington ordered: DGW II: 75.

103 "A likely young Virginia...: *Virginia Gazette*, April 22, 1737, April 7, 1738.

103 One visitor thought: Creswell, Journal, 52–53.

103 One Annapolis woman: Spruill, 92–93.

103 Wrote one bedazzled man: William Eddis, *Letters from America, Historical and Descriptive, Comprising Occurrences from 1769 to 1777*, Inclusive, London, 1792,
p, 113.

104 Philip Fithian, a tutor: Philip Fithian, 1774 notes, in Morgan, *Virginians at Home*, 78–80.

104 Wrote Boston's Nancy Winslow: Nancy Winslow, quoted in June Sprigg, *Domestick Beings*, New York: Alfred Knopf, 1984, 84.

105 A tutor wrote about: Philip Fithian notes, in Morgan, 18–19.

105 Anne Blair of Virginia: *William & Mary Quarterly*, vol XVI (1959, series 3), 177, in Mary Benson, *Women in Eighteenth Century America: A Study of Opinion and Social Usage*, Port Washington, NY: Kennikat Press, 1935, 296–297.

105 Some women did not agree: Hughes, I: 458; Molly Cooper, quoted in Sprigg, 82.

105 Adams frumped that men: E. B. Greene, *The Revolutionary Generation*, 1763–1790, 95.

105 One participant at such: Cresswell, in Hughes I: 452; Morgan, *Virginians at Home*, 81.

106 He scoffed at the lack: DGW I, February 15, 1760.

107 ...have been some disarray among the caps.": Flexner, 239.

107 None paid any: Isaacs, 100.

108 He often purchased: List of George Washington's cash accounts, March, 1772, PGW Col. Ser. IX: 19–21.

108 Washington was such: Breen, 339–357; *Virginia Gazette*, April 4, 1768.

108 He once bought: George Washington to George Fairfax, January 19, 1773, PGW Col. Ser. IX: 160–61; Walter Magowan to George Washington, May 9, 1773, PGW Col. Ser. IX: 230; Cash Accounts, PGW Col. Ser. IX: 19–20.

108 Card games were always: DGW I: 238.

108 His diaries showed that: DGW II: 57. Between March 9 and 17, 1772, Washington played cards for money on seven out of nine evenings.

108 The Washingtons enjoyed attending: Virginia Gazette, October, 1737.

109 It was a competition: George Washington Parke Custis,

Recollections, 384–386; Lossing, 116n; DGW I: 229; Flexner, *George Washington: Forge of Experience (1732–1775)*, Boston: Little, Brown and Company, 1965, 239–240.

110 Women also used: Spruill, 116–119, 128.

111 Clothing gave women: Brown, 202–203.

111 He took great pleasure: Kibler, *Washington in Williamsburg*, 26.

111 In 1761, Washington ordered: George Washington to Richard Washington, October 20, 1761, PGW, Col. Ser. VII: 81.

112 He complained often: George Washington to R. Washington, October 20, 1761, PGW, Col. Series, VII: 81.

112 He reveled in the image he projected: George Washington to Bushrod Washington, January 15, 1783, in Stephen Pucas, ed., *The Quotable George Washington: The Wisdom of an American Patriot*, Madison: Madison House Press, 1999, 15.

112 It was one of the finest: N.D. Mereness, ed., Lord Adam Gordon, Travels in the American Colonies, New York: Antiquarian Press, 1961, 365–453; Julia Spruill, Women's Life and Work in the Southern Colonies, 89–90.

112 As always, their visit: James Flexner, George Washington: The Forge of Experience (1732–1775), 236–237.

113 When finished, the portrait: George Washington to Jonathan Boucher, May 21, 1772, GWW III: 83–85.

CHAPTER SEVEN

116 "I am sure: George Washington to Mary Washington, February 15, 1787, GWW XXIX: 158–162.

116 He went so far: George Washington to George Augustine Washington, October 25, 1786, GWW XXVIIII: 28–29.

117 Among the gentry: Linda DePauw, Conover Hunt, and Miriam Schneir, *Remember the Ladies: Women in America, 1750–1815*, New York: Viking Press, 1976, 21.

117 The sometimes proved: "Invoice," October 12, 1761, GWW II: 369–371.

118 …she told her.: Martha Washington to Nancy Bassett, August 28, 1762, Fields 57.

118 This gave children: DePauw, Conover, Schneir, 33.

118 Lessons might be: Jack Custis to George Washington, August 30, 1770, Hamilton, IV: 31–32.

119 In most regions: Clinton, 133.

119 "Mrs. Washington is a most: Abigail Adams to her sister, October 11, 1789, Stewart Mitchell, *New Letters of Abigail Adams, 1788–1801*, Boston: Houghton Mifflin, 1947, 30.

119 One said that the grandchildren: George Washington Parke Custis, Recollections, 408n; letter of Augusta Berard, in Clayton Torrence, ed., "Arlington and Mount Vernon, 1856: As Described in a Letter of Augusta Berard," *Virginia Magazine of History and Biography* (April 1949), 162.

119 He once said of his reluctance: Bourne, 11.

120 At eleven, he ordered: Cash Accounts, GWW II: 334–35, 369–370; DGW I: 273.

120 Over the years: Lossing, 108–109.

120 Martha wrote: Martha Washington to Margaret Green, September 29, 1760, Fields, 131–132.

121 Martha wrote: Martha Washington to Anna Maria Bassett, April 6, 1762, Fields, 146–147.

122 …fit shook her frail body.: DGW II:15.

122 He came again: DGW II: 30.

122 The Washington's also implored: Mary Thompson, "First Father: George Washington as a Parent," Mount Vernon Ladies Association Paper, April, 2000, 28; George Washington to Thomas Jackson, July 20, 1770, GWW III: 17–20; Washington to Rev. Jonathan Boucher, Feb. 3, 20, 1771, GWW III: 40–41.

122 Another doctor suggested: Dr. John Johnson to Martha Washington, March 21, 1772, Fields, 150.

123 Patsy drank the mineral waters: Julia Spruill, *Women's Life and Work in the Southern Colonies*, 109; George Washington's Cash Accounts for July, 1769, PGW Col. Ser. VIII: 238–240.

123 Washington noted of one trip: Bourne, 34.

123 George described her feelings: Jared Sparks, *The Writing of George Washington*, 4 vols., Boston: John B. Russell, II: 262.

123 She learned to dance: George Washington's cash

accounts, May, 1766, PGW Col. Ser. VII: 437–439.

124 ...for pocked money, three pounds.": DGW II: 63.

124 "I can't help adding: Martha Washington to Mrs. S. Thorpe, July 15, 1772, GWW III: 88.

124 They should not be too genteel: Martha Washington to Mrs. Shelbury, August 10, 1764, PGW VII: 328–329.

125 She feared this catastrophe: George Washington to Jonathan Boucher, July 27, 1769, PGW Col. Ser. VIII: 237–238.

126 He told Boucher that young Jack: Bourne, 41.

126 The confident minister: Jonathan Boucher to George Washington, June 13, 1768, June 16, 1768, August 2, 1768, in Hamilton, III: 314–316, 317–318, 324–328.

127 And, in another letter: Bourne, 41–43.

127 Boucher wrote to Washington: Jonathan Boucher to George Washington, May 21, 1779, GWW VIII: 339.

127 "You will remember my: Jonathan Boucher to George Washington, July 20, 1769, Hamilton, III: 360–361.

127 "Traveling will be: Rev. Jonathan Boucher to George Washington, May 9, 1770, Hamilton, Letters IV: 18–19.

128 "He will be in less: Rev. Jonathan Boucher to George Washington, December 18, 1770, Hamilton, Letters IV: 41–46.

129 He wrote to Boucher: George Washington to Jonathan Boucher, December 16, 1770, GWW VIII: 411–412.

129 He had previously admitted: George Washington to Jonathan Boucher, July 31, 1768, PGW Col Ser. VIII: 120–121.

130 ...strong symptoms of health.": Rev. Jonathan Boucher to George Washington, May 9, 1771, Hamilton, Letters, IV: 59–60.

130 The, in the very next line: Jack Custis to George Washington, August 18, 1771, Hamilton, Letters, IV: 80–81.

130 "I have hitherto: Rev. Jonathan Boucher to George Washington, November 19, 1771, Hamilton, Letters, IV: 83–86.

131 He wrote, defensively: Rev. Jonathan Boucher to George Washington, April 8, 1773, George Washington Papers, Library of Congress, series 4, no. 915.

CHAPTER EIGHT

134 Uncle Jack arrived: DGW, II: 113–115.

135 ...or scarce a sigh.": George Washington to Burwell Bassett, June 19, 1773, GWW II: 138–139.

135 "Your own good sense: George Washington to Burwell Bassett, April 25, 1773, GWW III: 133–134.

135 "The shock, you may suppose: Dr. Myles Cooper to George Washington, July 2, 1773, PGW: Col. Ser. IX: 253–254.

136 "Her case is more: John Parke Custis to Martha Washington, July 5, 1773, in Fields, 152–153.

136 He wrote, "Poor Patsy's death: Fielding Lewis to George Washington, July 7, 1773, PGW, Col. Ser. IX: 268–269.

136 He added that: Lord Dunmore to George Washington, July 3, 1773, PGW, Col. Ser. IX: 258–259.

137 A very distraught George: Ferling, 80.

137 Cooper even volunteered: Jack Custis to George Washington, July 5, 1773, Hamilton, IV: 232–234.

139 ...to the completion of the marriage.": George Washington to Benedict Calvert, April 3, 1773, GWW III: 129–131.

139 He believed, too, that his stepson: George Washington to Burwell Bassett, April 25, 1773, GWW III: 133–134.

139 Boucher simply gushed: Jonathan Boucher to George Washington, April 8, 1773, George Washington Papers, Library of Congress, series 4.

139 He wrote that their campaign: George Washington to Myles Cooper, December 15, 1773, GWW, III: 167–168.

140 Friends as associates: Bartholomew Dandridge to George Washington, February 16, 1773, PGW, Col. Ser. IX: 478–480.

140 He wrote that: Dr. Cooper to George Washington, January 10, 1774, Hamilton, IV: 312–314.

140 He told him that: Jack Custis to George Washington, February 20, 1774, PGW, Col. Ser. IX: 491.

CHAPTER NINE

144 Several weeks later: DGW I: 159–160; Elswyth Thane, *Potomac Squire*, New York: Duell, Sloan and Pearce, 1963, 61–62.

145 Colonies passed laws: Brown, 250–252.

146 The other northern: Mark Boatner, *Encyclopedia of the American Revolution*, Mechanicsburg, Pa; Stackpole Books, 1994, 883.

146 All of the northern colonies: *Historical Sketches of the Town of Leicester, Massachusetts*, Boston, 1860, 442–443.

146 These religious groups: Stephen Weeks, *Southern Quakers and Slavery: A Study in Institutional History*, Baltimore: Johns Hopkins University Press, 1896, 201–215.

147 Virginia residents: Thad Tate Jr. "The Negro in Eighteenth Century Williamsburg," Williamsburg, 1965, 210–211; David Brion Davis, *The Problem of Slavery in the Age of Revolution, 1770–1823*, Ithaca: Cornell University Press, 1975, 196.

147 He often accused: George Washington to Daniel Adams, July 20, 1772, PGW IX, Col. Ser., 69–70; George Washington to Jacky Washington, September 2, 1787, GWW XXIX: 269; George Washington to Andrew Whiting, December 16, 1792, GWW XXXII: 263; George Washington to James Mercer, July 19, 1773, PGW IX, Col. Ser. 282; *Virginia Gazette*, May 4, 1775; George Washington to William Pearce, March 22, 1795, *Memoirs of Long Island: George Washington and Mount Vernon*, Brooklyn, 1899, 4 vols, IV: 206; George Washington to William Pearce, December 19, 1793, GWW XXXIII: 194.

148 He was also one: George Washington to William Pearce, December, 1793, *Memoirs of Long Island*, IV: 17–28; Walsh, 2–94.

148 His slaves' teeth: Lund Washington account book, May, 1784.

148 At one point he ordered: Walsh, 96.

149 He wrote of another: George Washington to William Pearce, February 15, 1795, *Memoirs of Long Island*, IV: 159; Humphrey Knight to George Washington, August 23, 1758, Hamilton III: 48–49; Fritz Hirschfield, *George Washington and Slavery: A Documentary Portrayal*, Columbia: University of Mis-

souri Press, 1997, 40–41; George Washington to William Pearce, March 22, 1795, *Memoirs of Long Island*, IV: 178.

149 Washington also fumed: George Washington to William Pearce, August 26, 1783, Memoirs of Long Island, IV: 5; George Washington to Arthur Young, June 18, 1792, GWW XXXII: 65.

149 Washington promptly barred: Walsh, 81.

150 He advised his overseers: Flexner, *George Washington: Forge of Experience*, 284–286; George Washington to Andrew Whiting, January 6, 1793, GWW XXXII: 392.

150 Washington wrote, adding that: George Washington to John Fairfax, January 1, 1789, PGW Pres. Ser. I: 223; George Washington to Andrew Whiting, January 6, 1793, GWW XXXII: 293.

151 Samuel Vaughn, who visited: Jean Lee, "Mount Vernon Plantation: A Model for the Republic," in Phililp Schwarz, ed., *Slavery at the Home of George Washington*, Mount Vernon: Mount Vernon Ladies Association, 2001, 29–30.

151 Washington's stepgrandson: Custis, *Recollections*, 157.

151 "Washington managed: Methie Budka, trans. Julian Niemcewicz, *Under the Vine and Fig Tree: Travels through America, 1797–1799*, 1805, *With Some Further Account of Life in New Jersey*, Elizabeth, NJ: Grassman, 1965, 101–102; Richard Parkinson, *A Tour in America in 1798, 1799 and 1800*, London, 1805, 2 vols., II: 436.

151 "Time, patience and education: "Letters of George Washington Bearing on the Negro," *Journal of Negro History*, October, 1917, 411–422; George Washington to David Stuart, March 28 and June 15, 1790, GWW XXXI: 30, 52; Jacques Pierre Brissot de Warville, *New Travels in the United States of America*, 1788, trans. Mara Vamos and Durand Echevarria, Durant Echevarria, ed., Cambridge: Harvard University Press, 1964, 329–330.

152 If a man's property: Alfred Cornwell and John Meyer, *The Economics of Slavery and Other Studies in Economic History*, Chicago: Aldine Co., 1964, 45–84; Ira Berlin and Philip Morgan, eds., *Cultivation and Culture: The Shaping of Slave Life in the Americas*, Charlottesville: University of Virginia Press, 1993,

2–3; David Brion Davis, The Problem of Slavery in the Age of Revolution, 261.

152 The two men offered: George Mercer to George Washington, December 23, 1764, PGW X Col. Ser. II: 424–425.

153 He wrote to Bryan Fairfax: Thomas Paine, "African Slavery in America," 6; George Washington to Bryan Fairfax, July 18, 1774, PGW X Col. Ser. 119–128; Fairfax Resolves, with George Mason, 154–156; *Virginia Gazette*, July 24, 1774; George Washington to Bryan Fairfax, August 24, 1774, PGW X, Col. Ser. 154–156, George Washington to Lund Washington, GWW IV: 147–149.

153 The institution would not be buried: Willard Sterne Randall, *George Washington: A Life*, New York: Henry Holt, 1997, 258–259.

154 The entire scheme: Dowdey, The Golden Age, 339.

154 Washington's opposition: David Mitros, "Shepard Kollock and the New Jersey Journal," *Morris County Circular*, 2001, 19; Koch and Peden, eds. *Life and Selected Writings of Thomas Jefferson*, 278–279.

154 Gouverneur Morris, a member: Henry Cooley, *A Study of Slavery in New Jersey: Johns Hopkins University Studies in Historical and Political Science*, 14th series, New York: Johnson Reprint, 1973, 23; John Jay to Elias Boudinot, 1819, Henry Johnson, ed., *Correspondence and Public Papers of John Jay*, 4 vols., New York: G.P, Putnam's Sons, 1893 IV: 430–443, reprint, New York: DeCapo Press, 1971.

154 He wrote that: William Nell, *The Colored Patriots of the American Revolution*, Boston: Robert Eallot, 1855, 388.

154 He wrote to his cousin: Thane, *Potomac Squire*, 188–189.

155 Washington was enthusiastic: George Washington to the Marquis de Lafayette, May 10, 1786, PGW III Confederation Series, 43.

155 Still, Washington would not free: Lucas, *Quotable George Washington*, 89; George Washington to John Mercer, December 5, 1786, December 19, 1786, GWW XXIX: 103, 112.

155 He wrote of his dilemma: George Washington to Robert

Lewis, August 18, 1799, GWW XXXVII: 338–339.

156 Desperate for troops: George Washington to General William Heath, June 29, 1780, GWW XIX: 93; Major Henry Lee to George Washington, July 26, 1779, GWW XV: 488.

156 Jacky did not find any: Jack Custis to Martha Washington, October 12, 1781, in Fields, 187.

156 He wrote that: Dowdey, 40–43.

157 He asked: Dowdey, 186–187.

157 Some two dozen worked: Thane, Potomac Squire, 47.

158 She wrote: Scott, 37.

158 Another wrote: Isabella Martin and Mary Avary, eds., Mary Chestnut, *Diary from Dixie*, New York, 1922, 163; *Laura Comer Diary*, Southern Historical Collection; *Catherine Broun Diary*, Southern Historical Collection, in Scott, 46–47.

158 She wrote that his abilities: Martha Washington to Elizabeth Powel, May 20, 1797, Fields, 302–303.

159 She was so fearful that her own: Fields, 302; Patricia Brady, *George Washington's Beautiful Nelly: The Letters of Eleanor Parke Custis Lewis to Elizabeth Bordley Gibson, 1794–1851*, 10.

159 George wrote in anger: George Washington to Andrew Whiting, December 23, 1792, GWW XXXII: 277.

159 In another ad: Advertisement, PGW Col. Ser. VII: 65–68; advertisement, GWW III: 289.

160 He first wrote of Oney: Fields, 307; George Washington to Oliver Wolcott Jr., September 1, 1796, GWW XXXV: 201–202.

160 She wrote: Fields, 394.

161 He could have easily: George Washington to George Augustine Washington, August 26, 1787, GWW XXIX: 264–266; Walsh, "Slavery and Agriculture at Mount Vernon," in Schwarz, *Slavery at the Home of George Washington*, 70.

CHAPTER TEN

164 He especially admired: Jefferson's remarks in JOHB X: xv-xvii. David McCants, *Patrick Henry: Orator*, Westport, CT: Greenwood Press, 1990, 121.

165 Parliament, they were convinced: J. Franklin Jameson, "The American Revolution: Revolutionary or Non-Revolutionary?" in Gerry Grob and George Billias, eds., *Interpretations of American Historical Patterns*, 2 vols., New York: Free Press, 1967, I:199–200; William Appleman Williams, *America Confronts a Revolutionary World*, New York: William Morrow Company, 1976, 28–31.

165 These freedoms: Daniel Boorstin, "American Revolution: Revolutionary or Non-Revolutionary?" in Grob and Billias, *Interpretations of American Historical Patterns* 221–228; Adrienne Koch, *Power, Morals and the Founding Fathers: Essays in the Interpretation of the American Enlightenment*, Ithaca: Cornell University Press, 1961, 122–126; Arthur Bryant, *The American Ideal*, Freeport, NY: Books for Libraries Press, 1969, 8–10; Gordon Wood, *The Creation of the American Republic*, New York: W.W. Norton Co., 1969, 108–114.

166 Its editor said the act: *Newport Mercury*, October 28, 1765; for opposition and riots, Pauline Maier, *From Resistance to Revolution: Colonial Radicals and the Development of American Opposition to Britain, 1765–1776*, New York: Alfred Knopf, 51–61.

166 He had written: Flexner, *George Washington: Forge of Experience*, 310.

166 Now he wrote to his mother-in-law: George Washington to Francis Dandridge, September 20, 1765, GWW II: 425–426.

166 The crusade against the act: *Virginia Gazette*, October 25, 1765, April 4, 1766.

166 Patrick Henry said: Paul Ford, *The True George Washington*, Philadelphia, 1898, 83; GW XI: 476.

168 For the first time: George Mason to George Washington, April 5, 1769, PGW Col. Ser. VIII: 182–183.

168 Virginia's leaders also: George Washington to Francis Dandridge, September 20, 1765, GWW II: 425; George Washington to George Mason, in Isaac, *Transformation of Virginia*, 251; Billings, Selby, Tate, 318–319.

169 He told his friends: George Washington to George Mason, April 28, 1769, PGW Col. Ser. VIII: 182.

169 The acts, denounced: Leckie, *George Washington's War*, 143; *Virginia Gazette*, January 6, 1774, and front page stories for the next several weeks.

170 His thinking had changed: Flexner, P., *George Washington: The Indispensable Man*, 58.

170 He told the House of Burgesses: Leckie, 143.

170 They argued with Washington: Billings, Shelby, Tate, 316–318; Paul Longmore, *The Invention of George Washington*, Berkeley: University of California Press, 1988, 77–79.

170 Washington and Mason organized: *Virginia Gazette*, August 4, 1774.

171 Lord Dunmore promptly: *Virginia Gazette*, May 26, 1774.

171 In Massachusetts, James Otis: David Burg, ed., *An Eyewitness History: The American Revolution*, Facts On File, Inc., New York: 2001, 40–46.

172 "Have we not addressed: George Washington to Bryan Fairfax, July 4, 1774, PGW Col. Ser. X: 212.

172 As a military man: George Washington to Captain Robert Mackenzie, October 9, 1774, GWW III: 244–247.

173 By the end of the First Continental Congress: DGW II: 164–166.

173 He replied: Henry's reply has been reprinted hundreds of times. This note is from an 1848 speech by Robert Winthrop on the Fourth of July to commemorate the laying of the cornerstone of the Washington Monument.

174 Typical was her rejoinder: Lebsock, *Virginia Women*, 54; Martha Washington to Anna Maria Bassett, February 25, 1788, Fields, 205–206.

174 Churches and teachers: Spruill, 232–242.

175 In a behavior book: Spruill, 244–245. Articles such as this appeared in dozens of colonial newspapers.

175 A group of women: *State Records of North Carolina*, XVI, 389–390.

175 Women who did none: Spruill, 246–354.

176 The crown also forbid: David Ramsay, "The View From Inside," Jack Greene, ed., *The Ambiguity of the American Revolu-*

tion, New York: Harper and Row, 1968, 33–34.

177 Later, Washington wrote to Joseph Reed: George Washington to Joseph Reed, February 10, 1776, GWW IV: 321.

178 "She seemed ready to make: Edmund Pendleton to anonymous corespondent, September, 1774, David Mays. Ed., *The Papers and Letters of Edmund Pendleton, 1774–1803*, 2 vols., Charlottesville, VA: University of Virginia Press, 1967, I: 98.

CHAPTER ELEVEN

179 Now he was not merely: Fleming, *First in Their Hearts*, 52.

182 His humility impressed everyone: Abigail Adams to John Adams, August 19, 1774, Charles Adams, *The Letters of Mrs. Adams, the Wife of John Adams*, 3rd ed. Vol. I, Boston: Little, Brown and Company, 1841, 201.

182 He wrote to his Fairfax Company Leckie, *George Washington's War*, 125; CONG I: 527.

182 The new commander told: Flexner, *Forge of Experience*, 340–341.

183 "There is something charming to me: John Adams to Elbridge Gerry, June 18, 1775, CONG I: 504.

183 He thought of Martha: George Washington to Burwell Bassett, CONG I: 515; Bourne, 57–61.

183 He wrote that it was: George Washington to Martha Washington, June 18, 23, 1775, CONG I: 509–511.

184 He urged Jacky: George Washington to Jack Custis, June 19, 1775, Custis, *Recollections*, 533–534; Randall, 284–286.

184 Now, though, a war: Randall, 274–274.

184 He told him to make sure: Elswyth Thane, *Potomac Squire*, 177.

CHAPTER TWELVE

187 He wrote to Massachusetts lawmakers: George Washington to the New York Legislature, June 26, 1775, GWW III: 305; to the Massachusetts Legislature, July 4, 1775, GWW III: 307.

188 American general: Worthington Ford, ed., *Journals of the Continental Congress, 1774–1789*, 24 vols., Washington, D.C.:

U.S. Government Printing Office, 1904, III: 395, 403; George Washington to Richard Henry Lee, December 26, 1775, R. H. Lee, *Memoir of the Life of Richard Henry Lee*, 2 vols., Philadelphia, 1825, II: 9.

188 Another twenty thousand: Benjamin Quarles, *The Negro in the American Revolution*, Chapel Hill: University of North Carolina Press, 1961, 26–28.

189 Lund told George: Lund Washington to George Washington, January 15, 1776, Thane, *Potomac Squire*, 164–165.

189 The two newspaper articles: Alice Desmond, *Martha Washington: Our First Lady*, New York: Dodd, Mead & Co., 1943, 142.

189 "Let no one: George Washington to Lund Washington, November 26, 1775, GWW IV: 114–116.

190 The nickname: *Virginia Gazette*, March 14, 1777.

190 Just outside the city: *Virginia Gazette*, December 8, 1775; *Pennsylvania Evening Post*, December issues, 1775.

190 She was astonished: Martha Washington to Elizabeth Ramsey, December 30, 1775, Fields, 164.

191 Her decision: Lossing, *Mary and Martha*, 136–145.

191 The woman who had never left: Martha Washington to Elizabeth Ramsey, December 30, 1775, Fields, 164.

192 ...to be observed among them.": *Pennsylvania Journal*, August 2, 1775.

192 A disgusted Washington: Bourne, 61.

192 He was particularly unhappy: George Washington to Richard Henry Lee, July 10, 1775, GWW III: 329–331; to Jack Custis, July 27, 1775, GWW III: 371–373; to General Phillip Schuyler, July 28, 1775, GWW III: 373–376; to Lund Washington, August 20, 1775, GWW III: 432–435.

193 He began to think about: George Washington to John Hancock, September 24, 1776, GWW VI: 110–111; George Washington to William Livingston, January 24, 1777, GWW VII: 56–57.

193 She lamented that: Martha Washington to Elizabeth Ramsay, December 30, 1775, Fields, 164.

194 The first impression: *Elizabeth Drinker Diary*, April 6, 1778.

195 ...smooth the rugged paths of war.": Wharton,   Anne, *Martha Washington*, London: John Murphy, 1897, 100.

195 "Her graceful and cheerful manners: Elswyth Thane, *Washington's Lady*, 158–161.

196 She understood the problems: Martha Washington to Anna Maria Bassett, January 31, 1776, Fields, 166–167.

CHAPTER THIRTEEN

197 The worst storm to hit the Atlantic Coast in thirty-five years arrived on the morning of February 24, 1777: Theodore Tappert and John Doberstein, *Journals of Henry Melchior Muhlenberg*, 6 vols., Philadelphia: Muhlenberg Press, 1959, I: 3, 16.

197 It followed a previous storm: Phineas Pemberton, notes for Metropolitan Observatory, Philadelphia, February, 1777; Hugh Gaines, *The Journal of Hugh Gaines*, New York: Dodd, Mead and Co., 1902, 19; David Ludlum, *Early American Winters*, 1604–1820, Boston: American Meteorological Society, 1966, 100.

198 Here in Morristown: Flexner, *George Washington: The Indispensable Man*, 181, 545.

198 The Americans suffered: Boatner, *Encyclopedia of the American Revolution*, 647–656.

199 He warned members of Congress: George Washington to Robert Morris, January 17, 1777, GWW VII: 32; Washington to Joseph Reed, February 23, 1777, GWW VII: 190–192.

199 John Adams warned his wife: Medical committee to George Washington, February 15, 1777, CONG VI: 271; John Adams to Abigail Adams, February 20, 1777, CONG VI: 326–327.

200 He did so without approval: George Washington to Robert Harrison, January 29, 1777, GWW VII: 37–38; Dr. Carl Binger, *Revolutionary Doctor: Benjamin Rush, 1746–1813*, New York: W.W. Norton, 1966, 122; Congressional Medical Committee to George Washington, February 13, 1777, CONG VI: 271–272.

200 The immediate inoculations: R. Torres-Reyes, "A Study of Medical Services in the 1779–1780 Winter Encampment,"

National Park Service, Washington Association, 1971, 52; Richard Henry Lee on Virginia success to Patrick Henry, April 22, 1777, CONG VI: 633.

200 He was outside in cold: Flexner, *George Washington in the American Revolution*, 202.

201 More phlegm filled: Morris Saffron, *Surgeon General to Washington: Dr. John Cochran 1730–1817*, New York: Columbia University Press, 1977, 33–38.

201 Hamilton and other aides: Nathanael Greene to William Livingston, March 8, 1777, Richard Showman, ed. *The Papers of Nathanael Greene*, 6 vols., Chapel Hill: University of North Carolina Press, 1989, II: 36; *Continental Journal*, March 27, 1777; Alexander Hamilton to Alexander McDougall, March 10, 1777, HAM I: 201–202.

202 Martha left Mount Vernon: Thane, *Washington's Lady*, 150–152.

202 Bundled up with blankets: *Virginia Gazette*, April 4, 1777. *The Gazette* wrote of her trip, but the general's brush with death was not printed until several weeks later.

204 "His worthy lady: Mrs. Martha Bland to her sister-in-law, Frances Randolph, May 12, 1777, *Proceedings of the New Jersey Historical Society*, July 1933, 152.

204 One woman wrote, "As she was said to be so grand: Nathaniel Hervey, *The Memory of Washington*, Boston: Munro, 1862, 87.

204 Her effect on her husband: George Washington Greene, *The Life of Nathanael Greene*, New York: G.P. Putnam and Sons, 1867, 309.

205 "Mother won't even go: Sally Fairfax to Bryan Fairfax, January, 1778, *Diary of a Little Colonial Girl*, Richmond: Virginia Historical Society, 1903, 3.

206 Martha also had the boys': Martha Washington to Anna Maria Bassett, November, 1777, Fields, 174.

206 Congress insisted that Washington: James Flexner, *George Washington in the American Revolution*, 229–234 on Lafayette shot; Joseph Clark, "Diary of Joseph Clark," *N.J.*

Historical Society Proceedings, VII: 96, 98–99.

CHAPTER FOURTEEN

210 "An inn at Brandywine Creek: Martha Washington to Mercy Otis Warren, March 7, 1778, Fields, 177–178; to an anonymous friend, February, 1778, Fields, 176–177.

211 ...my heart pains for them.": Fields, 176¬178.

211 One army doctor: Hugh Rankin, ed., "Albigence Waldo Diary," *Narratives of the American Revolution, as Told by a Young Soldier, a Home-sick Surgeon, a French Volunteer, and a German General's Wife*, Chicago: R.R. Donnelly and Sons Company, 1976, 182.

212 A Massachusetts general: Edward Fields, ed., *Diary of Colonel Israel Angell, Commanding the Second Rhode Island Continental Regiment during the American Revolution, 1778–1781*, Providence, 1899, xii-xiii; John Paterson to Thomas Marshall, February 23, 1778, Boyle II: 66–68.

212 "It is a sad: During the first week of March, a quartermaster, James Bradford, wrote to another soldier that the British had seized 133 head of cattle en route to Valley Forge, James Bradford to Thomas Wooster, March 4, 1778, Boyle II: 65–67; Robert Hinckley, ed., Christina Leach, *Diary of Christina Young Leach of Kingssessing, 1765–1796*, Philadelphia: Historical Society of Pennsylvania, 1911, 7.

212 "The inhabitants are only fit: Elias Boudinot to Elisha Boudinot, September 23, 1777, George Boyd, *Elias Boudinot, Patriot and Statesman, 1740–1821*, Princeton: Princeton University Press, 1952, reprint, New York: Greenwood Press, 1969, 43.

213 ...weak men without any character.": John Harvie to Thomas Jefferson, Julian Boyd, Ed., *The Papers of Thomas Jefferson*, 31 vols., Princeton: Princeton University Press, 1950, II: 125–127.

213 Many of its supervisors: Thomas Jones and John Chaloner to Thomas Wharton Jr. and the Supreme Executive Council of Pennsylvania, December 24, 1777, Boyle I: 5.

213 Jedediah Huntington wrote to: Richard Platt to Alexander McDougall, December 20, 1777, Boyle I: 9–11; Jedediah

Huntington to Jabez Huntington, January 7, 1778, Valley Forge Historical Papers; Thomas Jones to Charles Stewart, February 16, 1778, Charles Stewart Papers, New York Historical Society.

214 ...from my soul pity those miseries.": George Washington to Henry Laurens, December 23, 1777, GWW X: 192–198.

215 Conditions were so bad: Dr. Benjamin Rush to Patrick Henry, January 12, 1778, Carl Binger, *Revolutionary Doctor: Benjamin Rush, 1746–1813*, 133.

215 He wrote to Governor Livingston: George Washington to William Livingston, December 21, 1777, GWW X: 233.

215 When he asked her to join him: Martha Washington to Burwell Bassett, December 22, 1777, Mount Vernon Library Collection.

216 ...that dismal abode [Valley Forge]").: Pierre-Etienne Duponceau letter to a friend June 13, 1778, Gilbert Chinard, *George Washington as the French Knew Him: A Collection of Texts*, Princeton: Princeton University Press, 1940, 14.

216 Another wrote that to end: General John Armstrong to George Washington, December 30, 1777, Library of Congress, George Washington Papers.

217 Mrs. Washington again began: *Elizabeth Drinker Diary*, quoted in *200 Years Ago Today in Valley Forge*, Valley Forge Historical Park, 1979.

217 To entertain: Flexner, *George Washington in the American Revolution*, 283; John Trussel Jr. *Birthplace of an Army: A Study of the Valley Forge Encampment*, Harrisburg: Pennsylvania Historical and Museum Commission, 1998, 98.

217 Throughout the terrible winter: Marquis de Lafayette to his wife, January 6, 1776, Stanley Idzerda, ed., *Lafayette in the Age of the American Revolution: Selected Letters and Papers, 1776–1790*, Ithaca, NY: Cornell University Press, 1977, I: 225.

217 One woman said of her industry: Wharton, 122–123.

218 "She was dressed: Chastellux, I: 298.

218 The man remained: *Drinker Diary*.

219 ...estimable in female character.": Thacher, 152–153.

219 A member of the life guard: John Steele to William Steele, in Dennis Ryan, *A Salute to Courage: The American Revolution as*

Seen Through Wartime Writings of Officers of the Continental Army and Navy, New York: Columbia University Press, 1979, 186–187.

219 He recalled: Deponceau was interviewed at the Fiftieth anniversary of the Valley Forge winter. *Republican Star and General Advertiser*, August 19, 1828, 2.

219 Chastellux, the French diplomat: Chastellux, I: 298–299.

219 George Benet, who visited the camp: George Benet to his mother, April 15, 1783, GWW, 321n.

220 …a most heavenly sight.": John Hunter, "An Account of a Visit Made to Washington at Mount Vernon, by an English Gentleman, in 1785, from the Diary of John Hunter," *Pennsylvania Magazine of History and Biography* 17 (1893), 81.

220 "This leaves us: John Custis to Martha Washington, April 3, 1778, Fields, 178–179.

221 "[It] pleased us: Dr. James Craik to Dr. Jonathan Potts, May 15, 1778, Valley Forge Historical Park Papers.

221 William Gifford of New Jersey: William Gifford to Benjamin Holme, January 24, 1778,. Boyle I: 30–32.

221 Another asked his mother: William Weeks to a friend, February 16, 1778, Boyle I: 55–58.

221 Elias Boudinout wrote of them: Elias Boudinot to Elisha Boudinot, March 15, 1778, Boyle II: 78–79.

221 In January, in the height of the Valley Forge woes: John Crane to Eleazar Wheelock, January 6, 1778, Boyle I: 18.

222 Isaac Gibbs of New Hampshire: Isaac Gibbs to his brother, March 5, 1778, Boyle I: 72–75.

222 Artillery Lieutenant George Fleming: George Fleming to Sebastian Baumann, May 14, 1778, Boyle II: 126–127.

225 Hundreds of women participated: "The Sentiments of an American Woman," broadside, in John Dunlap, *The Sentiments of an American Woman*, Philadelphia, 1780, reprinted in Kerber and Mathews, *Women's America*, 80–82.

226 She urged women: *Virginia Gazette*, September 21, 1776.

227 …their businesses lost money—for years.: Clinton, 29–31.

227 Single women used the newspapers: Janet James, *Chang-*

ing Ideas about Women in the United States, 1776–1825, 66.

227 The people felt a close connection: *Virginia Gazette*, May 17, 1776.

CHAPTER FIFTEEN

229 He had sent her: George Scheer and Hugh Rankin, *Rebels and Redcoats*, New York: World Publishing Company, 1957 367.

229 There was nearly two feet: Almon Lauber, ed., *Orderly Books of the Fourth New York Regiment, With the Diaries of Samuel Tallmadge, 1780–1782, and John Barr, 1779–1782*, Albany, N.Y., 1932, 717.

229 It was one of twenty-six storms: Robert Parker Diary, *Pennsylvania Magazine of History and Biography* 28 (1904), 23; Earl Miers, *Crossroads of Freedom: The American Revolution and the Rise of a New Nation*, New Brunswick: Rutgers University Press, 1971, 101.

230 Herbert Muhlenberg, an amateur: David Ludlum, *History of Early American Winters*, 120–121.

230 Washington had again decided: George Washington to Alexander McDougall, November 13, 1779, GWW XVII: 100–102; to Nathanael Greeene, November 23, GWW XVII: 167–168.

230 Having removed the snow: Thacher, 180–181.

230 British officers traveled back: Ludlum, 114–116.

232 General Greene wrote to a friend: George Washington to Samuel Huntington, December 15, 1779, GWW XVII: 272–273; Nathanael Greene to Daniel Broadhead, December 18, 1779, GREENE: V: 182.

233 Business did decline: Thane, *Potomac Squire*, 162.

233 "[In] the last letter from Nelly...": Martha Washington to Eleanor and Jack Custis, March 19, 1778, Custis, 547–548.

234 George chastised him: George Washington to Jack Custis, Custis, 559–561.

234 Congress ordered some states: *Journals of the Continental Congress*, XV: 44–45, 1358–1359.

234 Regional food administrators: Jeremiah Wadsworth to

Nathanael Greene, December 23, 1779, GREENE V: 199–200.

234 Washington was so desperate for food: S. Sydney Bradford, "Hunger Menaces the Revolution," *Maryland Historical Magazine*, March 1966, 11.

234 He wrote to Governor George Clinton: Theodore Thayer, *Colonial and Revolutionary Morris County*, 224.

234 They had to keep themselves: "Quartermaster's Receipt Book in the Revolution," *New Jersey Historical Society Proceedings* (July 1920), 11: 364–368; *Claims to Damages Done by Americans*, Morris County, New Jersey State Library, Archives and History; Washington's accusation, General Orders, December 28, 1779, GWW XVII: 331–332.

234 Finally, on January 3: Nathanael Greene to Moore Furman, January 4, 1780, GREENE: 230.

235 Washington watched it fall: George Washington's weather diary, January 6, 1780, Morristown National Historial Park.

235 General Greene wrote: Nathanael Greene to Jeremiah Wadsworth, January 5, 1780, GREENE: 230; Freeman V: 152–153.

235 He also asked the Freeholders: GWW to the Justices of Morris County (and New Jersey), January 8, 1780, GWW XVII: 362–365.

236 Kitty was ill: Thane, *Fighting Quaker*, 269.

236 David Thompson wrote that his mother: Barbara Hoskins, Caroline Force, Dorothea Roberts, and Gladys Foster, *Washington Valley: An Informal History*, Ann Arbor, MI, 1960, 57–58.

237 It was a letter: Willard Wallace, *Traitor and Hero: The Life and Fortunes of Benedict Arnold*, New York: Harper Bros., 1954, 190–105; Washington letter in Lauren Paine, *Benedict Arnold, Hero and Traitor*, London: Robert Hale, 1963, 139.

238 These dances improved: Lt. Erkuries Beatty to Reading Beatty, March 13, 1780, Beatty Letters, Morristown National Historical Park Collection.

238 "Her many intercessions: Custis, 403.

239 She was thrilled by Olney Winsor: Varlo, in Baker, 17–18;

Blanchard, in Baker, 67; Hunter, Hunter Diary, 81; Chastellux, I: 134; Winsor in Kaminski and Saladino, 523.

240 The Washingtons remained: D.B. Read, *The Life and Times of General John Graves Simcoe*, Toronto: Virtue Publishing, 1890, 67–68; Washington wrote to Silas Condict that he was safe, February 1, 1780, GWW VII: 474.

241 "The poor general: George Washington to John Augustine Washington, July 6, 1780, XVIV: 335–337; Martha Washington to Burwell Bassett, July 18, 1780, Fields, 183.

CHAPTER SIXTEEN

244 (Throughout the rest of his life: DGW IV: 136.

245 One South Carolina woman: Mary Guerard to Susan Garvey, May 1779, *A Woman's Letters in 1779 and 1782*, Charleston: South Carolina Historical Society, 1909, 4.

245 The general and his aides: Thane, *Washington's Lady*, 228–229.

246 ...and entertained a houseful of strangers.: Bryan, 251.

246 A grinning Washington sent Lafayette: DGW II: 260.

248 George and Martha, who summoned: Thane, *Potomac Squire*, 231–233; Custis, 254–255, 504–505; Thane, *Potomac Squire*, 198.

249 "It is all over.": Thomas Fleming, *Beat the Last Drum*, 343.

249 King George III: Garry Wills, *Cincinnatus: George Washington and the Enlightenment*, Garden City, N.Y.: Doubleday, 1984, 13.

249 Washington assured friends: George Washington to the Marquis de Lafayette, February 1, 1784, GWW XXVII: 317.

250 "The glorious task for which we first flew to arms: General Orders, April 18, 1783, GWW XXVI: 334–337.

251 He told the crowd: George Washington to Congress, December 23, 1783, GWW XXVII: 284–285.

251 Army aide James McHenry: James McHenry to Margaret Caldwell, December 23, 1783, CONG XXI: 221.

CHAPTER SEVENTEEN

254 Calling the worker: George Washington to Lund Washington, August 13, 1783, in Dalzell and Dalzell, 113.

255 He was determined: Custis, 370–373; Lossing, 234–235.

255 Everything was planted with precision: DGW II: 343, 387, 370.

255 Instead of building new garden houses: Dalzell and Dalzell, 117–119.

256 They did not: Ferling, 330–333.

256 He groaned to a friend: Forrest McDonald, *We the People: The Economic Origins of the Constitution*, Chicago, 1958, 72.

256 His dream of breeding buffalo: George Washington to Charles Wilson Peale, March 13, 1787, GWW XXIX: 178; Ferling, 325.

257 (Houdon postponed the chance: Ferling, 340.

257 At times, the plantation: DGW II: 458n. Many stopped off at Mount Vernon on tours of the U.S. and returned home to write articles or books about the "new America."

258 Vander Kemp happily continued: Francis Vander Kemp, William Spohn Baker, ed., *Washington after the Revolution, 1784–1799*, Philadelphia: J.B. Lippincott Company, 1898, 107.

258 Some, in fact, recalled that the general: Ferling, 338–339.

258 His wife had to grab him: Custis, 41.

258 He loved his afternoon: According to his diary, he usually went on fox hunts about once a week depending upon the season and the weather, DGW II: 455, 459.

259 Nelly and Wash visited their mother: George Washington to David Stuart, April 9, 1793, GWW XXXII: 414,

259 She frequently wrote to friends: Martha Washington to Fanny Bassett, February 25, 1788, Fields, 205–206.

260 "I shall distrust my skill: Martha Washington to Fanny Bassett, August 7, 1784; Elizabeth Powel to Martha Washington, November 31, 1787, in Fields, 195, 198–200.

260 "Grandmamma always spoiled: Nelly Custis quoted by Wash in Custis, 38.

260 Just as Martha: Desmond, 208–210.

260 She wrote to Elizabeth Bordley Gibson: Patricia Brady, *George Washington's Beautiful Nelly: the Letters of Eleanor Parke Custis Lewis to Elizabeth Bordley Gibson, 1794–1851*, Columbia: University of South Carolina Press, 1991, 3.

260 In a letter a week later: Nelly Custis to Elizabeth Bordley, October 13 and 19, 1795, Brady, *George Washington's Beautiful Nelly*, 19–20, 20–24.

261 She wrote to a friend: Nelly Custis to Elizabeth Bordley, November 23, 1797, Brady, *George Washington's Beautiful Nelly*, 39–45.

261 In another letter, Nelly remembered: Brady, *George Washington's Beautiful Nelly*, 1; Nelly Lewis to Jared Sparks, February 26, 1833, *The Life of George Washington*, Boston: Ferdinand Andrews, 1830, 522.

262 In fact, when Henry Knox: Henry Knox to George Washington, March 19, 1787, John Kaminsky and Jill McCaughan, *A Great and Good Man: George Washington in the Eyes of His Contemporaries*, Madison: Madison House, 1989, 74.

262 When Nelly was older: Custis, 41, with Wash recalling what Nelly had said.

262 Lafayette wrote of Wash: Custis, 408n; Lafayette quoted in Woodrow Wilson, *George Washington*, New York: Harper & Brothers, 1897, 239, and in Mary Thompson paper "George Washington as a Parent," November 11, 2000, 11, 14.

263 George and Martha took her in: Fields, 216n

263 The general said he was: P. Bradley Nutting, "Tobias Lear, S.P.U.S.": First Secretary to the President," *Presidential Studies Quarterly*, XXIV, No. 4, Fall, 1994, 714; Diaries IV:337.

263 He wrote to his wartime friend: George Washington to the Marquis de Lafayette, December 8, 1784, GWW XXVIII: 7.

264 The rebellion had to be: Gordon Wood, *The Creation of the American Republic*, 1776–1787, 277–465.

265 He complained bitterly: Washington to Jay, August 1, 1786, GWW XXVIII: 502; Washington to Henry Knox, December 26, 1786, XXIX: 122; to David Humphreys, December 26, 1786, GWW XXIX: 124.

265 He had warned people: George Washington to Bushrod Washington, January 10, 1784, GWW XXVII: 417; George Washington to Rev. William Gordon, July 8, 1783, GWW XXVII: 49.

265 John Jay had been urging: John Schroeder, ed., *Maxims of George Washington: Military, Political, Social, Moral and Religious*, Mount Vernon: Mount Vernon Ladies Association, 1989, 193.

266 ...his health and fame.": *Pennsylvania Packet*, May 14, 1787 (thirty-one newspapers throughout the country reprinted the *Packet's* story); *Pennsylvania Herald*, May 16, 1787.

266 A newspaper editor: *Petersburg (Va.) Gazette*, July 26, 1787.

266 James Madison wrote that Washington: James Madison's notes, quoted in DGW (abridged), 317.

266 Madison wrote to Jefferson: Richard Harwell, ed., Douglas Southall Freeman, *George Washington*, abridged ed., New York: Collier Books, 1968, 554.

266 He wrote, "He is in perfect good health: Alexander Donald to Thomas Jefferson, November 12, 1787, in DGW (abridged), 326.

267 Later, Jefferson wrote that: Thomas Jefferson to Dr. Walter Jones, January 2, 1814, Andrew Lipscomb and Albert Bergh, *The Writings of Thomas Jefferson*, Washington, D.C., 1903, XIV:50.

267 And in Washington: Longman, 185.

267 British historian Archibald Alison: Archibald Alison, *History of Europe from the Commencement of the French Revolution to the Restoration of the Bourbons*, 10 vols., London, 1829–1842, vol. IV, Chapter XXI.

268 He wrote to him: George Washington to Henry Knox, April 1, 1789, PGW Pres. Ser., II: 2.

268 Some, such as Governor Morris: Elias Boudinot to George Washington, April 6, 1789, Washington Papers, Library of Congress; Boudinot to Washington, April 6, 1789, PGW, Pres. Ser. II: 24–25; Anthony Wayne to George Washington, April 6, 1789, Wayne Papers, Huntington Library, San Marino, California; Richard Henry Lee to George Washington, April 6, 1789, PGW

Pres. Ser. II: 29–30.

268 There was a groundswell: John Alden, *George Washington: A Biography*, Baton Rouge: Louisiana State University Press, 1984, 234.

269 ...and of an observing and reflecting turn of mind.": *Pennsylvania Gazette*, September 26, 1787, in an article reprinted across the U.S.; "Modestus," writing in the *Pennsylvania Gazette*, March 5, 1788.

269 In fact, he would break: Hamilton to George Washington, September, 1788, Harold Syrett, *The Papers of Alexander Hamilton*, V: 220–222.

269 She told others: Martha Washington to John Dandridge, April 20, 1789, Fields, 213; Martha Washington to Mercy Otis Warren, December 26, 1789, Fields, 223–224.

269 ...glory of the United States,": George Washington to Charles Thomson, April 14, 1789, PGW Pres. Ser.II: 56–57.

269 ...call of my country.": George Washington to John Langdon, April 14, 1789, John Langdon Papers, Lilly Library, Indiana University.

270 ...destiny was reaching out to him, and to her.: George Washington to Martha Washington, June 18, 1775, PGW Rev. Ser. I: 4.

CHAPTER EIGHTEEN

271 ...as he arrives to address Congress in 1792: Article signed Sigma, in a February 1847 edition of the *National Intelligencer*, Custis, 490–492n.

272 Washington had hoped to travel: George Washington to William Hartshorne, April 1, 1789, PGW, Pres. Ser. 2, 1–2.

272 "Unutterable sensations: George Washington to the Mayor, Corporation, and Citizens of Alexandria, April 16, 1789, PGW Pres. Ser. II: 59–60.

273 And, too, he hoped people: *Virginia Herald and Fredericksburg Advertiser*, April 30, 1789, George Washington to the citizens of Baltimore; April 17, 1789, PGW Pres. Ser. II: 62–63; He struck that same theme in an address to the judges of the Pennsylvania Supreme Court and other groups on his route to New York,

PGW Pres. Ser. II: 84–85; His "purity" quote is from an address to the Pennsylvania legislature on April 21, 1789, PGW Pres. Ser. II: 105–106.

273 And, wherever he went: George Washington to the Pennsylvania Society of the Cincinnati, April 20, 1789, PGW Pres. Ser. II: 80–81.

274 Soldiers had to hold: DGW V: 477–478; Philadelphia resident's letter to his nephew, *Gazette of the United States*, April 25–29, 1789; *Philadelphia Federal Gazette*, April 20, 1789, *New York Daily Gazette*, April 25, 1789, *New York Daily Advertiser*, April 24, 1789.

274 Wrote Elizabeth Quincy: Eliza Quincy, *Memoir of the Life of Eliza S.M. Quincy*, 50, in PGW Pres. Ser. II: 114n.

274 They were visible symbols: Isaacs, 268, describing the success of Patrick Henry, in what could have been an analysis of the Washingtons.

275 ...one of the best in the world.": George Washington to Lafayette, January 29, 1789, PGW I: Pres. Ser. 262.; Washington to Catherine Macauley Graham, January 9, 1790, GWW XXX: 496.

275 Now he saw: "Thirteen Heads" letter to Rev. William Gordon, July 8, 1783, GWW XXVI: 484–486

276 He refused to personally campaign: Longman, 67.

277 He told them to investigate: Nutting, 715.

278 This assumption, accepted by Congress: In Robert Hendickson, *Hamilton II: 1789—1804*, New York: Mason/Charter, 1976, 80–81.

278 Jefferson, who worked closely with him: Thomas Jefferson to Walter Jones, January 2, 1814, *Writings of Thomas Jefferson*, 9 vols., Washington, D.C., 1853–1855, from Vol. VI, in Baker, 168.

279 ...going through with his purpose.": Jefferson quoted in George Milton, *Use of Presidential Power, 1789—1943*, Boston: Little, Brown and Company, 1944, 25–26.

279 He wrote, "Thus when he had: From Guizot's essay on Washington, untitled, in Baker, 223.

279 Wrote one of his first biographers: Jared Sparks, *Writings*

of George Washington, with a Life of the Author, 12 vols., vol. I, Boston, 1837, in Baker, 203.

279 "There was not a moment: Nutting, "Tobias Lear, S.P.U.S.: First Secretary to the President," 715.

279 Wrote a French army chaplain: *In Familiar Letters on the Public Men of the Revolution*, Philadelphia, 1847; Longman, 206.

280 He begged off on an invitation: DGW (abridged version), 353; George Washington to James McHenry, April 1, 1789, PGW Pres. Ser. 2, 3.

280 Robert Morris, a friend: Robert Morris to George Washington, April 6, 1789, PGW Pres. Ser. 2: 32–33.

280 Savage had numerous engravings: Mary Thompson, "First Father: George Washington as a Parent," paper to the Arlington Medical Arts Society, April 11, 2000.

280 He was called that wherever he went: *Virginia Herald*, April 28, 1791.

280 In 1791, following his visit: Jean Pierre Brissot de Warville, *Nouveau Voyage dans Les Etats-Unis de L'Amerique Septentrionalefait en 1788*, Paris, 1791, vol. XI: 414. De Warville was guillotined in Paris in 1793.

280 And historian Henry Tuckerman: Henry Tuckerman, "Character and Portraits of Washington," *North American Review*, July, 1856; in Baker, 295.

281 He added that his face: Paul Norton and F.M. Halliday, "Latrobe's America," *American Heritage*, August, 1962; Thane, *Potomac Squire*, 356–358.

281 French Comte de Segur wrote: Greene, *Revolutionary Generation*, 303.

281 Another Frenchman, Claude Victor: From de Broglie's 1782 journal of his visit to America, published in the *Magazine of American History* (1877) I: 180. De Broglie was guillotined in 1794.

282 Again in Manhattan: Martha Washington to Fanny Bassett, June 8, 1789, Fields, 215–216.

282 The Macomb house: Richard Norton Smith, *Patriarch*, Boston: Houghton Mifflin Company, 1993, xiii-xiv.

282 The sight of the Washington family: DGW IV: 14, 56, 110.

283 ...in the pomp of sovereign power.": David Ramsey, *Life of George Washington*, New York, 1807, partially reprinted in Baker, 161.

283 He wrote of Long Island: DGW IV: 27, 120.

283 Later that day, his friend Governor Morris: DGW IV: 18–19.

284 ...which render hospitality so charming.": Jacque Pierre Brissot de Warville, *Nouveau Voyage*, 429.

285 ...funerals for that reason, too).: Richard Norton Smith, *Patriarch*, 25.

285 He, too, found Washington's conversation: Paul Norton and E.M. Halliday, "Latrobe's America," *American Heritage*, August, 1962; Thane, *Potomac Squire*, 356–358; Smith, 275; Isaac Weld spent Washington's sixty-fifth birthday with him in 1796 and wrote of his halting conversation in Isaac Weld, *Travels through the States of North America and the Provinces of Upper and Lower Canada during the Years 1795, 1796 and 1797*, in Baker, 51–53; Henry Wansey, *The Journal of an Excursion to the United States of North America in the Summer of 1794*, Salisbury, England, 1795.

285 "General Washington is more cheerful: Jedidiah Morse, D.D., *American Geography or a view of the present situation of the United States of America*, Elizabethtown, NJ, 1789, in Baker, 33.

285 One wrote that: Elkanah Watson, Winslow Watson, *Men and Times of the Revolution or Memoirs of Elkanah Watson*, New York, 1856.

286 ...wrote Isaac Weld of the president.: Isaac Weld, Baker, 51–52.

286 William Carey said that: William Carey, *Washingtoniana*, Baltimore, 1800.

286 Wrote on editor: *National Gazette*, January 30, 1793.

286 "The president exercises: Thomas Shippen to his father, September 16, 1790, Robert Lancaster Jr., *Historic Virginia Homes and Churches*, Philadelphia, J.B. Lippincott Company, 1915, 362.

287 She wrote that many of the receptions: Abigail Adams to Mary Cranch, August 9, 1789, Mitchell, *New Letters of Abigail Adams*, 55.

287 Sometimes the ostrich-plumed women: Charlotte Chambers to her mother, February 25, 1795, William Baker, *Washington after the Revolution, 1784–1799*, Philadelphia: J.B. Lippincott Company, 1898, 299–301.

287 When she bought her niece: Martha Washington to Fanny Bassett, October 23, 1789, Fields, 219–220.

288 Martha shrugged her shoulders: Jefferson to Vail, in Vail, 81–82.

288 "She is plain in her dress: Metchie Budka, Julian Niemcewicz, *Under Their Vine and Fig Tree: Travels through America in 1797–1799, 1805, with some further account of life in New Jersey*, 85; Vail, ed. "A Dinner at Mount Vernon: From the Unpublished Journal of Joshua Brookes (1773–1859)," 80; Abigail Adams to her sister, June 28, 1789, Mitchell, *New Letters of Abigail Adams*, 1788–1801, 13; Thane, *Washington's Lady*, 284.

288 After their first year as wives: Abigail Adams to her sister, June 18, 1789, July 12, 1789, and August 29, 1790, Mitchell, 13, 15, 57.

289 Murray wrote to her parents: Judith Sargent Murray to her parents, August 14, 1790, Bonnie Hurd Smith, ed., *From Gloucester to Philadelphia in 1790: Observations, Anecdotes and Thoughts from the 18th Century—Letters of Judith Sargent Murray*, Cambridge, Judith Sargent Murray Society, 1998, 250–254.

289 Julian Niemcewicz, a Polish diplomat: Budka, Niemcewicz, 84–90.

290 …if you could but see me.": Martha Washington to Fanny Bassett, June 8, 1789, Fields, 214–215.

290 He wrote proudly: Bryan, 295.

290 Mrs. Adams put it best: Abigail Adams to her sister, July 12, 1789, Mitchell, 15.

291 One visitor, William MacLay, wrote that he saw: DGW (abridged), 373n.

291 He coughed: Thane, *Washington's Lady*, 282–283.

291 Her granddaughter Eliza: DGW IV: 129; Bryan, 307.

291 Following his recovery: Martha Washington to Mercy Otis Warren, June 12, 1790, Fields, 225–226.

291 Thomas Jefferson said of Martha: Vail, 81–82.

291 He wrote, "She has no affectation: Benjamin Latrobe, The *Journal of Latrobe: Being the Notes and Sketches of an Architect, Naturalist, and Traveler in the United States from 1796—1820*, New York: D. Appleton and Company, 1905, 57.

292 Those women all connected to Martha: William Hemphill, ed., *State Records of South Carolina: Journals of the State Assembly and House of Representatives, 1776–1780*, Columbia: University of South Carolina Press, 1970, 279.

293 ..nearly bombarded on two occasions.: Cynthia Kierner, *Southern Women in Revolution, 1776–1783: Personal and Political Narratives*, Columbia: University of South Carolina Press, 4–5.

293 David Ramsey, a physician: Moultrie, Ramsay, quoted in Kierner, 20.

294 Women had to insist upon: Cott, 202–203; James, 83–101; Mary Wollstonecraft, *Vindication of the Rights of Man*, London, 1792, 38–39.

295 …paying $5 for them.: James, 107.

295 Powel and Mrs. Washington: Eliza Powel to Enos Hitchcock, May 20, 1790, Hitchcock Papers, Rhode Island Historical Society.

295 Most male views of the feminists: Alice Izard to Margaret Manigault, May 29, 1801, Manigault Papers, Duke University Library, Durham, North Carolina.

295 And then there were thousands: Joseph Hawes and Elizabeth Nybakken, eds., *Family and Society in American History*, Chicago: University of Illinois Press, 2001, 75–76.

295 Eliza Pinckney ran her father's farms: Harriott Ravenal, *Eliza Pinckney*, New York, 1909, 11.

296 Benjamin Rush put it best: Benjamin Rush, "Address to the People of the United States," in Hezekiah Niles, ed., *Principles and Acts of the Revolution in America*, Baltimore, 1822, 402;

Ronald Hoffman and Peter Albert, *Women in the Age of the American Revolution*, Charlottesville: University Press of Virginia, 16–17.

296 They read their Bibles: Mary Beth Norton, "Reflections on Women in the Age of the American Revolution," Hoffman, Albert, *Women in the Age of the American Revolution*, 491.

296 In her they saw: Pauline Maier, *Revolutionary Generation*, 324–325.

296 Nowhere was this more obvious: Anthony Rotundo, *American Manhood: Transformations in Masculinity from the Revolution to the Modern Era*, New York: Basic Books, 1993, 18–19; Cott, 69–71; Linda Kerber, "Separate Spheres, Female Worlds, Women's Place: The Rhetoric of Women's History," *Journal of American History*, 75 (1988).

297 He wrote, "In America: Janet James, *Changing Ideas about Women in the United States, 1776–1825*, New York: Garland Publishing, 1981, 78–83; Noah Webster, *A Collection of Essays and Fugitive Writings*, Boston, 1790, 27–28.

297 Her stepfather scoffed: Morgan, 17; Daniel Smith, *Inside the Great House: Planter Family Life in Eighteenth Century Chesapeake Society*, Ithaca: Cornell University Press, 1980, 63; in Lebsock, Virginia Women, 46.

297 Even so, in 1805: James, 110.

298 Martha was pleased: Edward Carter, ed., The Virginia *Journals of Benjamin Henry Latrobe, 1795–1798*, 2 vols., New Haven: Yale University Press for the Maryland Historical Society, 1977, I: 168.

298 "He is now well: Martha Washington to Fanny Bassett, August 29, 1791, Fields, 233.

298 The 1790s saw more public schools: Nancy Cott, *The Bonds of Womanhood: "Woman's Sphere" in New England, 1780–1835*, 3.

299 …is no less grateful.": John Kaminski and Jill Adair McCaughan, eds., *A Great and Good Man: George Washington in the Eyes of His Contemporaries*, Madison: Madison House, 1989, 150.

299 Washington, who continually proclaimed: DGW (abridged), 384–385.

299 When Washington left Annapolis: *Maryland Gazette*, March 31, 1791.

299 Three days later he was greeted: Dunlap's *Daily American Advertiser*, May 13, 1791; *Columbian Centinel*, June 11, 1791.

299 In Boston, he stood among dignitaries: DGW IV: 34–35.

300 "He had no need to seek: Samuel Stanhope Smith, "An Oration Upon the Death of General George Washington, Delivered in the State House at Trenton (N.J.), January 24, 1800."

300 On a later tour of the southern states: DGW V: 457; Virginia Herald, May 26, 1791.

300 Many of the soldiers: Custis, 507.

301 "If ever any government: Harris, ed., Judith Sargent Murray, *Selected Writings of Judith Sargent Murray*, New York: Oxford University Press, 1895, 55.

301 John Jay, the first chief justice: John Jay in an address to the New York legislature, January 28, 1800, in Baker, 162–165.

302 "I should have been very happy: Martha Washington to Abigail Adams, November 4, 1789, Fields, 221.

302 Just over a year later: Martha Washington to Fanny Bassett, October 23, 1789, Fields, 219–220; to Janet Montgomery, January 29, 1791, Fields, 229–230.

303 Theater managers even set aside: DGW IV: 54–55.

303 "From that expectation: Martha Washington to Mercy Otis Warren, June 12, 1790, Fields, 225–226.

304 She told Warren: Martha Washington to Mercy Otis Warren, December 26, 1789, Fields, 223–224.

304 Jared Sparks, one of the Washingtons' biographers: Jared Sparks, *The Life of George Washington*, Boston: Ferdinand Andrews, 1839, 98–99.

304 Virginia congressman John Page: Smith, 27, 36.

CHAPTER NINETEEN

307 His portraits hung in the capitals: Greene, *Revolutionary Generation*, 303.

308 This proclamation kept America: Neutrality Proclamation, XXXII: 439–431; Thane, *Washington's Lady*, 307.

308 Washington always defended: Smith, 112; Farewell Address, GWW XXXV: 214–238.

309 "We have experienced enough: George Washington to the Merchants and Traders of Baltimore, May 27, 1793, GWW XXII: 477; to the Merchants and Traders of Philadelphia, March 22, 1793, GWW XXXII: 430–431.

309 The president bluntly told a friend: George Washington to Dr. James Anderson, December 24, 1795, GWW XXXIV: 307.

310 The battle ended: Alden, 262–265.

311 A friend of Mrs. Adams's: William Bentley, *The Diary of William Bentley*, D.D., Salem, Mass, 1914, 4 vols., IV: 557.

311 During the final two years: Smith, Patriarch, 130.

312 Hamilton knew how to play: Alexander Hamilton to George Washington, July 30, 1792, Washington Papers, Library of Congress.

312 Martha's friend Elizabeth Powel: Washington Papers, Mount Vernon library collection; Smith, 150.

313 ...the virgin soil of America.": David Humphreys, *Life and Times of David Humphreys*, II: 169–173. New York: G. P. Putnam, 1917, 2 vols.

313 Aaron Bancroft of Massachusetts: Aaron Bancroft, *The Life of George Washington, Commander in Chief of the American Army, through the Revolutionary War; and the First President of the United States*, London, Stockdale, 1808.

313 Yet he could not: Alden, 212–213.

313 As an elderly couple: Lorena Walsh, "Slavery and Agriculture at Mount Vernon," in Schwartz, 73; Mary Thompson, "They Appear to Live Comfortable Together: Private Lives of the Mount Vernon Slaves," in Schawrtz, 79–81.

313 Inexplicably, he scoffed: George Washington to David Stuart, March 28 and June 15, 1790, GWW XXXI: 30, 52.

314 A nervous Washington: George Washington to Tobias Lear, September 5, 1790, GWW XXXI: 152.

314 "I would not, in twelve months: George Washington to Tobias Lear, May 6, 1794, GWW XXXIII: 358; George Washington to Alexander Spotswood, November 23, 1794, GWW XXXIV: 47.

314 An antislavery New Hampshire: Alden, 213; Hirschfield, *George Washington and Slavery*, 112–113.

314 These conflicted views: John Fitzpatrick, ed. *The Last Will and Testament of George Washington and Schedule of the Property, to which is appended the Last Will and Testament of Martha Washington*, Mount Vernon, VA: The Mount Vernon Ladies Association of the Union, 1972 2; Mary Thompson, "To Follow Her Departed Friend: The Last Years and Death of Martha Washington," paper for the Mount Vernon Ladies Association, April 25, 2000, 14.

315 He said that parties: Farewell Address, GWW XXXV: 226.

315 One virulent editor: *The Aurora*, August 22, September 27, October 21, 1795; National Gazette, December 12, 1792, March 2, 1793; Carol Sue Humphrey, "George Washington and the Press," in Mark Rozell, William Pederson, Frank Williams ed., *George Washington and the Origins of the American Presidency*, Westport, CT: Praeger Press, 2000, 157–169; Paine remarks in Marshall Smelser, "George Washington and the Alien and Sedition Acts," *American History Review*, January, 1954, 323–328; "debauched remarks," *Aurora*, December 23, 1796.

315 Of the critics he said: Ward, 26.

316 Near the end of his first term: Smelser, "George Washington and the Alien and Sedition Acts," 327, George Washington to Edmund Randolph, August 20, 1792, GWW XXXII: 136–137.

316 A British diplomat's wife: Bradford Perkins, ed., "A Diplomat's Wife in Philadelphia: Letters of Henrietta Liston, 1796–1800," *The William and Mary Quarterly* (October, 1954), 613.

316 She said that "in a hot day: Martha Washington to Eliza-

beth Powel, July 14, 1797, Fields, 305–306.

317 Then, after some thought: George Washington to Henry Knox, March 2, 1797, GWW XXXV: 408–410.

317 He added, "What I have recommended: George Washington talk to Cherokee Nation Representatives, August 29, 1796, GWW XXXV: 196.

319 "The situation in which I now stand: GWW XXXV: 214–238; Alden, 287–291; Smith, 279–283.

319 Wrote Samuel Smucker: Samuel Smucker, *Life of George Washington*, Philadelphia, 1860.

319 "His decisions: John Marshall, *Life of George Washington, Commander in Chief*, 5 vols., 1804–1807, reprinted from vol. V in Baker, 142–148.

320 ...political talents and wisdom?": John Jay to the New York Legislature, January 28, 1800.

320 Ames wrote that the entire: Fisher Ames to the Massachusetts Legislature, February 8, 1800.

320 He wrote to them that: George Washington to the committeemen of Shepherdstown, October 12, 1796, GWW XXXV: 242.

320 "I am fairly out: Smith, 273.

CHAPTER TWENTY

321 "Grandpapa is very well: Eleanor Parke Custis to Elizabeth Bordley Gibson, March 18, 1797, Brady, *George Washington's Beautiful Nelly*, 30–31.

322 ...for the president.: Thane, *Washington's Lady*, 301–302.

322 He wrote in his diary: DGW IV: 255.

322 "I have scarcely a room: George Washington to James McHenry, April 3, 1797, PGW Retirement Series, I:71–72.

322 Artist John Trumbull was thankful: John Trumbull to Martha Washington, April 25, 1797, Fields, 297–298.

322 Wrote a minister: Bancroft, *The Life of George Washington, Commander in Chief of the American Army; through the Revolutionary War; and the First President of the United States.*

323 He let everybody know: George Washington to Oliver Wolcott, May 15, 1797, PGW Retirement Series I: 142–143.

323 The general and his wife hosted the marriage: Brady, *George Washington's Beautiful Nelly*, 12–13.

324 He told Lear that: Bourne, 137.

324 Martha wrote to her niece Fanny: Martha Washington to Fanny Bassett, November 22, 1794, Fields, 280–281.

324 He wrote to his grandson: George Washington to Wash Custis, November 15, 1796, November 28, 1796, in Custis, 74–76.

325 "I could say nothing to him: George Washington to Dr. Samuel Smith, May 24, 1797, Custis, 83–84.

325 The gullible president: Wash Custis to George Washington, May 29, 1797, George Washington to Wash Custis, June 4, 1797, Custis, 84–86.

325 His grandfather reprimanded him: George Washington to Wash Custis, May 10, 1798, Wash Custis to George Washington May 26, 1798, Custis, 104; George Washington to Wash Custis, June 13, 1798, Custis, 106.

326 ...and can never be erased.": Wash Custis to George Washington, April 2, 1798, Custis, 101–102.

326 In a series of letters: Wash Custis to George Washington, July 14, 1797, Custis, 92–93.

326 He reminded them all too: George Washington to a Mr. McDowell, September 2, 1798, Custis, 111–113.

326 He wrote to Samuel Smith: Bryan, 358

326 His grandfather knew: George Washington to David Stuart, January 22, 1799, Custis, 114–116.

326 But his grandmother always downplayed: Martha Washington to Sally Cary Fairfax, May 17, 1798, Fields, 314–315.

327 ...three times a week.: Thane, *Washington's Lady*, 299.

327 She wrote to Sally: Martha Washington to Sally Fairfax, May 17, 1798, Fields, 314–315.

328 Others remembered too: Anonymous writer, Custis, 488n; Jeanne Pierre Brissot de Warville, *Travels in America* and in Baker, 41.

329 ...set aside money for their care.: Legally, Washington could only free slaves that he owned. He could not free those belonging to Martha and her estate from her marriage to Daniel

Custis. Martha freed George's slaves a year before her death, but the Custis dower slaves remained with the grandchildren.

329 "I shall soon: Diary of Tobias Lear, December 14¬25, 1799, in *Letters and Recollections of George Washington*, New York: Doubleday, Page and Company, 1906, 135; "To Follow Her Departed Friend: The Last Years and Death of Martha Washington," paper by Mary Thompson, April 25, 2000, for Mount Vernon Ladies Association, 1.

329 The editor of the British Register wrote: Oration of Major General Henry Lee, German Lutheran Church of Philadelphia, December 26, 1799; John Marshall's speech to the U.S. House of Representatives, December 19, 1799; Jefferson letter to Dr. Walter Jones, January 2, 1814, *The Writings of Thomas Jefferson*, 9 vols. Vol. VI., in Baker, 170; W. S. Baker, ed. *Character Portraits of Washington, as Delineated by Historians, Orators and Divines, Selected and Arranged in Chronological Order with Biographical Notes and References*, Philadelphia, Robert M. Lindsay, 1887, 54; *London Courier*, January 24, 1800; *Monthly Magazine or British Register*, January, 1800.

330 She told Manasseh Cutler: Ibid.

330 Mrs. William Thornton: Oliver Wolcott to Mrs. Wolcott, July 17, 1800, George Gibbs, ed., *Memoirs of the Administration of Washington and John Adams, Edited from the Papers of Oliver Wolcott, Secretary of the Treasury*, 2 vols., New York, 1846, II: 380–381; Henrieta Liston, "Mrs. Liston Returns to Virginia," *Virginia Cavalcade* (Summer, 1965), 40–47; "Diary of Mrs. William Thornton, 1800–1863," *Records of the Columbia Historical Society, Washington, D.C.* 10 vols., Washington, D.C., 1907, X:174, 213.

331 Without her: Eliza Cope Harrison, ed., *Philadelphia Merchant: the Diary of Thomas P. Cope, 1800–1851*, South Bend, IN: Gateway Editions, 1978, 111–113.

331 Extremely upset: Horace Binney, Bushrod Washington, Philadelphia: C. Sherman & Sons, 1858, 25–26.

331 Then Martha Washington died: Thomas Law to John Law, May 23, 1802, Ellen McCallister, "This Melancholy Scene,"

Annual Report, 1981, Mount Vernon: The Mount Vernon Ladies Association, 1982, 13–15.

331 He wrote that she was: Eliza Custis Law, "Self-Portrait: Eliza Custis, 1808," *The Virginia Magazine of History and Biography* (April, 1945), 91; Mary Custis Lee DeButts, *Growing Up in the 1850s: The Journal of Agnes Lee*, Chapel Hill: University of North Carolina Press, 1984, entry of March 23, 1856; Thomas Jefferson to a friend, May 31, 1802, Mount Vernon Library collection.

331 ...so well sustained on every occasion.": *Alexandria Advertiser* and *Commercial Intelligencer*, May 25, 1802.

INDEX

ABOUT THE AUTHOR

Bruce Chadwick is a former journalist and the author of seven works of history including *The First American Army* (Sourcebooks, 2005), *George Washington's War* (Sourcebooks, 2004), *Brother Against Brother, Two American Presidents, Traveling the Underground Railroad* and *The Reel Civil War*. He lectures in American History at Rutgers University and also teaches writing at New Jersey City University.